MW00603616

Mastering Embedded Linux Programming

Harness the power of Linux to create versatile
and robust embedded solutions

Chris Simmonds

[PACKT] open source ✳
PUBLISHING   community experience distilled

BIRMINGHAM - MUMBAI

Mastering Embedded Linux Programming

Copyright © 2015 Packt Publishing

All rights reserved. No part of this book may be reproduced, stored in a retrieval system, or transmitted in any form or by any means, without the prior written permission of the publisher, except in the case of brief quotations embedded in critical articles or reviews.

Every effort has been made in the preparation of this book to ensure the accuracy of the information presented. However, the information contained in this book is sold without warranty, either express or implied. Neither the author, nor Packt Publishing, and its dealers and distributors will be held liable for any damages caused or alleged to be caused directly or indirectly by this book.

Packt Publishing has endeavored to provide trademark information about all of the companies and products mentioned in this book by the appropriate use of capitals. However, Packt Publishing cannot guarantee the accuracy of this information.

First published: December 2015

Production reference: 1181215

Published by Packt Publishing Ltd.
Livery Place
35 Livery Street
Birmingham B3 2PB, UK.

ISBN 978-1-78439-253-6

www.packtpub.com

Credits

Author

Chris Simmonds

Reviewers

Robert Berger

Tim Bird

Mathieu Deschamps

Mark Furman

Klaas van Gend

Behan Webster

Commissioning Editor

Kartikey Pandey

Acquisition Editor

Sonali Vernekar

Content Development Editor

Samantha Gonsalves

Technical Editor

Dhiraj Chandanshive

Copy Editor

Kevin McGowan

Project Coordinator

Sanchita Mandal

Proofreader

Safis Editing

Indexer

Priya Sane

Production Coordinator

Manu Joseph

Cover Work

Manu Joseph

Foreword

Linux is an extremely flexible and powerful operating system and I suspect we've yet to truly see it used to full advantage in the embedded world. One possible reason is that there are many different facets to it and the learning curves can be steep and time consuming.

Its possible to figure your way own through the world of Embedded Linux, as I myself have done over the past decade, however I am pleased to see people like Chris putting together books like this which give people a good grounding on many useful topics. I certainly could have used a guide like this back when I started!

I obviously have a personal bias to the Yocto Project, it being my major contribution and attempt to make a difference to the Embedded Linux world. One of its core objectives is to try and make things easier for people building Embedded Linux systems. We've had some successes; there are also areas we know work is still needed. We're continually trying to simplify barriers to entry and let more people get involved, make the technology more accessible and encourage adoption.

In writing this book, Chris is supporting the same objectives. I hope you enjoy the book, enjoy Linux and that ultimately that we might see you becoming a part of the vibrant open source communities that make up many of the components you're about to learn about.

Richard Purdie
Yocto Project Architect, Linux Foundation Fellow

About the Author

Chris Simmonds is a software consultant and trainer who lives in southern England. He has been using Linux in embedded systems since the late 1990s, during which he has worked on many interesting projects, including a stereoscopic camera, intelligent weighing scales, various set-top boxes and home routers, and even a large walking robot.

He is a frequent presenter at open source and embedded conferences, including the Embedded Linux Conference, Embedded World, and the Android Builders' Summit. He has been conducting training courses and workshops in embedded Linux since 2002 and in embedded Android since 2010. He has delivered hundreds of sessions to many well-known companies. You can see some of his work on the "Inner Penguin" blog at www.2net.co.uk.

I would like to thank my editor, Samantha Gonsalves, for her tireless work in reviewing my work and keeping me on track. I would also like to thank the people who took time to review my early drafts and to see through my obfuscations to the core of what I was trying to say. So, I would like to thank Behan Webster, Klaas van Gend, Tim Bird, Robert Berger, Mathieu Deschamps, and Mark Furman. Last but not least, I would like to thank my wife, Shirley Simmonds, for her support and for understanding the fact that I really could not help her redecorate the house because I had a book to write.

About the Reviewers

Robert Berger has been gathering practical and managerial experience in software design and development for embedded systems with and without hard real-time requirements since 1993. Since the beginning of the 21st century, he has been using GNU/Linux on desktops and server class machines, but mainly for embedded practices (automotive, industrial control, robotics, telecoms, consumer electronics, and so on). He regularly attends international events, such as Embedded World, Embedded Software Engineering Congress, Embedded Systems Conference, and Embedded Linux Conference as an expert and lecturer. His specializes mainly in training, but also in consulting (in German or English) worldwide. Robert's expertise ranges from the smallest real-time systems (FreeRTOS) to setups with multiple processors/cores and embedded GNU/Linux (user-, kernel-space, device drivers, hardware interfacing, debugging, multi-core, and the Yocto project) with a focus on free and open source software. He is a globetrotter. He is the CEO and embedded software specialist at Reliable Embedded Systems, which is based in St. Barbara, Austria. When he is not traveling, he lives with his family in Athens, Greece. Feel free to contact him on his website at http://www.ReliableEmbeddedSystems.com.

He has reviewed the book *Embedded Linux Systems with the Yocto Project* (*Prentice Hall Open Source Software Development Series*) by *Rudolf J. Streif*.

Tim Bird works as a senior software engineer for Sony Mobile Communications, where he helps Sony improve the Linux kernel for use in Sony's products. He is also the chair of the Architecture Group of the CE Working Group of the Linux Foundation. He has been working with Linux for over 20 years. He helped found two different embedded Linux trade associations and is the creator of the Embedded Linux Conference, which he still leads. Earlier in his embedded Linux career, Tim coauthored the book *Using Caldera OpenLinux*.

Mathieu Deschamps is the founder of ScourGE (`www.scourge.fr`), which provides open source software/hardware innovation services to its clients. They are leaders in the fields of telecommunication, mobile communication, industrial processes, and decision support systems.

He is an R&D business consultant and a trainer. Also, since 2003, he has been an independent tech-driver, involved in many large and small scale projects around GNU/Linux, Android, embedded systems engineering, and security.

Mark Furman, author of OpenVZ Essentials, currently works as a systems engineer for Info-Link Technologies. He has been in the IT field for over 10 years and specializes in Linux and other open source technologies. In his spare time, he enjoys writing and reviewing books on Linux and other open source technologies as well as tinkering with Arduino, Python, and Raspberry Pi projects at Knox Labs, a Hackerspace located in Knox County, OH.

Klaas van Gend graduated in systems and control engineering at Eindhoven University of Technology in the Netherlands. He worked for companies, including Philips, Siemens, and Bosch, writing software for printer prototypes, video encryption, car infotainment, medical equipment, industrial automation, and navigation systems. In 2004, he switched over to MontaVista Software, which was the market leader for embedded Linux. As a systems architect and consultant, he worked with many companies all over Europe, integrating embedded Linux into their products.

For the last few years, he has been working as a trainer and consultant for Vector Fabrics, a small start-up specializing in multi-core programming and software dynamic analysis. He teaches multi-core programming in C and C++ and helps customers improve software performance by utilizing hardware resources in a better way. Vector Fabrics' Pareon tool suite also automatically finds hard-to-find dynamic bugs, including data races, buffer overruns, use-after-free for heap and stack variables, and memory leaks.

He has authored over 100 magazine articles and papers on (embedded) Linux, programming, performance, systems design, and computer games. He cofounded the Embedded Linux Conference Europe and was a lead developer for several open source projects, including UMTSmon for 3G cellular networks and the physics puzzle game *The Butterfly Effect*.

When not at work, he reads urban fantasy or can be found at Aeroclub Nistelrode, piloting glider planes.

Behan Webster has spent two decades in diverse tech industries such as telecom, datacom, optical, embedded, and automotive writing code for a range of hardware from the very small to the very large. His Linux experience spans kernel programming, Embedded Linux, and board bring-up. Currently, he is the lead consultant at Converse in Code Inc, an embedded Linux engineer and project lead working on the LLVMLinux project as well as being a trainer for The Linux Foundation.

www.PacktPub.com

Support files, eBooks, discount offers, and more

For support files and downloads related to your book, please visit www.PacktPub.com.

Did you know that Packt offers eBook versions of every book published, with PDF and ePub files available? You can upgrade to the eBook version at www.PacktPub.com and as a print book customer, you are entitled to a discount on the eBook copy. Get in touch with us at service@packtpub.com for more details.

At www.PacktPub.com, you can also read a collection of free technical articles, sign up for a range of free newsletters and receive exclusive discounts and offers on Packt books and eBooks.

https://www2.packtpub.com/books/subscription/packtlib

Do you need instant solutions to your IT questions? PacktLib is Packt's online digital book library. Here, you can search, access, and read Packt's entire library of books.

Why subscribe?

- Fully searchable across every book published by Packt
- Copy and paste, print, and bookmark content
- On demand and accessible via a web browser

Free access for Packt account holders

If you have an account with Packt at www.PacktPub.com, you can use this to access PacktLib today and view 9 entirely free books. Simply use your login credentials for immediate access.

Table of Contents

Preface

An embedded system is a device with a computer inside that doesn't look like a computer. Washing machines, televisions, printers, cars, aircraft, and robots are all controlled by a computer of some sort, and in some cases, more than one. As these devices become more complex, and as our expectations of the things that we can do with them expand, the need for a powerful operating system to control them grows. Increasingly, Linux is the operating system of choice.

The power of Linux stems from its open source model, which encourages sharing of code. This means that software engineers from many backgrounds, and often employed by competing companies, can cooperate to create an operating system kernel that is up-to-date and tracks the development of the hardware. From this one code base, there is support from the largest super computers down to a wristwatch. Linux is only one component of the operating system. Many other components are needed to create a working system, from basic tools, such as a command shell, to graphical user interfaces, with web content and communicating with cloud services. The Linux kernel together with an extensive range of other open source components allow you to build a system that can function in a wide range of roles.

However, flexibility is a double-edged sword. While it gives a system designer a wide choice of solutions to a particular problem, it also presents the problem of knowing which are the best choices. The propose of this book is to describe in detail how to construct an embedded Linux system using free, open source projects to produce a robust, reliable, and efficient system. It is based on the experience of the author as a consultant and trainer over a period of many years, using examples to illustrate best practices.

What this book covers

Mastering Embedded Linux Programming is organized along the lines of the life cycle of a typical embedded Linux project. The first six chapters tell you what you need to know about how to set up the project and how a Linux system is put together, culminating in selecting an appropriate Linux build system. Next, comes the stage where certain key decisions must be made about the system architecture and design choices, including flash memory, device drivers, and the init system. Following this is the phase of writing applications to make use of the embedded platform you have built, and for which there are two chapters on processes, threads, and memory management. Finally, we come to the stage of debugging and optimizing the platform, which is discussed in chapters 12 and 13. The last chapter describes how to configure Linux for real-time applications.

Chapter 1, Starting Out, sets the scene by describing the choices available to the system designer at the start of a project.

Chapter 2, Learning About Toolchains, describes the components of a toolchain with an emphasis on cross-compiling. It describes where to get a toolchain and provides details on how to build one from the source code.

Chapter 3, All About Bootloaders, explains the role of the bootloader to initialize the hardware of the device and uses U-Boot and Bareboot as examples. It also describes the device tree, which is a means of encoding the hardware configuration, used in many embedded systems.

Chapter 4, Porting and Configuring the Kernel, provides information on how to select a Linux kernel for an embedded system and configure it for the hardware within the device. It also covers how to port Linux to the new hardware.

Chapter 5, Building a Root Filesystem, introduces the ideas behind the user space part of an embedded Linux implementation by means of a step-by-step guide on how to configure a root filesystem.

Chapter 6, Selecting a Build System, covers two embedded Linux build systems, which automate the steps described in the previous four chapters and conclude the first section of the book.

Chapter 7, Creating a Storage Strategy, discusses the challenges created by managing flash memory, including raw flash chips and embedded MMC or eMMC packages. It describes the filesystems that are applicable to each type of technology. It also covers techniques on how to update the device firmware in the field.

Chapter 8, Introducing Device Drivers, describes how kernel device drivers interact with the hardware with worked examples of a simple driver. It also describes the various ways of calling device drivers from the user space.

Chapter 9, Starting up - the init Program, shows how the first user space program, init, which starts the rest of the system. It describes the three versions of the init program, each suitable for a different group of embedded systems, with increasing complexity from BusyBox init to systemd.

Chapter 10, Learning About Processes and Threads, describes embedded systems from the point of view of the application programmer. This chapter looks at processes and threads, inter-process communication, and scheduling policies.

Chapter 11, Managing Memory, introduces the ideas behind virtual memory and how the address space is divided into memory mappings. It also covers how to detect memory that is being used and memory leaks.

Chapter 12, Debugging with GDB, shows you how to use the GNU debugger, GDB, to interactively debug both the user space and kernel code. It also describes the kernel debugger, kdb.

Chapter 13, Profiling and Tracing, covers the techniques available to measure the system performance, starting from whole system profiles and then zeroing in on particular areas where bottlenecks are causing poor performance. It also describes Valgrind as a tool to check the correctness of an application's use of thread synchronization and memory allocation.

Chapter 14, Real-time Programming, provides a detailed guide to real-time programming on Linux, including the configuration of the kernel and the real-time kernel patch, and also provides a description of tools to measure real-time latencies. It also covers information on how to reduce the number of page faults by locking the memory.

What you need for this book

The software used in this book is entirely open source. The versions used are, in most cases, the latest stable versions available at the time of writing. While I have tried to describe the main features in a manner that are not specific to a particular version, it is inevitable that the examples of commands contain some details that will not work with the later versions. I hope that the descriptions that accompany them are sufficiently informative so that you can apply the same principles to the later versions of the package.

There are two systems involved in creating an embedded system: the host system that is used to cross-compile the software and the target system on which it runs. For the host system, I have used Ubuntu 14.04, but most Linux distributions will work with little modification. In the same way, I had to choose a target system to represent an embedded system. I chose two: the BeagelBone Black and the QEMU CPU emulator, emulating an ARM target. The latter target means that you can try out the examples without having to invest in the hardware for an actual target device. At the same time, it should be possible to apply the examples to a wide range of targets with adaptations for specifics, such as device names and memory layout.

The versions of the main packages for the target are U-Boot 2015.07, Linux 4.1, Yocto Project 1.8 "Fido", and Buildroot 2015.08.

Who this book is for

This book is ideal for Linux developers and system programmers who are already familiar with embedded systems and who want to know how to create best-in-class devices. A basic understanding of C programming and experience with systems programming is needed.

Conventions

In this book, you will find a number of text styles that distinguish between different kinds of information. Here are some examples of these styles and an explanation of their meaning.

Code words in text, database table names, folder names, filenames, file extensions, pathnames, dummy URLs, user input, and Twitter handles are shown as follows: "We could use the stream I/O functions `fopen(3)`, `fread(3)`, and `fclose(3)`."

A block of code is set as follows:

```
static struct mtd_partition omap3beagle_nand_partitions[] = {
  /* All the partition sizes are listed in terms of NAND block
size */
  {
    .name          = "X-Loader",
    .offset        = 0,
    .size          = 4 * NAND_BLOCK_SIZE,
    .mask_flags    = MTD_WRITEABLE,   /* force read-only */
  }
}
```

When we wish to draw your attention to a particular part of a code block, the relevant lines or items are set in bold:

```
static struct mtd_partition omap3beagle_nand_partitions[] = {
  /* All the partition sizes are listed in terms of NAND block
size */
  {
    .name        = "X-Loader",
    .offset      = 0,
    .size        = 4 * NAND_BLOCK_SIZE,
    .mask_flags  = MTD_WRITEABLE,  /* force read-only */
  }
}
```

Any command-line input or output is written as follows:

```
# flash_erase -j /dev/mtd6 0 0
# nandwrite /dev/mtd6 rootfs-sum.jffs2
```

New terms and **important words** are shown in bold. Words that you see on the screen, for example, in menus or dialog boxes, appear in the text like this: "The second line prints the message **Please press Enter to activate this console** on the console."

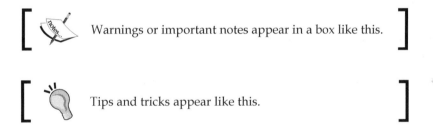

Warnings or important notes appear in a box like this.

Tips and tricks appear like this.

Reader feedback

Feedback from our readers is always welcome. Let us know what you think about this book — what you liked or disliked. Reader feedback is important for us as it helps us develop titles that you will really get the most out of.

To send us general feedback, simply e-mail feedback@packtpub.com, and mention the book's title in the subject of your message.

If there is a topic that you have expertise in and you are interested in either writing or contributing to a book, see our author guide at www.packtpub.com/authors.

Customer support

Now that you are the proud owner of a Packt book, we have a number of things to help you to get the most from your purchase.

Downloading the example code

You can download the example code files from your account at http://www. packtpub.com for all the Packt Publishing books you have purchased. If you purchased this book elsewhere, you can visit http://www.packtpub.com/support and register to have the files e-mailed directly to you.

Errata

Although we have taken every care to ensure the accuracy of our content, mistakes do happen. If you find a mistake in one of our books—maybe a mistake in the text or the code—we would be grateful if you could report this to us. By doing so, you can save other readers from frustration and help us improve subsequent versions of this book. If you find any errata, please report them by visiting http://www.packtpub. com/submit-errata, selecting your book, clicking on the **Errata Submission Form** link, and entering the details of your errata. Once your errata are verified, your submission will be accepted and the errata will be uploaded to our website or added to any list of existing errata under the Errata section of that title.

To view the previously submitted errata, go to https://www.packtpub.com/books/ content/support and enter the name of the book in the search field. The required information will appear under the **Errata** section.

Piracy

Piracy of copyrighted material on the Internet is an ongoing problem across all media. At Packt, we take the protection of our copyright and licenses very seriously. If you come across any illegal copies of our works in any form on the Internet, please provide us with the location address or website name immediately so that we can pursue a remedy.

Please contact us at copyright@packtpub.com with a link to the suspected pirated material.

We appreciate your help in protecting our authors and our ability to bring you valuable content.

Questions

If you have a problem with any aspect of this book, you can contact us at
questions@packtpub.com, and we will do our best to address the problem.

1
Starting Out

You are about to begin working on your next project, and this time it is going to be running Linux. What should you think about before you put finger to keyboard? Let's begin with a high-level look at embedded Linux and see why it is popular, what are the implications of open source licenses, and what kind of hardware you will need to run Linux.

Linux first became a viable choice for embedded devices around 1999. That was when Axis (www.axis.com) released their first Linux-powered network camera and TiVo (www.tivo.com) their first **DVR (Digital Video Recorder)**. Since 1999, Linux has become ever more popular, to the point that today it is the operating system of choice for many classes of product. At the time of writing, in 2015, there are about two billion devices running Linux. That includes a large number of smartphones running Android, which uses a Linux kernel, and hundreds of millions of set top boxes, smart TVs, and Wi-Fi routers, not to mention a very diverse range of devices such as vehicle diagnostics, weighing scales, industrial devices, and medical monitoring units that ship in smaller volumes.

So, why does your TV run Linux? At first glance, the function of a TV is simple: it has to display a stream of video on a screen. Why is a complex Unix-like operating system like Linux necessary?

The simple answer is Moore's Law: Gordon Moore, co-founder of Intel, observed in 1965 that the density of components on a chip will double about every two years. That applies to the devices that we design and use in our everyday lives just as much as it does to desktops, laptops, and servers. At the heart of most embedded devices is a highly integrated chip that contains one or more processor cores and interfaces with main memory, mass storage, and peripherals of many types. This is referred to as a System on Chip, or SoC, and they are increasing in complexity in accordance with Moore's Law. A typical SoC has a technical reference manual that stretches to thousands of pages. Your TV is not simply displaying a video stream as the old analog sets used to do.

The stream is digital, possibly encrypted, and it needs processing to create an image. Your TV is (or soon will be) connected to the Internet. It can receive content from smartphones, tablets, and home media servers. It can be (or soon will be) used to play games. And so on and so on. You need a full operating system to manage this degree of complexity.

Here are some points that drive the adoption of Linux:

- Linux has the necessary functionality. It has a good scheduler, a good network stack, support for USB, Wi-Fi, Bluetooth, many kinds of storage media, good support for multimedia devices, and so on. It ticks all the boxes.

- Linux has been ported to a wide range of processor architectures, including some that are very commonly found in SoC designs — ARM, MIPS, x86, and PowerPC.

- Linux is open source, so you have the freedom to get the source code and modify it to meet your needs. You, or someone working on your behalf, can create a board support package for your particular SoC board or device. You can add protocols, features, and technologies that may be missing from the mainline source code. You can remove features that you don't need to reduce memory and storage requirements. Linux is flexible.

- Linux has an active community; in the case of the Linux kernel, very active. There is a new release of the kernel every 10 to 12 weeks, and each release contains code from around 1,000 developers. An active community means that Linux is up to date and supports current hardware, protocols, and standards.

- Open source licenses guarantee that you have access to the source code. There is no vendor tie-in.

For these reasons, Linux is an ideal choice for complex devices. But there are a few caveats I should mention here. Complexity makes it harder to understand. Coupled with the fast moving development process and the decentralized structures of open source, you have to put some effort into learning how to use it and to keep on re-learning as it changes. I hope that this book will help in the process.

Selecting the right operating system

Is Linux suitable for your project? Linux works well where the problem being solved justifies the complexity. It is especially good where connectivity, robustness, and complex user interfaces are required. However it cannot solve every problem, so here are some things to consider before you jump in:

- Is your hardware up to the job? Compared to a traditional **RTOS (real-time operating system)** such as VxWorks, Linux requires a lot more resources. It needs at least a 32-bit processor, and lots more memory. I will go into more detail in the section on typical hardware requirements.

- Do you have the right skill set? The early parts of a project, board bring-up, require detailed knowledge of Linux and how it relates to your hardware. Likewise, when debugging and tuning your application, you will need to be able to interpret the results. If you don't have the skills in-house you may want to outsource some of the work. Of course, reading this book helps!

- Is your system real-time? Linux can handle many real-time activities so long as you pay attention to certain details, which I will cover in detail in *Chapter 14, Real-time Programming*.

Consider these points carefully. Probably the best indicator of success is to look around for similar products that run Linux and see how they have done it; follow best practice.

The players

Where does open source software come from? Who writes it? In particular, how does this relate to the key components of embedded development—the toolchain, bootloader, kernel, and basic utilities found in the root filesystem?

The main players are:

- The open source community. This, after all, is the engine that generates the software you are going to be using. The community is a loose alliance of developers, many of whom are funded in some way, perhaps by a not-for-profit organization, an academic institution, or a commercial company. They work together to further the aims of the various projects. There are many of them, some small, some large. Some that we will be making use of in the remainder of this book are Linux itself, U-Boot, BusyBox, Buildroot, the Yocto Project, and the many projects under the GNU umbrella.

- CPU architects — These are the organizations that design the CPUs we use. The important ones here are ARM/Linaro (ARM-based SoCs), Intel (x86 and x86_64), Imagination Technologies (MIPS), and Freescale/IBM (PowerPC). They implement or, at the very least, influence support for the basic CPU architecture.

- SoC vendors (Atmel, Broadcom, Freescale, Intel, Qualcomm, TI, and many others) — They take the kernel and toolchain from the CPU architects and modify it to support their chips. They also create reference boards: designs that are used by the next level down to create development boards and working products.

- Board vendors and OEMs — these people take the reference designs from SoC vendors and build them in to specific products, for instance set-top-boxes or cameras, or create more general purpose development boards, such as those from Avantech and Kontron. An important category are the cheap development boards such as BeagleBoard/BeagleBone and Raspberry Pi that have created their own ecosystems of software and hardware add-ons.

These form a chain, with your project usually at the end, which means that you do not have a free choice of components. You cannot simply take the latest kernel from kernel.org, except in a few rare cases, because it does not have support for the chip or board that you are using.

This is an ongoing problem with embedded development. Ideally, the developers at each link in the chain would push their changes upstream, but they don't. It is not uncommon to find a kernel which has many thousands of patches that are not merged upstream. In addition, SoC vendors tend to actively develop open source components only for their latest chips, meaning that support for any chip more than a couple of years old will be frozen and not receive any updates.

The consequence is that most embedded designs are based on old versions of software. They do not receive security fixes, performance enhancements, or features that are in newer versions. Problems such as Heartbleed (a bug in the OpenSSL libraries) and Shellshock (a bug in the bash shell) go unfixed. I will talk more about this later in this chapter under the topic of security.

What can you do about it? First, ask questions of your vendors: what is their update policy, how often do they revise kernel versions, what is the current kernel version, what was the one before that? What is their policy for merging changes up-stream? Some vendors are making great strides in this way. You should prefer their chips.

Secondly, you can take steps to make yourself more self-sufficient. This book aims to explain the dependencies in more detail and show you where you can help yourself. Don't just take the package offered to you by the SoC or board vendor and use it blindly without considering the alternatives.

Project lifecycle

This book is divided into four sections that reflect the phases of a project. The phases are not necessarily sequential. Usually they overlap and you will need to jump back to revisit things that were done previously. However, they are representative of a developer's preoccupations as the project progresses:

- Elements of embedded Linux (chapters 1 to 6) will help you set up the development environment and create a working platform for the later phases. It is often referred to as the "board bring-up" phase.

- System architecture and design choices (chapters 7 to 9) will help you to look at some of the design decisions you will have to make concerning the storage of programs and data, how to divide work between kernel device drivers and applications, and how to initialize the system.

- Writing embedded applications (chapters 10 and 11) show how to make effective use of the Linux process and threads model and how to manage memory in a resource-constrained device.

- Debugging and optimizing performance (chapters 12 and 13) describe how to trace, profile, and debug your code in both the applications and the kernel.

The fifth section on real-time (*Chapter 14, Real-time Programming*) stands somewhat alone because it is a small, but important, category of embedded systems. Designing for real-time behavior has an impact on each of the four main phases.

The four elements of embedded Linux

Every project begins by obtaining, customizing, and deploying these four elements: the toolchain, the bootloader, the kernel, and the root filesystem. This is the topic of the first section of this book:

- **Toolchain**: This consists of the compiler and other tools needed to create code for your target device. Everything else depends on the toolchain.

- **Bootloader**: This is necessary to initialize the board and to load and boot the Linux kernel.

- **Kernel**: This is the heart of the system, managing system resources and interfacing with hardware.

- **Root filesystem**: This contains the libraries and programs that are run once the kernel has completed its initialization.

Of course, there is also a fifth element, not mentioned here. That is the collection of programs that are specific to your embedded application which make the device do whatever it is supposed to do, be it weigh groceries, display movies, control a robot, or fly a drone.

Typically you will be offered some or all of these elements as a package when you buy your SoC or board. But, for the reasons mentioned in the preceding paragraph, they may not be the best choices for you. I will give you the background to make the right selections in the first six chapters and I will introduce you to two tools that automate the whole process for you: Buildroot and the Yocto Project.

Open source

The components of embedded Linux are open source, so now is a good time to consider what that means, why open sources work the way they do and how this affects the often proprietary embedded device you will be creating from it.

Licenses

When talking about open source, the word, "free" is often used. People new to the subject often take it to mean nothing to pay, and open source software licenses do indeed guarantee that you can use the software to develop and deploy systems for no charge. However, the more important meaning here is freedom, since you are free to obtain the source code and modify it in any way you see fit and redeploy it in other systems. These licenses give you this right. Compare that with shareware licenses which allow you to copy the binaries for no cost but do not give you the source code, or other licenses that allow you to use the software for free under certain circumstances, for example, for personal use but not commercial.
These are not open source.

I will provide the following comments in the interest of helping you understand the implications of working with open source licenses, but I would like to point out that I am an engineer and not a lawyer. What follows is my understanding of the licenses and the way they are interpreted.

Open source licenses fall broadly into two categories: the **GPL (General Public License)** from the Free Software Foundation and the permissive licenses derived from **BSD (Berkeley Software Distribution)**, the Apache Foundation, and others.

The permissive licenses say, in essence, that you may modify the source code and use it in systems of your own choosing so long as you do not modify the terms of the license in any way. In other words, with that one restriction, you can do with it what you want, including building it into possibly proprietary systems.

The GPL licenses are similar, but have clauses which compel you to pass the rights to obtain and modify the software on to your end users. In other words you share your source code. One option is to make it completely public by putting it onto a public server. Another is to offer it only to your end users by means of a written offer to provide the code when requested. The GPL goes further to say that you cannot incorporate GPL code into proprietary programs. Any attempt to do so would make the GPL apply to the whole. In other words, you cannot combine GPL and proprietary code in one program.

So, what about libraries? If they are licensed with the GPL, any program linked with them becomes GPL also. However, most libraries are licensed under the **Lesser General Public License (LGPL)**. If this is the case, you are allowed to link with them from a proprietary program.

All of the preceding description relates specifically to GPL v2 and LGPL v2.1. I should mention the latest versions of GPL v3 and LGPL v3. These are controversial, and I will admit that I don't fully understand the implications. However, the intention is to ensure that the GPLv3 and LGPL v3 components in any system can be replaced by the end user, which is in the spirit of open source software for everyone. It does pose some problems though. Some Linux devices are used to gain access to information according to a subscription level or another restriction, and replacing critical parts of the software may compromise that. Set-top boxes fit into this category. There are also issues with security. If the owner of a device has access to the system code, then so might an unwelcome intruder. Often the defense is to have kernel images that are signed by an authority, the vendor, so that unauthorized updates are not possible. Is that an infringement of my right to modify my device? Opinions differ.

The TiVo set-top box is an important part of this debate. It uses a Linux kernel, which is licensed under GPL v2. TiVo release the source code of their version of the kernel and so comply with the license. TiVo also have a bootloader that will only load a kernel binary that is signed by them. Consequently, you can build a modified kernel for a TiVo box, but you cannot load it on the hardware. The FSF take the position that this is not in the spirit of open source software and refer to this procedure as "tivoization". The GPL v3 and LGPL v3 were written to explicitly prevent this happening. Some projects, the Linux kernel in particular, have been reluctant to adopt the version three licenses because of the restrictions it would place on device manufacturers.

Hardware for embedded Linux

If you are designing or selecting hardware for an embedded Linux project, what do you look out for?

Firstly, a CPU architecture that is supported by the kernel – unless you plan to add a new architecture yourself of course! Looking at the source code for Linux 4.1, there are 30 architectures, each represented by a sub-directory in the arch/ directory. They are all 32- or 64-bit architectures, most with a **memory management unit (MMU)**, but some without. The ones most often found in embedded devices are ARM, MIPS, PowerPC, and X86, each in 32- and 64-bit variants, and all of which have memory management units.

Most of this book is written with this class of processor in mind. There is another group that doesn't have an MMU that runs a subset of Linux known as micro controller Linux or uClinux. These processor architectures include ARC, Blackfin, Microblaze, and Nios. I will mention uClinux from time to time but I will not go into details because it is a rather specialized topic.

Secondly, you will need a reasonable amount of RAM. 16 MiB is a good minimum, although it is quite possible to run Linux using half that. It is even possible to run Linux with 4 MiB if you are prepared to go to the trouble of optimizing every part of the system. It may even be possible to get lower, but there comes a point at which it is no longer Linux.

Thirdly, there is non-volatile storage, usually flash memory. 8 MiB is enough for a simple device such as a webcam or a simple router. As with RAM, you can create a workable Linux system with less storage if you really want to but, the lower you go, the harder it becomes. Linux has extensive support for flash storage devices, including raw NOR and NAND flash chips and managed flash in the form of SD cards, eMMC chips, USB flash memory, and so on.

Fourthly, a debug port is very useful, most commonly an RS-232 serial port. It does not have to be fitted on production boards, but makes board bring-up, debugging, and development much easier.

Fifthly, you need some means of loading software when starting from scratch. A few years ago, boards would have been fitted with a JTAG interface for this purpose, but modern SoCs have the ability to load boot code directly from removable media, especially SD and micro SD cards, or serial interfaces such as RS-232 or USB.

In addition to these basics, there are interfaces to the specific bits of hardware your device needs to get its job done. Mainline Linux comes with open source drivers for many thousands of different devices, and there are drivers (of variable quality) from the SoC manufacturer and drivers from the OEMs of third-party chips that may be included in the design, but remember my comments on the commitment and ability of some manufacturers. As a developer of embedded devices, you will find that you spend quite a lot of time evaluating and adapting third-party code, if you have it, or liaising with the manufacturer if you don't. Finally, you will have to write the device support for any interfaces that are unique to the device, or find someone to do it for you.

Hardware used in this book

The worked examples in this book are intended to be generic, but to make them relevant and easy to follow, I have had to choose a specific device as an example. I have used two exemplar devices: the BeagleBone Black and QEMU. The first is a widely-available and cheap development board which can be used in serious embedded hardware. The second is a machine emulator that can be used to create a range of systems that are typical of embedded hardware. It was tempting to use QEMU exclusively, but, like all emulations, it is not quite the same as the real thing. Using a BeagleBone, you have the satisfaction of interacting with real hardware and seeing real LEDs flash. It was also tempting to select a more up-to-date board than the BeagleBone Black, which is several years old now, but I believe that its popularity gives it a degree of longevity and means that it will continue to be available for some years yet.

In any case, I encourage you to try out as many of the examples as you can using either of these two platforms, or indeed any embedded hardware you may have to hand.

The BeagleBone Black

The BeagleBone and the later BeagleBone Black are open hardware designs for a small, credit card sized development board produced by Circuitco LLC. The main repository of information is at www.beagleboard.org. The main points of the specification are:

- TI AM335x 1GHz ARM® Cortex-A8 Sitara SoC
- 512 MiB DDR3 RAM
- 2 or 4 GiB 8-bit eMMC on-board flash storage
- Serial port for debug and development

- MicroSD connector, which can be used as the boot device
- Mini USB OTG client/host port that can also be used to power the board
- Full size USB 2.0 host port
- 10/100 Ethernet port
- HDMI for video and audio output

In addition, there are two 46-pin expansion headers for which there are a great variety of daughter boards, known as capes, which allow you to adapt the board to do many different things. However, you do not need to fit any capes in the examples in this book.

In addition to the board itself, you will need:

- a mini USB to full-size USB cable (supplied with the board) to provide power, unless you have the last item on this list.
- an RS-232 cable that can interface with the 6-pin 3.3 volt TTL level signals provided by the board. The Beagleboard website has links to compatible cables.
- a microSD card and a means of writing to it from your development PC or laptop, which will be needed to load software onto the board.
- an Ethernet cable, as some of the examples require network connectivity.
- optional, but recommended, a 5V power supply capable of delivering 1 A or more.

QEMU

QEMU is a machine emulator. It comes in a number of different flavors, each of which can emulate a processor architecture and a number of boards built using that architecture. For example, we have the following:

- **qemu-system-arm**: ARM
- **qemu-system-mips**: MIPS
- **qemu-system-ppc**: PowerPC
- **qemu-system-x86**: x86 and x86_64

For each architecture, QEMU emulates a range of hardware, which you can see by using the option `-machine help`. Each machine emulates most of the hardware that would normally be found on that board. There are options to link hardware to local resources, such as using a local file for the emulated disk drive. Here is a concrete example:

```
$ qemu-system-arm -machine vexpress-a9 -m 256M -drive
file=rootfs.ext4,sd -net nic -net use -kernel zImage -dtb vexpress-
v2p-ca9.dtb -append "console=ttyAMA0,115200 root=/dev/mmcblk0" -
serial stdio -net nic,model=lan9118 -net tap,ifname=tap0
```

The options used in the preceding command line are:

- `-machine vexpress-a9`: creates an emulation of an ARM Versatile Express development board with a Cortex A-9 processor
- `-m 256M`: populates it with 256 MiB of RAM
- `-drive file=rootfs.ext4,sd`: connect the `sd` interface to the local file `rootfs.ext4` (which contains a filesystem image)
- `-kernel zImage`: loads the Linux kernel from the local file named `zImage`
- `-dtb vexpress-v2p-ca9.dtb`: loads the device tree from the local file `vexpress-v2p-ca9.dtb`
- `-append "..."`: supplies this string as the kernel command line
- `-serial stdio`: connects the serial port to the terminal that launched QEMU, usually so that you can log on to the emulated machine via the serial console
- `-net nic,model=lan9118`: creates a network interface
- `-net tap,ifname=tap0`: connects the network interface to the virtual network interface `tap0`

To configure the host side of the network, you need the `tunctl` command from the **User Mode Linux (UML)** project; on Debian and Ubuntu the package is named `uml-utilities`. You use it to create a virtual network using the following command:

```
$ sudo tunctl -u $(whoami) -t tap0
```

This creates a network interface named `tap0` which is connected to the network controller in the emulated QEMU machine. You configure `tap0` in exactly the same way as any other interface.

All of these options are described in detail in the following chapters. I will be using Versatile Express for most of my examples, but it should be easy to use a different machine or architecture.

Software used in this book

I have used only open source software both for the development tools and the target operating system and applications. I assume that you will be using Linux on your development system. I tested all the host commands using Ubuntu 14.04 and so there is a slight bias towards that particular version, but any modern Linux distribution is likely to work just fine.

Summary

Embedded hardware will continue to get more complex, following the trajectory set by Moore's Law. Linux has the power and the flexibility to make use of hardware in an efficient way.

Linux is just one component of open source software out of the many that you need to create a working product. The fact that the code is freely available means that people and organizations at many different levels can contribute. However, the sheer variety of embedded platforms and the fast pace of development lead to isolated pools of software which are not shared as efficiently as they should be. In many cases, you will become dependent on this software, especially the Linux kernel that is provided by your SoC or Board vendor, and to a lesser extent the toolchain. Some SoC manufacturers are getting better at pushing their changes upstream and the maintenance of these changes is getting easier.

Fortunately, there are some powerful tools that can help you create and maintain the software for your device. For example, Buildroot is ideal for small systems and the Yocto Project for larger ones.

Before I describe these build tools, I will describe the four elements of embedded Linux, which you can apply to all embedded Linux projects, however they are created. The next chapter is all about the first of these, the toolchain, which you need to compile code for your target platform.

2
Learning About Toolchains

The toolchain is the first element of embedded Linux and the starting point of your project. The choices you make at this early stage will have a profound impact on the final outcome. Your toolchain should be capable of making effective use of your hardware by using the optimum instruction set for your processor, using the floating point unit if there is one, and so on. It should support the languages that you require and have a solid implementation of POSIX and other system interfaces. Not only that, but it should be updated when security flaws are discovered or bugs found. Finally, it should be constant throughout the project. In other words, once you have chosen your toolchain it is important to stick with it. Changing compilers and development libraries in an inconsistent way during a project will lead to subtle bugs.

Obtaining a toolchain is as simple as downloading and installing a package. But, the toolchain itself is a complex thing, as I will show you in this chapter.

What is a toolchain?

A toolchain is the set of tools that compiles source code into executables that can run on your target device, and includes a compiler, a linker, and run-time libraries. Initially, you need one to build the other three elements of an embedded Linux system: the bootloader, the kernel, and the root filesystem. It has to be able to compile code written in assembly, C, and C++ since these are the languages used in the base open source packages.

Usually, toolchains for Linux are based on components from the GNU project (http://www.gnu.org) and that is still true in the majority of cases at the time of writing. However, over the past few years, the Clang compiler and the associated LLVM project (http://llvm.org) have progressed to the point that it is now a viable alternative to a GNU toolchain. One major distinction between LLVM and GNU-based toolchains is in the licensing; LLVM has a BSD license, while GNU has the GPL. There are some technical advantages to Clang as well, such as faster compilation and better diagnostics, but GNU GCC has the advantage of compatibility with the existing code base and support for a wide range of architectures and operating systems. Indeed, there are still some areas where Clang cannot replace the GNU C compiler, especially when it comes to compiling a mainline Linux kernel. It is probable that, in the next year or so, Clang will be able to compile all the components needed for embedded Linux and so will become an alternative to GNU. There is a good description of how to use Clang for cross compilation at http://clang.llvm.org/docs/CrossCompilation. html. If you would like to use it as part of an embedded Linux build system, the EmbToolkit (https://www.embtoolkit.org) fully supports both GNU and LLVM/ Clang toolchains and various people are working on using Clang with Buildroot and the Yocto Project. I will cover embedded build systems in *Chapter 6, Selecting a Build System*. Meanwhile, this chapter focuses on the GNU toolchain as it is the only complete option at this time.

A standard GNU toolchain consists of three main components:

- **Binutils**: A set of binary utilities including the assembler, and the linker, ld. It is available at http://www.gnu.org/software/binutils/.

- **GNU Compiler Collection (GCC)**: These are the compilers for C and other languages which, depending on the version of GCC, include C++, Objective-C, Objective-C++, Java, Fortran, Ada, and Go. They all use a common back-end which produces assembler code which is fed to the GNU assembler. It is available at http://gcc.gnu.org/.

- **C library**: A standardized API based on the POSIX specification which is the principle interface to the operating system kernel from applications. There are several C libraries to consider, see the following section.

As well as these, you will need a copy of the Linux kernel headers, which contain definitions and constants that are needed when accessing the kernel directly. Right now, you need them to be able to compile the C library, but you will also need them later when writing programs or compiling libraries that interact with particular Linux devices, for example to display graphics via the Linux frame buffer driver. This is not simply a question of making a copy of the header files in the include directory of your kernel source code. Those headers are intended for use in the kernel only and contain definitions that will cause conflicts if used in their raw state to compile regular Linux applications.

Instead, you will need to generate a set of sanitized kernel headers which I have illustrated in *Chapter 5, Building a Root Filesystem*.

It is not usually crucial whether the kernel headers are generated from the exact version of Linux you are going to be using or not. Since the kernel interfaces are always backwards-compatible, it is only necessary that the headers are from a kernel that is the same as or older than the one you are using on the target.

Most people would consider the GNU debugger, GDB, to be part of the toolchain as well, and it is usual that it is built at this point. I will talk about GDB in *Chapter 12, Debugging with GDB*.

Types of toolchain - native versus cross toolchain

For our purposes, there are two types of toolchain:

- **Native**: This toolchain runs on the same type of system, sometimes the same actual system, as the programs it generates. This is the usual case for desktops and servers, and it is becoming popular on certain classes of embedded devices. The Raspberry Pi running Debian for ARM, for example, has self-hosted native compilers.

- **Cross**: This toolchain runs on a different type of system than the target, allowing the development to be done on a fast desktop PC and then loaded onto the embedded target for testing.

Almost all embedded Linux development is done using a cross development toolchain, partly because most embedded devices are not well suited to program development since they lack computing power, memory, and storage, but also because it keeps the host and target environments separate. The latter point is especially important when the host and the target are using the same architecture, X86_64, for example. In this case, it is tempting to compile natively on the host and simply copy the binaries to the target. This works up to a point but it is likely that the host distribution will receive updates more often than the target, that different engineers building code for the target will have slightly different versions of the host development libraries and so you will violate the principle that the toolchain should remain constant throughout the life of the project. You can make this approach work if you ensure that the host and target build environments are in lockstep with each other, but a much better approach is to keep the host and the target separate, and a cross toolchain is a way to do that.

However, there is a counter argument in favor of native development. Cross development creates the burden of cross-compiling all the libraries and tools that you need for your target. We will see later on in this chapter that cross-compiling is not always simple because most open source packages are not designed to be built in this way. Integrated build tools, including Buildroot and the Yocto Project, help by encapsulating the rules to cross compile a range of packages that you need in typical embedded systems but, if you want to compile a large number of additional packages, then it is better to natively compile them. For example, to provide a Debian distribution for the Raspberry Pi or BeagleBone using a cross compiler is impossible, they have to be natively compiled. Creating a native build environment from scratch is not easy and involves creating a cross compiler first to bootstrap a native build environment on the target and using that to build packages. You would need a build farm of well-provisioned target boards or you may be able to use QEMU to emulate the target. If you want to look into this further, you may want to look at the Scratchbox project, now in its second incarnation as Scratchbox2 (`https://maemo.gitorious.org/scratchbox2`). It was developed by Nokia to build their Maemo Linux operating system, and is used today by the Mer project and the Tizen project, among others.

Meanwhile, in this chapter, I will focus on the more mainstream cross compiler environment, which is relatively easy to set up and administer.

CPU architectures

The toolchain has to be built according to the capabilities of the target CPU, which includes:

- **CPU architecture**: arm, mips, x86_64, and so on
- **Big- or little-endian operation**: Some CPUs can operate in both modes, but the machine code is different for each
- **Floating point support**: Not all versions of embedded processors implement a hardware floating point unit, in which case, the toolchain can be configured to call a software floating point library instead
- **Application Binary Interface (ABI)**: The calling convention used for passing parameters between function calls

With many architectures, the ABI is constant across the family of processors. One notable exception is ARM. The ARM architecture transitioned to the **Extended Application Binary Interface (EABI)** in the late 2000's, resulting in the previous ABI being named the **Old Application Binary Interface (OABI)**. While the OABI is now obsolete, you continue to see references to EABI. Since then, the EABI has split into two, based on the way that floating point parameters are passed. The original EABI uses general purpose (integer) registers while the newer EABIHF uses floating point registers. The EABIHF is significantly faster at floating point operations since it removes the need for copying between integer and floating point registers, but it is not compatible with CPUs that do not have a floating point unit. The choice, then, is between two incompatible ABIs: you cannot mix and match the two and so you have to decide at this stage.

GNU uses a prefix to the tools to identify the various combinations that can be generated, consisting of a tuple of three or four components separated by dashes, as described here:

- **CPU**: The CPU architecture, such as arm, mips, or x86_64. If the CPU has both endian modes, they may be differentiated by adding el for little-endian, or eb for big-endian. Good examples are little-endian MIPS, mipsel and big-endian ARM, armeb.
- **Vendor**: This identifies the provider of the toolchain. Examples include buildroot, poky, or just unknown. Sometimes it is left out altogether.
- **Kernel**: For our purposes, it is always 'linux'.
- **Operating system**: A name for the user space component, which might be gnu or uclibcgnu. The ABI may be appended here as well so, for ARM toolchains, you may see gnueabi, gnueabihf, uclibcgnueabi, or uclibcgnueabihf.

You can find the tuple used when building the toolchain by using the -dumpmachine option of gcc. For example, you may see the following on the host computer:

```
$ gcc -dumpmachine
x86_64-linux-gnu
```

> When a native compiler is installed on a machine, it is normal to create links to each of the tools in the toolchain with no prefixes so that you can call the compiler with the command gcc.

Here is an example using a cross compiler:

```
$ mipsel-unknown-linux-gnu-gcc -dumpmachine
mipsel-unknown-linux-gnu
```

Choosing the C library

The programming interface to the Unix operating system is defined in the
C language, which is now defined by the POSIX standards. The C library is
the implementation of that interface; it is the gateway to the kernel for Linux
programs, as shown in the following diagram. Even if you are writing programs
in another language, maybe Java or Python, the respective run-time support
libraries will have to call the C library eventually:

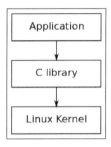

The C library is the gateway to the kernel for applications

Whenever the C library needs the services of the kernel it will use the kernel `system call` interface to transition between user space and kernel space. It is possible to bypass the C library by making kernel system calls directly, but that is a lot of trouble and almost never necessary.

There are several C libraries to choose from. The main options are as follows:

- **glibc**: Available at `http://www.gnu.org/software/libc`. It is the standard GNU C library. It is big and, until recently, not very configurable, but it is the most complete implementation of the POSIX API.

- **eglibc**: Available at `http://www.eglibc.org/home`. This is the embedded GLIBC. It was a series of patches to glibc which added configuration options and support for architectures not covered by glibc (specifically, the PowerPC e500). The split between eglibc and glibc was always rather artificial and, fortunately, the code base from eglibc has been merged back into glibc as of version 2.20, leaving us with one improved library. eglibc is no longer maintained.

- **uClibc**: Available at `http://www.uclibc.org`. The 'u' is really a Greek 'mu' character, indicating that this is the micro controller C library. It was first developed to work with uClinux (Linux for CPUs without memory management units), but has since been adapted to be used with full Linux. There is a configuration utility which allows you to fine-tune its features to your needs. Even a full configuration is smaller than glibc but it is not as complete an implementation of the POSIX standards.

- **musl libc**: Available at `http://www.musl-libc.org`. It is a new C library designed for embedded systems.

So, which to choose? My advice is to use uClibc only if you are using uClinux or if you have very limited amounts of storage or RAM and so the small size would be an advantage. Otherwise, I prefer to use an up-to-date glibc, or eglibc. I have no experience of musl libc but if you find that glibc/eglibc is not suitable, by all means give it a go. This process is summarized in the following figure:

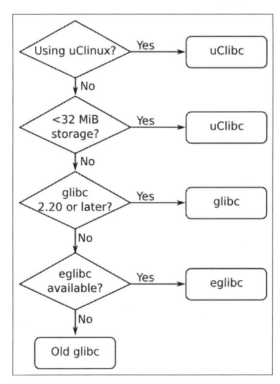

Choosing a C library

Finding a toolchain

You have three choices for your cross development toolchain: you may find a ready built toolchain that matches your needs, you can use the one generated by an embedded build tool which is covered in *Chapter 6, Selecting a Build System*, or you can create one yourself as described later in this chapter.

A pre-built cross toolchain is an attractive option in that you only have to download and install it, but you are limited to the configuration of that particular toolchain and you are dependent on the person or organization you got it from. Most likely, it will be one of these:

- SoC or board vendor. Most vendors offer a Linux toolchain.

- A consortium dedicated to providing system-level support for a given architecture. For example, Linaro, (https://www.linaro.org) have pre-built toolchains for the ARM architecture.

- Third-party Linux tool vendors such as Mentor Graphics, TimeSys, or MontaVista.

- Cross tool packages for your desktop Linux distribution, for example, Debian-based distributions have packages for cross compiling for ARM, MIPS, and PowerPC targets.

- A binary SDK produced by one of the integrated embedded build tools, the Yocto Project has some examples at http://autobuilder.yoctoproject.org/pub/releases/CURRENT/toolchain and there is also the Denx Embedded Linux Development Kit at ftp://ftp.denx.de/pub/eldk/.

- A link from a forum that you can't find any more.

In all of these cases, you have to decide whether the pre-built toolchain on offer meets your requirements. Does it use the C library you prefer? Will the provider give you updates for security fixes and bugs, bearing in mind my comments on support and updates from *Chapter 1, Starting Out*. If your answer is no to any of these then you should consider creating your own.

Unfortunately, building a toolchain is no easy task. If you truly want to do the whole thing yourself, take a look at *Cross Linux From Scratch* (http://trac.clfs.org). There, you will find step-by-step instructions on how to create each component.

A simpler alternative is to use crosstool-NG, which encapsulates the process into a set of scripts and has a menu-driven front-end. You still need a fair degree of knowledge, though, just to make the right choices.

It is simpler still to use a build system such as Buildroot or the Yocto Project since they generate a toolchain as part of the build process. This is my preferred solution as I have shown in *Chapter 6, Selecting a Build System*.

Building a toolchain using crosstool-NG

I am going to begin with crosstool-NG because it allows you to see the process of creating the toolchain and to create several different sorts.

Some years ago, Dan Kegel wrote a set of scripts and makefiles for generating cross development toolchains and called it crosstool (`kegel.com/crosstool`). In 2007, Yann E. Morin used that base to create the next generation of crosstool, crosstool-NG (`crosstool-ng.org`). Today it is, by far, the most convenient way to create a stand-alone cross toolchain from source.

Installing crosstool-NG

Before you begin, you will need a working native toolchain and build tools on your host PC. To work with crosstool-NG on an Ubuntu host, you will need to install the packages using the following command:

```
$ sudo apt-get install automake bison chrpath flex g++ git gperf
gawk libexpat1-dev libncurses5-dev libsdl1.2-dev libtool
python2.7-dev texinfo
```

Next, get the current release from the croostool-NG downloads section, `http://crosstool-ng.org/download/crosstool-ng`. In my examples I have used 1.20.0. Extract it and create the front-end menu system, ct-ng, as shown in the following commands:

```
$ tar xf crosstool-ng-1.20.0.tar.bz2
$ cd crosstool-ng-1.20.0
$ ./configure --enable-local
$ make
$ make install
```

The `--enable-local` option means that the program will be installed into the current directory, which avoids the need for root permissions as would be required if you were to install it in the default location, `/usr/local/bin`. Type `./ct-ng` from the current directory to launch the crosstool menu.

Selecting the toolchain

Crosstool-NG can build many different combinations of toolchains. To make the initial configuration easier, it comes with a set of samples that cover many of the common use-cases. Use ./ct-ng list-samples to generate the list.

As an example, suppose that your target is a BeagleBone Black which has an ARM Cortex A8 core and a VFPv3 floating point unit, and that you want to use a current version of glibc. The closest sample is arm-cortex_a8-linux-gnueabi. You can see the default configuration by prefixing the name with show-:

```
$ ./ct-ng show-arm-cortex_a8-linux-gnueabi

[L..] arm-cortex_a8-linux-gnueabi

OS              : linux-3.15.4

Companion libs  : gmp-5.1.3 mpfr-3.1.2 cloog-ppl-0.18.1 mpc-1.0.2
libelf-0.8.13

binutils        : binutils-2.22

C compiler      : gcc-4.9.1 (C,C++)

C library       : glibc-2.19 (threads: nptl)

Tools           : dmalloc-5.5.2 duma-2_5_15 gdb-7.8 ltrace-
0.7.3 strace-4.8
```

To select this as the target configuration, you would type:

```
$ ./ct-ng  arm-cortex_a8-linux-gnueabi
```

At this point, you can review the configuration and make changes using the configuration menu command menuconfig:

```
$ ./ct-ng menuconfig
```

The menu system is based on the Linux kernel menuconfig and so navigation of the user interface will be familiar to anyone who has configured a kernel. If not, please refer to *Chapter 4, Porting and Configuring the Kernel* for a description of menuconfig.

There are a few configuration changes that I would recommend you make at this point:

- In **Paths and misc** options, disable **Render the toolchain read-only**
  (CT_INSTALL_DIR_RO)

- In **Target options | Floating point,** select **hardware (FPU)**
  (CT_ARCH_FLOAT_HW)

- In **C-library | extra config**, add **--enable-obsolete-rpc**
  (CT_LIBC_GLIBC_EXTRA_CONFIG_ARRAY)

The first is necessary if you want to add libraries to the toolchain after it has been installed, which I will describe later in this chapter. The next is to select the optimum floating point implementation for a processor with a hardware floating point unit. The last forces the toolchain to be generated with an obsolete header file, `rpc.h`, which is still used by a number of packages (note that this is only a problem if you selected glibc). The names in parentheses are the configuration labels stored in the configuration file. When you have made the changes, exit `menuconfig`, and save the configuration as you do so.

The configuration data is saved into a file named `.config`. Looking at the file, you will see that the first line of text reads *Automatically generated make config: don't edit* which is generally good advice, but I recommend that you ignore it in this case. Do you remember from the discussion about toolchain ABIs that ARM has two variants, one which passes floating point parameters in integer registers and one that uses the VFP registers? The float configuration you have just chosen is of the latter type and so the ABI part of the tuple should read `eabihf`. There is a configuration parameter that does exactly what you want but it is not enabled by default, neither does it appear in the menu, at least not in this version of crosstool. Consequently, you will have to edit `.config` and add the line shown in bold as follows:

```
[...]
#
# arm other options
#
CT_ARCH_ARM_MODE="arm"
CT_ARCH_ARM_MODE_ARM=y
# CT_ARCH_ARM_MODE_THUMB is not set
# CT_ARCH_ARM_INTERWORKING is not set
CT_ARCH_ARM_EABI_FORCE=y
CT_ARCH_ARM_EABI=y
CT_ARCH_ARM_TUPLE_USE_EABIHF=y
[...]
```

Now you can use crosstool-NG to get, configure, and build the components according to your specification by typing the following command:

```
$ ./ct-ng build
```

The build will take about half an hour, after which you will find your toolchain is present in `~/x-tools/arm-cortex_a8-linux-gnueabihf/`.

Anatomy of a toolchain

To get an idea of what is in a typical toolchain, I want to examine the crosstool-NG toolchain you have just created.

The toolchain is in the directory `~/x-tools/arm-cortex_a8-linux-gnueabihf/bin`. In there you will find the cross compiler, `arm-cortex_a8-linux-gnueabihf-gcc`. To make use of it, you need to add the directory to your path using the following command:

```
$ PATH=~/x-tools/arm-cortex_a8-linux-gnueabihf/bin:$PATH
```

Now you can take a simple `hello world` program that looks like this:

```
#include <stdio.h>
#include <stdlib.h>
int main (int argc, char *argv[])
{
  printf ("Hello, world!\n");
  return 0;
}
```

And compile it like this:

```
$ arm-cortex_a8-linux-gnueabihf-gcc helloworld.c -o helloworld
```

You can confirm that it has been cross compiled by using the `file` command to print the type of the file:

```
$ file helloworld
```

```
helloworld: ELF 32-bit LSB executable, ARM, version 1 (SYSV),
dynamically linked (uses shared libs), for GNU/Linux 3.15.4, not
stripped
```

Finding out about your cross compiler

Imagine that you have just received a toolchain, and that you would like to know more about how it was configured. You can find out a lot by querying gcc. For example, to find the version, you use `--version`:

```
$ arm-cortex_a8-linux-gnueabi-gcc --version
```

```
arm-cortex_a8-linux-gnueabi-gcc (crosstool-NG 1.20.0) 4.9.1
```

```
Copyright (C) 2014 Free Software Foundation, Inc.
```

```
This is free software; see the source for copying conditions. There
is NO warranty; not even for MERCHANTABILITY or FITNESS FOR A PARTICULAR
PURPOSE.
```

To find how it was configured, use -v:

```
$ arm-cortex_a8-linux-gnueabi-gcc -v
Using built-in specs.
COLLECT_GCC=arm-cortex_a8-linux-gnueabihf-gcc
COLLECT_LTO_WRAPPER=/home/chris/x-tools/arm-cortex_a8-linux-
gnueabihf/libexec/gcc/arm-cortex_a8-linux-gnueabihf/4.9.1/lto-wrapper
Target: arm-cortex_a8-linux-gnueabihf
Configured with:
/home/chris/hd/home/chris/build/MELP/build/crosstool-ng-
1.20.0/.build/src/gcc-4.9.1/configure --build=x86_64-build_unknown-
linux-gnu --host=x86_64-build_unknown-linux-gnu --target=arm-
cortex_a8-linux-gnueabihf --prefix=/home/chris/x-tools/arm-cortex_a8-
linux-gnueabihf --with-sysroot=/home/chris/x-tools/arm-cortex_a8-
linux-gnueabihf/arm-cortex_a8-linux-gnueabihf/sysroot --enable-
languages=c,c++ --with-arch=armv7-a --with-cpu=cortex-a8 --with-
tune=cortex-a8 --with-float=hard --with-pkgversion='crosstool-NG
1.20.0' --enable-__cxa_atexit --disable-libmudflap --disable-libgomp
--disable-libssp --disable-libquadmath --disable-libquadmath-support
--disable-libsanitizer --with-
gmp=/home/chris/hd/home/chris/build/MELP/build/crosstool-ng-
1.20.0/.build/arm-cortex_a8-linux-gnueabihf/buildtools --with-
mpfr=/home/chris/hd/home/chris/build/MELP/build/crosstool-ng-
1.20.0/.build/arm-cortex_a8-linux-gnueabihf/buildtools --with-
mpc=/home/chris/hd/home/chris/build/MELP/build/crosstool-ng-
1.20.0/.build/arm-cortex_a8-linux-gnueabihf/buildtools --with-
isl=/home/chris/hd/home/chris/build/MELP/build/crosstool-ng-
1.20.0/.build/arm-cortex_a8-linux-gnueabihf/buildtools --with-
cloog=/home/chris/hd/home/chris/build/MELP/build/crosstool-ng-
1.20.0/.build/arm-cortex_a8-linux-gnueabihf/buildtools --with-
libelf=/home/chris/hd/home/chris/build/MELP/build/crosstool-ng-
1.20.0/.build/arm-cortex_a8-linux-gnueabihf/buildtools --with-host-
libstdcxx='-static-libgcc -Wl,-Bstatic,-lstdc++,-Bdynamic -lm' --
enable-threads=posix --enable-target-optspace --enable-plugin --
enable-gold --disable-nls --disable-multilib --with-local-
prefix=/home/chris/x-tools/arm-cortex_a8-linux-gnueabihf/arm-
cortex_a8-linux-gnueabihf/sysroot --enable-c99 --enable-long-long
Thread model: posix
gcc version 4.9.1 (crosstool-NG 1.20.0)
```

There is a lot of output there but the interesting things to note are:

- --with-sysroot=/home/chris/x-tools/arm-cortex_a8-linux-gnueabihf/arm-cortex_a8-linux-gnueabihf/sysroot: This is the default sysroot directory, see the following section for an explanation

- --enable-languages=c,c++: Using this we have both C and C++ languages enabled

- `--with-arch=armv7-a`: The code is generated using the ARM v7a instruction set
- `--with-cpu=cortex-a8` and `--with-tune=cortex-a8`: The the code is further tweaked for a Cortex A8 core
- `--with-float=hard`: Generate opcodes for the floating point unit and uses the VFP registers for parameters
- `--enable-threads=posix`: Enable POSIX threads

These are the default settings for the compiler. You can override most of them on the gcc command line so, for example, if you want to compile for a different CPU, you can override the configured setting, `--with-cpu`, by adding `-mcpu` to the command line, as follows:

```
$ arm-cortex_a8-linux-gnueabihf-gcc -mcpu=cortex-a5 helloworld.c -o
helloworld
```

You can print out the the range of architecture-specific options available using `--target-help`, as follows:

```
$ arm-cortex_a8-linux-gnueabihf-gcc --target-help
```

You may be wondering if it matters whether or not you get the exact configuration right at the time you generate the toolchain if you can change it later on, and the answer depends on the way you anticipate using it. If you plan to create a new toolchain for each target, then it makes sense to set everything up at the beginning because it will reduce the risks of getting it wrong later on. Jumping ahead a little to *Chapter 6, Selecting a Build System*, I call this the Buildroot philosophy. If, on the other hand, you want to build a toolchain that is generic and you are prepared to provide the correct settings when you build for a particular target, then you should make the base toolchain generic, which is the way the Yocto Project handles things. The preceding examples follow the Buildroot philosophy.

The sysroot, library, and header files

The toolchain sysroot is a directory which contains subdirectories for libraries, header files, and other configuration files. It can be set when the toolchain is configured through `--with-sysroot=` or it can be set on the command line, using `--sysroot=`. You can see the location of the default sysroot by using `-print-sysroot`:

```
$ arm-cortex_a8-linux-gnueabi-gcc -print-sysroot
```

```
/home/chris/x-tools/arm-cortex_a8-linux-gnueabihf/arm-cortex_a8-
linux-gnueabihf/sysroot
```

You will find the following in the sysroot:

- `lib`: Contains the shared objects for the C library and the dynamic linker/loader, `ld-linux`
- `usr/lib`: the static library archives for the C library and any other libraries that may be installed subsequently
- `usr/include`: Contains the headers for all the libraries
- `usr/bin`: Contains the utility programs that run on the target, such as the `ldd` command
- `/usr/share`: Used for localization and internationalization
- `sbin`: Provides the ldconfig utility, used to optimize library loading paths

Plainly, some of these are needed on the development host to compile programs, and others – for example the shared libraries and `ld-linux` – are needed on the target at runtime.

Other tools in the toolchain

The following table shows various other commands in the toolchain together with a brief description:

Command	Description
addr2line	Converts program addresses into filenames and numbers by reading the debug symbol tables in an executable file. It is very useful when decoding addresses printed out in a system crash report.
ar	The archive utility is used to create static libraries.
as	This is the GNU assembler.
c++filt	This is used to demangle C++ and Java symbols.
cpp	This is the C preprocessor, and is used to expand #define, #include, and other similar directives. You seldom need to use this by itself.
elfedit	This is used to update the ELF header of ELF files.
g++	This is the GNU C++ front-end, which assumes source files contain C++ code.
gcc	This is the GNU C front-end, which assumes source files contain C code.

Command	Description
gcov	This is a code coverage tool.
gdb	This is the GNU debugger.
gprof	This is a program profiling tool.
ld	This is the GNU linker.
nm	This lists symbols from object files.
objcopy	This is used to copy and translate object files.
objdump	This is used to display information from object files.
ranlib	This creates or modifies an index in a static library, making the linking stage faster.
readelf	This displays information about files in ELF object format.
size	This lists section sizes and the total size.
strings	This display strings of printable characters in files.
strip	This is used to strip an object file of debug symbol tables, thus making it smaller. Typically, you would strip all the executable code that is put onto the target.

Looking at the components of the C library

The C library is not a single library file. It is composed of four main parts that together implement the POSIX functions API:

- libc: The main C library that contains the well-known POSIX functions such as printf, open, close, read, write, and so on
- libm: Maths functions such as cos, exp, and log
- libpthread: All the POSIX thread functions with names beginning with pthread_
- librt: The real-time extensions to POSIX, including shared memory and asynchronous I/O

The first one, `libc`, is always linked in but the others have to be explicitly linked with the `-l` option. The parameter to `-l` is the library name with `lib` stripped off. So, for example, a program that calculates a sine function by calling `sin()` would be linked with `libm` using `-lm`:

```
arm-cortex_a8-linux-gnueabihf-gcc myprog.c -o myprog -lm
```

You can verify which libraries have been linked in this or any other program by using the `readelf` command:

```
$ arm-cortex_a8-linux-gnueabihf-readelf -a myprog | grep "Shared
library"
0x00000001 (NEEDED)           Shared library: [libm.so.6]
0x00000001 (NEEDED)           Shared library: [libc.so.6]
```

Shared libraries need a run-time linker, which you can expose using:

```
$ arm-cortex_a8-linux-gnueabihf-readelf -a myprog | grep "program
interpreter"
    [Requesting program interpreter: /lib/ld-linux-armhf.so.3]
```

This is so useful that I have a script file with these commands into a shell script:

```
#!/bin/sh
${CROSS_COMPILE}readelf -a $1 | grep "program interpreter"
${CROSS_COMPILE}readelf -a $1 | grep "Shared library"
```

Linking with libraries: static and dynamic linking

Any application you write for Linux, whether it be in C or C++, will be linked with the C library, libc. This is so fundamental that you don't even have to tell gcc or g++ to do it because it always links libc. Other libraries that you may want to link with have to be explicitly named through the `-l` option.

The library code can be linked in two different ways: statically, meaning that all the library functions your application calls and their dependencies are pulled from the library archive and bound into your executable; and dynamically, meaning that references to the library files and functions in those files are generated in the code but the actual linking is done dynamically at runtime.

Static libraries

Static linking is useful in a few circumstances. For example, if you are building a small system which consists of only BusyBox and some script files, it is simpler to link BusyBox statically and avoid having to copy the runtime library files and linker. It will also be smaller because you only link in the code that your application uses rather than supplying the entire C library. Static linking is also useful if you need to run a program before the filesystem that holds the runtime libraries is available.

You tell gcc to link all libraries statically by adding -static to the command line:

```
$ arm-cortex_a8-linux-gnueabihf-gcc -static helloworld.c -o
helloworld-static
```

You will notice that the size of the binary increases dramatically:

```
$ ls -l
-rwxrwxr-x 1 chris chris   5323 Oct  9 09:01 helloworld
-rwxrwxr-x 1 chris chris 625704 Oct  9 09:01 helloworld-static
```

Static linking pulls code from a library archive, usually named lib[name].a. In the preceding case it is libc.a, which is in [sysroot]/usr/lib:

```
$ ls -l $(arm-cortex_a8-linux-gnueabihf-gcc -print-
sysroot)/usr/lib/libc.a
-r--r--r-- 1 chris chris 3434778 Oct  8 14:00 /home/chris/x-
tools/arm-cortex_a8-linux-gnueabihf/arm-cortex_a8-linux-
gnueabihf/sysroot/usr/lib/libc.a
```

Note that the syntax $(arm-cortex_a8-linux-gnueabihf-gcc -print-sysroot) places the output of the program on the command line. I am using it as a generic way to refer to the files in the sysroot.

Creating a static library is as simple as creating an archive of object files using the ar command. If I had two source files named test1.c and test2.c and I want to create a static library named libtest.a, then I would do this:

```
$ arm-cortex_a8-linux-gnueabihf-gcc -c test1.c
$ arm-cortex_a8-linux-gnueabihf-gcc -c test2.c
$ arm-cortex_a8-linux-gnueabihf-ar rc libtest.a test1.o test2.o
$ ls -l
total 24
-rw-rw-r-- 1 chris chris 2392 Oct  9 09:28 libtest.a
-rw-rw-r-- 1 chris chris  116 Oct  9 09:26 test1.c
```

```
-rw-rw-r-- 1 chris chris 1080 Oct  9 09:27 test1.o
-rw-rw-r-- 1 chris chris  121 Oct  9 09:26 test2.c
-rw-rw-r-- 1 chris chris 1088 Oct  9 09:27 test2.o
```

Then I could link `libtest` into my `helloworld` program using:

```
$ arm-cortex_a8-linux-gnueabihf-gcc helloworld.c -ltest -L../libs -
I../libs -o helloworld
```

Shared libraries

A more common way to deploy libraries is as shared objects that are linked at runtime, which makes more efficient use of storage and system memory, since only one copy of the code needs to be loaded. It also makes it easy to update library files without having to re-link all the programs that use them.

The object code for a shared library must be position-independent so that the runtime linker is free to locate it in memory at the next free address. To do this, add the `-fPIC` parameter to gcc, and then link it using the `-shared` option:

```
$ arm-cortex_a8-linux-gnueabihf-gcc -fPIC -c test1.c
$ arm-cortex_a8-linux-gnueabihf-gcc -fPIC -c test2.c
$ arm-cortex_a8-linux-gnueabihf-gcc -shared -o libtest.so test1.o
test2.o
```

To link an application with this library, you add `-ltest`, exactly as in the static case mentioned in the preceding paragraph but, this time, the code is not included in the executable, but there is a reference to the library that the runtime linker will have to resolve:

```
$ arm-cortex_a8-linux-gnueabihf-gcc helloworld.c -ltest -L../libs -
I../libs -o helloworld
$ list-libs helloworld
[Requesting program interpreter: /lib/ld-
linux-armhf.so.3]
0x00000001 (NEEDED)                      Shared library: [libtest.so]
0x00000001 (NEEDED)                      Shared library: [libc.so.6]
```

The runtime linker for this program is `/lib/ld-linux-armhf.so.3`, which must be present in the target's filesystem. The linker will look for `libtest.so` in the default search path: `/lib` and `/usr/lib`. If you want it to look for libraries in other directories as well, you can place a colon-separated list of paths in the shell variable `LD_LIBRARY_PATH`:

```
# export LD_LIBRARY_PATH=/opt/lib:/opt/usr/lib
```

Understanding shared library version numbers

One of the benefits of shared libraries is that they can be updated independently of the programs that use them. Library updates are of two types: those that fix bugs or add new functions in a backwards-compatible way, and those that break compatibility with existing applications. GNU/Linux has a versioning scheme to handle both these cases.

Each library has a release version and an interface number. The release version is simply a string that is appended to the library name, for example the JPEG image library, libjpeg, is currently at release 8.0.2 and so the library is named libjpeg. so.8.0.2. There is a symbolic link named libjpeg.so to libjpeg.so.8.0.2 so that, when you compile a program with -ljpeg, you link with the current version. If you install version 8.0.3, the link is updated and you will link with that one instead.

Now, suppose that version 9.0.0 comes along and that breaks backwards compatibility. The link from libjpeg.so now points to libjpeg.so.9.0.0, so that any new programs are linked with the new version, possibly throwing compile errors when the interface to libjpeg changes, which the developer can fix. Any programs on the target that are not recompiled are going to fail in some way because they are still using the old interface. This is where the soname helps. The soname encodes the interface number when the library was built and is used by the runtime linker when it loads the library. It is formatted as <library name>.so.<interface number>. For libjpeg. so.8.0.2, the soname is libjpeg.so.8:

```
$ readelf -a /usr/lib/libjpeg.so.8.0.2 | grep SONAME
0x000000000000000e (SONAME)            Library soname:
[libjpeg.so.8]
```

Any program compiled with it will request libjpeg.so.8 at runtime which will be a symbolic link on the target to libjpeg.so.8.0.2. When version 9.0.0 of libjpeg is installed, it will have a soname of libjpeg.so.9, and so it is possible to have two incompatible versions of the same library installed on the same system. Programs that were linked with libjpeg.so.8.*.* will load libjpeg.so.8, and those linked with libjpeg.so.9.*.* will load libjpeg.so.9.

This is why, when you look at the directory listing of <sysroot>/usr/lib/libjpeg*, you find these four files:

- libjpeg.a: This is the library archive used for static linking
- libjpeg.so -> libjpeg.so.8.0.2: This is a symbolic link, used for dynamic linking

- `libjpeg.so.8 -> libjpeg.so.8.0.2`: This is a symbolic link used when loading the library at runtime
- `libjpeg.so.8.0.2`: This is the actual shared library, used at both compile time and runtime

The first two are only needed on the host computer for building, the last two are needed on the target at runtime.

The art of cross compiling

Having a working cross toolchain is the starting point of a journey, not the end of it. At some point, you will want to begin cross compiling the various tools, applications, and libraries that you need on your target. Many of them will be open source packages, each of which has its own method of compiling, and each with its own peculiarities. There are some common build systems, including:

- Pure makefiles where the toolchain is controlled by the `make` variable `CROSS_COMPILE`
- The GNU build system known as Autotools
- CMake (`https://cmake.org`)

I will cover only the first two here since these are the ones needed for even a basic embedded Linux system. For CMake, there are some excellent resources on the CMake website referenced in the preceding point.

Simple makefiles

Some important packages are very simple to cross compile, including the Linux kernel, the U-Boot bootloader, and Busybox. For each of these, you only need to put the toolchain prefix in the `make` variable `CROSS_COMPILE`, for example `arm-cortex_a8-linux-gnueabi-`. Note the trailing dash `-`.

So, to compile Busybox, you would type:

```
$ make CROSS_COMPILE=arm-cortex_a8-linux-gnueabi-
```

Or, you can set it as a shell variable:

```
$ export CROSS_COMPILE=arm-cortex_a8-linux-gnueabi-
$ make
```

In the case of U-Boot and Linux, you also have to set the `make` variable `ARCH` to one of the machine architectures they support, which I will cover in *Chapter 3, All About Bootloaders* and *Chapter 4, Porting and Configuring the Kernel*.

Autotools

The name, Autotools, refers to a group of tools that are used as the build system in many open source projects. The components, together with the appropriate project pages, are:

- GNU Autoconf
  (`http://www.gnu.org/software/autoconf/autoconf.html`)
- GNU Automake
  (`http://www.gnu.org/savannah-checkouts/gnu/automake`)
- GNU Libtool (`http://www.gnu.org/software/libtool/libtool.html`)
- Gnulib (`https://www.gnu.org/software/gnulib`)

The role of Autotools is to smooth over the differences between the many different types of system that the package may be compiled for, accounting for different versions of compilers, different versions of libraries, different locations of header files, and dependencies with other packages. Packages that use Autotools come with a script named `configure` that checks dependencies and generates makefiles according to what it finds. The configure script may also give you the opportunity to enable or disable certain features. You can find the options on offer by running `./configure --help`.

To configure, build, and install a package for the native operating system, you would typically run these three commands:

```
$ ./configure
$ make
$ sudo make install
```

Autotools is able to handle cross development as well. You can influence the behavior of the configure script by setting these shell variables:

- `CC`: The C compiler command
- `CFLAGS`: Additional C compiler flags
- `LDFLAGS`: Additional linker flags, for example if you have libraries in a non-standard directory `<lib dir>` you would add it to the library search path by adding `-L<lib dir>`
- `LIBS`: Contains a list of additional libraries to pass to the linker, for instance `-lm` for the math library

- CPPFLAGS: Contains C/C++ preprocessor flags, for example you would add `-I<include dir>` to search for headers in a non-standard directory `<include dir>`
- CPP: The C preprocessor to use

Sometimes it is sufficient to set only the CC variable, as follows:

```
$ CC=arm-cortex_a8-linux-gnueabihf-gcc ./configure
```

At other times, that will result in an error like this:

```
[...]
checking whether we are cross compiling... configure: error: in '/home/
chris/MELP/build/sqlite-autoconf-3081101':
configure: error: cannot run C compiled programs.
If you meant to cross compile, use '--host'.
See 'config.log' for more details
```

The reason for the failure is that `configure` often tries to discover the capabilities of the toolchain by compiling snippets of code and running them to see what happens, which cannot work if the program has been cross compiled. Nevertheless, there is a hint in the error message of how to solve the problem. Autotools understands three different types of machine that may be involved when compiling a package:

- **Build**: This is the computer that is to build the package, which defaults to the current machine.
- **Host**: This is the computer the program will run on: for a native compile this is left blank and it defaults to be the same computer as build. For a cross compile you set it to be the tuple of your toolchain.
- **Target**: This is the computer the program will generate code for: you would set this when building a cross compiler, for example.

So, to cross compile, you just need to override host, as follows:

```
$ CC=arm-cortex_a8-linux-gnueabihf-gcc \
./configure --host=arm-cortex_a8-linux-gnueabihf
```

One final thing to note is that the default install directory is `<sysroot>/usr/local/*`. You would usually install it in `<sysroot>/usr/*` so that the header files and libraries would be picked up from their default locations. The complete command to configure a typical Autotools package is:

```
$ CC=arm-cortex_a8-linux-gnueabihf-gcc \
./configure --host=arm-cortex_a8-linux-gnueabihf --prefix=/usr
```

An example: SQLite

The SQLite library implements a simple relational database and is quite popular on embedded devices. You begin by getting a copy of SQLite:

```
$ wget http://www.sqlite.org/2015/sqlite-autoconf-3081101.tar.gz
$ tar xf sqlite-autoconf-3081101.tar.gz
$ cd sqlite-autoconf-3081101
```

Next, run the configure script:

```
$ CC=arm-cortex_a8-linux-gnueabihf-gcc \
./configure --host=arm-cortex_a8-linux-gnueabihf --prefix=/usr
```

That seems to work! If it failed, there would be error messages printed to the terminal and recorded in `config.log`. Note that several makefiles have been created, so now you can build it:

```
$ make
```

Finally, you install it into the toolchain directory by setting the make variable DESTDIR. If you don't, it will try to install it into the host computer's /usr directory which is not what you want.

```
$ make DESTDIR=$(arm-cortex_a8-linux-gnueabihf-gcc -print-sysroot)
install
```

You may find that final command fails with a file permissions error. A crosstool-NG toolchain will be read-only by default, which is why it is useful to set CT_INSTALL_ DIR_RO to y when building it. Another common problem is that the toolchain is installed in a system directory such as /opt or /usr/local in which case you will need root permissions when running the install.

After installing, you should find that various files have been added to your toolchain:

- `<sysroot>/usr/bin`: sqlite3. This is a command-line interface for SQLite that you can install and run on the target.
- `<sysroot>/usr/lib`: libsqlite3.so.0.8.6, libsqlite3.so.0, libsqlite3.so libsqlite3. la libsqlite3.a. These are the shared and static libraries.
- `<sysroot>/usr/lib/pkgconfig`: sqlite3.pc: This is the package configuration file, as described in the following section.
- `<sysroot>/usr/lib/include`: sqlite3.h, sqlite3ext.h: These are the header files.
- `<sysroot>/usr/share/man/man1`: sqlite3.1. This is the manual page.

Now you can compile programs that use sqlite3 by adding `-lsqlite3` at the link stage:

```
$ arm-cortex_a8-linux-gnueabihf-gcc -lsqlite3 sqlite-test.c -o
sqlite-test
```

Where, `sqlite-test.c` is a hypothetical program that calls SQLite functions. Since sqlite3 has been installed into the sysroot, the compiler will find the header and library files without any problem. If they had been installed elsewhere you would have to add `-L<lib dir>` and `-I<include dir>`.

Naturally, there will be runtime dependencies as well, and you will have to install the appropriate files into the target directory as described in *Chapter 5, Building a Root Filesystem*.

Package configuration

Tracking package dependencies is quite complex. The package configuration utility, `pkg-config` (`http://www.freedesktop.org/wiki/Software/pkg-config`) helps track which packages are installed and which compile flags each needs by keeping a database of Autotools packages in `[sysroot]/usr/lib/pkgconfig`. For instance, the one for SQLite3 is named `sqlite3.pc` and contains essential information needed by other packages that need to make use of it:

```
$ cat $(arm-cortex_a8-linux-gnueabihf-gcc -print-
sysroot)/usr/lib/pkgconfig/sqlite3.pc
# Package Information for pkg-config
prefix=/usr
exec_prefix=${prefix}
libdir=${exec_prefix}/lib
includedir=${prefix}/include
Name: SQLite
Description: SQL database engine
Version: 3.8.11.1
Libs: -L${libdir} -lsqlite3
Libs.private: -ldl -lpthread
Cflags: -I${includedir}
```

You can use the utility `pkg-config` to extract information in a form that you can feed straight to gcc. In the case of a library like libsqlite3, you want to know the library name (`--libs`) and any special C flags (`--cflags`):

```
$ pkg-config sqlite3 --libs --cflags
Package sqlite3 was not found in the pkg-config search path.
Perhaps you should add the directory containing `sqlite3.pc'
to the PKG_CONFIG_PATH environment variable
No package 'sqlite3' found
```

Oops! That failed because it was looking in the host's sysroot and the development package for libsqlite3 has not been installed on the host. You need to point it at the sysroot of the target toolchain by setting the shell variable `PKG_CONFIG_LIBDIR`:

```
$ PKG_CONFIG_LIBDIR=$(arm-cortex_a8-linux-gnueabihf-gcc -print-
sysroot)/usr/lib/pkgconfig \
pkg-config sqlite3 --libs --cflags
 -lsqlite3
```

Now the output is `-lsqlite3`. In this case, you knew that already, but generally you wouldn't, so this is a valuable technique. The final command to compile would be:

```
$ PKG_CONFIG_LIBDIR=$(arm-cortex_a8-linux-gnueabihf-gcc -print-
sysroot)/usr/lib/pkgconfig \
arm-cortex_a8-linux-gnueabihf-gcc $(pkg-config sqlite3 --cflags --
libs) sqlite-test.c -o sqlite-
```

Problems with cross compiling

Sqlite3 is a well-behaved package and cross compiles nicely but not all packages are so tame. Typical pain points include:

- Home-grown build systems, zlib, for example, has a configure script but it does not behave like the Autotools configure described in the previous section
- Configure scripts that read `pkg-config` information, headers, and other files from the host, disregarding the `--host` override
- Scripts that insist on trying to run cross compiled code

Each case requires careful analysis of the error and additional parameters to the configure script to provide the correct information or patches to the code to avoid the problem altogether. Bear in mind that one package may have many dependencies, especially with programs that have a graphical interface using GTK or QT or handle multimedia content. As an example, mplayer, which is a popular tool for playing multimedia content, has dependencies on over 100 libraries. It would take weeks of effort to build them all.

Therefore, I would not recommend manually cross compiling components for the target in this way except when there is no alternative, or the number of packages to build is small. A much better approach is to use a build tool such as Buildroot or the Yocto Project, or, avoid the problem altogether by setting up a native build environment for your target architecture. Now you can see why distributions like Debian are always compiled natively.

Summary

The toolchain is always your starting point: everything that follows from that is dependent on having a working, reliable toolchain.

Most embedded build environments are based on a cross development toolchain which creates a clear separation between a powerful host computer building the code and a target computer on which it runs. The toolchain itself consists of the GNU binutils, a C compiler from the GNU compiler collection – and quite likely the C++ compiler as well – plus one of the C libraries I have described. Usually the GNU debugger, gdb, will be generated at this point, which I describe in *Chapter 12, Debugging with GDB*. Also, keep a watch out for the Clang compiler, as it will develop over the next few years.

You may start with nothing but a toolchain – perhaps built using crosstool-NG or downloaded from Linaro – and use it to compile all of the packages that you need on your target, accepting the amount of hard work this will entail. Or, you may obtain the toolchain as part of a distribution which includes a range of packages. A distribution can be generated from source code using a build system such as Buildroot or the Yocto Project, or it can be a binary distribution from a third party, maybe a commercial enterprise like Mentor Graphics or an open source project such as the Denx ELDK. Beware of toolchains or distributions that are offered to you for free as part of a hardware package: they are often poorly configured and not maintained. In any case, you should make the choice according to your situation, and then be consistent in its use throughout the project.

Once you have a toolchain, you can use it to build the other components of your embedded Linux system. In the next chapter, you will learn about the bootloader, which brings your device to life and begins the boot process.

3
All About Bootloaders

The bootloader is the second element of embedded Linux. It is the part that starts the system up and loads the operating system kernel. In this chapter, I will look at the role of the bootloader and, in particular, how it passes control from itself to the kernel using a data structure called a device tree, also known as a **flattened device tree** or **FDT**. I will cover the basics of device trees so that you will be able to follow the connections described in a device tree and relate it to real hardware.

I will look at the popular open source bootloader U-Boot and see how to use it to boot a target device and also how to customize it to a new device. Finally, I will take a quick look at Barebox, a bootloader that shares its past with U-Boot but which has, arguably, a cleaner design.

What does a bootloader do?

In an embedded Linux system, the bootloader has two main jobs: basic system initialization and the loading of the kernel. In fact, the first job is somewhat subsidiary to the second in that it is only necessary to get as much of the system working as is needed to load the kernel.

When the first lines of bootloader code are executed, following power-on or a reset, the system is in a very minimal state. The DRAM controller will not have been set up so main memory is not accessible, likewise other interfaces will not have been configured so storage accessed via NAND flash controllers, MMC controllers, and so on, are also not usable. Typically, the only resources operational at the beginning are a single CPU core and some on-chip static memory. As a result, system bootstrap consists of several phases of code, each bringing more of the system into operation.

The early boot phase stops once the interfaces required to load a kernel are working. That includes main memory and the peripherals used to access the kernel and other images, be they mass storage or network. The final act of the bootloader is to load the kernel into RAM and create an execution environment for it. The details of the interface between the bootloader and the kernel are architecture-specific but, in all cases, it means passing a pointer to information about the hardware that the bootloader knows about and passing a kernel command line, which is an ASCII string containing essential information for Linux. Once the kernel has begun executing, the bootloader is no longer needed and all the memory it was using can be reclaimed.

A subsidiary job of the bootloader is to provide a maintenance mode for updating boot configurations, loading new boot images into memory and, maybe, running diagnostics. This is usually controlled by a simple command-line user interface, commonly over a serial interface.

The boot sequence

In simpler times, some years ago, it was only necessary to place the bootloader in non-volatile memory at the reset vector of the processor. NOR flash memory was common at that time and, since it can be mapped directly into the address space, it was the ideal method of storage. The following diagram shows such a configuration, with the reset vector at 0xfffffffc at the top end of an area of flash memory. The bootloader is linked so that there is a jump instruction at that location that points to the start of the bootloader code:

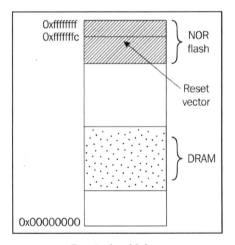

Boot in the old days

From that point, it can initialize the memory controller so that the main memory, the DRAM, becomes available and copies itself into DRAM. Once fully operational, the bootloader can load the kernel from flash memory into DRAM and transfer control to it.

However, once you move away from a simple linearly addressable storage medium like NOR flash, the boot sequence becomes a complex, multi-stage procedure. The details are very specific to each SoC, but they generally follow each of the following phases.

Phase 1: ROM code

In the absence of reliable external memory, the code that runs immediately after a reset or power-on has to be stored on-chip in the SoC; this is known as ROM code. It is programmed into the chip when it is manufactured, hence ROM code is proprietary and cannot be replaced by an open source equivalent. The ROM code can make very few assumptions about any hardware that is not on the chip, because it will be different from one design to another. This applies even to the DRAM chips used for the main system memory. Consequently, the only RAM that the ROM code has access to is the small amount of static RAM (SRAM) found in most SoC designs. The size of the SRAM varies from as little as 4 KiB up to a few hundred KiB:

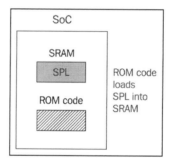

Phase 1 bootloader

The ROM code is capable of loading a small chunk of code from one of several preprogrammed locations into the SRAM. As an example, TI OMAP and Sitara chips will try to load code from the first few pages of NAND flash memory, or from flash memory connected through **SPI (Serial Peripheral Interface)**, or from the first sectors of an MMC device (which could be an eMMC chip or an SD card), or from a file named MLO on the first partition of an MMC device. If reading from all of those memory devices fails, then it will try reading a byte stream from Ethernet, USB, or UART; the latter is provided mainly as a means of loading code into flash memory during production rather than for use in normal operation. Most embedded SoCs have ROM code that works in a similar way. In SoCs where the SRAM is not large enough to load a full bootloader like U-Boot, there has to be an intermediate loader called the secondary program loader, or SPL.

At the end of this phase, the next stage bootloader is present in on-chip memory and the ROM code jumps to the beginning of that code.

Phase 2: SPL

The SPL must set up the memory controller and other essential parts of the system preparatory to loading the **third stage program loader** (TPL) into main memory, the DRAM. The functionality of the SPL is limited by its size. It can read a program from a list of storage devices, as can the ROM code, once again using preprogrammed offsets from the start of a flash device, or a well known file name such as u-boot.bin. The SPL usually doesn't allow for any user interaction but it may print version information and progress messages which you will see on the console. The following diagram explains the phase 2 architecture:

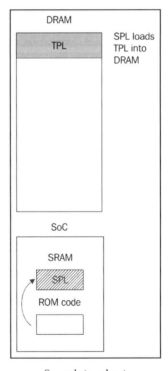

Second stage boot

The SPL may be open source, as is the case with the TI x-loader and Atmel AT91Bootstrap, but it is quite common for it to contain proprietary code that is supplied by the manufacturer as a binary blob.

At the end of the second phase, the third stage loader is present in DRAM, and the SPL can make a jump to that area.

Phase 3: TPL

Now, at last, we are running a full bootloader like U-Boot or Barebox. Usually, there is a simple command-line user interface that will let you perform maintenance tasks such as loading new boot and kernel images into flash storage, loading and booting a kernel, and there is a way to load the kernel automatically without user intervention. The following diagram explains the phase 3 architecture:

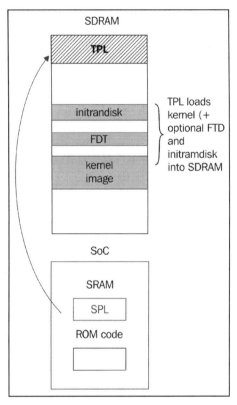

Third stage boot

At the end of the third phase, there is a kernel in memory, waiting to be started. Embedded bootloaders usually disappear from memory once the kernel is running and perform no further part in the operation of the system.

Booting with UEFI firmware

Most embedded PC designs and some ARM designs have firmware based on the **Universal Extensible Firmware Interface (UEFI)** standard, see the official website at `http://www.uefi.org` for more information. The boot sequence is fundamentally the same as described in the preceding section:

Phase 1: The processor loads the UEFI boot manager firmware from flash memory. In some designs, it is loaded directly from NOR flash memory, in others there is ROM code on-chip which loads the boot manager from SPI flash memory. The boot manager is roughly equivalent to the SPL, but may allow user interaction through a text-based or graphical interface.

Phase 2: The boot manager loads the boot firmware from the **EFI System Partition (ESP)** or a hard disk or SSD, or from a network server via PXE boot. If loading from a local disk drive, the EXP is identified by a well-known GUID value of C12A7328-F81F-11D2-BA4B-00A0C93EC93B. The partition should be formatted using the FAT32 format. The third stage bootloader should be in a file named `<efi_system_partition>/boot/boot<machine_type_short_name>.efi`.

For example, the file path to the loader on an x86_64 system is: `/efi/boot/bootx64.efi`

Phase 3: The TPL in this case has to be a bootloader that is capable of loading a Linux kernel and an optional RAM disk into memory. Common choices are:

- **GRUB 2**: This is the GNU Grand Unified Bootloader, version 2, and it is the most commonly used Linux loader on PC platforms. However, there is one controversy in that it is licensed under GPL v3, which may make it incompatible with secure booting since the license requires the boot keys to to be supplied with the code. The website is `https://www.gnu.org/software/grub/`.

- **gummiboot**: This is a simple UEFI-compatible bootloader which has since been integrated into systemd, and is licensed under LGPL v2.1 The website is `https://wiki.archlinux.org/index.php/Systemd-boot`.

Moving from bootloader to kernel

When the bootloader passes control to the kernel it has to pass some basic information to the kernel, which may include some of the following:

- On PowerPC and ARM architectures: a number unique to the type of the SoC
- Basic details of the hardware detected so far, including at least the size and location of the physical RAM, and the CPU clock speed

- The kernel command line
- Optionally, the location and size of a device tree binary
- Optionally, the location and size of an initial RAM disk

The kernel command line is a plain ASCII string which controls the behavior of Linux, setting, for example, the device that contains the root filesystem. I will look at the details of this in the next chapter. It is common to provide the root filesystem as a RAM disk, in which case it is the responsibility of the bootloader to load the RAM disk image into memory. I will cover the way you create initial RAM disks in *Chapter 5, Building a Root Filesystem*.

The way this information is passed is dependent on the architecture and has changed in recent years. For instance, with PowerPC, the bootloader simply used to pass a pointer to a board information structure, whereas, with ARM, it passed a pointer to a list of "A tags". There is a good description of the format of the kernel source in Documentation/arm/Booting.

In both cases, the amount of information passed was very limited, leaving the bulk of it to be discovered at runtime or hard-coded into the kernel as "platform data". The widespread use of platform data meant that each device had to have a kernel configured and modified for that platform. A better way was needed, and that way is the device tree. In the ARM world, the move away from A tags began in earnest in February 2013 with the release of Linux 3.8 but there are still quite a lot of devices in the field, and even in development, still using A tags.

Introducing device trees

You are almost certainly going to encounter device trees at some point. This section aims to give you a quick overview of what they are and how they work but there are many details that are not discussed.

A device tree is a flexible way to define the hardware components of a computer system. Usually, the device tree is loaded by the bootloader and passed to the kernel, although it is possible to bundle the device tree with the kernel image itself to cater for bootloaders that are not capable of handling them separately.

The format is derived from a Sun Microsystems bootloader known as OpenBoot, which was formalized as the Open Firmware specification, IEEE standard IEEE1275-1994. It was used in PowerPC-based Macintosh computers and so was a logical choice for the PowerPC Linux port. Since then, it has been adapted on a large scale by the many ARM Linux implementations and, to a lesser extent, by MIPS, MicroBlaze, ARC, and other architectures.

I would recommend visiting http://devicetree.org for more information.

Device tree basics

The Linux kernel contains a large number of device tree source files in
arch/$ARCH/boot/dts, and this is a good starting point for learning about
device trees. There are also a smaller number of sources in the U-boot source
code in arch/$ARCH/dts. If you acquired your hardware from a third party,
the dts file forms part of a board support package and you should expect to
receive one along with the other source files.

The device tree represents a computer system as a collection of components
joined together in a hierarchy, like a tree. The device tree begins with a root
node, represented by a forward slash, /, which contains subsequent nodes
representing the hardware of the system. Each node has a name and contains a
number of properties in the form name = "value". Here is a simple example:

```
/dts-v1/;
/ {
  model = "TI AM335x BeagleBone";
  compatible = "ti,am33xx";
  #address-cells = <1>;
  #size-cells = <1>;
  cpus {
    #address-cells = <1>;
    #size-cells = <0>;
    cpu@0 {
      compatible = "arm,cortex-a8";
      device_type = "cpu";
      reg = <0>;
    };
  };
  memory@0x80000000 {
    device_type = "memory";
    reg = <0x80000000 0x20000000>; /* 512 MB */
  };
};
```

Here we have a root node which contains a cpus node and a memory node. The cpus
node contains a single CPU node named cpu@0. It is a common convention that the
names of nodes include an @ followed by an address that distinguishes them from
any others.

Both the root and CPU nodes have a compatible property. The Linux kernel uses this to match this name against the strings exported by device drivers in a `struct of_device_id` (more on this in *Chapter 8, Introducing Device Drivers*). It is a convention that the value is composed of a manufacturer name and a component name to reduce confusion between similar devices made by different manufacturers, hence `ti,am33xx` and `arm,cortex-a8`. It is also quite common to have more than one value for `compatible` where there is more than one driver that can handle this device. They are listed with the most suitable first.

The CPU node and the memory node have a `device_type` property which describes the class of device. The node name is often derived from the `device_type`.

The reg property

The memory and CPU nodes have a `reg` property, which refers to a range of units in a register space. A `reg` property consists of two values representing the start address and the size (length) of the range. Both are written down as zero or more 32-bit integers, called cells. Hence, the memory node refers to a single bank of memory that begins at 0x80000000 and is 0x20000000 bytes long.

Understanding `reg` properties becomes more complex when the address or size values cannot be represented in 32 bits. For example, on a device with 64-bit addressing, you need two cells for each:

```
/ {
    #address-cells = <2>;
    #size-cells = <2>;
    memory@80000000 {
        device_type = "memory";
        reg = <0x00000000 0x80000000 0 0x80000000>;
    };
}
```

The information about the number of cells required is held in `#address-cells` and `#size_cells` declarations in an ancestor node. In other words, to understand a `reg` property, you have to look backwards down the node hierarchy until you find `#address-cells` and `#size_cells`. If there are none, the default values are 1 for each – but it is bad practice for device tree writers to depend on fall-backs.

Now, let's return to the cpu and cpus nodes. CPUs have addresses as well: in a quad core device they might be addressed as 0, 1, 2, and 3. That can be thought of as a one-dimensional array without any depth so the size is zero. Therefore, you can see that we have `#address-cells = <1>` and `#size-cells = <0>` in the cpus node, and in the child node, cpu@0, we assign a single value to the `reg` property: node `reg = <0>`.

Phandles and interrupts

The structure of the device tree described so far assumes that there is a single hierarchy of components, whereas in fact there are several. As well as the obvious data connection between a component and other parts of the system, it might also be connected to an interrupt controller, to a clock source and to a voltage regulator. To express these connections, we have phandles.

Take an example of a system containing a serial port which can generate interrupts and the interrupt controller:

```
/dts-v1/;
{
  intc: interrupt-controller@48200000 {
    compatible = "ti,am33xx-intc";
    interrupt-controller;
    #interrupt-cells = <1>;
    reg = <0x48200000 0x1000>;
  };
  serial@44e09000 {
    compatible = "ti,omap3-uart";
    ti,hwmods = "uart1";
    clock-frequency = <48000000>;
    reg = <0x44e09000 0x2000>;
    interrupt-parent = <&intc>;
    interrupts = <72>;
  };
};
```

We have an interrupt-controller node which has the special property `#interrupt-cells`, which tells us how many 4-byte values are needed to represent an interrupt line. In this case, it is just one giving the IRQ number, but it is quite common to use additional values to characterize the interrupt, for example `1 = low-to-high edge triggered`, `2 = high-to-low edge triggered`, and so on.

Looking at the serial node, it has an `interrupt-parent` property which references the interrupt-controller it is connected to by using its label. This is the phandle. The actual IRQ line is given by the `interrupts` property, `72` in this case.

The `serial` node has other properties that we have not seen before: `clock-frequency` and `ti,hwmods`. These are part of the bindings for this particular type of device, in other words, the kernel device driver will read these properties to manage the device. The bindings can be found in the Linux kernel source, in directory `Documentation/devicetree/bindings/`.

Device tree include files

A lot of hardware is common between SoCs of the same family and between boards using the same SoC. This is reflected in the device tree by splitting out common sections into include files, usually with the extension .dtsi. The Open Firmware standard defines /include/ as the mechanism to be used, as in this snippet from vexpress-v2p-ca9.dts:

```
/include/ "vexpress-v2m.dtsi"
```

Look through the .dts files in the kernel, though, and you will find an alternative include statement that is borrowed from C, for example in am335x-boneblack.dts:

```
#include "am33xx.dtsi"
#include "am335x-bone-common.dtsi"
```

Here is another example from am33xx.dtsi:

```
#include <dt-bindings/gpio/gpio.h>
#include <dt-bindings/pinctrl/am33xx.h>
```

Lastly, include/dt-bindings/pinctrl/am33xx.h contains normal C macros:

```
#define PULL_DISABLE (1 << 3)
#define INPUT_EN (1 << 5)
#define SLEWCTRL_SLOW (1 << 6)
#define SLEWCTRL_FAST 0
```

All of this is resolved if the device tree sources are built using kernel kbuild, which first runs them through the C pre-processor, cpp, where the #include and #define statements are processed into plain text that is suitable for the device tree compiler. The motivation is shown in the previous example: it means that device tree sources can use the same constant definitions as the kernel code.

When we include files in this way the nodes are overlaid on top of one another to create a composite tree in which the outer layers extend or modify the inner ones. For example, am33xx.dtsi, which is general to all am33xx SoCs, defines the first MMC controller interface like this:

```
mmc1: mmc@48060000 {
    compatible = "ti,omap4-hsmmc";
    ti,hwmods = "mmc1";
    ti,dual-volt;
    ti,needs-special-reset;
    ti,needs-special-hs-handling;
    dmas = <&edma 24    &edma 25>;
```

```
    dma-names = "tx", "rx";
    interrupts = <64>;
    interrupt-parent = <&intc>;
    reg = <0x48060000 0x1000>;
    status = "disabled";
};
```

 Note that the status is disabled, meaning that no device driver should be bound to it, and also that it has the label mmc1.

In am335x-bone-common.dtsi, which is included with both BeagleBone and BeagleBone Black, the same node is referenced by its phandle:

```
&mmc1 {
  status = "okay";
  bus-width = <0x4>;
  pinctrl-names = "default";
  pinctrl-0 = <&mmc1_pins>;
  cd-gpios = <&gpio0 6 GPIO_ACTIVE_HIGH>;
  cd-inverted;
};
```

Here, mmc1 is enabled (status="okay") because both variants have a physical MMC1 device, and the pinctrl is established. Then, in am335x-boneblack.dts, you will see another reference to mmc1 which associates it with a voltage regulator:

```
&mmc1 {
  vmmc-supply = <&vmmcsd_fixed>;
};
```

So, layering source files like this gives flexibility and reduces the need for duplicated code.

Compiling a device tree

The bootloader and kernel require a binary representation of the device tree, so it has to be compiled using the device tree compiler, dtc. The result is a file ending with .dtb, which is referred to as a device tree binary or a device tree blob.

There is a copy of dtc in the Linux source, in scripts/dtc/dtc, and it is also available as a package on many Linux distributions. You can use it to compile a simple device tree (one that does not use #include) like this:

```
$ dtc simpledts-1.dts -o simpledts-1.dtb
DTC: dts->dts on file "simpledts-1.dts"
```

Be wary of the fact that `dtc` does not give helpful error messages and it makes no checks other than on the basic syntax of the language, which means that debugging a typing error in a source file can be a lengthy business.

To build more complex examples, you will have to use the kernel `kbuild`, as shown in the next chapter.

Choosing a bootloader

Bootloaders come in all shapes and sizes. The kind of characteristics you want from a bootloader are that they be simple and customizable with lots of sample configurations for common development boards and devices. The following table shows a number of them that are in general use:

Name	Architectures
Das U-Boot	ARM, Blackfin, MIPS, PowerPC, SH
Barebox	ARM, Blackfin, MIPS, PowerPC
GRUB 2	X86, X86_64
RedBoot	ARM, MIPS, PowerPC, SH
CFE	Broadcom MIPS
YAMON	MIPS

We are going to focus on U-Boot because it supports a good number of processor architectures and a large number of individual boards and devices. It has been around for a long time and has a good community for support.

It may be that you received a bootloader along with your SoC or board. As always, take a good look at what you have and ask questions about where you can get the source code from, what the update policy is, how they will support you if you want to make changes, and so on. You may want to consider abandoning the vendor-supplied loader and use the current version of an open source bootloader instead.

U-Boot

U-Boot, or to give its full name, Das U-Boot, began life as an open source bootloader for embedded PowerPC boards. Then, it was ported to ARM-based boards and later to other architectures, including MIPS, SH, and x86. It is hosted and maintained by Denx Software Engineering. There is plenty of information available, and a good place to start is `www.denx.de/wiki/U-Boot`. There is also a mailing list at `u-boot@lists.denx.de`.

Building U-Boot

Begin by getting the source code. As with most projects, the recommended way is to clone the git archive and check out the tag you intend to use which, in this case, is the version that was current at the time of writing:

```
$ git clone git://git.denx.de/u-boot.git
$ cd u-boot
$ git checkout v2015.07
```

Alternatively, you can get a tarball from `ftp://ftp.denx.de/pub/u-boot/`.

There are more than 1,000 configuration files for common development boards and devices in the `configs/` directory. In most cases, you can make a good guess of which to use, based on the filename, but you can get more detailed information by looking through the per-board `README` files in the `board/` directory, or you can find information in an appropriate web tutorial or forum. Beware, though, the way U-Boot is configured has undergone a lot of changes since the 2014.10 release. Double-check that the instructions you are following are appropriate.

Taking the BeagleBone Black as an example, we find that there is a likely configuration file named `am335x_boneblack_defconfig` in `configs/` and we find the text **The binary produced by this board supports ... Beaglebone Black** in the board `README` files for the am335x chip, `board/ti/am335x/README`. With this knowledge, building U-Boot for a BeagleBone Black is simple. You need to inform U-Boot of the prefix for your cross compiler by setting the `make` variable `CROSS_COMPILE` and then select the configuration file using a command of the type `make [board]_defconfig`, as follows:

```
$ make CROSS_COMPILE=arm-cortex_a8-linux-gnueabihf-
am335x_boneblack_defconfig
$ make CROSS_COMPILE=arm-cortex_a8-linux-gnueabihf-
```

The results of the compilation are:

- `u-boot`: This is U-Boot in ELF object format, suitable for use with a debugger
- `u-boot.map`: This is the symbol table
- `u-boot.bin`: This is U-Boot in raw binary format, suitable for running on your device
- `u-boot.img`: This is `u-boot.bin` with a U-Boot header added, suitable for uploading to a running copy of U-Boot
- `u-boot.srec`: This is U-Boot in Motorola `srec` format, suitable for transferring over a serial connection

The BeagleBone Black also requires a **Secondary Program Loader** (SPL), as described earlier. This is built at the same time and is named `MLO`:

```
$ ls -l MLO u-boot*
-rw-rw-r-- 1 chris chris 76100 Dec 20 11:22 MLO
-rwxrwxr-x 1 chris chris 2548778 Dec 20 11:22 u-boot
-rw-rw-r-- 1 chris chris 449104 Dec 20 11:22 u-boot.bin
-rw-rw-r-- 1 chris chris 449168 Dec 20 11:22 u-boot.img
-rw-rw-r-- 1 chris chris 434276 Dec 20 11:22 u-boot.map
-rw-rw-r-- 1 chris chris 1347442 Dec 20 11:22 u-boot.srec
```

The procedure is similar for other targets.

Installing U-Boot

Installing a bootloader on a board for the first time requires some outside assistance. If the board has a hardware debug interface, such as JTAG, it is usually possible to load a copy of U-Boot directly into RAM and set it running. From that point, you can use U-Boot commands to copy it into flash memory. The details of this are very board-specific and outside the scope of this book.

Some SoC designs have a boot ROM built in which can be used to read boot code from various external sources such as SD cards, serial interfaces, or USBs, and this is the case with the AM335x chip in the BeagleBone Black. Here is how to load U-Boot via the micro-SD card.

Firstly, format a micro-SD card so that the first partition is in FAT32 format, and mark it as bootable. If you have a direct SD slot available, the card appears as `/dev/mmcblk0`, otherwise, if you are using a memory card reader, it will be seen as `/dev/sdb`, or `/dev/sdc`, and so on. Now, type the following command to partition the micro-SD card, assuming that the card is seen as `/dev/mmcblk0`:

```
$ sudo sfdisk -D -H 255 -S 63 /dev/mmcblk0 << EOF
,9,0x0C,*
,,,-
EOF
```

Format the first partition as `FAT16`:

```
$ sudo mkfs.vfat -F 16 -n boot /dev/mmcblk0p1
```

Now, mount the partition you have just formatted: on some systems it is enough to simply remove the micro-SD card and then plug it back in again, on others you may have to click on an icon. On current versions of Ubuntu, it should be mounted as `/media/[user]/boot` so I would copy U-Boot and the SPL to it like this:

```
cp MLO u-boot.img /media/chris/boot
```

Finally, unmount it.

With no power on the BeagleBone board, insert the micro-SD card.

Plug in the serial cable. A serial port should appear on your PC as `/dev/ttyUSB0` or similar.

Start a suitable terminal program such as `gtkterm`, `minicom`, or `picocom` and attach to the port at 115,200 bps with no flow control:

```
$ gtkterm -p /dev/ttyUSB0 -s 115200
```

Press and hold the **Boot Switch** button on the Beaglebone, power up the board using the external 5V power connector, and release the button after about 5 seconds. You should see a U-Boot prompt on the serial console:

```
U-Boot#
```

Using U-Boot

In this section, I will describe some of the common tasks that you can use U-Boot to perform.

Usually, U-Boot offers a command-line interface over a serial port. It gives a command prompt which is customized for each board. In the examples, I will use `U-Boot#`. Typing `help` prints out all the commands configured in this version of U-Boot; typing `help <command>` prints out more information about a particular command.

The default command interpreter is quite simple. There is no command-line editing by pressing cursor left or right keys; there is no command completion by pressing the *Tab* key; there is no command history by pressing the cursor up key. Pressing any of these keys will disrupt the command you are currently trying to type and you will have to type `Ctrl+C` and start over again. The only line editing key you can safely use is the back space. As an option, you can configure a different command shell called Hush, which has more sophisticated interactive support.

The default number format is hexadecimal. For example, as shown in this command:

```
nand read 82000000 400000 200000
```

This command will read 0x200000 bytes from offset 0x400000 from the start of the NAND flash memory into RAM address 0x82000000.

Environment variables

U-Boot uses environment variables extensively to store and pass information between functions and even to create scripts. Environment variables are simple `name=value` pairs that are stored in an area of memory. The initial population of variables may be coded in the board configuration header file, like this:

```
#define CONFIG_EXTRA_ENV_SETTINGS \
"myvar1=value1\0" \
"myvar2=value2\0"
```

You can create and modify variables from the U-Boot command line using `setenv`. For example `setenv foo bar` creates the variable `foo` with the value `bar`. Note that there is no = sign between the variable name and the value. You can delete a variable by setting it to a null string, `setenv foo`. You can print all the variables to the console using `printenv`, or a single variable using `printenv foo`.

Usually, it is possible to use the `saveenv` command to save the entire environment to permanent storage of some kind. If there is raw NAND or NOR flash, then an erase block is reserved for this purpose, often with another used for a redundant copy to guard against corruption. If there is eMMC or SD card storage it can be stored in a file in a partition of the disk. Other options include storing in a serial EEPROM connected via an I2C or SPI interface or non-volatile RAM.

Boot image format

U-Boot doesn't have a filesystem. Instead, it tags blocks of information with a 64-byte header so that it can track the contents. You prepare files for U-Boot using the `mkimage` command. Here is a brief summary of its usage:

```
$ mkimage
Usage: mkimage -l image
-l ==> list image header information
mkimage [-x] -A arch -O os -T type -C comp -a addr -e ep -n name -d
data_file[:data_file...] image
-A ==> set architecture to 'arch'
```

```
-O ==> set operating system to 'os'

-T ==> set image type to 'type'

-C ==> set compression type 'comp'

-a ==> set load address to 'addr' (hex)

-e ==> set entry point to 'ep' (hex)

-n ==> set image name to 'name'

-d ==> use image data from 'datafile'

-x ==> set XIP (execute in place)

mkimage [-D dtc_options] -f fit-image.its fit-image

mkimage -V ==> print version information and exit
```

For example, to prepare a kernel image for an ARM processor, the command is:

```
$ mkimage -A arm -O linux -T kernel -C gzip -a 0x80008000 \
-e 0x80008000 -n 'Linux' -d zImage uImage
```

Loading images

Usually, you will load images from removable storage such as an SD card or a network. SD cards are handled in U-Boot by the mmc driver. A typical sequence to load an image into memory would be:

```
U-Boot# mmc rescan

U-Boot# fatload mmc 0:1 82000000 uimage

reading uimage

4605000 bytes read in 254 ms (17.3 MiB/s)

U-Boot# iminfo 82000000


## Checking Image at 82000000 ...

Legacy image found

Image Name: Linux-3.18.0

Created: 2014-12-23 21:08:07 UTC

Image Type: ARM Linux Kernel Image (uncompressed)

Data Size: 4604936 Bytes = 4.4 MiB

Load Address: 80008000

Entry Point: 80008000

Verifying Checksum ... OK
```

The command `mmc rescan` re-initializes the `mmc` driver, perhaps to detect that an SD card has recently been inserted. Next, `fatload` is used to read a file from a FAT-formatted partition on the SD card. The format is:

```
fatload <interface> [<dev[:part]> [<addr> [<filename> [bytes
[pos]]]]]
```

If `<interface>` is `mmc`, as in our case, `<dev:part>` is the device number of the `mmc` interface counting from zero, and the partition number counting from one. Hence `<0:1>` is the first partition on the first device. The memory location, `0x82000000`, is chosen to be in an area of RAM that is not being used at this moment. If we intend to boot this kernel, we have to make sure that this area of RAM will not be overwritten when the kernel image is decompressed and located at the runtime location, `0x80008000`.

To load image files over a network you use the **Trivial File Transfer Protocol (TFTP)**. This requires you to install a TFTP daemon, tftpd, on your development system and start it running. You also have to configure any firewalls between your PC and the target board to allow the TFTP protocol on UDP port 69 to pass through. The default configuration of tftpd allows access only to the directory `/var/lib/tftpboot`. The next step is to copy the files you want to transfer to the target into that directory. Then, assuming that you are using a pair of static IP addresses, which removes the need for further network administration, the sequence of commands to load a set of kernel image files should look like this:

```
U-Boot# setenv ipaddr 192.168.159.42
U-Boot# setenv serverip 192.168.159.99
U-Boot# tftp 82000000 uImage
link up on port 0, speed 100, full duplex
Using cpsw device
TFTP from server 192.168.159.99; our IP address is 192.168.159.42
Filename 'uImage'.
Load address: 0x82000000
Loading:
#################################################################
#################################################################
#################################################################
###########################################################
3 MiB/s
done
Bytes transferred = 4605000 (464448 hex)
```

Finally, let's look at how to program images into NAND flash memory and read them back, which is is handled by the `nand` command. This example loads a kernel image via TFTP and programs it into flash:

```
U-Boot# fatload mmc 0:1 82000000 uimage
reading uimage
4605000 bytes read in 254 ms (17.3 MiB/s)

U-Boot# nandecc hw
U-Boot# nand erase 280000 400000

NAND erase: device 0 offset 0x280000, size 0x400000
Erasing at 0x660000 -- 100% complete.
OK
U-Boot# nand write 82000000 280000 400000

NAND write: device 0 offset 0x280000, size 0x400000
4194304 bytes written: OK
```

Now you can load the kernel from flash memory using `nand read`:

```
U-Boot# nand read 82000000 280000 400000
```

Booting Linux

The `bootm` command starts a kernel image running. The syntax is:

```
bootm [address of kernel] [address of ramdisk] [address of dtb].
```

The address of the kernel image is necessary, but the address of ramdisk and dtb can be omitted if the kernel configuration does not need them. If there is a dtb but no ramdisk, the second address can be replaced with a dash (-). That would look like this:

```
U-Boot# bootm 82000000 - 83000000
```

Automating the boot with U-Boot scripts

Plainly, typing a long series of commands to boot your board each time it is turned on is not acceptable. To automate the process, U-Boot stores a sequence of commands in environment variables. If the special variable named bootcmd contains a script, it is run at power-up after a delay of bootdelay seconds. If you are watching this on the serial console, you will see the delay counting down to zero. You can press any key during this period to terminate the countdown and enter into an interactive session with U-Boot.

The way that you create scripts is simple, though not easy to read. You simply append commands separated by semicolons, which must be preceded by a backslash escape character. So, for example, to load a kernel image from an offset in flash memory and boot it, you might use the following command:

```
setenv bootcmd nand read 82000000 400000 200000\;bootm 82000000
```

Porting U-Boot to a new board

Let's assume that your hardware department has created a new board called "Nova" that is based on the BeagleBone Black and that you need to port U-Boot to it. You will need to understand the layout of the U-Boot code and how the board configuration mechanism works. In the 2014.10 release, U-Boot adopted the same configuration mechanism as the Linux kernel, Kconfig. Over the next few releases, the existing configuration settings will be moved from the current location in the header files in include/configs into Kconfig files. As of the 2014.10 release, each board had a Kconfig file which contains minimal information derived from the old boards.cfg file.

The main directories you will be dealing with are:

- arch: Contains code specific to each supported architecture in directories arm, mips, powerpc, and so on. Within each architecture, there is a subdirectory for each member of the family, for example, in arch/arm/cpu, there are directories for the architecture variants, including amt926ejs, armv7, and armv8.

- board: Contains code specific to a board. Where there are several boards from the same vendor, they can be collected together into a subdirectory, hence the support for the am335x evm board, on which the BeagleBone is based, is in board/ti/am335x.

- common: Contains core functions including the command shells and the commands that can be called from them, each in a file named cmd_[command name].c.

- doc: Contains several README files describing various aspects of U-Boot. If you are wondering how to proceed with your U-Boot port, this is a good place to start.

- include: In addition to many shared header files, this contains the very important subdirectory include/configs where you will find the majority of the board configuration settings. As the move to Kconfig progresses, the information will be moved out into Kconfig files but, at the time of writing, that process has only just begun.

Kconfig and U-Boot

The way that Kconfig extracts configuration information from Kconfig files and stores the total system configuration in a file named .config is described in some detail in *Chapter 4, Porting and Configuring the Kernel*. U-Boot has adopted kconfig and kbuild with one change. A U-Boot build can produce up to three binaries: a normal u-boot.bin, a **Secondary Program Loader (SPL)**, and a **Tertiary Program Loader (TPL)**, each with possibly different configuration options. Consequently, lines in .config and default configuration files can be prefixed with the codes shown in the following table to indicate which target they apply to:

None	Normal image only
S:	SPL image only
T:	TPL image only
ST:	SPL and TPL images
+S:	Normal and SPL images
+T:	Normal and TPL images
+ST:	Normal, SPL and TPL images

Each board has a default configuration stored in configs/[board name}_defconfig. For your Nova board, you will have to create a file named nova_defonfig. for example, and add these lines to it:

```
CONFIG_SPL=y
CONFIG_SYS_EXTRA_OPTIONS="SERIAL1,CONS_INDEX=1,EMMC_BOOT"
+S:CONFIG_ARM=y
+S:CONFIG_TARGET_NOVA=y
```

On the first line, CONFIG_SPL=y causes the SPL binary, MLO, to be generated, CONFIG_ARM=y causes the contents of arch/arm/Kconfig to be included on line three. On line four, CONFIG_TARGET_NOVA=y selects your board. Note that lines three and four are prefixed by +S: so that they apply to both the SPL and normal binaries.

You should also add a menu option to the ARM architecture Kconfig that allows people to select Nova as a target:

```
CONFIG_SPL=y
config TARGET_NOVA
bool "Support Nova!"
```

Board-specific files

Each board has a subdirectory named board/[board name] or board/[vendor]/[board name] which should contain:

- Kconfig: Contains configuration options for the board
- MAINTAINERS: Contains a record of whether the board is currently maintained and, if so, by whom
- Makefile: Used to build the board-specific code
- README: Contains any useful information about this port of U-Boot, for example, which hardware variants are covered

In addition, there may be source files for board specific functions.

Your Nova board is based on a BeagleBone which, in turn, is based on a TI AM335x EVM, so, you can start by taking a copy of the am335x board files:

```
$ mkdir board/nova
```

```
$ cp -a board/ti/am335x board/nova
```

Next, change the Kconfig file to reflect the Nova board:

```
if TARGET_NOVA

config SYS_CPU
default "armv7"

config SYS_BOARD
default "nova"

config SYS_SOC
default "am33xx"

config SYS_CONFIG_NAME
default "nova"
endif
```

Setting `SYS_CPU` to `armv7` causes the code in `arch/arm/cpu/armv7` to be compiled and linked. Setting `SYS_SOC` to `am33xx` causes the code in `arch/arm/cpu/armv7/am33xx` to be included, setting `SYS_BOARD` to `nova` brings in `board/nova` and setting `SYS_CONFIG_NAME` to `nova` means that the header file `include/configs/nova.h` is used for further configuration options.

There is one other file in `board/nova` that you need to change, the linker script placed at `board/nova/u-boot.lds`, which has a hard-coded reference to `board/ti/am335x/built-in.o`. Change this to use the copy local to `nova`:

```
diff --git a/board/nova/u-boot.lds b/board/nova/u-boot.lds
index 78f294a..6689b3d 100644
--- a/board/nova/u-boot.lds
+++ b/board/nova/u-boot.lds
@@ -36,7 +36,7 @@ SECTIONS
*(.__image_copy_start)
*(.vectors)
CPUDIR/start.o (.text*)
- board/ti/am335x/built-in.o (.text*)
+ board/nova/built-in.o (.text*)
*(.text*)
}
```

Configuration header files

Each board has a header file in `include/configs` which contains the majority of the configuration. The file is named by the `SYS_CONFIG_NAME` identifier in the board's `Kconfig`. The format of this file is described in detail in the `README` file at the top level of the U-Boot source tree.

For the purposes of your Nova board, simply copy `am335x_evm.h to nova.h` to `nova.h` and make a small number of changes:

```
diff --git a/include/configs/nova.h b/include/configs/nova.h
index a3d8a25..8ea1410 100644
--- a/include/configs/nova.h
+++ b/include/configs/nova.h
@@ -1,5 +1,5 @@
/*
- * am335x_evm.h
+ * nova.h, based on am335x_evm.h
*
* Copyright (C) 2011 Texas Instruments Incorporated -
http://www.ti.com/
*
```

```
@@ -13,8 +13,8 @@
 * GNU General Public License for more details.
 */
-#ifndef __CONFIG_AM335X_EVM_H
-#define __CONFIG_AM335X_EVM_H
+#ifndef __CONFIG_NOVA
+#define __CONFIG_NOVA
 #include <configs/ti_am335x_common.h>
@@ -39,7 +39,7 @@
 #define V_SCLK (V_OSCK)
 /* Custom script for NOR */
-#define CONFIG_SYS_LDSCRIPT "board/ti/am335x/u-boot.lds"
+#define CONFIG_SYS_LDSCRIPT "board/nova/u-boot.lds"
 /* Always 128 KiB env size */
 #define CONFIG_ENV_SIZE (128 << 10)
@@ -50,6 +50,9 @@
 #define CONFIG_PARTITION_UUIDS
 #define CONFIG_CMD_PART
+#undef CONFIG_SYS_PROMPT
+#define CONFIG_SYS_PROMPT "nova!> "
+
 #ifdef CONFIG_NAND
 #define NANDARGS \
 "mtdids=" MTDIDS_DEFAULT "\0" \
```

Building and testing

To build for the Nova board, select the configuration you have just created:

```
$ make CROSS_COMPILE=arm-cortex_a8-linux-gnueabi- nova_defconfig
$ make CROSS_COMPILE=arm-cortex_a8-linux-gnueabi-
```

Copy MLO and u-boot.img to the FAT partition of the micro-SD card you created earlier and boot the board.

Falcon mode

We are used to the idea that booting a modern embedded processor involves the CPU boot ROM loading an SPL which loads u-boot.bin which then loads a Linux kernel. You may be wondering if there is a way to reduce the number of steps, thereby simplifying and speeding up the boot process. The answer is U-Boot "Falcon mode", named after the Peregrine falcon which is claimed to be the fastest of all birds.

The idea is simple: have the SPL load a kernel image directly, missing out u-boot.bin. There is no user interaction and there are no scripts. It just loads a kernel from a known location in flash or eMMC into memory, passes it a pre-prepared parameter block and starts it running. The details of configuring Falcon mode are beyond this book. If you would like more information, take a look at doc/README.falcon.

Barebox

I will complete this chapter with a look at another bootloader that has the same roots as U-Boot but takes a new approach to bootloaders. It is derived from U-Boot and was actually called U-Boot v2 in the early days. The Barebox developers aimed to combine the best parts of U-Boot and Linux, including a POSIX-like API and mountable filesystems.

The Barebox project website is www.barebox.org and the developer mailing list is barebox@lists.infradead.org.

Getting Barebox

To get Barebox, clone the git repository and check out the version you want to use:

```
$ git clone git://git.pengutronix.de/git/barebox.git
$ cd barebox
$ git checkout v2014.12.0
```

The layout of the code is similar to U-Boot:

- arch: Contains code specific to each supported architecture, which includes all the major embedded architectures. SoC support is in arch/[architecture]/ mach-[SoC]. Support for individual boards is in arch/[architecture]/boards.

- common: Contains core functions, including the shell.

- commands: Contains the commands that can be called from the shell.

- Documentation: Contains the templates for documentation files. To build it, type "make docs". The results are put in Documentation/html.

- drivers: Contains the code for the device drivers.

- include: Contains header files.

Building Barebox

Barebox has used `kconfig/kbuild` for a long time. There are default configuration files in `arch/[architecture]/configs`. As an example, assume that you want to build Barebox for the BeagleBoard C4. You need two configurations, one for the SPL, and one for the main binary. Firstly, build MLO:

```
$ make ARCH=arm CROSS_COMPILE=arm-cortex_a8-linux-gnueabi-
omap3530_beagle_xload_defconfig
$ make ARCH=arm CROSS_COMPILE=arm-cortex_a8-linux-gnueabi-
```

The result is the secondary program loader, MLO.

Next, build Barebox:

```
$ make ARCH=arm CROSS_COMPILE=arm-cortex_a8-linux-gnueabi-
omap3530_beagle_defconfig
$ make ARCH=arm CROSS_COMPILE=arm-cortex_a8-linux-gnueabi-
```

Copy both to an SD card:

```
$ cp MLO /media/boot/
$ cp barebox-flash-image /media/boot/barebox.bin
```

Then, boot up the board and you should see messages like these on the console:

```
barebox 2014.12.0 #1 Wed Dec 31 11:04:39 GMT 2014


Board: Texas Instruments beagle
nand: Trying ONFI probe in 16 bits mode, aborting !
nand: NAND device: Manufacturer ID: 0x2c, Chip ID: 0xba (Micron ),
256MiB, page
size: 2048, OOB size: 64
omap-hsmmc omap3-hsmmc0: registered as omap3-hsmmc0
mci0: detected SD card version 2.0
mci0: registered disk0
malloc space: 0x87bff400 -> 0x87fff3ff (size 4 MiB)
booting from MMC


barebox 2014.12.0 #2 Wed Dec 31 11:08:59 GMT 2014


Board: Texas Instruments beagle
netconsole: registered as netconsole-1
```

```
i2c-omap i2c-omap30: bus 0 rev3.3 at 100 kHz
ehci ehci0: USB EHCI 1.00
nand: Trying ONFI probe in 16 bits mode, aborting !
nand: NAND device: Manufacturer ID: 0x2c, Chip ID: 0xba (Micron NAND
256MiB 1,8V
16-bit), 256MiB, page size: 2048, OOB size: 64
omap-hsmmc omap3-hsmmc0: registered as omap3-hsmmc0
mci0: detected SD card version 2.0
mci0: registered disk0
malloc space: 0x85e00000 -> 0x87dfffff (size 32 MiB)
environment load /boot/barebox.env: No such file or directory
Maybe you have to create the partition.
no valid environment found on /boot/barebox.env. Using default
environment
running /env/bin/init...


Hit any key to stop autoboot: 0
```

Barebox is continuing to evolve. At the time of writing, it lacks the breadth of
hardware support that U-Boot has, but it is worth considering for new projects.

Summary

Every system needs a bootloader to bring the hardware to life and to load a kernel.
U-Boot has found favor with many developers because it supports a useful
range of hardware and it is fairly easy to port to a new device. Over the last few
years, the complexity and ever increasing variety of embedded hardware has led
to the introduction of the device tree as a way of describing hardware. The device
tree is simply a textual representation of a system that is compiled into a **device
 tree binary** (**dtb**) and which is passed to the kernel when it loads. It is up to the
kernel to interpret the device tree and to load and initialize drivers for the devices
it finds there.

In use, U-Boot is very flexible, allowing images to be loaded from mass storage, flash
memory, or a network, and booted. Likewise, Barebox can achieve the same but with
a smaller base of hardware support. Despite its cleaner design and POSIX-inspired
internal APIs, at the time of writing it does not seem to have been accepted beyond
its own small but dedicated community.

Having covered some of the intricacies of booting Linux, in the next chapter you will
see the next stage of the process as the third element of your embedded project, the
kernel, comes into play.

4

Porting and Configuring the Kernel

The kernel is the third element of embedded Linux. It is the component that is responsible for managing resources and interfacing with hardware and so affects almost every aspect of your final software build. It is usually tailored to your particular hardware configuration although, as we saw in *Chapter 3*, *All About Bootloaders*, device trees allow you to create a generic kernel that is tailored to particular hardware by the contents of the device tree.

In this chapter, we will look at how to get a kernel for a board and how to configure and compile it. We will look again at bootstrap, this time focusing on the part the kernel plays. We will also look at device drivers and how they pick up information from the device tree.

What does the kernel do?

Linux began in 1991 when Linus Torvalds started writing an operating system for Intel 386 and 486-based personal computers. He was inspired by the Minix operating system written by Andrew S. Tanenbaum four years earlier. Linux differed in many ways from Minix, the main differences being that it was a 32-bit virtual memory kernel and the code was open source, later released under the GPL 2 license.

He announced it on the 25th August 1991 on the *comp.os.minix* newsgroup in a famous post that begins as *Hello everybody out there using minix - I'm doing a (free) operating system (just a hobby, won't be big and professional like gnu) for 386(486) AT clones. This has been brewing since april, and is starting to get ready. I'd like any feedback on things people like/dislike in minix, as my OS resembles it somewhat (same physical layout of the file-system (due to practical reasons) among other things).*

To be strictly accurate, Linus did not write an operating system, he wrote a kernel instead, which is one component of an operating system. To create a working system, he used components from the GNU project, especially the toolchain, C library, and basic command-line tools. That distinction remains today, and gives Linux a lot of flexibility in the way it is used. It can be combined with a GNU user space to create a full Linux distribution that runs on desktops and servers, which is sometimes called GNU/Linux; it can be combined with an Android user space to create the well-known mobile operating system or it can be combined with a small Busybox-based user space to create a compact embedded system. Contrast this with the BSD operating systems, FreeBSD, OpenBSD, and NetBSD, in which the kernel, the toolchain, and the user space are combined into a single code base.

The kernel has three main jobs: to manage resources, to interface with hardware, and to provide an API that offers a useful level of abstraction to user space programs, as summarized in the following diagram:

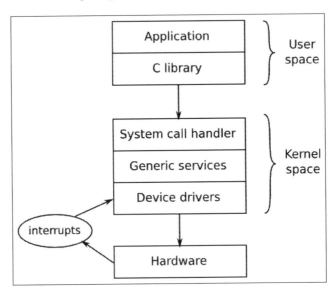

Applications running in user space run at a low CPU privilege level. They can do very little other than make library calls. The primary interface between the user space and the kernel space is the C library, which translates user level functions such as those defined by POSIX into kernel system calls. The system call interface uses an architecture-specific method such as a trap or a software interrupt to switch the CPU from the low privilege user mode to the high privilege kernel mode, which allows access to all memory addresses and CPU registers.

The system call handler dispatches the call to the appropriate kernel subsystem: scheduling calls to the scheduler, the filesystem, calls to the filesystem code, and so on. Some of those calls require input from the underlying hardware and will be passed down to a device driver. In some cases, the hardware itself invokes a kernel function by raising an interrupt. Interrupts can only be handled in a device driver, never by a user space application.

In other words, all the useful things that your application does, it does them through the kernel. The kernel, then, is one of the most important elements in the system.

Choosing a kernel

The next step is to choose the kernel for your project, balancing the desire to always use the latest version of software against the need for vendor-specific additions.

Kernel development cycle

Linux has been developed at a fast pace, with a new version being released every 8 to 12 weeks. The way that the version numbers are constructed has changed a bit in recent years. Before July 2011, there was a three number version scheme with version numbers that looked like 2.6.39. The middle number indicated whether it was a developer or stable release, odd numbers (2.1.x, 2.3.x, 2.5.x) were for developers and even numbers were for end users. From version 2.6 onwards, the idea of a long-lived development branch (the odd numbers) was dropped as it slowed down the rate at which new features were made available to users. The change in numbering from 2.6.39 to 3.0 in July 2011 was purely because Linus felt that the numbers were becoming too large: there was no huge leap in the features or architecture of Linux between those two versions. He also took the opportunity to drop the middle number. Since then, in April 2015, he bumped the major from 3 to 4, again purely for neatness, not because of any large architectural shift.

Linus manages the development kernel tree. You can follow him by cloning his git tree like so:

```
$ git clone \
git://git.kernel.org/pub/scm/linux/kernel/git/torvalds/linux.git
```

This will check out into subdirectory `linux`. You can keep up to date by running the command `git pull` in that directory from time to time.

Currently, a full cycle of kernel development begins with a merge window of two weeks, during which Linus will accept patches for new features. At the end of the merge window, a stabilization phase begins, during which Linus will produce release candidates with version numbers ending in -rc1, -rc2, and so on, usually up to -rc7 or -rc8. During this time, people test the candidates and submit bug reports and fixes. When all significant bugs have been fixed, the kernel is released.

The code incorporated during the merge window has to be fairly mature already. Usually, it is pulled from the repositories of the many subsystem and architecture maintainers of the kernel. By keeping to a short development cycle, features can be merged when they are ready. If a feature is deemed not sufficiently stable or well developed by the kernel maintainers, it can simply be delayed until the next release.

Keeping a track of what has changed from release to release is not easy. You can read the commit log in Linus' git repository but, with roughly 10,000 or more entries per release, it is not easy to get an overview. Thankfully, there is the *Linux Kernel Newbies* website, `http://kernelnewbies.org` where you will find a succinct overview of each version, at `http://kernelnewbies.org/LinuxVersions`.

Stable and long term support releases

The rapid rate of change of Linux is a good thing in that it brings new features into the mainline code base, but it does not fit very well with the longer life cycle of embedded projects. Kernel developers address this in two ways. Firstly, it is acknowledged that a release may contain bugs that need to be fixed before the next kernel release comes around. That is the role of the stable Linux kernel, maintained by Greg Kroah-Hartman. After release, the kernel moves from being **mainline** (maintained by Linus) to **stable** (maintained by Greg). Bug fix releases of the stable kernel are marked by a third number, 3.18.1, 3.18.2, and so on. Before version 3, there were four release numbers, 2.6.29.1, 2.6.39.2, and so on.

You can get the stable tree by using the following command:

```
$ git clone \
git://git.kernel.org/pub/scm/linux/kernel/git/stable/linux-
stable.git
```

You can use `git chckout` to get a particular version, for example version 4.1.10:

```
$ cd linux-stable
$ git checkout v4.1.10
```

Usually, the stable kernel is maintained only until the next mainline release, 8 to 12 weeks later, so you will see that there is just one or sometimes two stable kernels at kernel.org. To cater for those users who would like updates for a longer period of time and be assured that any bugs will be found and fixed, some kernels are labeled **long term** and maintained for two or more years. There is at least one long term kernel each year. Looking at kernel.org at the time of writing, there are a total of eight long term kernels: 4.1, 3.18, 3.14, 3.12, 3.10, 3.4, 3.2, and 2.6.32. The latter has been maintained for five years and is at version 2.6.32.68. If you are building a product that you will have to maintain for this length of time the latest long term kernel might well be a good choice.

Vendor support

In an ideal world, you would be able to download a kernel from kernel.org and configure it for any device that claims to support Linux. However, that is not always possible: in fact mainline Linux has solid support for only a small subset of the many devices that can run Linux. You may find support for your board or SoC from independent open source projects, Linaro or the Yocto Project, for example, or from companies providing third party support for embedded Linux, but in many cases you will be obliged to look to the vendor of your SoC or board for a working kernel. As we also know, some are better than others.

 My only advice at this point is to choose vendors who give good support or who, even better, take the trouble to get their kernel changes into the mainline.

Licensing

The Linux source code is licensed under GPL v2, which means that you must make the source code of your kernel available in one of the ways specified in the license.

The actual text of the license for the kernel is in the file COPYING. It begins with an addendum written by Linus that states that code calling the kernel from user space via the system call interface is not considered a derivative work of the kernel and so is not covered by the license. Hence, there is no problem with proprietary applications running on top of Linux.

However, there is one area of Linux licensing that causes endless confusion and debate: kernel modules. A kernel module is simply a piece of code that is dynamically linked with the kernel at runtime, thereby extending the functionality of the kernel. The GPL makes no distinction between static and dynamic linking, so it would appear that the source for kernel modules is covered by the GPL. But, in the early days of Linux, there were debates about exceptions to this rule, for example, in connection with the Andrew filesystem. This code predates Linux and therefore (it was argued) is not a derivative work, and so the license does not apply. Similar discussions took place over the years with respect to other pieces of code, with the result that it is now accepted practice that the GPL does not necessarily apply to kernel modules. This is codified by the kernel `MODULE_LICENSE` macro, which may take the value `Proprietary` to indicate that it is not released under the GPL. If you plan to use the same arguments yourself, you may want to read though an oft-quoted email thread titled *Linux GPL and binary module exception clause?* (`http://yarchive.net/comp/linux/gpl_modules.html`).

The GPL should be considered a good thing because it guarantees that when you and I are working on embedded projects, we can always get the source code for the kernel. Without it, embedded Linux would be much harder to use and more fragmented.

Building the kernel

Having decided which kernel to base your build on, the next step is to build it.

Getting the source

Let's assume that you have a board that is supported in mainline. You can get the source code through git or by downloading a tarball. Using git is better because you can see the commit history, you can easily see any changes you may make and you can switch between branches and versions. In this example, we are cloning the stable tree and checking out the version tag 4.1.10:

```
$ git clone
git://git.kernel.org/pub/scm/linux/kernel/git/stable/linux-
stable.git linux
$ cd linux
$ git checkout v4.1.10
```

Alternatively, you could download the tarball from `https://https://cdn.kernel.org/pub/linux/kernel/v4.x/linux-4.1.10.tar.xz`.

There is a lot of code here. There are over 38,000 files in the 4.1 kernel containing C source code, header files, and assembly code, amounting to a total of over 12.5 million lines of code (as measured by the cloc utility). Nevertheless, it is worth knowing the basic layout of the code and to know, approximately, where to look for a particular component. The main directories of interest are:

- `arch`: This contains architecture-specific files. There is one subdirectory per architecture.
- `Documentation`: This contains kernel documentation. Always look here first if you want to find more information about an aspect of Linux.
- `drivers`: This contains device drivers, thousands of them. There is a subdirectory for each type of driver.
- `fs`: This contains filesystem code.
- `include`: This contains kernel header files, including those required when building the toolchain.
- `init`: This contains the kernel start-up code.
- `kernel`: This contains core functions, including scheduling, locking, timers, power management, and debug/trace code.
- `mm`: This contains memory management.
- `net`: This contains network protocols.
- `scripts`: This contains many useful scripts including the device tree compiler, dtc, which I described in *Chapter 3*, *All About Bootloaders*.
- `tools`: This contains many useful tools, including the Linux performance counters tool, perf, which I will describe in *Chapter 13*, *Profiling and Tracing*.

Over a period of time, you will become familiar with this structure, and realize that, if you are looking for the code for the serial port of a particular SoC, you will find it in `drivers/tty/serial` and not in `arch/$ARCH/mach-foo` because it is a device driver and not something central to the running of Linux on that SoC.

Understanding kernel configuration

One of the strengths of Linux is the degree to which you can configure the kernel to suit different jobs, from a small dedicated device such as a smart thermostat to a complex mobile handset. In current versions there are many thousands of configuration options. Getting the configuration right is a task in itself but, before that, I want to show you how it works so that you can better understand what is going on.

The configuration mechanism is called `Kconfig`, and the build system that it integrates with is called `Kbuild`. Both are documented in `Documentation/kbuild/`. `Kconfig/Kbuild` is used in a number of other projects as well as the kernel, including crosstool-NG, U-Boot, Barebox, and BusyBox.

The configuration options are declared in a hierarchy of files named `Kconfig` using a syntax described in `Documentation/kbuild/kconfig-language.txt`. In Linux, the top level `Kconfig` looks like this:

```
mainmenu "Linux/$ARCH $KERNELVERSION Kernel Configuration"
config SRCARCH
    string
    option env="SRCARCH"
    source "arch/$SRCARCH/Kconfig"
```

The last line includes the architecture-dependent configuration file which sources other `Kconfig` files depending on which options are enabled. Having the architecture play such a role has two implications: firstly, that you must specify an architecture when configuring Linux by setting `ARCH=[architecture]`, otherwise it will default to the local machine architecture, and second that the layout of the top level menu is different for each architecture.

The value you put into `ARCH` is one of the subdirectories you find in directory `arch`, with the oddity that `ARCH=i386` and `ARCH=x86_64` both have the source `arch/x86/Kconfig`.

The `Kconfig` files consist largely of menus, delineated by `menu`, `menu title`, and `endmenu` keywords, and menu items marked by `config`. Here is an example, taken from `drivers/char/Kconfig`:

```
menu "Character devices"
[...]
config DEVMEM
    bool "/dev/mem virtual device support"
    default y
      help
      Say Y here if you want to support the /dev/mem device.
      The /dev/mem device is used to access areas of physical
      memory.
      When in doubt, say "Y".
```

The parameter following `config` names a variable that, in this case, is `DEVMEM`. Since this option is a Boolean, it can only have two values: if it is enabled it is assigned to `y`, if not the variable is not defined at all. The name of the menu item that is displayed on the screen is the string following the `bool` keyword.

This configuration item, along with all the others, is stored in a file named `.config` (note that the leading dot `.` means that it is a hidden file that will not be shown by the `ls` command unless you type `ls -a` to show all files). The variable names stored in `.config` are prefixed with `CONFIG_`, so if `DEVMEM` is enabled, the line reads:

```
CONFIG_DEVMEM=y
```

There are several other data types in addition to `bool`. Here is the list:

- `bool`: This is either `y` or not defined.
- `tristate`: This is used where a feature can be built as a kernel module or built into the main kernel image. The values are `m` for a module, `y` to be built in, and not defined if the feature is not enabled.
- `int`: This is an integer value written using decimal notation.
- `hex`: This is an unsigned integer value written using hexadecimal notation.
- `string`: This is a string value.

There may be dependencies between items, expressed by the `depends on` phrase, as shown here:

```
config MTD_CMDLINE_PARTS
    tristate "Command line partition table parsing"
    depends on MTD
```

If `CONFIG_MTD` has not been enabled elsewhere, this menu option is not shown and so cannot be selected.

There are also reverse dependencies: the `select` keyword enables other options if this one is enabled. The `Kconfig` file in `arch/$ARCH` has a large number of `select` statements that enable features specific to the architecture, as can be seen here for arm:

```
config ARM
    bool
default y
    select ARCH_HAS_ATOMIC64_DEC_IF_POSITIVE
    select ARCH_HAS_ELF_RANDOMIZE
[...]
```

There are several configuration utilities that can read the `Kconfig` files and produce a `.config` file. Some of them display the menus on screen and allow you to make choices interactively. `Menuconfig` is probably the one most people are familiar with, but there is also `xconfig` and `gconfig`.

You launch each one via `make`, remembering that, in the case of the kernel, you have to supply an architecture, as illustrated here:

```
$ make ARCH=arm menuconfig
```

Here, you can see `menuconfig` with the `DEVMEM` `config` option highlighted in the previous paragraph:

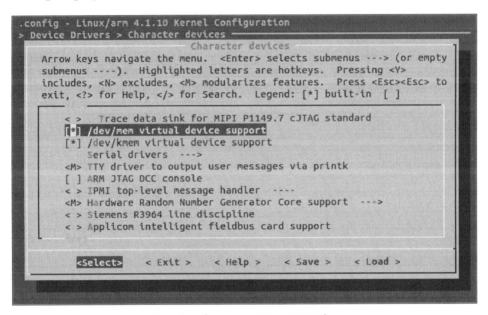

```
.config - Linux/arm 4.1.10 Kernel Configuration
> Device Drivers > Character devices
                       Character devices
   Arrow keys navigate the menu.  <Enter> selects submenus ---> (or empty
   submenus ----).  Highlighted letters are hotkeys.  Pressing <Y>
   includes, <N> excludes, <M> modularizes features.  Press <Esc><Esc> to
   exit, <?> for Help, </> for Search.  Legend: [*] built-in  [ ]

      < >    Trace data sink for MIPI P1149.7 cJTAG standard
      [*]  /dev/mem virtual device support
      [*] /dev/kmem virtual device support
           Serial drivers  --->
      <M> TTY driver to output user messages via printk
      [ ] ARM JTAG DCC console
      < > IPMI top-level message handler  ----
      <M> Hardware Random Number Generator Core support  --->
      < > Siemens R3964 line discipline
      < > Applicom intelligent fieldbus card support

        <Select>    < Exit >    < Help >    < Save >    < Load >
```

Kernel configuration using menuconfig

The star (`*`) to the left of an item means that it is selected (`="y"`) or, if it is an `M`, that it has been selected to be built as a kernel module.

You often see instructions like `enable CONFIG_BLK_DEV_INITRD`, but with so many menus to browse through, it can take a while to find the place where that configuration is set. All configuration editors have a `search` function. You can access it in `menuconfig` by pressing the forward slash key, `/`. In xconfig, it is in the edit menu but, in this case make sure you miss off the `CONFIG_` part of the variable you are searching for.

With so many things to configure, it is unreasonable to start with a clean sheet each time you want to build a kernel so there are a set of known working configuration files in `arch/$ARCH/configs`, each containing suitable configuration values for a single SoC or a group of SoCs. You can select one with `make [configuration file name]`. For example, to configure Linux to run on a wide range of SoCs using the armv7-a architecture, which includes the BeagleBone Black AM335x, you would type:

```
$ make ARCH=arm multi_v7_defconfig
```

This is a generic kernel that runs on various different boards. For a more specialized application, for example when using a vendor-supplied kernel, the default configuration file is part of the board support package; you will need to find out which one to use before you can build the kernel.

There is another useful configuration target named `oldconfig`. This takes an exiting `.config` file and asks you to supply configuration values for any options that don't have them. You would use it when moving a configuration to a newer kernel version: copy `.config` from the old kernel to the new source directory and run `make ARCH=arm oldconfig` to bring it up to date. It can also be used to validate a `.config` file that you have edited manually (ignoring the text `Automatically generated file; DO NOT EDIT` that occurs at the top: sometimes it is OK to ignore warnings).

If you do make changes to the configuration, the modified `.config` file becomes part of your device and needs to be placed under source code control.

When you start the kernel build, a header file, `include/generated/autoconf.h`, is generated which contains a `#define` for each configuration value so that it can be included in the kernel source, exactly as with U-Boot.

Using LOCALVERSION to identify your kernel

You can discover the kernel version that you have built using the `make kernelversion` target:

```
$ make kernelversion
4.1.10
```

This is reported at runtime through the `uname` command and is also used in naming the directory where kernel modules are stored.

If you change the configuration from the default it is advisable to append your own version information, which you can configure by setting CONFIG_LOCALVERSION, which you will find in the **General setup configuration** menu. It is also possible (but discouraged) to do the same by editing the top level makefile and appending it to the line that begins with EXTRAVERSION. As an example, if I wanted to mark the kernel I am building with an identifier melp and version 1.0, I would define the local version in the .config file like this:

```
CONFIG_LOCALVERSION="-melp-v1.0"
```

Running make kernelversion produces the same output as before but now, if I run make kernelrelease, I see:

```
$ make kernelrelease
4.1.10-melp-v1.0
```

It is also printed at the beginning of the kernel log:

```
Starting kernel ...
[    0.000000] Booting Linux on physical CPU 0x0
[    0.000000] Linux version 4.1.10-melp-v1.0 (chris@builder) (gcc
version 4.9.1 (crosstool-NG 1.20.0) ) #3 SMP Thu Oct 15 21:29:35 BST 2015
```

I can now identify and track my custom kernel.

Kernel modules

I have mentioned kernel modules several times already. Desktop Linux distributions use them extensively so that the correct device and kernel functions can be loaded at runtime depending on the hardware detected and features required. Without them, every single driver and feature would have to be statically linked in to the kernel, making it unfeasibly large.

On the other hand, with embedded devices, the hardware and kernel configuration is usually known at the time the kernel is built so modules are not so useful. In fact, they cause a problem because they create a version dependency between the kernel and the root filesystem which can cause boot failures if one is updated but not the other. Consequently, it is quite common for embedded kernels to be built without any modules at all. Here are a few cases where kernel modules are a good idea:

- When you have proprietary modules, for the licensing reasons given in the preceding section.
- To reduce boot time by deferring the loading of non-essential drivers.

- When there are a number of drivers that could be loaded and it would take up too much memory to compile them statically. For example, you have a USB interface to support a range of devices. This is essentially the same argument as is used in desktop distributions.

Compiling

The kernel build system, kbuild, is a set of make scripts that take the configuration information from the .config file, work out the dependencies and compile everything that is necessary to produce a kernel image containing all the statically linked components, possibly a device tree binary and possibly one or more kernel modules. The dependencies are expressed in the makefiles that are in each directory with buildable components. For instance, these two lines are taken from drivers/char/Makefile:

```
obj-y                    += mem.o random.o
obj-$(CONFIG_TTY_PRINTK) += ttyprintk.o
```

The obj-y rule unconditionally compiles a file to produce the target, so mem.c and random.c are always part of the kernel. In the second line, ttyprintk.c is dependent on a configuration parameter. If CONFIG_TTY_PRINTK is y it is compiled as a built in, if it is m it is built as a module and, if the parameter is undefined, it is not compiled at all.

For most targets, just typing make (with the appropriate ARCH and CROSS_COMPILE) will do the job, but it is instructive to take it one step at a time.

Compiling the kernel image

To build a kernel image, you need to know what your bootloader expects. This is a rough guide:

- **U-Boot**: Traditionally U-Boot has required a uImage, but newer versions can load a zImage file using the bootz command
- **x86 targets**: It requires a bzImage file
- **Most other bootloaders**: It requires a zImage file

Here is an example of building a zImage file:

```
$ make -j 4 ARCH=arm CROSS_COMPILE=arm-cortex_a8-linux-gnueabihf-
zImage
```

 The -j 4 option tells make how many jobs to run in parallel, which reduces the time taken to build. A rough guide is to run as many jobs as you have CPU cores.

It is the same when building bzImage and uImage targets.

There is a small issue with building a uImage file for ARM with multi-platform support, which is the norm for the current generation of ARM SoC kernels. Multi-platform support for ARM was introduced in Linux 3.7. It allows a single kernel binary to run on multiple platforms and is a step on the road toward having a small number of kernels for all ARM devices. The kernel selects the correct platform by reading the machine number or the device tree passed to it by the bootloader. The problem occurs because the location of physical memory might be different for each platform, and so the relocation address for the kernel (usually 0x8000 bytes from the start of physical RAM) might also be different. The relocation address is coded into the uImage header by the mkimage command when the kernel is built, but it will fail if there is more than one relocation address to choose from. To put it another way, the uImage format is not compatible with multi-platform images. You can still create a uImage binary from a multi-platform build so long as you give the LOADADDR of the particular SoC you are hoping to boot this kernel on. You can find the load address by looking in mach-[your SoC]/Makefile.boot and noting the value of zreladdr-y.

In the case of a BeagleBone Black, the full command would look like this:

```
$ make -j 4 ARCH=arm CROSS_COMPILE=arm-cortex_a8-linux-gnueabihf-
LOADADDR=0x80008000 uImage
```

A kernel build generates two files in the top level directory: vmlinux and System. map. The first, vmlinux, is the kernel as an ELF binary. If you have compiled your kernel with debug enabled (CONFIG_DEBUG_INFO=y), it will contain debug symbols which can be used with debuggers like kgdb. You can also use other ELF binary tools such as size:

```
$ arm-cortex_a8-linux-gnueabihf-size vmlinux
   text      data       bss        dec       hex     filename
8812564    790692   8423536   18026792   1131128     vmlinux
```

System.map contains the symbol table in human readable form.

Most bootloaders cannot handle ELF code directly. There is a further stage of processing which takes vmlinux and places those binaries in arch/$ARCH/boot that are suitable for the various bootloaders:

- Image: vmlinux converted to raw binary.
- zImage: For the PowerPC architecture, this is just a compressed version of Image, which implies that the bootloader must do the decompression. For all other architectures, the compressed Image is piggybacked onto a stub of code that decompresses and relocates it.
- uImage: zImage plus a 64-byte U-Boot header.

While the build is running, you will see a summary of the commands being executed:

```
$ make -j 4 ARCH=arm CROSS_COMPILE=arm-cortex_a8-linux-gnueabihf-
zImage
CC      init/main.o
CHK     include/generated/compile.h
CC      init/version.o
CC      init/do_mounts.o
CC      init/do_mounts_rd.o
CC      init/do_mounts_initrd.o
LD      init/mounts.o
[...]
```

Sometimes, when the kernel build fails, it is useful to see the actual commands being executed. To do that, add `V=1` to the command line:

```
$ make ARCH=arm CROSS_COMPILE=arm-cortex_a8-linux-gnueabihf- V=1
zImage
[...]
arm-cortex_a8-linux-gnueabihf-gcc -Wp,-
MD,init/.do_mounts_initrd.o.d  -nostdinc -isystem /home/chris/x-
tools/arm-cortex_a8-linux-gnueabihf/lib/gcc/arm-cortex_a8-linux-
gnueabihf/4.9.1/include -I./arch/arm/include -
Iarch/arm/include/generated/uapi -Iarch/arm/include/generated  -
Iinclude -I./arch/arm/include/uapi -
Iarch/arm/include/generated/uapi -I./include/uapi -
Iinclude/generated/uapi -include ./include/linux/kconfig.h -
D__KERNEL__ -mlittle-endian -Wall -Wundef -Wstrict-prototypes -
Wno-trigraphs -fno-strict-aliasing -fno-common -Werror-implicit-
function-declaration -Wno-format-security -std=gnu89 -fno-dwarf2-
cfi-asm -mabi=aapcs-linux -mno-thumb-interwork -mfpu=vfp -funwind-
tables -marm -D__LINUX_ARM_ARCH__=7 -march=armv7-a -msoft-float -
Uarm -fno-delete-null-pointer-checks -O2 --param=allow-store-data-
races=0 -Wframe-larger-than=1024 -fno-stack-protector -Wno-unused-
but-set-variable -fomit-frame-pointer -fno-var-tracking-
assignments -Wdeclaration-after-statement -Wno-pointer-sign -fno-
strict-overflow -fconserve-stack -Werror=implicit-int -
Werror=strict-prototypes -Werror=date-time -DCC_HAVE_ASM_GOTO    -
D"KBUILD_STR(s)=#s" -
D"KBUILD_BASENAME=KBUILD_STR(do_mounts_initrd)"  -
D"KBUILD_MODNAME=KBUILD_STR(mounts)" -c -o init/do_mounts_initrd.o
init/do_mounts_initrd.c
[...]
```

Compiling device trees

The next step is to build the device tree, or trees if you have a multi-platform build. The dtbs target builds device trees according to the rules in `arch/$ARCH/boot/dts/Makefile` using the device tree source files in that directory:

```
$ make ARCH=arm dtbs
...
DTC     arch/arm/boot/dts/omap2420-h4.dtb
DTC     arch/arm/boot/dts/omap2420-n800.dtb
DTC     arch/arm/boot/dts/omap2420-n810.dtb
DTC     arch/arm/boot/dts/omap2420-n810-wimax.dtb
DTC     arch/arm/boot/dts/omap2430-sdp.dtb
...
```

The `.dtb` files are generated in the same directory as the sources.

Compiling modules

If you have configured some features to be built as modules, you can build them separately using the `modules` target:

```
$ make -j 4 ARCH=arm CROSS_COMPILE=arm-cortex_a8-linux-gnueabihf-
modules
```

The compiled modules have a `.ko` suffix and are generated in the same directory as the source code, meaning that they are scattered all around the kernel source tree. Finding them is a little tricky but you can use the `modules_install` make target to install them in the right place. The default location is `/lib/modules` in your development system, which is almost certainly not what you want. To install them into the staging area of your root filesystem (we will talk about root filesystems in the next chapter), provide the path using `INSTALL_MOD_PATH`:

```
$ make -j4 ARCH=arm CROSS_COMPILE=arm-cortex_a8-linux-gnueabihf-
INSTALL_MOD_PATH=$HOME/rootfs modules_install
```

Kernel modules are put into the directory `/lib/modules/[kernel version]`, relative to the root of the filesystem.

Cleaning kernel sources

There are three make targets for cleaning the kernel source tree:

- `clean`: removes object files and most intermediates.

- `mrproper`: removes all intermediate files, including the `.config` file. Use this target to return the source tree to the state it was in immediately after cloning or extracting the source code. If you are curious about the name, Mr Proper is a cleaning product common in some parts of the world. The meaning of `make mrproper` is to give the kernel sources a really good scrub.

- `distclean`: This is the same as mrproper but also deletes editor backup files, patch leftover files, and other artifacts of software development.

Booting your kernel

Booting is highly device-dependent, but here is an example using U-Boot on a BeagleBone Black and QEMU:.

BeagleBone Black

The following U-Boot commands show how to boot Linux on a BeagleBone Black:

```
U-Boot# fatload mmc 0:1 0x80200000 zImage
reading zImage
4606360 bytes read in 254 ms (17.3 MiB/s)
U-Boot# fatload mmc 0:1 0x80f00000 am335x-boneblack.dtb
reading am335x-boneblack.dtb
29478 bytes read in 9 ms (3.1 MiB/s)
U-Boot# setenv bootargs console=ttyO0,115200
U-Boot# bootz 0x80200000 - 0x80f00000
Kernel image @ 0x80200000 [ 0x000000 - 0x464998 ]
## Flattened Device Tree blob at 80f00000
   Booting using the fdt blob at 0x80f00000
   Loading Device Tree to 8fff5000, end 8ffff325 ... OK
Starting kernel ...
[    0.000000] Booting Linux on physical CPU 0x0
...
```

Note that we set the kernel command line to `console=ttyO0,115200`. That tells Linux which device to use for console output which, in this case, is the first UART on the board, device `ttyO0`, at a speed of 115,200 bits per second. Without this, we would not see any messages after `Starting the kernel` ... and therefore would not know if it was working or not.

QEMU

Assuming that you have already installed `qemu-system-arm`, you can launch it with the multi_v7 kernel and the `.dtb` file for the ARM Versatile Express, as follows:

```
$ QEMU_AUDIO_DRV=none \
qemu-system-arm -m 256M -nographic -M vexpress-a9 -kernel zImage -
dtb vexpress-v2p-ca9.dtb -append "console=ttyAMA0"
```

Note that setting `QEMU_AUDIO_DRV` to `none` is just to suppress error messages from QEMU about missing configurations for the audio drivers, which we do not use.

To exit from QEMU, type `Ctrl-A` then `x` (two separate keystrokes).

Kernel panic

While things started off well, they ended badly:

```
[    1.886379] Kernel panic - not syncing: VFS: Unable to mount
root fs on unknown-block(0,0)
[    1.895105] ---[ end Kernel panic - not syncing: VFS: Unable to
mount root fs on unknown-block(0, 0)
```

This is a good example of a kernel panic. A panic occurs when the kernel encounters an unrecoverable error. By default, it will print out a message to the console and then halt. You can set the `panic` command line parameter to allow a few seconds before it reboots following a panic.

In this case, the unrecoverable error is because there is no root filesystem, illustrating that a kernel is useless without a user space to control it. You can supply a user space by providing a root filesystem either as a ramdisk or on a mountable mass storage device. We will talk about how to create a root filesystem in the next chapter but, to get things up and running, assume that we have a ramdisk in the file uRamdisk and you can then boot to a shell prompt by entering these commands into U-Boot:

```
fatload mmc 0:1 0x80200000 zImage

fatload mmc 0:1 0x80f00000 am335x-boneblack.dtb

fatload mmc 0:1 0x81000000 uRamdisk

setenv bootargs console=tty00,115200 rdinit=/bin/sh

bootz 0x80200000 0x81000000 0x80f00000
```

Here, I have added `rdinit=/bin/sh` to the command line so that the kernel will run a shell and give us a shell prompt. Now, the output on the console looks like this:

```
...
[    1.930923] sr_init: No PMIC hook to init smartreflex

[    1.936424] sr_init: platform driver register failed for SR

[    1.964858] Freeing unused kernel memory: 408K (c0824000 -
c088a000)

/ # uname -a

Linux (none) 3.18.3 #1 SMP Wed Jan 21 08:34:58 GMT 2015 armv7l
GNU/Linux

/ #
```

At last, we have a prompt and can interact with our device.

Early user space

In order to transition from kernel initialization to user space, the kernel has to mount a root filesystem and execute a program in that root filesystem. This can be via a ramdisk, as shown in the previous section, or by mounting a real filesystem on a block device. The code for all of this is in init/main.c, starting with the function rest_init() which creates the first thread with PID 1 and runs the code in kernel_init(). If there is a ramdisk, it will try to execute the program /init, which will take on the task of setting up the user space.

If it fails to find and run /init, it tries to mount a filesystem by calling the function prepare_namespace() in init/do_mounts.c. This requires a root= command line to give the name of the block device to use for mounting, usually in the form:

- root=/dev/<disk name><partition number>
- root=/dev/<disk name>p<partition number>

For example, for the first partition on an SD card, that would be root=/dev/mmcblk0p1. If the mount succeeds, it will try to execute /sbin/init, followed by /etc/init, /bin/init, and then /bin/sh, stopping at the first one that works.

The init program can be overridden on the command line. For a ramdisk, use rdinit=, (I used rdinit=/bin/sh earlier to execute a shell) and, for a filesystem, use init=.

Kernel messages

Kernel developers are fond of printing out useful information through liberal use of printk() and similar functions. The messages are categorized according to importance, 0 being the highest:

Level	Value	Meaning
KERN_EMERG	0	The system is unusable
KERN_ALERT	1	Action must be taken immediately
KERN_CRIT	2	Critical conditions
KERN_ERR	3	Error conditions
KERN_WARNING	4	Warning conditions
KERN_NOTICE	5	Normal but significant conditions
KERN_INFO	6	Informational
KERN_DEBUG	7	Debug-level messages

They are first written to a buffer, `__log_buf`, the size of which is two to the power of `CONFIG_LOG_BUF_SHIFT`. For example, if it is 16, then `__log_buf` is 64 KiB. You can dump the entire buffer using the command `dmesg`.

If the level of a message is less than the console log level, it is displayed on the console as well as being placed in `__log_buf`. The default console log level is 7, meaning that messages of level 6 and lower are displayed, filtering out `KERN_DEBUG` which is level 7. You can change the console log level in several ways, including by using the kernel parameter `loglevel=<level>` or the command `dmesg -n <level>`.

Kernel command line

The kernel command line is a string that is passed to the kernel by the bootloader, via the `bootargs` variable in the case of U-Boot; it can also be defined in the device tree, or set as part of the kernel configuration in `CONFIG_CMDLINE`.

We have seen some examples of the kernel command line already but there are many more. There is a complete list in `Documentation/kernel-parameters.txt`. Here is a smaller list of the most useful ones:

Name	Description
debug	Sets the console log level to the highest level, eight, to ensure that you see all the kernel messages on the console.
init=	The `init` program to run from a mounted root filesystem, which defaults to `/sbin/init`.
lpj=	Sets the `loops_per_jiffy` to a given constant, see the following paragraph.
panic=	Behavior when the kernel panics: if it is greater than zero, it gives the number of seconds before rebooting; if it is zero, it waits forever (this is the default); or if it is less than zero, it reboots without any delay.
quiet	Sets the console log level to one, suppressing all but emergency messages. Since most devices have a serial console, it takes time to output all those strings. Consequently, reducing the number of messages using this option reduces boot time.
rdinit=	The `init` program to run from a ramdisk, it defaults to `/init`.
ro	Mounts the root device as read-only. Has no effect on a ramdisk which is always read/write.
root=	Device to mount the root filesystem.
rootdelay=	The number of seconds to wait before trying to mount the root device, defaults to zero. Useful if the device takes time to probe the hardware, but also see `rootwait`.

Name	Description
`rootfstype=`	The filesystem type for the root device. In many cases, it is auto-detected during mount, but it is required for `jffs2` filesystems.
`rootwait`	Waits indefinitely for the root device to be detected. Usually necessary with `mmc` devices.
`rw`	Mounts the root device as read-write (default).

The `lpj` parameter is often mentioned in connection with reducing the kernel boot time. During initialization, the kernel loops for approximately 250 ms to calibrate a delay loop. The value is stored in the variable `loops_per_jiffy`, and reported like this:

```
Calibrating delay loop... 996.14 BogoMIPS (lpj=4980736)
```

If the kernel always runs on the same hardware it will always calculate the same value. You can shave 250 ms off the boot time by adding `lpj=4980736` to the command line.

Porting Linux to a new board

The scope of the task depends on how similar your board is to an existing development board. In *Chapter 3*, *All About Bootloaders* we ported U-Boot to a new board, named Nova, which is based on the BeagleBone Black (when I say based, it actually is one) so, in this case, there are very few changes to the kernel code to be made. If you are porting to completely new and innovative hardware, there will be more to do. I am only going to consider the simple case.

The organization of architecture-specific code in `arch/$ARCH` differs from one system to another. The x86 architecture is pretty clean because hardware details are detected at runtime. The PowerPC architecture puts SoC and board-specific files in subdirectory platforms. The ARM architecture has the most board and SoC-specific files of all because there are a lot of ARM boards and SoCs. Platform-dependent code is in directories named `mach-*` in `arch/arm`, approximately one per SoC. There are other directories named `plat-*` which contain code common to several versions of an SoC. In the case of the Nova board, the relevant directory is `mach-omap2`. Don't be fooled by the name, though, it contains support for OMAP2, 3, and 4 chips.

In the following sections, I am going do the port to the Nova board in two different ways. Firstly, I am going to show you how to do this with a device tree, and then without, since there are a lot of devices in the field that fit in this category. You will see that it is much simpler when you have a device tree.

With a device tree

The first thing to do is create a device tree for the board and modify it to describe the additional or changed hardware on the board. In this simple case, we will just copy am335x-boneblack.dts to nova.dts and change the board name:

```
/dts-v1/;
#include "am33xx.dtsi"
#include "am335x-bone-common.dtsi"
/ {
    model = "Nova";
    compatible = "ti,am335x-bone-black", "ti,am335x-bone", "ti,am33xx";
};
...
```

We can build nova.dtb explicitly:

`$ make  ARCH=arm nova.dtb`

Or, if we want nova.dtb to be produced by default for the OMAP2 platform with make ARCH=arm dtbs then we could add the following line to arch/arm/boot/dts/Makefile:

```
dtb-$(CONFIG_SOC_AM33XX) += \
[...]
nova.dtb \
[...]
```

Now we can boot the same zImage file as before, configured with multi_v7_defconfig, but load the nova.dtb as we can see here:

```
Starting kernel ...

[    0.000000] Booting Linux on physical CPU 0x0
[    0.000000] Initializing cgroup subsys cpuset
[    0.000000] Initializing cgroup subsys cpu
[    0.000000] Initializing cgroup subsys cpuacct
[    0.000000] Linux version 3.18.3-dirty (chris@builder) (gcc
version 4.9.1 (crosstool-N
G 1.20.0) ) #1 SMP Wed Jan 28 07:50:50 GMT 2015
[    0.000000] CPU: ARMv7 Processor [413fc082] revision 2 (ARMv7),
cr=10c5387d
[    0.000000] CPU: PIPT / VIPT nonaliasing data cache, VIPT
aliasing instruction cache
[    0.000000] Machine model: **Nova**
...
```

We could create a custom configuration by taking a copy of multi_v7_defconfig and adding in those features we need, and cutting down code size by leaving out those we don't.

Without a device tree

Firstly, we need to create a configuration name for the board, in this case, it is NOVABOARD. We need to add this to the Kconfig file of the mach- directory for your SoC and we need to add a dependency for the SoC support itself, which is OMAPAM33XX.

These lines are added to arch/arm/mach-omap2/Kconfig:

```
config MACH_NOVA BOARD
bool "Nova board"
depends on SOC_OMAPAM33XX
default n
```

There is a source file named board-*.c for each board, which contains code and configurations which are specific to the target. In our case, it is board-nova.c, based on a copy of board-am335xevm.c. There must be a rule to compile it, conditional on CONFIG_MACH_NOVABOARD, which this addition to arch/arm/mach-omap2/Makefile takes care of:

```
obj-$(CONFIG_MACH_NOVABOARD) += board-nova.o
```

Since we are not using the device tree to identify the board, we will have to use the older machine number mechanism. This is a number unique to each board that is passed by the bootloader in register r1, and which the ARM start code will use to select the correct board support. The definitive list of ARM machine numbers is held at: www.arm.linux.org.uk/developer/machines/download.php. You can request a new machine number from: www.arm.linux.org.uk/developer/machines/?action=new#.

If we hijack machine number 4242, we could add it to arch/arm/tools/mach-types, as shown:

```
machine_is_xxx    CONFIG_xxxx       MACH_TYPE_xxx        number
...
nova_board        MACH_NOVABOARD    NOVABOARD            4242
```

When we build the kernel, it will be used to create the mach-types.h header file present in include/generated/.

The machine number and the board support are tied together by a structure which is defined like this:

```
MACHINE_START(NOVABOARD, "nova_board")
/* Maintainer: Chris Simmonds */
.atag_offset    = 0x100,
```

```
.map_io          = am335x_evm_map_io,
.init_early      = am33xx_init_early,
.init_irq        = ti81xx_init_irq,
.handle_irq      = omap3_intc_handle_irq,
.timer           = &omap3_am33xx_timer,
.init_machine    = am335x_evm_init,
MACHINE_END
```

Note that there may be more than one machine structure in a board file, allowing us to create a kernel that will run on several different boards. The machine number passed by the bootloader selects the correct one.

Finally, we need a new default configuration for our board, which selects CONFIG_MACH_NOVABOARD and other configuration options specific to it. In the following example, it would be in `arch/arm/configs/novaboard_defconfig`. Now you can build the kernel image as usual:

```
$ make ARCH=arm novaboard_defconfig
$ make -j 4 ARCH=arm CROSS_COMPILE=arm-cortex_a8-linux-gnueabi-
zImage
```

There is still one step before the job is finished. The bootloader needs to be modified to pass the right machine number. Assuming that you are using U-Boot, you need to copy the machine numbers generated by Linux in `arch/arm/include/asm/mach-types.h` to U-Boot file `arch/arm/include/asm/mach-types.h`. Then you need to update the configuration header file for Nova, `include/configs/nova.h`, and add the following line:

```
#define CONFIG_MACH_TYPE         MACH_TYPE_NOVABOARD
```

Now, at last, you can build U-Boot and use it to boot the new kernel on the Nova board:

```
Starting kernel ...

[    0.000000] Linux version 3.2.0-00246-g0c74d7a-dirty
(chris@builder) (gcc version 4.9.
1 (crosstool-NG 1.20.0) ) #3 Wed Jan 28 11:45:10 GMT 2015
[    0.000000] CPU: ARMv7 Processor [413fc082] revision 2 (ARMv7),
cr=10c53c7d
[    0.000000] CPU: PIPT / VIPT nonaliasing data cache, VIPT
aliasing instruction cache
[    0.000000] Machine: nova_board
```

Additional reading

The following resources have further information about the topics introduced in this chapter:

- *Linux Kernel Newbies*, kernelnewbies.org
- *Linux Weekly News*, www.lwn.net

Summary

Linux is a very powerful and complex operating system kernel that can be married to various types of user space ranging from a simple embedded device, to increasingly complex mobile devices using Android, to a full server operating system. One of its strengths is the degree of configurability. The definitive place to get the source code is www.kerenl.org, but you will probably need to get the source for a particular SoC or board from the vendor of that device or a third-party that supports that device. The customization of the kernel for a particular target may consist of changes to the core kernel code, additional drivers for devices that are not in mainline Linux, a default kernel configuration file and, a device tree source file.

Normally you start with the default configuration for your target board, and then tweak it by running one of the configuration tools such as menuconfig. One of the things you should consider at this point is whether kernel features and drivers should be compiled as modules or built-in. Kernel modules are usually no great advantage for embedded systems, where the feature set and hardware are usually well defined. However, modules are often used as a way to import proprietary code into the kernel, and also to reduce boot time by loading non-essential drivers after boot. Building the kernel produces a compressed kernel image file, named zImage, bzImage, or uImage depending on the bootloader you will be using and the target architecture. A kernel build will also generate any kernel modules (as .ko files) that you have configured, and device tree binaries (as .dtb files) if your target requires them.

Porting Linux to a new target board can be quite simple or very difficult depending on how different the hardware is from that in the mainline or vendor supplied kernel. If your hardware is based on a well-known reference design, then it may be just a question of making changes to the device tree or to the platform data. You may well need to add device drivers, which I discuss in *Chapter 8, Introducing Device Drivers*. However, if the hardware is radically different to a reference design, you may need additional core support, which is outside the scope of this book.

The kernel is the core of a Linux based system, but it cannot work by itself. It requires a root filesystem that contains user space. The root filesystem can be a ramdisk or a filesystem accessed via a block device, which will be the subject of the next chapter. As we have seen, booting a kernel without a root filesystem results in a kernel panic.

5
Building a Root Filesystem

The root filesystem is the fourth and final element of embedded Linux. Once you have read this chapter, you will be able build, boot, and run a simple embedded Linux system.

This chapter explores the fundamental concepts behind the root filesystem by building one from scratch. The main aim is to provide the background information that you need to understand and make best use of build systems like Buildroot and the Yocto Project, which I will cover in *Chapter 6, Selecting a Build System*.

The techniques I will describe here are broadly known as **roll your own** or **RYO**. Back in the earlier days of embedded Linux, it was the only way to create a root filesystem. There are still some use cases where an RYO root filesystem is applicable, for example, when the amount of RAM or storage is very limited, for quick demonstrations, or for any case in which your requirements are not (easily) covered by the standard build system tools. Nevertheless, these cases are quite rare. Let me emphasize that the purpose of this chapter is educational, it is not meant to be a recipe for building everyday embedded systems: use the tools described in the next chapter for that.

The first objective is to create a minimal root filesystem that will give us a shell prompt. Then, using that as a base, we will add scripts to start up other programs and configure a network interface and user permissions. Knowing how to build the root filesystem from scratch is a useful skill and it will help you to understand what is going on when we look at more complex examples in later chapters.

What should be in the root filesystem?

The kernel will get a root filesystem, either as a ramdisk, passed as a pointer from the bootloader, or by mounting the block device given on the kernel command line by the `root=` parameter. Once it has a root filesystem, the kernel will execute the first program, by default named `init`, as described in the section *Early Userspace* in *Chapter 4*, *Porting and Configuring the Kernel*. Then, as far as the kernel is concerned, its job is complete. It is up to the `init` program to begin processing scripts, start other programs, and so on, by calling system functions in the C library, which translate into kernel system calls.

To make a useful system, you need these components as a minimum:

- **init**: The program that starts everything off, usually by running a series of scripts.

- **shell**: Needed to give you a command prompt but, more importantly, to run the shell scripts called by `init` and other programs.

- **daemons**: Various server programs, started by `init`.

- **libraries**: Usually, the programs mentioned so far are linked with shared libraries which must be present in the root filesystem.

- **Configuration files**: The configuration for `init` and other daemons is stored in a series of ASCII text files, usually in the `/etc` directory.

- **Device nodes**: The special files that give access to various device drivers.

- **/proc and /sys**: Two pseudo filesystems that represent kernel data structures as a hierarchy of directories and files. Many programs and library functions read these files.

- **kernel modules**: If you have configured some parts of your kernel to be modules, they will be here, usually in `/lib/modules/[kernel version]`.

In addition, there are the system application or applications that make the device do the job it is intended for, and the runtime end user data that they collect.

As an aside, it is possible to condense all of the above into a single program. You could create a statically linked program that is started instead of `init` and runs no others. I have come across such a configuration only once. For example, if your program was named `/myprog`, you would put the following command in the kernel command line:

```
init=/myprog
```

Or, if the root filesystem was loaded as a ramdisk, you would put the following command:

```
rdinit=/myprog
```

The downside of this approach is that you can't make use of the many tools that normally go into an embedded system; you have to do everything yourself.

Directory layout

Interestingly, Linux does not care about the layout of files and directories beyond the existence of the program named by `init=` or `rdinit=`, so you are free to put things wherever you like. As an example, compare the file layout of a device running Android to that of a desktop Linux distribution: they are almost completely different.

However, many programs expect certain files to be in certain places, and it helps us developers if devices use a similar layout, Android aside. The basic layout of a Linux system is defined in the **Filesystem Hierarchy Standard (FHS)**, see the reference at the end of this chapter. The FHS covers all implementations of Linux operating systems from the largest to the smallest. Embedded devices have a sub-set based on need but it usually includes the following:

- `/bin`: programs essential for all users
- `/dev`: device nodes and other special files
- `/etc`: system configuration
- `/lib`: essential shared libraries, for example, those that make up the C library
- `/proc`: the `proc` filesystem
- `/sbin`: programs essential to the system administrator
- `/sys`: the `sysfs` filesystem
- `/tmp`: a place to put temporary or volatile files
- `/usr`: as a minimum, this should contain the directories `/usr/bin`, `/usr/lib` and `/usr/sbin`, which contain additional programs, libraries, and system administrator utilities
- `/var`: a hierarchy of files and directories that may be modified at runtime, for example, log messages, some of which must be retained after boot

There are some subtle distinctions here. The difference between /bin and /sbin is simply that /sbin need not be included in the search path for non-root users. Users of Red Hat-derived distributions will be familiar with this. The significance of /usr is that it may be in a separate partition from the root filesystem so it cannot contain anything that is needed to boot the system up. That is what essential means in the preceding description: it contains files that are needed at boot time and so must be part of the root filesystem.

> While it might seem like overkill to have four directories to store programs, a counter argument would be that it does no harm, and it may even do some good because it allows you to store /usr in a different filesystem.

Staging directory

You should begin by creating a staging directory on your host computer where you can assemble the files that will eventually be transferred to the target. In the following examples, I have used ~/rootfs. You need to create a skeleton directory structure in that, for example:

```
$ mkdir ~/rootfs
$ cd ~/rootfs
$ mkdir bin dev etc home lib proc sbin sys tmp usr var
$ mkdir usr/bin usr/lib usr/sbin
$ mkdir var/log
```

To see the directory hierarchy more clearly you can use the handy tree command, used in the following example with the -d option to show only directories:

```
$ tree -d

├── bin
├── dev
├── etc
├── home
├── lib
├── proc
├── sbin
├── sys
```

```
├── tmp
├── usr
│   ├── bin
│   ├── lib
│   └── sbin
└── var
    └── log
```

POSIX file access permissions

Every process which, in the context of this discussion, means every running program, belongs to a user and one or more groups. The user is represented by a 32-bit number called the **user ID** or **UID**. Information about users, including the mapping from a UID to a name, is kept in /etc/passwd. Likewise, groups are represented by a **group ID** or **GID**, with information kept in /etc/group. There is always a root user with a UID of 0 and a root group with a GID of 0. The root user is also called the super-user because, in a default configuration, it bypasses most permission checks and can access all the resources in the system. Security in Linux-based systems is mainly about restricting access to the root account.

Each file and directory also has an owner and belongs to exactly one group. The level of access a process has to a file or directory is controlled by a set of access permission flags, called the mode of the file. There are three collections of three bits: the first collection applies to the owner of the file, the second to members of the same group as the file, and the last to everyone else, the rest of the world. The bits are for read (r), write (w), and execute (x) permissions on the file. Since three bits fit neatly into an octal digit, they are usually represented in octal, as shown in the following figure:

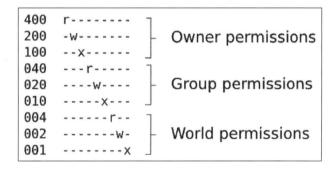

There is a further group of three bits that have special meanings:

- **SUID (4)**: If the file is an executable, change the effective UID of the process to that of the owner of the file.

- **SGID (2)**: If the file is an executable, change the effective GID of the process to that of the group of the file.

- **Sticky (1)**: In a directory, restrict deletion so that one user cannot delete files that are owned by another user. This is usually set on /tmp and /var/tmp.

The SUID bit is probably the most often used. It gives non-root users a temporary privilege escalation to super-user to perform a task. A good example is the ping program: ping opens a raw socket which is a privileged operation. In order for normal users to use ping, it is normally owned by the root and has the SUID bit set so that, when you run ping, it executes with UID 0 regardless of your UID.

To set these bits, use the octal numbers, 4, 2, 1, with the chmod command. For example, to set SUID on /bin/ping in your staging root directory, you could use the following:

```
$ cd ~/rootfs
$ ls -l bin/ping
-rwxr-xr-x 1 root root 35712 Feb  6 09:15 bin/ping
$ sudo chmod 4755 bin/ping
$ ls -l bin/ping
-rwsr-xr-x 1 root root 35712 Feb  6 09:15 bin/ping
```

 Note the s in the last file listing: that is the indication that SUID is set.

File ownership permissions in the staging directory

For security and stability reasons, it is vitally important to pay attention to the ownership and permissions of the files that will be placed on the target device. Generally speaking, you want to restrict sensitive resources to be accessible only by the root and to run as many of the programs using non-root users so that, if they are compromised by an outside attack, they offer as few system resources to the attacker as possible. For example, the device node /dev/mem gives access to system memory, which is necessary in some programs. But, if it is readable and writeable by everyone, then there is no security because everyone can access everything. So /dev/mem should be owned by root, belong to the root group and have a mode of 600, which denies read and write access to all but the owner.

There is a problem with the staging directory though. The files you create there will be owned by you but, when they are installed on the device, they should belong to specific owners and groups, mostly the root user. An obvious fix is to change the ownership at this stage with the command shown here:

```
$ cd ~/rootfs
$ sudo chown -R root:root *
```

The problem is that you need root privileges to run that command and, from that point onward, you will need to be root to modify any files in the staging directory. Before you know it, you are doing all your development logged on as root, which is not a good idea. This is a problem that we will come back to later.

Programs for the root filesystem

Now, it is time to start populating the root filesystem with the essential programs and the supporting libraries, configuration, and data files that it needs to operate, beginning with an overview of the types of program you will need.

The init program

You have seen in the previous chapter that init is the first program to be run and so has PID 1. It runs as the root user and so has maximum access to system resources. Usually, it runs shell scripts which start daemons: a daemon is a program that runs in the background with no connection to a terminal, in other places it would be called a server program.

Shell

We need a shell to run scripts and to give us a command-line prompt so that we can interact with the system. An interactive shell is probably not necessary in a production device, but it is useful for development, debugging, and maintenance. There are various shells in common use in embedded systems:

- bash: is the big beast that we all know and love from desktop Linux. It is a superset of the Unix Bourne shell, with many extensions or *bashisms*.

- ash: also based on the Bourne shell, and has a long history with the BSD variants of Unix. Busybox has a version of ash which has been extended to make it more compatible with bash. It is much smaller than bash and hence is a very popular choice for embedded systems.

- hush: is a very small shell that we briefly looked at in the chapter on bootloaders. It is useful on devices with very little memory. There is a version in BusyBox.

 If you are using ash or hush as the shell on the target, make sure that you test your shell scripts on the target. It is very tempting to test them only on the host, using bash, and then be surprised that they don't work when you copy them to the target.

Utilities

The shell is just a way of launching other programs and a shell script is little more than a list of programs to run, with some flow control and a means of passing information between programs. To make a shell useful, you need the utility programs that the Unix command-line is based on. Even for a basic root filesystem, there are approximately 50 utilities, which presents two problems. Firstly, tracking down the source code for each and cross compiling it would be quite a big job. Secondly, the resulting collection of programs would take up several tens of megabytes, which was a real problem in the early days of embedded Linux when a few megabytes was all you had. To solve this problem, BusyBox was born.

BusyBox to the rescue!

The genesis of BusyBox had nothing to do with embedded Linux. The project was instigated in 1996 by Bruce Perens for the Debian installer so that he could boot Linux from a 1.44 MB floppy disk. Coincidentally, that was about the size of the storage on contemporary devices and so the embedded Linux community quickly took it up. BusyBox has been at the heart of embedded Linux ever since.

BusyBox was written from scratch to perform the essential functions of those essential Linux utilities. The developers took advantage of the 80:20 rule: the most useful 80% of a program is implemented in 20% of the code. Hence, BusyBox tools implement a subset of the functions of the desktop equivalents, but they do enough to be useful in the majority of cases.

Another trick BusyBox employs is to combine all the tools together into a single binary, making it easy to share code between them. It works like this: BusyBox is a collection of applets, each of which exports its main function in the form [applet]_main. For example, the cat command is implemented in coreutils/cat.c and exports cat_main. The main function of BusyBox itself dispatches the call to the correct applet based on the command-line arguments.

So, to read a file, you can launch `busybox` with the name of the applet you want to run, followed by any arguments the applet expects, as shown here:

```
$ busybox cat my_file.txt
```

You can also run `busybox` with no arguments to get a list of all the applets that have been compiled.

Using BusyBox in this way is rather clumsy. A better way to get BusyBox to run the `cat` applet is to create a symbolic link from `/bin/cat` to `/bin/busybox`:

```
$ ls -l bin/cat bin/busybox
-rwxr-xr-x 1 chris chris 892868 Feb  2 11:01 bin/busybox
lrwxrwxrwx 1 chris chris      7 Feb  2 11:01 bin/cat -> busybox
```

When you type `cat` at the command line, `busybox` is the program that actually runs. BusyBox only has to check the command tail passed in `argv[0]`, which will be `/bin/cat`, extract the application name, `cat`, and do a table look-up to match `cat` with `cat_main`. All this is in `libbb/appletlib.c` in this section of code (slightly simplified):

```
    applet_name = argv[0];
    applet_name = bb_basename(applet_name);
    run_applet_and_exit(applet_name, argv);
```

BusyBox has over three hundred applets including an `init` program, several shells of varying levels of complexity, and utilities for most admin tasks. There is even a simple version of the `vi` editor so you can change text files on your device.

To summarize, a typical installation of BusyBox consists of a single program with a symbolic link for each applet, but which behaves exactly as if it were a collection of individual applications.

Building BusyBox

BusyBox uses the same `Kconfig` and `Kbuild` system of the kernel, so cross compiling is straightforward. You can get the source by cloning the git archive and checking out the version you want (1_24_1 was the latest at the time of writing), like this:

```
$ git clone git://busybox.net/busybox.git
$ cd busybox
$ git checkout 1_24_1
```

You can also download the corresponding `tarball` file from `http://busybox.net/downloads`. Then, configure BusyBox, starting in this case with the default configuration, which enables pretty much all of the features of BusyBox:

```
$ make distclean
```

```
$ make defconfig
```

At this point, you probably want to run `make menuconfig` to fine tune the configuration. You almost certainly want to set the install path in **Busybox Settings | Installation Options** (`CONFIG_PREFIX`) to point to the staging directory. Then, you can cross compile in the usual way:

```
$ make -j 4 ARCH=arm CROSS_COMPILE=arm-cortex_a8-linux-gnueabihf-
```

The result is the executable, `busybox`. For a `defconfig` build for ARM v7a, it comes out at about 900 KiB. If that is too big for you, you can slim it down by configuring out the utilities you don't need.

To install BusyBox, use the following command:

```
$ make install
```

This will copy the binary to the directory configured in `CONFIG_PREFIX` and create all the symbolic links to it.

ToyBox – an alternative to BusyBox

BusyBox is not the only game in town. For example, Android has an equivalent named Toolbox, but it is more tuned to the needs of Android and not useful in a general purpose embedded environment. A more useful option is ToyBox, a project started and maintained by Rob Landley, who was previously a maintainer of BusyBox. ToyBox has the same aim as BusyBox, but with more emphasis on complying with standards, especially POSIX-2008 and LSB 4.1, and less on compatibility with GNU extensions to those standards. ToyBox is smaller than BusyBox, partly because it implements fewer applets.

However, the main difference is the license, BSD rather than GPL v2, which makes it license-compatible with operating systems with a BSD-licensed user space, such as Android itself.

Libraries for the root filesystem

Programs are linked with libraries. You could link them all statically, in which case, there would be no libraries on the target device. But, that takes up an unnecessarily large amount of storage if you have more than two or three programs. So, you need to copy shared libraries from the toolchain to the staging directory. How do you know which libraries?

One option is to copy all of them since they must be of some use, otherwise they wouldn't exist! That is certainly logical and, if you are creating a platform to be used by others for a range of applications, that would be the correct approach. Be aware, though, that a full `glibc` is quite large. In the case of a CrossTool-NG build of `glibc` 2.19, the space taken by `/lib` and `/usr/lib` is 33 MiB. Of course, you could cut down on that considerably by using uClibc or Musel `libc` libraries.

Another option is to cherry pick only those libraries that you require, for which you need a means of discovering library dependencies. Using some of our knowledge from *Chapter 2, Learning About Toolchains* libraries, you can use `readelf` for that task:

```
$ cd ~/rootfs
$ arm-cortex_a8-linux-gnueabihf-readelf -a bin/busybox | grep "program
interpreter"
      [Requesting program interpreter: /lib/ld-linux-armhf.so.3]
$ arm-cortex_a8-linux-gnueabihf-readelf -a bin/busybox | grep "Shared
library"
0x00000001 (NEEDED)                 Shared library: [libm.so.6]
0x00000001 (NEEDED)                 Shared library: [libc.so.6]
```

Now you need to find these files in the toolchain and copy them to the staging directory. Remember that you can find `sysroot` like this:

```
$ arm-cortex_a8-linux-gnueabihf-gcc -print-sysroot
/home/chris/x-tools/arm-cortex_a8-linux-gnueabihf/arm-cortex_a8-
linux-gnueabihf/sysroot
```

To reduce the amount of typing, I am going to keep a copy of that in a shell variable:

```
$ export SYSROOT=`arm-cortex_a8-linux-gnueabihf-gcc -print-
sysroot`
```

If you look at `/lib/ld-linux-armhf.so.3`, in `sysroot`, you will see that, it is, in fact, a symbolic link:

```
$ ls -l $SYSROOT/lib/ld-linux-armhf.so.3
[...]/sysroot/lib/ld-linux-armhf.so.3 -> ld-2.19.so
```

Repeat the exercise for `libc.so.6` and `libm.so.6` and you will end up with a list of three files and three symbolic links. Copy them using `cp -a`, which will preserve the symbolic link:

```
$ cd ~/rootfs
$ cp -a $SYSROOT/lib/ld-linux-armhf.so.3 lib
$ cp -a $SYSROOT/lib/ld-2.19.so lib
$ cp -a $SYSROOT/lib/libc.so.6 lib
$ cp -a $SYSROOT/lib/libc-2.19.so lib
$ cp -a $SYSROOT/lib/libm.so.6 lib
$ cp -a $SYSROOT/lib/libm-2.19.so lib
```

Repeat this procedure for each program.

 It is only worth doing this to get the very smallest embedded footprint possible. There is a danger that you will miss libraries that are loaded through `dlopen(3)` calls - plugins mostly. We will look at an example with the NSS libraries when we come to configure network interfaces later on in this chapter.

Reducing size by stripping

Libraries and programs are often compiled with a symbol table information built in, more so if you have compiled with the debug switch, `-g`. You seldom need these on the target. A quick and easy way to save space is to strip them. This example shows `libc` before and after stripping:

```
$ file rootfs/lib/libc-2.19.so
rootfs/lib/libc-2.19.so: ELF 32-bit LSB shared object, ARM, version 1
(SYSV), dynamically linked (uses shared libs), for GNU/Linux 3.15.4,
not stripped
$ ls -og rootfs/lib/libc-2.19.so
-rwxrwxr-x 1 1547371 Feb  5 10:18 rootfs/lib/libc-2.19.so
$ arm-cortex_a8-linux-gnueabi-strip rootfs/lib/libc-2.19.so
$ file rootfs/lib/libc-2.19.so
rootfs/lib/libc-2.19.so: ELF 32-bit LSB shared object, ARM, version 1
(SYSV), dynamically linked (uses shared libs), for GNU/Linux 3.15.4,
stripped
$ ls -l rootfs/lib/libc-2.19.so
-rwxrwxr-x 1 chris chris 1226024 Feb  5 10:19 rootfs/lib/libc-2.19.so
$ ls -og rootfs/lib/libc-2.19.so
-rwxrwxr-x 1 1226024 Feb  5 10:19 rootfs/lib/libc-2.19.so
```

In this case, we saved 321,347 bytes, which was about 20%.

When stripping kernel modules, use the following command:

```
strip --strip-unneeded <module name>
```

Otherwise, you will strip out the symbols needed to relocate the module code and it will fail to load.

Device nodes

Most devices in Linux are represented by device nodes, in accordance with the Unix philosophy that *everything is a file* (except network interfaces, which are sockets). A device node may refer to a block device or a character device. Block devices are mass storage devices such as SD cards or hard drives. A character device is pretty much anything else, once again with the exception of network interfaces. The conventional location for device nodes is the directory /dev. For example, a serial port may be represented by the device node /dev/ttyS0.

Device nodes are created using the program mknod (short for make node):

```
mknod <name> <type> <major> <minor>
```

name is the name of the device node that you want to create, type is either, c for character devices, and b for block. They each have a major number and a minor number which is used by the kernel to route file requests to the appropriate device driver code. There is a list of standard major and minor numbers in the kernel source in Documentation/devices.txt.

You will need to create device nodes for all the devices you want to access on your system. You can do that manually by using the mknod command as I will illustrate here, or you can use one of the device managers mentioned later to create them automatically, at runtime.

You need just two nodes to boot with BusyBox: console and null. The console only needs to be accessible to root, the owner of the device node, so the access permissions are 600. The null device should be readable and writable by everyone, so the mode is 666. You can use the -m option to mknod to set the mode when creating the node. You need to be root to create a device node:

```
$ cd ~/rootfs
$ sudo mknod -m 666 dev/null c 1 3
$ sudo mknod -m 600 dev/console c 5 1
$ ls -l dev
total 0
crw------- 1 root root 5, 1 Oct 28 11:37 console
crw-rw-rw- 1 root root 1, 3 Oct 28 11:37 null
```

You delete device nodes by using the standard rm command: there is no rmnod command because, once created, they are just files.

The proc and sysfs filesystems

proc and sysfs are two pseudo filesystems that give a window onto the inner workings of the kernel. They both represent kernel data as files in a hierarchy of directories: when you read one of the files, the contents you see do not come from disk storage, it has been formatted on-the-fly by a function in the kernel. Some files are also writable, meaning that a kernel function is called with the new data you have written and, if it is of the correct format and you have sufficient permissions, it will modify the value stored in the kernel's memory. In other works, proc and sysfs provide another way to interact with device drivers and other kernel code.

proc and sysfs should be mounted on the directories /proc and /sys:

```
mount -t proc proc /proc
mount -t sysfs sysfs /sys
```

Although they are very similar in concept, they perform different functions. proc has been part of Linux since the early days. Its original purpose was to expose information about processes to user space, hence the name. To this end, there is a directory for each process named /proc/<PID> which contains information about its state. The process list command, ps, reads these files to generate its output. In addition, there are files that give information about other parts of the kernel, for example, /proc/cpuinfo tells you about the CPU, /proc/interrupts has information about interrupts, and so on. Finally, in /proc/sys, there are files that display and control the state and behavior of kernel sub-systems, especially scheduling, memory management, and networking. The best reference for the files you will find in proc is man page proc(5).

In fact, over time, the number of files in proc and their layout has become rather chaotic. In Linux 2.6, sysfs was introduced to export a subset of the data in an ordered way.

In contrast, sysfs exports a very ordered hierarchy of files relating to devices and the way they are connected to each other.

Mounting filesystems

The mount command allows us to attach one filesystem to a directory within another, forming a hierarchy of filesystems. The one at the top, which was mounted by the kernel when it booted, is called the root filesystem. The format of the mount command is as follows:

```
mount [-t vfstype] [-o options] device directory
```

You need to specify the type of the filesystem, `vfstype`, the block device node it resides on, and the directory you want to mount it to. There are various options you can give after the `-o`, have a look at the manual for more information. As an example, if you want to mount an SD card containing an `ext4` filesystem in the first partition onto directory `/mnt`, you would type the following:

```
mount -t ext4 /dev/mmcblk0p1 /mnt
```

Assuming the mount succeeds, you would be able to see the files stored on the SD card in the directory `/mnt`. In some cases, you can leave out the filesystem type and let the kernel probe the device to find out what is stored there.

Looking at the example of mounting the `proc` filesystem, there is something odd: there is no device node, `/dev/proc`, since it is a pseudo filesystem, not a real one. But the `mount` command requires a device as a parameter. Consequently we have to give a string where the device should go, but it does not matter much what that string is. These two commands achieve exactly the same result:

```
mount -t proc proc /proc
mount -t proc nodevice /proc
```

It is fairly common to use the filesystem type in the place of the device when mounting pseudo filesystems.

Kernel modules

If you have kernel modules, they need to be installed into the root filesystem, using the kernel `make modules_install` target, as we saw in the last chapter. This will copy them into the directory `/lib/modules/<kernel version>` together with the configuration files needed by the `modprobe` command.

Be aware that you have just created a dependency between the kernel and the root filesystem. If you update one, you will have to update the other.

Transfering the root filesystem to the target

Having created a skeleton root filesystem in your staging directory, the next task is to transfer it to the target. In the sections that follow, I will describe three possibilities:

- **ramdisk**: a filesystem image that is loaded into RAM by the bootloader. Ramdisks are easy to create and have no dependencies on mass storage drivers. They can be used in fall-back maintenance mode when the main root filesystem needs updating. They can even be used as the main root filesystem in small embedded devices and, of course, as the early user space in mainstream Linux distributions. A compressed ramdisk uses the minimum amount of storage but still consumes RAM. The contents are volatile so you need another storage type to store permanent data such as configuration parameters.

- **disk image**: a copy of the root filesystem formatted and ready to be loaded onto a mass storage device on the target. For example, it could be an image in ext4 format ready to be copied onto an SD card, or it could be in jffs2 format ready to be loaded into flash memory via the bootloader. Creating a disk image is probably the most common option. There is more information about the different types of mass storage in *Chapter 7, Creating a Storage Strategy*.

- **network filesystem**: the staging directory can be exported to the network via an NFS server and mounted by the target at boot-time. This is often done during the development phase in preference to repeated cycles of creating a disk image and reloading it onto the mass storage device, which is quite a slow process.

I will start with ramdisk and use it to illustrate a few refinements to the root filesystem, like adding user names and a device manager to create device nodes automatically. Then, I will show you how to create a disk image and, finally, how to use NFS to mount the root filesystem over a network.

Creating a boot ramdisk

A Linux boot ramdisk, strictly speaking, an **initial RAM filesystem** or **initramfs**, is a compressed cpio archive. cpio is an old Unix archive format, similar to TAR and ZIP but easier to decode and so requiring less code in the kernel. You need to configure your kernel with CONFIG_BLK_DEV_INITRD to support initramfs.

In fact, there are three different ways to create a boot ramdisk: as a standalone `cpio` archive, as a `cpio` archive embedded in the kernel image, and as a device table which the kernel build system processes as part of the build. The first option gives the most flexibility because we can mix and match kernels and ramdisks to our hearts content. However, it means that you have two files to deal with instead of one and not all bootloaders have the facility to load a separate ramdisk. I will show you how to build one into the kernel later.

Standalone ramdisk

The following sequence of instructions creates the archive, compresses it and adds a U-Boot header ready for loading onto the target:

```
$ cd ~/rootfs
$ find . | cpio -H newc -ov --owner root:root > ../initramfs.cpio
$ cd ..
$ gzip initramfs.cpio
$ mkimage -A arm -O linux -T ramdisk -d initramfs.cpio.gz uRamdisk
```

Note that we ran `cpio` with the option `--owner root:root`. This is a quick fix for the file ownership problem mentioned earlier, making everything in the `cpio` file UID and GID 0.

The final size of the `uRamdisk` file is ~ 2.9 MiB, with no kernel modules. Add to that 4.4 MiB for the kernel `zImage` file, and 440 KiB for U-Boot and this gives a total of 7.7 MiB of storage needed to boot this board. We are a little way off the 1.44 MiB floppy that started it all off. If size was a real problem, you could use one of these options:

- Make the kernel smaller by leaving out drivers and functions you don't need
- Make BusyBox smaller by leaving out utilities you don't need
- Use uClibc or musl libc in place of glibc
- Compile BusyBox statically

Booting the ramdisk

The simplest thing we can do is to run a shell on the console so that we can interact with the device. We can do that by adding `rdinit=/bin/sh` to the kernel command line. Now, you can boot the device.

Booting with QEMU

QEMU has the option `-initrd` to load `initframfs` into memory, so the full command is now as follows:

```
$ cd ~/rootfs

$ QEMU_AUDIO_DRV=none \

qemu-system-arm -m 256M -nographic -M vexpress-a9 -kernel zImage
-append "console=ttyAMA0 rdinit=/bin/sh" -dtb vexpress-v2p-ca9.dtb
-initrd initramfs.cpio.gz
```

Booting the BeagleBone Black

To boot the BeagleBone Black, boot to the U-Boot prompt and enter these commands:

```
fatload mmc 0:1 0x80200000 zImage

fatload mmc 0:1 0x80f00000 am335x-boneblack.dtb

fatload mmc 0:1 0x81000000 uRamdisk

setenv bootargs console=tty00,115200 rdinit=/bin/sh

bootz 0x80200000 0x81000000 0x80f00000
```

If all goes well, you will get a root shell prompt on the console.

Mounting proc

Note that the `ps` command doesn't work: that is because the `proc` filesystem has not been mounted yet. Try mounting it and run `ps` again.

A refinement to this setup is to write a shell script that contains things that need to be done at boot-up and give that as the parameter to `rdinit=`. The script would look like the following snippet:

```
#!/bin/sh

/bin/mount -t proc proc /proc

/bin/sh
```

Using a shell as `init` in this way is very handy for quick hacks, for example, when you want to rescue a system with a broken `init` program. However, in most cases, you would use an `init` program, which we will cover further down.

Building a ramdisk cpio into the kernel image

In some cases, it is preferable to build the ramdisk into the kernel image, for example, if the bootloader cannot handle a ramdisk file. To do this, change the kernel configuration and set CONFIG_INITRAMFS_SOURCE to the full path of the cpio archive you created earlier. If you are using menuconfig, it is in **General setup | Initramfs source file(s)**. Note that it has to be the uncompressed cpio file ending in .cpio; not the gzipped version. Then, build the kernel. You should see that it is larger than before.

Booting is the same as before, except that there is no ramdisk file. For QEMU, the command is like this:

```
$ cd ~/rootfs
$ QEMU_AUDIO_DRV=none \
qemu-system-arm -m 256M -nographic -M vexpress-a9 -kernel zImage -
append "console=ttyAMA0 rdinit=/bin/sh" -dtb vexpress-v2p-ca9.dtb
```

For the BeagleBone Black, enter these commands into U-Boot:

```
fatload mmc 0:1 0x80200000 zImage
fatload mmc 0:1 0x80f00000 am335x-boneblack.dtb
setenv bootargs console=ttyO0,115200 rdinit=/bin/sh
bootz 0x80200000 - 0x80f00000
```

Of course, you must remember to rebuild the kernel each time you change the contents of the ramdisk and regenerate the .cpio file.

Another way to build a kernel with ramdisk

An interesting way to build the ramdisk into the kernel image is by using a **device table** to generate a cpio archive. A device table is a text file which lists the files, directories, device nodes, and links that go into the archive. The overwhelming advantage is that you can create entries in the cpio file that are owned by root, or any other UID, without having root privileges yourself. You can even create device nodes. All this is possible because the archive is just a data file. It is only when it is expanded by Linux at boot time that real files and directories get created, using the attributes you have specified.

Here is a device table for our simple rootfs, but missing most of the symbolic links to busybox to make it manageable:

```
dir /proc 0755 0 0
dir /sys 0755 0 0
```

```
dir /dev 0755 0 0
nod /dev/console 0600 0 0 c 5 1
nod /dev/null 0666 0 0 c 1 3
nod /dev/tty00 0600 0 0 c 252 0
dir /bin 0755 0 0
file /bin/busybox /home/chris/rootfs/bin/busybox 0755 0 0
slink /bin/sh /bin/busybox 0777 0 0
dir /lib 0755 0 0
file /lib/ld-2.19.so /home/chris/rootfs/lib/ld-2.19.so 0755 0 0
slink /lib/ld-linux.so.3 /lib/ld-2.19.so 0777 0 0
file /lib/libc-2.19.so /home/chris/rootfs/lib/libc-2.19.so 0755 0 0
slink /lib/libc.so.6 /lib/libc-2.19.so 0777 0 0
file /lib/libm-2.19.so /home/chris/rootfs/lib/libm-2.19.so 0755 0 0
slink /lib/libm.so.6 /lib/libm-2.19.so 0777 0 0
```

The syntax is fairly obvious:

- `dir <name> <mode> <uid> <gid>`
- `file <name> <location> <mode> <uid> <gid>`
- `nod <name> <mode> <uid> <gid> <dev_type> <maj> <min>`
- `slink <name> <target> <mode> <uid> <gid>`

The kernel provides a tool that reads this file and creates a `cpio` archive. The source is in `usr/gen_init_cpio.c`. There is a handy script in `scripts/gen_initramfs_list.sh` that creates a device table from a given directory, which saves a lot of typing.

To complete, the task, you need to set `CONFIG_INITRAMFS_SOURCE` to point to the device table file and then build the kernel. Everything else is the same as before.

The old initrd format

There is an older format for a Linux ramdisk, known as `initrd`. It was the only format available before Linux 2.6 and is still needed if you are using the mmu-less variant of Linux, uCLinux. It is pretty obscure and I will not cover it here. There is more information in the kernel source, in `Documentation/initrd.txt`.

The init program

Running a shell, or even a shell script, at boot time is fine for simple cases, but really you need something more flexible. Normally, Unix systems run a program called init that starts up and monitors other programs. Over the years, there have been many init programs, some of which I will describe in *Chapter 9, Starting up - the init Program*. For now, I will briefly introduce the init from BusyBox.

init begins by reading the configuration file, /etc/inittab. Here is a simple example which is adequate for our needs:

```
::sysinit:/etc/init.d/rcS
::askfirst:-/bin/ash
```

The first line runs a shell script, rcS, when init is started. The second line prints the message **Please press Enter to activate this console** to the console, and starts a shell when you press *Enter*. The leading - before /bin/ash means that it will be a login shell, which sources /etc/profile and $HOME/.profile before giving the shell prompt. One of the advantages of launching the shell like this is that job control is enabled. The most immediate effect is that you can use *Ctrl + C* to terminate the current program. Maybe you didn't notice it before but, wait until you run the ping program and find you can't stop it!

BusyBox init provides a default inittab if none is present in the root filesystem. It is a little more extensive than the preceding one.

The script /etc/init.d/rcS is the place to put initialization commands that need to be performed at boot, for example, mounting the proc and sysfs filesystems:

```
#!/bin/sh
mount -t proc proc /proc
mount -t sysfs sysfs /sys
```

Make sure that you make rcS executable, like this:

```
$ cd ~/rootfs
$ chmod +x etc/init.d/rcS
```

You can try it out on QEMU by changing the -append parameter, like this:

```
-append "console=ttyAMA0 rdinit=/sbin/init"
```

To achieve the same on the BeagleBone Black, you need to change the bootargs variable in U-Boot as shown:

```
setenv bootargs console=ttyO0,115200 rdinit=/sbin/init
```

Configuring user accounts

As I have hinted already, it is not good practice to run all programs as root since, if one is compromised by an outside attack, then the whole system is at risk and a misbehaving program can do more damage if it is running as root. It is preferable to create unprivileged user accounts and use them where full root is not necessary.

User names are configured in /etc/passwd. There is one line per user, with seven fields of information separated by colons:

- The login name
- A hash code used to verify the password , or more usually an x to indicate that the password is stored in /etc/shadow
- UID
- GID
- A comment field, often left blank
- The user's home directory
- (Optional) the shell this user will use

For example, this creates users root with UID 0 and daemon with UID 1:

```
root:x:0:0:root:/root:/bin/sh
daemon:x:1:1:daemon:/usr/sbin:/bin/false
```

Setting the shell for user daemon to /bin/false ensures that any attempt to log on with that name will fail.

Various programs have to read /etc/passwd so as to be able to look up UIDs and names, and so it has to be word-readable. That is a problem if the password hashes are stored in there because a malicious program would be able to take a copy and discover the actual passwords using a variety of cracker programs. Therefore, to reduce the exposure of this sensitive information, the passwords are stored in /etc/shadow and an x is placed in the password field to indicate that this is the case. /etc/shadow is only accessible as root, and, so as long as the root user is restricted, the passwords are safe.

The shadow password file consists of one entry per user, made up of nine fields. Here is an example that mirrors the passwd file shown in the preceding paragraph:

```
root::10933:0:99999:7:::
daemon:*:10933:0:99999:7:::
```

The first two fields are the username and the password hash. The remaining seven are related to password aging, which is not usually an issue on embedded devices. If you are curious about the full details, refer to the manual page *shadow(5)*.

In the example, the password for `root` is empty, meaning that `root` can log on without giving a password, which is useful during development, but not for production! You can generate a password hash by using the command `mkpasswd` or by running the `passwd` command on the target and copy and pasting the hash field from `/etc/shadow` on the target into the default shadow file in the staging directory.

The password for daemon is `*`, which will not match any logon password, once again ensuring that the daemon cannot be used as a regular user account.

Group names are stored in a similar way in `/etc/group`. The format is as follows:

- The name of the group
- The group password, usually an x character, indicating that there is no group password
- The GID
- An optional list of users who belong to this group, separated by commas.

Here is an example:

```
root:x:0:
daemon:x:1:
```

Adding user accounts to the root filesystem

Firstly, you have to add to your staging directory `etc/passwd`, `etc/shadow`, and `etc/group`, as shown in the preceding section. Make sure that the permissions of shadow are 0600.

The login procedure is started by a program called `getty`, which is part of BusyBox. You launch it from `inittab` using the keyword `respawn`, which restarts `getty` when a login shell is terminated, so `inittab` should read like this:

```
::sysinit:/etc/init.d/rcS
::respawn:/sbin/getty 115200 console
```

Then rebuild the ramdisk and try it out using QEMU or BeagelBone Black as before.

Starting a daemon process

Typically, you would want to run certain background processes at start up. Let's take the log daemon, `syslogd`, as an example. The purpose of `syslogd` is to accumulate log messages from other programs, mostly other daemons. Naturally, BusyBox has an applet for that!

Starting the daemon is as simple as adding a line like this to `etc/inittab`:

```
::respawn:syslogd -n
```

`respawn` means that, if the program terminates, it will be automatically restarted; `-n` means that it should run as a foreground process. The log is written to `/var/log/messages`.

You may also want to start `klogd` in the same way: `klogd` sends kernel log messages to `syslogd` so that they can be logged to permanent storage.

As an aside, I should mention that, in the case of a typical embedded Linux system, writing log files to flash memory is not such a good idea as it will wear it out. I will cover the options for logging in *Chapter 7, Creating a Storage Strategy*.

A better way of managing device nodes

Creating device nodes statically with `mknod` is quite hard work and inflexible. There are other ways to create device nodes automatically on demand:

- `devtmpfs`: This is a pseudo filesystem that you mount over `/dev` at boot time. The kernel populates it with device nodes for all the devices that the kernel currently knows about and creates nodes for new devices as they are detected at runtime. The nodes are owned by `root` and have default permissions of 0600. Some well-known device nodes, such as `/dev/null` and `/dev/random`, override the default to 0666 (see `struct memdev` in `drivers/char/mem.c`).

- `mdev`: This is a BusyBox applet that is used to populate a directory with device nodes and to create new nodes as needed. There is a configuration file, `/etc/mdev.conf`, which contains rules for ownership and the mode of the nodes.

- `udev`: This is now part of `systemd` and is the solution you will find on desktop Linux and some embedded devices. It is very flexible and a good choice for higher end embedded devices.

Although both `mdev` and `udev` create the device nodes themselves, it is more usual to let `devtmpfs` do that job and use `mdev`/`udev` as a layer on top to implement the policy for setting ownership and permissions.

An example using devtmpfs

If you have booted up one of the earlier ramdisk examples, trying out `devtmpfs` is as simple as entering this command:

```
# mount -t devtmpfs devtmpfs /dev
```

You should see that `/dev` is full of device nodes. For a permanent fix, add this to `/etc/init.d/rcS`:

```
#!/bin/sh
mount -t proc proc /proc
mount -t sysfs sysfs /sys
mount -t devtmpfs devtmpfs /dev
```

In point of fact, kernel initialization does this automatically unless you have supplied an `initramfs` ramdisk as we have done! To see the code, look in the `init/do_mounts.c`, function `prepare_namespace()`.

An example using mdev

While `mdev` is a bit more complex to set up, it does allow you to modify the permissions of device nodes as they are created. Firstly, there is a startup phase, selected by the `-s` option, when `mdev` scans the `/sys` directory looking for information about current devices and populates the `/dev` directory with the corresponding nodes.

If you want to keep track of new devices coming on line and create nodes for them as well, you need to make `mdev` a hotplug client by writing to `/proc/sys/kernel/hotplug`. These additions to `/etc/init.d/rcS` will achieve all of that:

```
#!/bin/sh
mount -t proc proc /proc
mount -t sysfs sysfs /sys
mount -t devtmpfs devtmpfs /dev
echo /sbin/mdev > /proc/sys/kernel/hotplug
mdev -s
```

The default mode is 660 and ownership is `root:root`. You can change that by adding rules in `/etc/mdev.conf`. For example, to give the `null`, `random`, and `urandom` devices their correct modes, you would add this to `/etc/mdev.conf`:

```
null      root:root 666
random    root:root 444
urandom   root:root 444
```

The format is documented in the BusyBox source code in `docs/mdev.txt` and there are more examples in the directory named `examples`.

Are static device nodes so bad after all?

Statically created device nodes do have one advantage: they don't take any time during boot to create, whereas the other methods do. If minimizing boot time is a priority, using statically-created device nodes will save a measurable amount of time.

Configuring the network

Next, let's look at some basic network configurations so that we can communicate with the outside world. I am assuming that there is an Ethernet interface, `eth0`, and that we only need a simple IP v4 configuration.

These examples use the network utilities that are part of BusyBox, and are sufficient for a simple use case, using the `old-but-reliable ifup` and `ifdown` programs. You can read the man pages on both for more details. The main network configuration is stored in `/etc/network/interfaces`. You will need to create these directories in the staging directory:

```
etc/network
etc/network/if-pre-up.d
etc/network/if-up.d
var/run
```

For a static IP address, `etc/network/interfaces` would look like this:

```
auto lo
iface lo inet loopback
auto eth0
iface eth0 inet static
  address 10.0.0.42
  netmask 255.255.255.0
  network 10.0.0.0
```

For a dynamic IP address allocated using DHCP, `etc/network/interfaces` would look like this:

```
auto lo
iface lo inet loopback
auto eth0
iface eth0 inet dhcp
```

You will also have to configure a DHCP client program. BusyBox has one named `udchpcd`. It needs a shell script that should go in `/usr/share/udhcpc/default.script`. There is a suitable default in the BusyBox source code in the directory `examples//udhcp/simple.script`.

Network components for glibc

`glibc` uses a mechanism known as the **name service switch** (**NSS**) to control the way that names are resolved to numbers for networking and users. User names, for example, may be resolved to UIDs via the file `/etc/passwd`; network services such as HTTP can be resolved to the service port number via `/etc/services`, and so on. All this is configured by `/etc/nsswitch.conf`, see the manual page, *nss(5)* for full details. Here is a simple example that will suffice for most embedded Linux implementations:

```
passwd:       files
group:        files
shadow:       files
hosts:        files dns
networks:     files
protocols:    files
services:     files
```

Everything is resolved by the correspondingly named file in `/etc`, except for the host names, which may additionally be resolved by a DNS lookup.

To make this work, you need to populate `/etc` with those files. Networks, protocols, and services are the same across all Linux systems, so they can be copied from `/etc` in your development PC. `/etc/hosts` should, at least contain, the loopback address:

```
127.0.0.1 localhost
```

We will come to the others, `passwd`, `group`, and `shadow`, later.

The last piece of the jigsaw is the libraries that perform the name resolution. They are plugins that are loaded as needed based on the contents of `nsswitch.conf`, meaning that they do not show up as dependencies if you use `readelf` or similar. You will simply have to copy them from the toolchain's `sysroot`:

```
$ cd ~/rootfs
$ cp -a $TOOLCHAIN_SYSROOT/lib/libnss* lib
$ cp -a $TOOLCHAIN_SYSROOT/lib/libresolv* lib
```

Creating filesystem images with device tables

The kernel has a utility, `gen_init_cpio`, that creates a `cpio` file based on format instructions set out in a text file, called a `device table`, which allows a non-root user to create device nodes and to allocate arbitrary UID and GID values to any file or directory.

The same concept has been applied to tools that create other filesystem image formats:

- `jffs2`: `mkfs.jffs2`
- `ubifs`: `mkfs.ubifs`
- `ext2`: `genext2fs`

We will look at `jffs2` and `ubifs` in *Chapter 7, Creating a Storage Strategy*, when we look at filesystems for flash memory. The third, `ext2`, is a fairly old format for hard drives.

They each take a device table file with the format `<name> <type> <mode> <uid> <gid> <major> <minor> <start> <inc> <count>` in which the following applies:

- `name`: Filename
- `type`: One of the following:
    - `f`: A regular file
    - `d`: A directory
    - `c`: A character special device file
    - `b`: A block special device file
    - `p`: A FIFO (named pipe)
- `uid` The UID of the file
- `gid`: The GID of the file

- `major` and `minor`: the device numbers (device nodes only)
- `start`, `inc`, and `count`: (device nodes only) allow you to create a group of device nodes starting from the `minor` number in `start`

You do not have to specify every file, as with `gen_init_cpio`: you just have to point them at a directory – the staging directory – and list the changes and exceptions you need to make in the final filesystem image.

A simple example which populates static device nodes for us is as follows:

```
/dev            d   755  0    0    -     -     -     -    -
/dev/null       c   666  0    0    1     3     0     0    -
/dev/console    c   600  0    0    5     1     0     0    -
/dev/tty00      c   600  0    0    252   0     0     0    -
```

Then, use `genext2fs` to generate a filesystem image of 4 MiB (that is 4,096 blocks of the default size, 1,024 bytes):

```
$ genext2fs -b 4096 -d rootfs -D device-table.txt -U rootfs.ext2
```

Now, you can copy the resulting image, `rootfs.ext`, to an SD card or similar.

Putting the root filesytem onto an SD card

This is an example of mounting a filesystem from a normal block device, such as an SD card. The same principles apply to other filesystem types and we will look at them in more detail in *Chapter 7, Creating a Storage Strategy*.

Assuming that you have a device with an SD card, and that the first partition is used for the boot files, `MLO` and `u-boot.img` – as on a BeagleBone Black. Assume also that you have used `genext2fs` to create a filesystem image. To copy it to the SD card, insert the card and identify the block device it has been assigned: typically `/dev/sd` or `/dev/mmcblk0`. If it is the latter, copy the filesystem image to the second partition:

```
$ sudo dd if=rootfs.ext2 of=/dev/mmcblk0p2
```

Then, slot the SD card into the device, and set the kernel command line to `root=/dev/mmcblk0p2`. The complete boot sequence is as follows:

```
fatload mmc 0:1 0x80200000 zImage
fatload mmc 0:1 0x80f00000 am335x-boneblack.dtb
setenv bootargs console=tty00,115200 root=/dev/mmcblk0p2
bootz 0x80200000 - 0x80f00000
```

Mounting the root filesystem using NFS

If your device has a network interface, it is best to mount the root filesystem over the network during development. It gives you access to almost unlimited storage so you can add in debug tools and executables with large symbol tables. As an added bonus, updates made to the root filesystem hosted on the development machine are made available on the target immediately. You also have a copy of log files.

For this to work, your kernel has to be configured with CONFIG_ROOT_NFS. Then, you can configure Linux to do the mount at boot time by adding the following to the kernel command line:

```
root=/dev/nfs
```

Give the details of the NFS export as follows:

```
nfsroot=<host-ip>:<root-dir>
```

Configure the network interface that connects to the NFS server so that it is available at boot time, before the init program runs by using this command:

```
ip=<target-ip>
```

There is more information about NFS root mounts in the kernel source in Documentation/filesystems/nfs/nfsroot.txt.

You also need to install and configure an NFS server on your host which, for Ubuntu, you can do with this command:

```
$ sudo apt-get install nfs-kernel-server
```

The NFS server needs to be told which directories are being exported to the network, which is controlled by /etc/exports. Add a line like this one to that file:

```
/<path to staging> *(rw,sync,no_subtree_check,no_root_squash)
```

Then, restart the server to pick up the change which, for Ubuntu, is:

```
$ sudo /etc/init.d/nfs-kernel-server restart
```

Testing with QEMU

The following script creates a virtual network between the network device `tap0` on the host and `eth0` on the target using a pair of static IPv4 addresses and then launches QEMU with the parameters to use `tap0` as the emulated interface. You will need to change the path to the root filesystem to be the full path to your staging directory, and maybe the IP addresses if they conflict with your network configuration:

```
#!/bin/bash

KERNEL=zImage
DTB=vexpress-v2p-ca9.dtb
ROOTDIR=/home/chris/rootfs

HOST_IP=192.168.1.1
TARGET_IP=192.168.1.101
NET_NUMBER=192.168.1.0
NET_MASK=255.255.255.0

sudo tunctl -u $(whoami) -t tap0
sudo ifconfig tap0 ${HOST_IP}
sudo route add -net ${NET_NUMBER} netmask ${NET_MASK} dev tap0
sudo sh -c "echo  1 > /proc/sys/net/ipv4/ip_forward"

QEMU_AUDIO_DRV=none \
qemu-system-arm -m 256M -nographic -M vexpress-a9 -kernel $KERNEL
-append "console=ttyAMA0 root=/dev/nfs rw
nfsroot=${HOST_IP}:${ROOTDIR} ip=${TARGET_IP}" -dtb ${DTB} -net
nic -net tap,ifname=tap0,script=no
```

The script is available as `run-qemu-nfs.sh`.

It should boot up as before, but now using the staging directory directly via the NFS export. Any files that you create in that directory will be immediately visible to the target device and any files created in the device will be visible to the development PC.

Testing with BeagleBone Black

In a similar way, you can enter these commands at the U-Boot prompt of the BeagleBone Black:

```
setenv serverip 192.168.1.1

setenv ipaddr 192.168.1.101

setenv npath [path to staging directory]

setenv bootargs console=ttyO0,115200 root=/dev/nfs rw
nfsroot=${serverip}:${npath} ip=${ipaddr}
```

Then; to boot it, load the kernel and `dtb` from `sdcard`, as before:

```
fatload mmc 0:1 0x80200000 zImage

fatload mmc 0:1 0x80f00000 am335x-boneblack.dtb

bootz 0x80200000 - 0x80f00000
```

Problems with file permissions

The files that were already in the staging directory are owned by you and will show up on the target when you run `ls -l` with whatever your UID is, typically 1,000. Any files created by the target device will be owned by root. The whole thing is a mess.

Unfortunately, there is no simple way out. The best advice is to make a copy of the staging directory and change ownership to `root:root` (using `sudo chown -R 0:0 *`) and export this directory as the NFS mount. It reduces the inconvenience of having just one copy of the root filesystem shared between development and target systems.

Using TFTP to load the kernel

When working with real hardware such as the BeagleBone Black, it is best to load the kernel over the network, especially when the root filesystem is mounted via NFS. In this way, you are not using any local storage on the device. It saves time if you don't have to keep re-flashing the memory and means that you can get work done while the flash storage drivers are still being developed (it happens).

U-Boot has supported the **Trivial File Transfer Protocol** (**TFTP**) for many years. Firstly, you need to install a `tftp` daemon on your development machine. On Ubuntu, you would install the `tftpd-hpa` package, which grants read access to files in the directory `/var/lib/tftpboot` to `tftp` clients like U-Boot.

Assuming that you have copied `zImage` and `am335x-boneblack.dtb` into `/var/lib/tftpboot`, enter these commands into U-Boot to load and boot:

```
setenv serverip 192.168.1.1
setenv ipaddr 192.168.1.101
tftpboot 0x80200000 zImage
tftpboot 0x80f00000 am335x-boneblack.dtb
setenv npath [path to staging]
setenv bootargs console=tty00,115200 root=/dev/nfs rw
nfsroot=${serverip}:${npath} ip=${ipaddr}
bootz 0x80200000 - 0x80f00000
```

It is fairly common for the response to `tftpboot` to look like this:

```
setenv ipaddr 192.168.1.101
nova!> setenv serverip 192.168.1.1
nova!> tftpboot 0x80200000 zImage
link up on port 0, speed 100, full duplex
Using cpsw device
TFTP from server 192.168.1.1; our IP address is 192.168.1.101
Filename 'zImage'.
Load address: 0x80200000
Loading: T T T T
```

The row of `T` characters on the last line indicate that there is something wrong and the TFTP requests are timing out. The most common reasons are as follows:

- Incorrect IP address for server.
- TFTP daemon not running on server.
- Firewall on server is blocking the TFTP protocol. Most firewalls do indeed block the TFTP port, 69, by default.

In this case, the tftp daemon was not running, so I started it with the following command:

```
$ sudo service tftpd-hpa restart
```

Additional reading

- *Filesystem Hierarchy Standard*, currently at version 3.0 available at `http://refspecs.linuxfoundation.org/fhs.shtml`.

- *ramfs, rootfs and initramfs , Rob Landley*, October 17, 2005, which is part of the Linux source code available at `Documentation/filesystems/ramfs-rootfs-initramfs.txt`.

Summary

One of the strengths of Linux is that it can support a wide range of root filesystems which allow it to be tailored to suit a wide range of needs. We have seen that it is possible to construct a simple root filesystem manually with a small number of components, and that BusyBox is especially useful in this regard. By going through the process one step at a time, it has given us insight into some of the basic workings of Linux systems, including network configuration and user accounts. However, the task rapidly becomes unmanageable as devices get more complex. And, there is the ever-present worry that there may be a security hole in the implementation which we have not noticed. In the next chapter, we will look at using embedded build systems to help us out.

6

Selecting a Build System

The preceding chapters covered the four elements of embedded Linux and showed you, step-by-step, how to build a toolchain, a bootloader, a kernel, and a root filesystem, and then combine them into a basic embedded Linux system. And there are a lot of steps! Now it is time to look at ways to simplify the process by automating it as much as possible. I will look at how embedded build systems can help, and look at two in particular: Buildroot and the Yocto Project. Both are complex and flexible tools which would require an entire book to adequately describe how they work. In this chapter, I only want to show you the general ideas behind build systems. I will show you how to build a simple device image to get an overall feel of the system and then how to make some useful changes, using the Nova board example from the previous chapters.

No more rolling your own embedded Linux

The process of creating a system manually, as described in *Chapter 5*, *Building a Root Filesystem,* is called the **roll your own** (**RYO**) process. It has the advantage that you are in complete control of the software and you can tailor it to do anything you like. If you want it to do something truly odd but innovative, or if you want to reduce the memory footprint to the smallest possible, RYO is the way to go. But, in the vast majority of situations, building manually is a waste of time and produces inferior, unmaintainable systems.

They are usually built incrementally over a period of months, often undocumented and seldom recreated from scratch because nobody had a clue where each part came from.

Build systems

The idea of a build system is to automate all the steps I have described up to this point. A build system should be able to build, from upstream source code, some or all of the following:

- The toolchain
- The bootloader
- The kernel
- The root filesystem

Building from an upstream source is important for a number of reasons. It means that you have peace of mind that you can rebuild at any time, without external dependencies. It also means that you have the source code for debugging and that you can meet your license requirements to distribute that to users where necessary.

Therefore to do its job, a build system has to be able to do the following:

- Download a source from upstream, either directly from the source code control system or as an archive, and cache it locally
- Apply patches to enable cross compilation, fix architecture-dependent bugs, apply local configuration policies, and so on
- Build the various components
- Create a staging area and assemble a root filesystem
- Create image files in various formats ready to be loaded onto the target

Other things that are useful are as follows:

- Add your own packages containing, for example, applications or kernel changes
- Select various root filesystem profiles: large or small, with and without graphics or other features
- Create a standalone SDK that you can distribute to other developers so that they don't have to install the complete build system
- Track which open source licenses are used by the various packages you have selected
- Allow you to create updates for in-field updating
- Have a user-friendly user interface

In all cases, they encapsulate the components of a system into packages, some for the host and some for the target. Each package is defined by a set of rules to get the source, build it, and install the results in the correct location. There are dependencies between the packages and a build mechanism to resolve the dependencies and build the set of packages required.

Open source build systems have matured considerably over the last few years. There are many around, including:

- **Buildroot**: An easy-to-use system using GNU `make` and `Kconfig` (`http://buildroot.org`)
- **EmbToolkit**: A simple system for generating root filesystems; the only one at the time of writing that supports LLVM/Clang out of the box (`https://www.embtoolkit.org`)
- **OpenEmbedded**: A powerful system which is also a core component of the Yocto Project and others (`http://openembedded.org`)
- **OpenWrt**: A build tool oriented towards building firmware for wireless routers (`https://openwrt.org`)
- **PTXdist**: An open source build system sponsored by Pengutronix (`http://www.pengutronix.de/software/ptxdist/index_en.html`)
- **Tizen**: A comprehensive system, with emphasis on mobile, media, and in-vehicle devices (`https://www.tizen.org`)
- **The Yocto Project**: This extends the OpenEmbedded core with configuration, layers, tools, and documentation: probably the most popular system (`http://www.yoctoproject.org`)

I will concentrate on two of these: Buildroot and The Yocto Project. They approach the problem in different ways and with different objectives.

Buildroot has the primary aim of building root filesystem images, hence the name, although it can build bootloader and kernel images as well. It is easy to install and configure, and generates target images quickly.

The Yocto Project, on the other hand, is more general in the way it defines the target system and so it can build fairly complex embedded devices. Every component is generated as a package in RPM, `.dpkg` or `.ipk` format (see the following section) and then the packages are combined together to make the filesystem image. Furthermore, you can install a package manager in the filesystem image, which allows you to update packages at runtime. In other words, when you build with the Yocto Project, you are, in effect, creating your own custom Linux distribution.

Package formats and package managers

Mainstream Linux distributions are, in most cases, constructed from collections of binary (precompiled) packages in either RPM or deb format. **RPM** stands for **Red Hat Package Manager** and is used in Red Hat, Suse, Fedora, and other distributions based on them. Debian-derived distributions, including Ubuntu and Mint, use the Debian package manager format, deb. In addition, there is a light-weight format specific to embedded devices known as the **Itsy PacKage** format, or **ipk**, which is based on deb.

The ability to include a package manager on the device is one of the big differentiators between build systems. Once you have a package manager on the target device, you have an easy path to deploy new packages to it and to update existing ones. I will talk about the implications of this in the next chapter.

Buildroot

The Buildroot project website is at http://buildroot.org.

Current versions of Buildroot are capable of building a toolchain, a bootloader (U-Boot, Barebox, GRUB2, or Gummiboot), a kernel, and a root filesystem. It uses GNU make as the principal build tool.

There is good online documentation at http://buildroot.org/docs.html, including *The Buildroot User Manual*.

Background

Buildroot was one of the first build systems. It began as part of the uClinux and uClibc projects as a way of generating a small root filesystem for testing. It became a separate project in late 2001 and continued to evolve through to 2006, after which it went into a rather dormant phase. However, since 2009, when Peter Korsgaard took over stewardship, it has been developing rapidly, adding support for glibc-based toolchains and the ability to build a bootloader and a kernel.

Buildroot is also the foundation of another popular build system, OpenWrt (http://wiki.openwrt.org) which forked from Buildroot around 2004. The primary focus of OpenWrt is to produce software for wireless routers and so the package mix is oriented towards networking infrastructure. It also has a runtime package manager using the .ipk format so that a device can be updated or upgraded without a complete re-flash of the image.

Stable releases and support

The Buildroot developers produce stable releases four times a year, in February, May, August, and November. They are marked by `git` tags of the form `<year>.02`, `<year>.05`, `<year>.08`, and `<year>.11`. Typically, when you start your project, you will be using the latest stable release. However, the stable releases are seldom updated after release. To get security fixes and other bug fixes you will have to either continually update to the next stable release as they become available or backport the fixes into your version.

Installing

As usual, you can install Buildroot either by cloning the repository or downloading an archive. Here is an example of obtaining version 2015.08.1, which was the latest stable version at the time of writing:

```
$ git clone git://git.buildroot.net/buildroot
$ cd buildroot
$ git checkout 2015.08.1
```

The equivalent TAR archive is available from `http://buildroot.org/downloads`.

Next, you should read the section titled *System Requirement* from *The Buildroot User Manual*, available at `http://buildroot.org/downloads/manual/manual.html` and make sure that you have installed all the packages listed there.

Configuring

Buildroot uses the `Kconfig` and `Kbuild` mechanisms as the kernel, which I described in the section *Understanding kernel configuration* in *Chapter 4, Porting and Configuring the Kernel*. You can configure it from scratch directly using `make menuconfig` (or `xconfig` or `gconfig`), or you can choose one of the 90 or so configurations for various development boards and the QEMU emulator which you can find stored in the directory `configs/`. Typing `make help` lists all the targets including the default configurations.

Let's begin by building a default configuration that you can run on the ARM QEMU emulator:

```
$ cd buildroot
$ make qemu_arm_versatile_defconfig
$ make
```

Note that you do not tell `make` how many parallel jobs to run with a `-j` option: Buildroot will make optimum use of your CPUs all by itself. If you want to limit the number of jobs, you can run `make menuconfig` and look under **Build** options.

The build will take half an hour to an hour, depending on the capabilities of your host system and the speed of your link to the Internet. When it is complete, you will find that two new directories have been created:

- `dl/`: This contains archives of the upstream projects that Buildroot has built
- `output/`: This contains all the intermediate and final compiled resources

You will see the following in `output/`:

- `build/`: This is the build directory for each component.
- `host/`: This contains various tools required by Buildroot that run on the host, including the executables of the toolchain (in `output/host/usr/bin`).
- `images/`: This is the most important of all and contains the results of the build. Depending on what you selected when configuring, you will find a bootloader, a kernel, and one or more root filesystem images.
- `staging/`: This is a symbolic link to the `sysroot` of the toolchain. The name of the link is a little confusing because it does not point to a staging area as I defined it in *Chapter 5, Building a Root Filesystem*.
- `target/`: This is the staging area for the root directory. Note that you cannot use this as a root filesystem, as it stands, because the file ownership and permissions are not set correctly. Buildroot uses a device table, as described in the previous chapter, to set ownership and permissions when the filesystem image is created.

Running

Some of the sample configurations have a corresponding entry in the directory `boards/`, which contains custom configuration files and information about installing the results on the target. In the case of the system you have just built, the relevant file is `board/qemu/arm-vexpress/readme.txt`, which tells you how to start QEMU with this target.

Assuming that you have already installed `qemu-system-arm` as described in *Chapter 1, Starting Out*, you can run it using this command:

```
$ qemu-system-arm -M vexpress-a9 -m 256 \
-kernel output/images/zImage \
-dtb output/images/vexpress-v2p-ca9.dtb \
-drive file=output/images/rootfs.ext2,if=sd \
-append "console=ttyAMA0,115200 root=/dev/mmcblk0" \
-serial stdio -net nic,model=lan9118 -net user
```

You should see the kernel boot messages appear in the same terminal window where you started QEMU, followed by a login prompt:

```
Booting Linux on physical CPU 0x0
Initializing cgroup subsys cpuset


Linux version 4.1.0 (chris@builder) (gcc version 4.9.3 (Buildroot
2015.08) ) #1 SMP Fri Oct 30 13:55:50 GMT 2015


CPU: ARMv7 Processor [410fc090] revision 0 (ARMv7), cr=10c5387d


CPU: PIPT / VIPT nonaliasing data cache, VIPT aliasing instruction
cache
Machine model: V2P-CA9
[...]
VFS: Mounted root (ext2 filesystem) readonly on device 179:0.
devtmpfs: mounted
Freeing unused kernel memory: 264K (8061e000 - 80660000)
random: nonblocking pool is initialized
Starting logging: OK
Starting mdev...
Initializing random number generator... done.
Starting network...


Welcome to Buildroot
buildroot login:
```

Log in as `root`, no password.

You will see that QEMU launches a black window in addition to the one with the kernel boot messages. It is there to display the graphics frame buffer of the target. In this case, the target never writes to the `framebuffer`, which is why it appears black. To close QEMU, either type `poweroff` at the root prompt or just close the `framebuffer` window. This works with QEMU 2.0 (default on Ubuntu 14.04), but fails with earlier versions including QEMU 1.0.50 (default on Ubuntu 12.04) because of problems with the SCSI emulation.

Creating a custom BSP

Next, let's use Buildroot to create a BSP for our Nova board, using the same versions of U-Boot and Linux from earlier chapters. The recommended places to store your changes are:

- `board/<organization>/<device>`: contains any patches, binary blobs, extra build steps, configuration files for Linux, U-Boot, and other components
- `configs/<device>_defconfig`: contains the default configuration for the board
- `packages/<organization>/<package_name>`: is the place to put any additional packages for this board

We can use the BeagleBone configuration file as a base, since Nova is a close cousin:

```
$ make clean    #  Always do a clean when changing targets
$ make beaglebone_defconfig
```

Now the `.config` file is set for BeagleBone. Next, create a directory for the board configuration:

```
$ mkdir -p board/melp/nova
```

U-Boot

In *Chapter 3, All About Bootloaders*, we created a custom bootloader for Nova, based on the 2015.07 of U-Boot version and created a patch file for it. We can configure Buildroot to select the same version, and apply our patch. Begin by by copying the patch file into `board/melp/nova`, and then use `make menuconfig` to set the U-Boot version to 2015.07, the patch directory to `board/melp/nova` and the board name to nova, as shown in this screenshot:

```
● ● ●   chris@builder: ~/buildroot
/home/chris/buildroot/.config - Buildroot 2015.08.1 Configuration
> Bootloaders
                            Bootloaders
   Arrow keys navigate the menu.  <Enter> selects submenus ---> (or empty
   submenus ----).  Highlighted letters are hotkeys.  Pressing <Y>
   selectes a feature, while <N> will exclude a feature.  Press
   <Esc><Esc> to exit, <?> for Help, </> for Search.  Legend: [*] feature

       [ ] Barebox
           *** gummiboot needs a toolchain w/ wchar ***
       [ ] mxs-bootlets
       [*] U-Boot
             Build system (Legacy)  --->
       (nova) U-Boot board name
             U-Boot Version (2015.07)  --->
       (board/melp/nova) Custom U-Boot patches
             U-Boot binary format (u-boot.img)  --->
       [*]   Install U-Boot SPL binary image

           <Select>    < Exit >    < Help >    < Save >    < Load >
```

Linux

In *Chapter 4, Porting and Configuring the Kernel*, we based the kernel on Linux 4.1.10 and supplied a new device tree, named `nova.dts`. Copy the device tree to `board/melp/nova` and change the Buildroot kernel configuration to use this version and the nova device tree as show in in this screenshot:

```
● ● ●   chris@builder: ~/buildroot
/home/chris/buildroot/.config - Buildroot 2015.08.1 Configuration
> Kernel
                              Kernel
   Arrow keys navigate the menu.  <Enter> selects submenus ---> (or empty
   submenus ----).  Highlighted letters are hotkeys.  Pressing <Y>
   selectes a feature, while <N> will exclude a feature.  Press
   <Esc><Esc> to exit, <?> for Help, </> for Search.  Legend: [*] feature

       [*] Linux Kernel
             Kernel version (Custom version)  --->
       (4.1.10) Kernel version
       ()    Custom kernel patches
             Kernel configuration (Using an in-tree defconfig file)  ---
       (multi_v7) Defconfig name
       ()    Additional configuration fragment files
             Kernel binary format (zImage)  --->
       [*]   Build a Device Tree Blob (DTB)
             Device tree source (Use a device tree present in the kern
       (nova)  Device Tree Source file names
       [ ]   Install kernel image to /boot in target
             Linux Kernel Extensions  --->

           <Select>    < Exit >    < Help >    < Save >    < Load >
```

Build

Now you can build the system for the Nova board just by typing `make`, which produces these files in the directory `output/images`:

```
MLO   nova.dtb   rootfs.ext2   u-boot.img   uEnv.txt   zImage
```

The last step is to save a copy of the configuration so that you and others can use it again:

```
$ make savedefconfig BR2_DEFCONFIG=configs/nova_defconfig
```

Now, you have a Buildroot configuration for the Nova board.

Adding your own code

Suppose that there are some programs that you have developed that you want to include in the build. You have two options: firstly to build them separately, using their own build systems, and then roll the binary into the final build as an overlay. Secondly you could create a Buildroot package that can be selected from the menu and built like any other.

Overlay

An overlay is simply a directory structure that is copied over the top of the Buildroot root filesystem at a late stage in the build process. It can contain executables, libraries and anything else you may want to include. Note that any compiled code must be compatible with the libraries deployed at runtime, which means that it must be compiled with the same toolchain that Buildroot uses. Using the Buildroot toolchain is quite easy: just add it to the path:

```
$ PATH=<path_to_buildroot>/output/host/usr/bin:$PATH
```

The prefix for the tools is `<ARCH>-linux-`.

The overlay directory is set by `BR2_ROOTFS_OVERLAY`, which contains a list of directories separated by spaces, which you should overlay on the Buildroot root filesystem. It can be configured in `menuconfig` with the option **System configuration | Root filesystem overlay directories**.

For example, if you add a `helloworld` program to the `bin` directory, and a script to start it at boot time, you would create an overlay directory with the following contents:

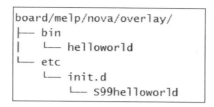

```
board/melp/nova/overlay/
├── bin
│   └── helloworld
└── etc
    └── init.d
        └── S99helloworld
```

Then you would add `board/melp/nova/overlay` to the overlay options.

The layout of the root filesystem is controlled by the `system/skeleton` directory, and the permissions are set in `device_table_dev.txt` and `device_table.txt`.

Adding a package

Buildroot packages are stored in the `package` directory, over 1,000 of them, each in its own subdirectory. A package consists of at least two files: `Config.in`, containing the snippet of `Kconfig` code required to make the package visible in the **configuration** menu, and a `makefile` named `<package_name>.mk`. Note that the package does not contain the code, just the instructions to get the code by downloading a tarball, doing a git pull, and so on.

The `makefile` is written in a format expected by Buildroot and contains directives that allow Buildroot to download, configure, compile, and install the program. Writing a new package `makefile` is a complex operation which is covered in detail in the *Buildroot User Manual*. Here is an example which shows you how to create a package for a simple program stored locally, such as our `helloworld` program.

Begin by creating the subdirectory `package/helloworld` with a configuration file, `Config.in`, that looks like this:

```
config BR2_PACKAGE_HELLOWORLD
bool "helloworld"
help
  A friendly program that prints Hello World! every 10s
```

The first line must be of the format BR2_PACKAGE_<uppercase package name>. That is followed by a Boolean and the package name as it will appear in the **configuration** menu and which will allow a user to select this package. The *Help* section is optional (but hopefully useful).

Next, link the new package into the **Target Packages** menu by editing package/Config.in and sourcing the configuration file as mentioned in the preceding section. You could append this to an existing sub-menu but, in this case, it seems neater to create a new sub-menu which only contains our package:

```
menu "My programs"
   source "package/helloworld/Config.in"
endmenu
```

Then, create a makefile, package/helloworld/helloworld.mk, to supply the data needed by Buildroot:

```
HELLOWORLD_VERSION:= 1.0.0
HELLOWORLD_SITE:= /home/chris/MELP/helloworld/
HELLOWORLD_SITE_METHOD:=local
HELLOWORLD_INSTALL_TARGET:=YES

define HELLOWORLD_BUILD_CMDS
  $(MAKE) CC="$(TARGET_CC)" LD="$(TARGET_LD)" -C $(@D) all
endef

define HELLOWORLD_INSTALL_TARGET_CMDS
  $(INSTALL) -D -m 0755 $(@D)/helloworld $(TARGET_DIR)/bin
endef

$(eval $(generic-package))
```

The location of the code is hard-coded to a local path name. In a more realistic case, you would get the code from a source code system or from a central server of some kind: there are details of how to do this in the *Buildroot User Guide* and plenty of examples in other packages.

License compliance

Buildroot is based on open source software, as are the packages it compiles. At some point during the project, you should check the licenses, which you can do by running:

```
$ make legal-info
```

The information is gathered into `output/legal-info`. There are summaries of the licenses used to compile the host tools in `host-manifest.csv` and, on the target, in `manifest.csv`. There is more information in the `README` file and in the *Buildroot User Manual*.

The Yocto Project

The Yocto Project is a more complex beast than Buildroot. Not only can it build toolchains, bootloaders, kernels, and root filesystems, as Buildroot can, but it can generate an entire Linux distribution for you, with binary packages that can be installed at runtime.

The Yocto Project is primarily a group of recipes, similar to Buildroot packages but written using a combination of Python and shell script, and a task scheduler called BitBake that produces whatever you have configured, from the recipes.

There is plenty of online documentation at `https://www.yoctoproject.org/`.

Background

The structure of the Yocto Project makes more sense if you look at the background first. Its roots are in OpenEmbedded, `http://openembedded.org/` which, in turn, grew out of a number of projects to port Linux to various hand-held computers, including the Sharp Zaurus and Compaq iPaq. OpenEmbedded came to life in 2003 as the build system for those hand-held computers but quickly expanded to encompass other embedded boards. It was developed and continues to be developed by an enthusiastic community of programmers.

The OpenEmbedded project set out to create a set of binary packages using the compact `.ipk` format, which could then be combined in various ways to create a target system and be installed on the target at runtime. It did this by creating recipes for each piece of software and using BitBake as the task scheduler. It was, and is, very flexible. By supplying the right metadata, you can create an entire Linux distribution to your own specification. One that is fairly well known is *The Ångström Distribution*, `http://www.angstrom-distribution.org`, but there are many others.

At some time in 2005 Richard Purdie, then a developer at OpenedHand, created a fork of OpenEmbedded which had a more conservative choice of packages and created releases that were stable over a period of time. He named it Poky, after the Japanese snack (if you are worried about these things, Poky is pronounced to rhyme with hockey). Although Poky was a fork, OpenEmbedded and Poky continued to run alongside each other, sharing updates and keeping the architectures more or less in step. Intel brought out OpenedHand in 2008 and they transferred Poky Linux to the Linux Foundation in 2010 when they formed the Yocto Project.

Since 2010, the common components of OpenEmbedded and Poky have been combined into a separate project known as OpenEmbedded core, or just oe-core.

Therefore, the Yocto Project collects together several components, the most important of which are the following:

- **Poky**: The reference distribution
- **oe-core**: The core metadata, which is shared with OpenEmbedded
- **BitBake**: The task scheduler, which is shared with OpenEmbedded and other projects
- **Documentation**: User manuals and developer's guides for each component
- **Hob**: A graphical user interface to OpenEmbedded and BitBake
- **Toaster**: A web-based interface to OpenEmbedded and BitBake
- **ADT Eclipse**: A plug-in for Eclipse that makes it easier to build projects using the Yocto Project SDK

Strictly speaking, the Yocto Project is an umbrella for these sub-projects. It uses OpenEmbedded as its build system, and Poky as its default configuration and reference environment. However, people often use the term "the Yocto Project" to refer to the build system alone. I feel that it is too late for me to turn this tide, so for brevity I will do the same. I apologise in advance to the developers of OpenEmbedded.

The Yocto Project provides a stable base which can be used as it is or which can be extended using meta layers, which I will discuss later in this chapter. Many SoC vendors provide board support packages for their devices in this way. Meta layers can also be used to create extended, or just different, build systems. Some are open source, such as the Angstrom Project, others are commercial, such as MontaVista Carrier Grade Edition, Mentor Embedded Linux, and Wind River Linux. The Yocto Project has a branding and compatibility testing scheme to ensure that there is interoperability between components. You will see statements like *Yocto Project Compatible 1.7* on various web pages.

Consequently, you should think of the Yocto Project as the foundation of a whole sector of embedded Linux, as well as being a complete build system in its own right. You may be wondering about the name, *yocto*. A yocto is the SI prefix for 10^{-24}, in the same way that micro is 10^{-6}. Why name the project yocto? It was partly to indicate that it could build very small Linux systems (although, to be fair, so can other build systems), but also, perhaps, to steal a march on the Ångström distribution which is based on OpenEmbedded. An Ångström is 10^{-10}. That's huge, compared to a yocto!

Stable releases and support

Usually, there is a release of the Yocto Project every six months, in April and October. They are principally known by the code name, but it is useful to know the version numbers of the Yocto Project and Poky as well. Here is a table of the four most recent releases at the time of writing:

Code name	Release date	Yocto version	Poky version
Fido	April 2015	1.8	13
Dizzy	October 2014	1.7	12
Daisy	April 2014	1.6	11
Dora	October 2013	1.5	10

The stable releases are supported with security and critical bug fixes for the current release cycle and the next cycle, that is approximately twelve months after release. No toolchain or kernel version changes are allowed for these updates. As with Buildroot, if you want continued support, you can update to the next stable release or you can backport changes to your version. You also also have the option of commercial support for periods of several years with the Yocto Project from operating system vendors such as Mentor Graphics, Wind River, and many others.

Installing the Yocto Project

To get a copy of the Yocto Project, you can either clone the repository, choosing the code name as the branch which is `fido` in this case:

```
$ git clone -b fido git://git.yoctoproject.org/poky.git
```

You can also download the archive from `http://downloads.yoctoproject.org/releases/yocto/yocto-1.8/poky-fido-13.0.0.tar.bz2`.

In the first case, you will find everything in the `poky` directory, in the second case, `poky-fido-13.0.0/`.

In addition, you should read the section titled *System Requirements* from the *Yocto Project Reference Manual* (http://www.yoctoproject.org/docs/current/ref-manual/ref-manual.html#detailed-supported-distros) and, in particular, you should make sure that the packages listed there are installed on your host computer.

Configuring

As with Buildroot, let's begin with a build for the ARM QEMU emulator. Begin by sourcing a script to set up the environment:

```
$ cd poky
$ source oe-init-build-env
```

That creates a working directory for you named `build` and makes it the current directory. All of the configuration, intermediate, and deployable files will be put in this directory. You must source this script each time you want to work on this project.

You can choose a different working directory by adding it as a parameter to `oe-init-build-env`, for example:

```
$ source oe-init-build-env build-qemuarm
```

That will put you into the `build-qemuarm` directory. You can then have several projects on the go at the same time: you choose which one you want to work with through the parameter to `oe-init-build-env`.

Initially, the `build` directory contains only one subdirectory named `conf`, which contains the configuration files for this project:

- `local.conf`: Contains a specification of the device you are going to build and the build environment.

- `bblayers.conf`: Contains a list of the directories that contain the layers you are going to use. There will be more on layers later on.

- `templateconf.cfg`: Contains the name of a directory which contains various `conf` files. By default, it points to `meta-yocto/conf`.

For now, we just need to set the `MACHINE` variable in `local.conf` to `qemuarm` by removing the comment character at the start of this line:

```
MACHINE ?= "qemuarm"
```

Building

To actually perform the build, you need to run `bitbake`, telling it which root filesystem image you want to create. Some common images are as follows:

- **core-image-minimal**: A small console-based system which is useful for tests and as the basis for custom images.

- **core-image-minimal-initramfs**: This is similar to core-image-minimal, but built as a ramdisk.

- **core-image-x11**: A basic image with support for graphics through an X11 server and the xterminal terminal app.

- **core-image-sato**: A full graphical system based on Sato, which is a mobile graphical environment built on X11, and GNOME. The image includes several apps including a terminal, an editor, and a file manager.

By giving BitBake the final target, it will work backwards and build all the dependencies first, beginning with the toolchain. For now, we just want to create a minimal image to see whether or not it works:

```
$ bitbake core-image-minimal
```

The build is likely to take some time, maybe more than an hour. When it is complete, you will find several new directories in the build directory including `build/downloads`, which contains all the source downloaded for the build, and `build/tmp` which contains most of the build artifacts. You should see the following in `tmp`:

- `work`: Contains the build directory and the staging area for all components, including the root filesystem

- `deploy`: Contains the final binaries to be deployed on the target:
    - `deploy/images/[machine name]`: Contains the bootloader, the kernel, and the root filesystem images ready to be run on the target
    - `deploy/rpm`: Contains the RPM packages that went to make up the images
    - `deploy/licenses`: Contains the license files extracted from each package

Running

When you build a QEMU target, an internal version of QEMU is generated, which removes the need to install the QEMU package for your distribution and thus avoids version dependencies. There is a wrapper script named `runqemu` for this internal QEMU.

To run the QEMU emulation, make sure that you have sourced `oe-init-build-env` and then just type:

```
$ runqemu qemuarm
```

In this case, QEMU has been configured with a graphic console so that the boot messages and login prompt appear in the black framebuffer screen:

```
QEMU
md: Scanned 0 and added 0 devices.
md: autorun ...
md: ... autorun DONE.
EXT4-fs (sda): recovery complete
EXT4-fs (sda): mounted filesystem with ordered data mode. Opts: (null)
VFS: Mounted root (ext4 filesystem) on device 8:0.
devtmpfs: mounted
Freeing unused kernel memory: 364K (c08cb000 - c0926000)
INIT: version 2.88 booting

Please wait: booting...
Starting udev
udev: Not using udev cache because of changes detected in the following files:
udev:     /proc/version /proc/cmdline /proc/devices
udev:     lib/udev/rules.d/* etc/udev/rules.d/*
udev: The udev cache will be regenerated. To identify the detected changes,
udev: compare the cached sysconf at   /etc/udev/cache.data
udev: against the current sysconf at  /dev/shm/udev.cache
udevd[73]: starting version 182
EXT4-fs (sda): re-mounted. Opts: data=ordered
random: dd urandom read with 117 bits of entropy available
Populating dev cache
random: nonblocking pool is initialized
INIT: Entering runlevel: 5
Configuring network interfaces... done.
Starting syslogd/klogd: done

Poky (Yocto Project Reference Distro) 1.8.1 qemuarm /dev/tty1

qemuarm login:
```

You can log on as `root`, without a password. You can close down QEMU by closing the framebuffer window. You can launch QEMU without the graphic window by adding `nographic` to the command line:

```
$ runqemu qemuarm nographic
```

In this case, you close QEMU using the key sequence *Ctrl + A + X*.

The `runqemu` script has many other options, type `runqemu help` for more information.

Layers

The metadata for the Yocto Project is structured into layers, by convention, each with a name beginning with `meta`. The core layers of the Yocto Project are as follows:

- **meta**: This is the OpenEmbedded core
- **meta-yocto**: Metadata specific to the Yocto Project, including the Poky distribution
- **meta-yocto-bsp**: Contains the board support packages for the reference machines that the Yocto Project supports

The list of layers in which BitBake searches for recipes is stored in `<your build directory>/conf/bblayers.conf` and, by default, includes all three layers mentioned in the preceding list.

By structuring the recipes and other configuration data in this way, it is very easy to extend the Yocto Project by adding new layers. Additional layers are available from SoC manufacturers, the Yocto Project itself, and a wide range of people wishing to add value to the Yocto Project and OpenEmbedded. There is a useful list of layers at `http://layers.openembedded.org`. Here are some examples:

- **meta-angstrom**: The Ångström distribution
- **meta-qt5**: Qt5 libraries and utilities
- **meta-fsl-arm**: BSPs for Freescale ARM-based SoCs
- **meta-fsl-ppc**: BSPs for Freescale PowerPC-based SoCs
- **meta-intel**: BSPs for Intel CPUs and SoCs
- **meta-ti**: BSPs for TI ARM-based SoCs

Adding a layer is as simple as copying the meta directory into a suitable location, usually alongside the default meta layers, and adding it to `bblayers.conf`. Just make sure it is compatible with the version of the Yocto Project you are using.

To illustrate the way layers work, let's create a layer for our Nova board which we can use for the remainder of the chapter as we add features. Each meta layer has to have at least one configuration file, `conf/layer.conf`, and should also have a README file and a license. There is a handy helper script that does the basics for us:

```
$ cd poky
$ scripts/yocto-layer create nova
```

The script asks for a priority, and if you want to create sample recipes. In the example here, I just accepted the defaults:

```
Please enter the layer priority you'd like to use for the layer:
[default: 6]

Would you like to have an example recipe created? (y/n) [default: n]

Would you like to have an example bbappend file created? (y/n)
[default: n]

New layer created in meta-nova.

Don't forget to add it to your BBLAYERS (for details see meta-
nova\README).
```

That will create a layer named `meta-nova` with a `conf/layer.conf`, an outline README and a MIT license in COPYING.MIT. The `layer.conf` file looks like this:

```
# We have a conf and classes directory, add to BBPATH
BBPATH .= ":${LAYERDIR}"

# We have recipes-* directories, add to BBFILES
BBFILES += "${LAYERDIR}/recipes-*/*/*.bb \
${LAYERDIR}/recipes-*/*/*.bbappend"

BBFILE_COLLECTIONS += "nova"
BBFILE_PATTERN_nova = "^${LAYERDIR}/"
BBFILE_PRIORITY_nova = "6"
```

It adds itself to BBPATH and the recipes it contains to BBFILES. From looking at the code, you can see that the recipes are found in the directories with names beginning `recipes-` and have file names ending in `.bb` (for normal BitBake recipes), or `.bbappend` (for recipes that extend existing normal recipes by adding and overriding instructions). This layer has the name `nova` which is added to the list of layers in BBFILE_COLLECTIONS and it has a priority of 6. The layer priority is used if the same recipe appears in several layers: the one in the layer with the highest priority wins.

Since you are about to build a new configuration, it is best to begin by creating a new build directory named `build-nova`:

```
$ cd ~/poky
$ . oe-init-build-env build-nova
```

Now you need to add this layer to your build configuration, `conf/bblayers.conf`:

```
LCONF_VERSION = "6"

BBPATH = "${TOPDIR}"
BBFILES ?= ""

BBLAYERS ?= " \
  /home/chris/poky/meta \
  /home/chris/poky/meta-yocto \
  /home/chris/poky/meta-yocto-bsp \
  /home/chris/poky/meta-nova \
  "
BBLAYERS_NON_REMOVABLE ?= " \
  /home/chris/poky/meta \
  /home/chris/poky/meta-yocto \
  "
```

You can confirm that it is set up correctly by using another helper script:

```
$ bitbake-layers show-layers
layer                 path                              priority
================================================================
meta                  /home/chris/poky/meta             5
meta-yocto            /home/chris/poky/meta-yocto        5
meta-yocto-bsp        /home/chris/poky/meta-yocto-bsp   5
meta-nova             /home/chris/poky/meta-nova         6
```

There you can see the new layer. It has priority 6 which means that we could override recipes in the other layers, which have a lower priority.

At this point it would be a good idea to run a build, using this empty layer. The final target will be the Nova board but, for now, build for a BeagelBone Black by removing the comment before `MACHINE ?= "beaglebone"` in `conf/local.conf`. Then, build a small image using `bitbake core-image-minimal` as before.

As well as recipes, layers may contain BitBake classes, configuration files for machines, distributions, and more. I will look at recipes next and show you how to create a customized image and how to create a package.

BitBake and recipes

BitBake processes metadata of several different types, which include the following:

- **recipes**: Files ending in `.bb`. These contain information about building a unit of software, including how to get a copy of the source code, the dependencies on other components, and how to build and install it.

- **append**: Files ending in `.bbappend`. These allow some details of a recipe to be overridden or extended. A `.bbappend` file simply appends its instructions to the end of a recipe (`.bb`) file of the same root name.

- **include**: Files ending in `.inc`. These contain information that is common to several recipes, allowing information to be shared among them. The files may be included using the `include` or `require` keywords. The difference is that `require` produces an error if the file does not exist, whereas `include` does not.

- **classes**: Files ending in `.bbclass`. These contain common build information, for example how to build a kernel or how to build an `autotools` project. The classes are inherited and extended in recipes and other classes using the `inherit` key word. The class `classes/base.bbclass` is implicitly inherited in every recipe.

- **configuration**: Files ending in `.conf`. They define various configuration variables that govern the project's build process.

A recipe is a collection of tasks written in a combination of Python and shell code. The tasks have names like `do_fetch`, `do_unpack`, `do_patch`, `do_configure`, `do_compile`, `do_install`, and so on. You use BitBake to execute these tasks.

The default task is `do_build`, so that you are running the build task for that recipe. You can list the tasks available in a recipe by running `bitbake core-image-minimal` like this:

```
$ bitbake -c listtasks core-image-minimal
```

The `-c` option allows you to specify the task, missing off the `do_` part. A common use is `-c fetch` to get the code needed by a recipe:

```
$ bitbake -c fetch busybox
```

You can also use `fetchall` to get the code for the target and all the dependencies:

```
$ bitbake -c fetchall core-image-minimal
```

The recipe files are are usually named `<package-name>_version.bb`. They may have dependencies on other recipes, which would allow BitBake to work out all the subtasks that need to be executed to complete the top level job. Unfortunately, I don't have the space in this book to describe the dependency mechanism, but you will find a full description in the Yocto Project documentation.

As an example, to create a recipe for our `helloworld` program in `meta-nova`, you would create a directory structure like this:

```
meta-nova/recipes-local/helloworld
├── files
│   └── helloworld.c
└── helloworld_1.0.bb
```

The recipe is `helloworld_1.0.bb` and the source is local to the recipe directory in the subdirectory files. The recipe contains these instructions:

```
DESCRIPTION = "A friendly program that prints Hello World!"
PRIORITY = "optional"
SECTION = "examples"

LICENSE = "GPLv2"
LIC_FILES_CHKSUM = "file://${COMMON_LICENSE_DIR}/GPL-
2.0;md5=801f80980d171dd6425610833a22dbe6"

SRC_URI = "file://helloworld.c"
S = "${WORKDIR}"

do_compile() {
  ${CC} ${CFLAGS} -o helloworld helloworld.c
}

do_install() {
  install -d ${D}${bindir}
  install -m 0755 helloworld ${D}${bindir}
}
```

The location of the source code is set by `SRC_URI`: in this case it will search directories, files, `helloworld`, and `helloworld-1.0` in the recipe directory. The only tasks that need to be defined are `do_compile` and `do_install`, which compile the one source file simply and install it into the target root filesystem: `${D}` expands to the staging area of the target device and `${bindir}` to the default binary directory, `/usr/bin`.

Every recipe has a license, defined by LICENSE, which is set to GPLv2 here. The file containing the text of the license and a checksum is defined by LIC_FILES_CHKSUM. BitBake will terminate the build if the checksum does not match, indicating that the license has changed in some way. The license file may be part of the package or it may point to one of the standard license texts in meta/files/common-licenses, as is the case here.

By default, commercial licenses are disallowed, but it is easy to enable them. You need to specify the license in the recipe, as shown here:

```
LICENSE_FLAGS = "commercial"
```

Then, in your conf/local.conf, you would explicitly allow this license, like so:

```
LICENSE_FLAGS_WHITELIST = "commercial"
```

To make sure that it compiles correctly, you can ask BitBake to build it, like so:

```
$ bitbake  helloworld
```

If all goes well, you should see that it has created a working directory for it in tmp/work/cortexa8hf-vfp-neon-poky-linux-gnueabi/helloworld/.

You should also see there is an RPM package for it in tmp/deploy/rpm/cortexa8hf_vfp_neon/helloworld-1.0-r0.cortexa8hf_vfp_neon.rpm.

It is not part of the target image yet, though. The list of packages to be installed is held in a variable named IMAGE_INSTALL. You can append to the end of that list by adding this line to your conf/local.conf:

```
IMAGE_INSTALL_append = " helloworld"
```

Note that there has to be a space between the first double quote and the first package name. Now, the package will be added to any image that you bitbake:

```
$ bitbake core-image-minimal
```

If you look in tmp/deploy/images/beaglebone/core-image-minimal-beaglebone.tar.bz2 you will see that /usr/bin/helloworld has indeed been installed.

Customizing images via local.conf

You may often want to add a package to an image during development or tweak it in other ways. As shown previously, you can simply append to the list of packages to be installed by adding a statement like this:

```
IMAGE_INSTALL_append = " strace helloworld"
```

It should be no surprise that you can also do the opposite: you can remove a package using this syntax:

```
IMAGE_INSTALL_remove = "someapp"
```

You can make more sweeping changes via EXTRA_IMAGE_FEATURES. There are too many to list here, I recommend you look at the *Image Features* section of the *Yocto Project Reference Manual* and the code in meta/classes/core-image.bbclass. Here is a short list which should give you an idea of the features you can enable:

- dbg-pkgs: installs debug symbol packages for all the packages installed in the image.

- debug-tweaks: allows root logins without passwords and other changes that make development easier.

- package-management: installs package management tools and preserves the package manager database.

- read-only-rootfs: makes the root filesystem read-only. We will cover this in more detail in *Chapter 7, Creating a Storage Strategy*.

- x11: installs the X server.

- x11-base: installs the X server with a minimal environment.

- x11-sato: installs the OpenedHand Sato environment.

Writing an image recipe

The problem with making changes to local.conf is that they are, well, local. If you want to create an image that is to be shared with other developers, or to be loaded onto a production system, then you should put the changes into an image recipe.

An image recipe contains instructions about how to create the image files for a target, including the bootloader, the kernel, and the root filesystem images. You can get a list of the images that are available by using this command:

```
$ ls meta*/recipes*/images/*.bb
```

The recipe for core-image-minimal is in meta/recipes-core/images/core-image-minimal.bb.

A simple approach is to take an existing image recipe and modify it using statements similar to those you used in local.conf.

For example, imagine that you want an image that is the same as `core-image-minimal` but includes your `helloworld` program and the `strace` utility. You can do that with a two-line recipe file which includes (using the `require` keyword) the base image and adds the packages you want. It is conventional to put the image in a directory named `images`, so add the recipe `nova-image.bb` with this content in `meta-nova/recipes-local/images`:

```
require recipes-core/images/core-image-minimal.bb
IMAGE_INSTALL += "helloworld strace"
```

Now you can remove the `IMAGE_INSTALL_append` line from your `local.conf` and build it using:

```
$ bitbake nova-image
```

If you want to go further and take total control of the contents of the root filesystem, you can start from scratch with an empty `IMAGE_INSTALL` variable and populate it like this:

```
SUMMARY = "A small image with helloworld and strace packages"
IMAGE_INSTALL = "packagegroup-core-boot helloworld strace"
IMAGE_LINGUAS = " "
LICENSE = "MIT"
IMAGE_ROOTFS_SIZE ?= "8192"
inherit core-image
```

`IMAGE_LINGUAS` contains a list of `glibc` locales to be installed in the target image. They can take up a lot of space so, in this case, we set the list to be empty, which is fine so long as we do not need locale-dependent library functions. `IMAGE_ROOTFS_SIZE` is the size of the resulting disk image, in KiB. Most of the work is done by the `core-image` class which we inherit at the end.

Creating an SDK

It is very useful to be able to create a standalone toolchain that other developers can install, avoiding the need for everyone in the team to have a full installation of the Yocto Project. Ideally, you want the toolchain to include development libraries and header files for all the libraries installed on the target. You can do that for any image using the `populate_sdk` task, as shown here:

```
$ bitbake nova-image -c populate_sdk
```

The result is a self-installing shell script in `tmp/deploy/sdk` named:

```
poky-<c_library>-<host_machine>-<target_image><target_machine>-
toolchain-<version>.sh
```

Here is an example:

```
poky-glibc-x86_64-nova-image-cortexa8hf-vfp-neon-toolchain-
1.8.1.sh
```

Note that, by default, the toolchain does not include static libraries. You can enable them individually by adding lines like this to your `local.conf` or the image recipe:

```
TOOLCHAIN_TARGET_TASK_append = " glibc-staticdev"
```

You can also enable them globally as shown:

```
SDKIMAGE_FEATURES_append = " staticdev-pkgs"
```

If you only want a basic toolchain with just C and C++ cross compilers, the C library and header files, you can instead run:

```
$ bitbake meta-toolchain
```

To install the SDK, just run the shell script. The default install directory is `/opt/poky`, but the install script allows you to change that:

```
$ tmp/deploy/sdk/poky-glibc-x86_64-nova-image-cortexa8hf-vfp-neon-
toolchain-1.8.1.sh


Enter target directory for SDK (default: /opt/poky/1.8.1):

You are about to install the SDK to "/opt/poky/1.8.1". Proceed[Y/n]?

[sudo] password for chris:

Extracting SDK...done

Setting it up...done

SDK has been successfully set up and is ready to be used.
```

To make use of the toolchain, first source the environment set up script:

```
. /opt/poky/1.8.1/environment-setup-cortexa8hf-vfp-neon-poky-linux-
gnueabi
```

Toolchains generated in this way are not configured with a valid `sysroot`:

```
$ arm-poky-linux-gnueabi-gcc -print-sysroot


/not/exist
```

Consequently, if you try to cross compile as I have shown in previous chapters, it will fail like this:

```
$ arm-poky-linux-gnueabi-gcc helloworld.c -o helloworld

helloworld.c:1:19: fatal error: stdio.h: No such file or directory

#include <stdio.h>
                  ^

compilation terminated.
```

This is because the compiler has been configured to be generic to a wide range of ARM processors, and the fine tuning is done when you launch it using the right set of gcc flags. So long as you use $CC to compile, everything should work fine:

```
$ $CC helloworld.c -o helloworld
```

License audit

The Yocto Project insists that each package has a license. A copy of the license is in tmp/deploy/licenses/[packagenam.e] for each package, as it is built. In addition, a summary of the packages and licenses used in an image are in the <image name>-<machine name>-<date stamp> directory. This is shown here:

```
$ ls tmp/deploy/licenses/nova-image-beaglebone-20151104150124
license.manifest  package.manifest
```

The first file lists the licenses used by each package, the second lists the package names only.

Further reading

You can have look at the following documentation for more information:

- *The Buildroot User Manual*, http://buildroot.org/downloads/manual/manual.html

- *Yocto Project* documentation: there are nine reference guides plus a tenth which is a composite of the others (the so-called *Mega-manual*") at https://www.yoctoproject.org/documentation

- *Instant Buildroot*, by *Daniel Manchón Vizuete*, Packt Publishing, 2013
- *Embedded Linux Development with Yocto Project*, by *Otavio Salvador* and *Daianne Angolini*, Packt Publishing, 2014

Summary

Using a build system takes the hard work out of creating an embedded Linux system, and it is almost always better than hand crafting a roll your own system. There is a range of open source build systems available these days: Buildroot and the Yocto Project represent two different approaches. Buildroot is simple and quick, making it a good choice for fairly simple single-purpose devices: traditional embedded Linux as I like to think of them.

The Yocto Project is more complex and flexible. It is package based, meaning that you have the option to install a package manager and perform updates of individual packages in the field. The meta layer structure makes it easy to extend the metadata and indeed there is good support throughout the community and industry for the Yocto Project. The downside is that there is a very steep learning curve: you should expect it to take several months to become proficient with it, and even then it will sometimes do things that you didn't expect, or at least that is my experience.

Don't forget that any devices you create using these tools will need to be maintained in the field for a period of time, often many years. The Yocto Project will provide point releases for about one year after a release, Buildroot usually does not provide any point releases. In either case you will find yourself having to maintain your release yourself or else paying for commercial support. The third possibility, ignoring the problem, should not be considered an option!

In the next chapter I will look at file storage and filesystems, and at the way that the choices you make there will affect the stability and maintainability of your embedded Linux.

7
Creating a Storage Strategy

The mass storage options for embedded devices have a great impact on the rest of the system in terms of robustness, speed, and methods of in-field updates.

Most devices employ flash memory in some form or other. Flash memory has become much less expensive over the past few years as storage capacities have increased from tens of megabytes to tens of gigabytes.

In this chapter, I will begin with a detailed look at the technology behind flash memory and how different memory organization affects the low level driver software that has to manage it, including the Linux memory technology device layer, MTD.

For each flash technology, there are different choices of filesystem. I will describe those most commonly found on embedded devices and complete the survey with a section giving a summary of choices for each type of flash.

The last sections consider techniques to make the best use of flash memory, look at how to update devices in the field, and draw everything together into a coherent storage strategy.

Storage options

Embedded devices need storage that takes little power, is physically compact, robust, and reliable over a lifetime of perhaps tens of years. In almost all cases, that means solid state storage, which was introduced many years ago with **read-only memory (ROM)**, but for the past 20 years it has been flash memory of some kind. There have been several generations of flash memory in that time, progressing from NOR to NAND to managed flash such as eMMC.

NOR flash is expensive but reliable and can be mapped into the CPU address space, which allows you to execute code directly from flash. NOR flash chips are low-capacity, ranging from a few megabytes to a gigabyte or so.

NAND flash memory is much cheaper than NOR and is available in higher capacities, in the range of tens of megabytes to tens of gigabytes. However, it needs a lot of hardware and software support to turn it into a useful storage medium.

Managed flash memory consists of one or more NAND flash chips packaged with a controller which handles the complexities of flash memory and presents a hardware interface similar to that of a hard disk. The attraction is that it removes complexity from the driver software and insulates the system designer against the frequent changes in flash technology. SD cards, eMMC chips, and USB flash drives fit into this category. Almost all of the current generation of smartphones and tablets have eMMC storage, and that trend is likely to progress with other categories of embedded devices.

Hard drives are seldom found in embedded systems. One exception is digital video recording in set-top boxes and smart TVs in which a large amount of storage is needed with fast write times.

In all cases, robustness is of prime importance: you want the device to boot and reach a functional state despite power failures and unexpected resets. You should choose filesystems that behave well under such circumstances.

NOR flash

The memory cells in NOR flash chips are arranged into erase blocks of, for example, 128 KiB. Erasing a block sets all the bits to 1. It can be programmed one word at a time (8, 16 or 32 bits, depending on the data bus width). Each erase cycle damages the memory cells slightly and, after a number of cycles, the erase block becomes unreliable and cannot be used anymore. The maximum number of erase cycles should be given in the data sheet for the chip but is usually in the range of 100K to 1M.

The data can be read word by word. The chip is usually mapped into the CPU address space which means that you can execute code directly from NOR flash. This makes it a convenient place to put the bootloader code as it needs no initialization beyond hardwiring the address mapping. SoCs that support NOR flash in this way have configurations that give a default memory mapping such that it encompasses the reset vector of the CPU.

The kernel, and even the root filesystem, can also be located in flash memory, avoiding the need for copying them into RAM and thus creating devices with small memory footprints. The technique is known as **eXecute In Place**, or **XIP**. It is very specialized and I will not examine it further here. There are some references at the end of the chapter.

There is a standard register-level interface for NOR flash chips called the **common flash interface** or **CFI**, which all modern chips support.

NAND flash

NAND flash is much cheaper than NOR flash and has a higher capacity. First generation NAND chips stored one bit per memory cell in what is now known as an **SLC** or **single level cell** organization. Later generations moved on to two bits per cell in **multi-level cell** (**MLC**) chips and now to three bits per cell in **tri-level cell** (**TLC**) chips. As the number of bits per cell has increased, the reliability of the storage has decreased, requiring more complex controller hardware and software to compensate.

As with NOR flash, NAND flash is organized into erase blocks ranging in size from 16 KiB to 512 KiB and, once again, erasing a block sets all the bits to 1. However, the number of erase cycles before the block becomes unreliable is lower, typically as few as 1K cycles for TLC chips and up to 100K for SLC. NAND flash can only be read and written in pages, usually of 2 or 4 KiB. Since they cannot be accessed byte-by-byte, they cannot be mapped into the address space and so code and data have to be copied into RAM before they can be accessed.

Data transfers to and from the chip are prone to bit flips, which can be detected and corrected using Error Correction Codes. SLC chips generally use a simple hamming code which can be implemented efficiently in software and can correct a single bit error in a page read. MLC and TLC chips need more sophisticated codes such as **BCH** (**Bose-Chaudhuri-Hocquenghem**) which can correct up to 8-bit errors per page. These need hardware support.

The error correction codes have to be stored somewhere and so there is an extra area of memory per page known as the **out of band** (**OOB**) area, or also the spare area. MLC designs usually have 1 byte of OOB per 32 bytes of main storage so, for a 2 KiB page device, the OOB is 64 bytes per page and for a 4 KiB page, 128 bytes. MLC and TLC chips have proportionally larger OOB areas to accommodate more complex error correction codes. The following diagram shows the organization of a chip with a 128 KiB erase block and 2 KiB pages:

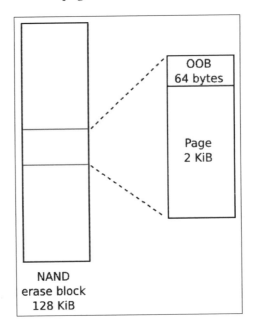

During production, the manufacturer tests all the blocks and marks any that fail by setting a flag in the OOB area of each page in the block. It is not uncommon to find that brand new chips have up to 2% of their blocks marked bad in this way. Furthermore, it is within the specification for a similar proportion of blocks to give errors on erase before the erase cycle limit is reached. The NAND flash driver should detect this and mark it as bad.

After space has been taken in the OOB area for a bad block flag and ECC bytes, there are still some bytes left. Some flash filesystems make use of these free bytes to store filesystem metadata. Consequently, lots of people are interested in the layout of the OOB area: the SoC ROM boot code, the bootloader, the kernel MTD driver, the filesystem code, and the tools to create filesystem images. There is not much standardization so it is easy to get into a situation in which the bootloader writes data using an OOB format that cannot be read by the kernel MTD driver. It is up to you to make sure that they all agree.

Access to NAND flash chips requires a NAND flash controller, which is usually part of the SoC. You will need the corresponding driver in the bootloader and kernel. The NAND flash controller handles the hardware interface to the chip, transferring data to and from pages, and may include hardware for error correction.

There is a standard register-level interface for NAND flash chips known as the **open NAND flash interface** or **ONFi** which most modern chips adhere to. See `http://www.onfi.org`.

Managed flash

The burden of supporting flash memory in the operating system, NAND in particular, becomes less if there is a well-defined hardware interface and a standard flash controller that hides the complexities of the memory. This is managed flash memory and it is becoming more and more common. In essence, it means combining one or more flash chips with a micro controller that offers an ideal storage device with a small sector size that is compatible with conventional filesystems. The most important types of managed flash for embedded systems are **Secure Digital** (**SD**) cards and the embedded variant known as **eMMC**.

MultiMediaCard and secure digital cards

The **MultiMediaCard** (**MMC**) was introduced in 1997 by SanDisk and Siemens as a form of packaged storage using flash memory. Shortly after, in 1999, SanDisk, Matsushita, and Toshiba created the SD card which is based on MMC but adds encryption and DRM (that is the secure part). Both were intended for consumer electronics such as digital cameras, music players, and similar devices. Currently, SD cards are the dominant form of managed flash for consumer and embedded electronics, even though the encryption features are seldom used. Newer versions of the SD specification allow for smaller packaging (mini SD and micro SD which is often written as uSD) and larger capacities: high capacity, SDHC, up to 32 GB and extended capacity, SDXC, up to 2 TB.

The hardware interface for MMC and SD cards is very similar, and it is possible to use fully-sized MMC in full-sized SD card slots (but not the other way round). Early incarnations used a 1-bit **Serial Peripheral Interface (SPI)**; more recent cards use a 4-bit interface. There is a command set for reading and writing memory in sectors of 512 bytes. Inside the package there is a microcontroller and one or more NAND flash chips, as shown in the diagram that follows:

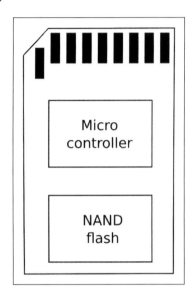

The microcontroller implements the command set and manages the flash memory, performing the function of a flash translation layer, as described later on in this chapter. They are pre-formatted with a FAT filesystem: FAT16 on SDSC cards, FAT32 on SDHC, and exFAT on SDXC. The quality of the NAND flash chips and the software on the microcontroller varies greatly between cards. It is questionable whether any of them are sufficiently reliable for deep embedded use, and certainly not with a FAT filesystem which is prone to file corruption. Remember that the prime use case for MMC and SD cards is for removable storage on cameras, tablets, and phones.

eMMC

eMMC or **Embedded MMC** is simply MMC memory packaged so that it can be soldered on to the motherboard, using a 4- or 8-bit interface for data transfer. However, they are intended to be used as storage for an operating system so the components are capable of performing that task. The chips are usually not pre-formatted with any filesystem.

Other types of managed flash

One of the first managed flash technologies was **CompactFlash (CF)**, using a subset of the **PCMCIA (Personal Computer Memory Card International Association)** interface. CF exposes the memory through a parallel ATA interface and appears to the operating system as a standard hard disk. They are common in x86-based single board computers and professional video and camera equipment.

One other format which we use every day is the USB flash drive. In this case, the memory is accessed through a USB interface and the controller implements the USB mass storage specification as well as the flash translation layer and interface to the flash chip or chips. The USB mass storage protocol, in turn, is based on the SCSI disk command set. As with MMC and SD cards, they are usually pre-formatted with a FAT filesystem. Their main use case in embedded systems is exchanging data with PCs.

A recent addition to the list of options for managed flash storage is **universal flash storage (UFS)**. Like eMMC, it is packaged in a chip that is mounted on the motherboard. It has a high-speed serial interface and can achieve data rates greater than eMMC. It supports a SCSI disk command set.

Accessing flash memory from the bootloader

In *Chapter 3*, *All About Bootloaders*, I mentioned the need for the bootloader to load kernel binaries and other images from various flash devices and to be able to perform system maintenance tasks such as erasing and reprogramming flash memory. It follows that the bootloader must have the drivers and infrastructure to support read, erase, and write operations on the type of memory you have, whether it be NOR, NAND, or managed. I will use U-Boot in the following example; other bootloaders follow a similar pattern.

U-Boot and NOR flash

U-Boot has drivers for NOR CFI chips in `drivers/mtd` and has the commands `erase` to erase memory and `cp.b` to copy data byte by byte, programming the flash. Suppose that you have NOR flash memory mapped from 0x40000000 to 0x48000000, of which 4MiB starting at 0x40040000 is a kernel image, then you would load a new kernel into flash using these U-Boot commands:

```
U-Boot# tftpboot 100000 uImage
U-Boot# erase 40040000 403fffff
U-Boot# cp.b 100000 40040000 $(filesize)
```

The variable `filesize` in the preceding example is set by the `tftpboot` command to the size of the file just downloaded.

U-Boot and NAND flash

For NAND flash, you need a driver for the NAND flash controller on your SoC, which you can find in `drivers/mtd/nand`. You use the `nand` command to manage the memory using the sub-commands `erase`, `write`, and `read`. This example shows a kernel image being loaded into RAM at 0x82000000 and then placed into flash starting at offset 0x280000:

```
U-Boot# tftpboot 82000000 uImage
U-Boot# nand erase 280000 400000
U-Boot# nand write 82000000 280000 $(filesize)
```

U-Boot can also read files stored in the JFFS2, YAFFS2, and UBIFS filesystems.

U-Boot and MMC, SD and eMMC

U-Boot has drivers for several MMC controllers in `drivers/mmc`. You can access the raw data using `mmc read` and `mmc write` at the user interface level, which allows you to handle raw kernel and filesystem images.

U-boot can also read files from the FAT32 and ext4 filesystems on MMC storage.

Accessing flash memory from Linux

Raw NOR and NAND flash memory is handled by the memory technology device sub-system, or MTD, which provides basic interfaces to read, erase, and write blocks of flash memory. In the case of NAND flash, there are functions to handle the OOB area and to identify bad blocks.

For managed flash, you need drivers to handle the particular hardware interface. MMC/SD cards and eMMC use the mmcblk driver; CompactFlash and hard drives use the SCSI Disk driver, sd. USB flash drives use the usb_storage driver together with the sd driver.

Memory technology devices

The **memory technology devices** (**MTD**), sub-system was started by David Woodhouse in 1999 and has been extensively developed over the intervening years. In this section, I will concentrate on the way it handles the two main technologies, NOR and NAND flash.

MTD consists of three layers: a core set of functions, a set of drivers for various types of chips, and user-level drivers that present the flash memory as a character device or a block device, as shown in the following diagram:

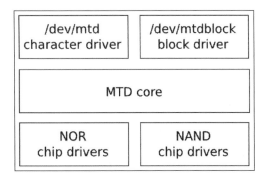

The chip drivers are at the lowest level and interface with flash chips. Only a small number of drivers are needed for NOR flash chips, enough to cover the CFI standard and variations plus a few non-compliant chips which are now mostly obsolete. For NAND flash, you will need a driver for the NAND flash controller you are using; this is usually supplied as part of the board support package. There are drivers for about 40 of them in the current mainline kernel in the directory `drivers/mtd/nand`.

MTD partitions

In most cases, you will want to partition the flash memory into a number of areas, for example, to provide space for a bootloader, a kernel image, or a root filesystem. In MTD, there are several ways to specify the size and location of partitions, the main ones being:

- Through the kernel command line using `CONFIG_MTD_CMDLINE_PARTS`
- Via the device tree using `CONFIG_MTD_OF_PARTS`
- With a platform mapping driver

In the case of the first option, the kernel command line option to use is `mtdparts`, which is defined as follows in the Linux source code in `drivers/mtd/cmdlinepart.c`:

```
mtdparts=<mtddef>[;<mtddef]
<mtddef>   := <mtd-id>:<partdef>[,<partdef>]
<mtd-id>   := unique name for the chip
<partdef>  := <size>[@<offset>][<name>][ro][lk]
<size>     := size of partition OR "-" to denote all remaining
              space
<offset>   := offset to the start of the partition; leave blank
              to follow the previous partition without any gap
<name>     := '(' NAME ')'
```

Perhaps an example will help. Imagine that you have one flash chip of 128 MB that is to be divided into five partitions. A typical command line would be:

```
mtdparts=:512k(SPL)ro,780k(U-Boot)ro,128k(U-BootEnv),
4m(Kernel),-(Filesystem)
```

The first element, before the colon, `:`, is `mtd-id`, which identifies the flash chip, either by number or by the name assigned by the board support package. If there is only one chip, as here, it can be left empty. If there is more than one chip, the information for each is separated by a semicolon, `;`. Then, for each chip, there is a comma-separated list of partitions, each with a size in bytes, kilobytes, `k`, or megabytes, `m`, and a name in brackets. The `ro` suffix makes the partition read-only to MTD and is often used to prevent accidental overwriting of the bootloader. The size of the last partition for the chip may be replaced by a dash, `-`, indicating that it should take up all the remaining space.

You can see a summary of the configuration at runtime by reading `/proc/mtd`:

```
# cat /proc/mtd
dev:    size      erasesize     name
mtd0: 00080000 00020000   "SPL"
mtd1: 000C3000 00020000   "U-Boot"
mtd2: 00020000 00020000   "U-BootEnv"
mtd3: 00400000 00020000   "Kernel"
mtd4: 07A9D000 00020000   "Filesystem"
```

There is more detailed information for each partition in `/sys/class/mtd`, including the erase block size and the page size, and it is nicely summarized using `mtdinfo`:

```
# mtdinfo /dev/mtd0
mtd0
Name:                         SPL
Type:                         nand
```

```
Eraseblock size:                    131072 bytes, 128.0 KiB
Amount of eraseblocks:              4 (524288 bytes, 512.0 KiB)
Minimum input/output unit size:     2048 bytes
Sub-page size:                      512 bytes
OOB size:                           64 bytes
Character device major/minor:       90:0
Bad blocks are allowed:             true
Device is writable:                 false
```

The equivalent partition information can be written as part of the device tree like so:

```
nand@0,0 {
  #address-cells = <1>;
  #size-cells = <1>;
  partition@0 {
    label = "SPL";
    reg = <0 0x80000>;
  };
  partition@80000 {
    label = "U-Boot";
    reg = <0x80000 0xc3000>;
  };
  partition@143000 {
    label = "U-BootEnv";
    reg = <0x143000 0x20000>;
  };
  partition@163000 {
    label = "Kernel";
    reg = <0x163000 0x400000>;
  };
  partition@563000 {
    label = "Filesystem";
    reg = <0x563000 0x7a9d000>;
  };
};
```

A third alternative is to code the partition information as platform data in an `mtd_partition` structure, as shown in this example taken from `arch/arm/mach-omap2/board-omap3beagle.c` (NAND_BLOCK_SIZE is defined elsewhere to be 128K):

```
static struct mtd_partition omap3beagle_nand_partitions[] = {
  {
    .name           = "X-Loader",
```

```
        .offset          = 0,
        .size            = 4 * NAND_BLOCK_SIZE,
        .mask_flags      = MTD_WRITEABLE,    /* force read-only */
    },
    {
        .name            = "U-Boot",
        .offset          = 0x80000;
        .size            = 15 * NAND_BLOCK_SIZE,
        .mask_flags      = MTD_WRITEABLE,    /* force read-only */
    },
    {
        .name            = "U-Boot Env",
        .offset          = 0x260000;
        .size            = 1 * NAND_BLOCK_SIZE,
    },
    {
        .name            = "Kernel",
        .offset          = 0x280000;
        .size            = 32 * NAND_BLOCK_SIZE,
    },
    {
        .name            = "File System",
        .offset          = 0x680000;
        .size            = MTDPART_SIZ_FULL,
    },
};
```

MTD device drivers

The upper level of the MTD sub-system is a pair of device drivers:

- A character device, with a major number of 90. There are two device nodes per MTD partition number, N: /dev/mtdN (*minor number=N*2*) and /dev/mtdNro (*minor number=(N*2 + 1)*). The latter is just a read-only version of the former.

- A block device, with a major number of 31 and a minor number of N. The device nodes are in the form /dev/mtdblockN.

The MTD character device, mtd

The character devices are the most important: they allow you to access the underlying flash memory as an array of bytes so that you can read and write (program) the flash. It also implements a number of `ioctl` functions that allow you to erase blocks and to manage the OOB area on NAND chips. The following list is in `include/uapi/mtd/mtd-abi.h`:

IOCTL	Description
MEMGETINFO	Gets basic MTD characteristic information
MEMERASE	Erases blocks in the MTD partition
MEMWRITEOOB	Writes out-of-band data for the page
MEMREADOOB	Reads out-of-band data for the page
MEMLOCK	Locks the chip (if supported)
MEMUNLOCK	Unlocks the chip (if supported)
MEMGETREGIONCOUNT	Gets the number of erase regions: non-zero if there are erase blocks of differing sizes in the partition, which is common for NOR flash, rare on NAND
MEMGETREGIONINFO	If MEMGETREGIONCOUNT is non-zero, this can be used to get the offset, size, and block count of each region
MEMGETOOBSEL	Deprecated
MEMGETBADBLOCK	Gets the bad block flag
MEMSETBADBLOCK	Sets the bad block flag
OTPSELECT	Sets OTP (one-time programmable) mode, if the chip supports it
OTPGETREGIONCOUNT	Gets the number of OTP regions
OTPGETREGIONINFO	Gets information about an OTP region
ECCGETLAYOUT	Deprecated

There is a set of utility programs known as `mtd-utils` for manipulating flash memory that makes use of these `ioctl` functions. The source is available from `git://git.infradead.org/mtd-utils.git` and is available as a package in the Yocto Project and Buildroot. The essential tools are shown in the following list. The package also contains utilities for the JFFS2 and UBI/UBIFS filesystems which I will cover later. For each of these tools, the MTD character device is one of the parameters:

- **flash_erase**: Erases a range of blocks.
- **flash_lock**: Locks a range of blocks.
- **flash_unlock**: Unlocks a range of blocks.

- **nanddump**: Dumps memory from NAND flash, optionally including the OOB area. Skips bad blocks.

- **nandtest**: Tests and diagnostics for NAND flash.

- **nandwrite**: Writes (program) from a data file to NAND flash, skipping bad blocks.

 You must always erase flash memory before writing new contents to it: `flash_erase` is the command to do that.

To program NOR flash, you simply copy bytes to the MTD device node using the `cp` command or similar.

Unfortunately, this doesn't work with NAND memory as the copy will fail at the first bad block. Instead, use `nandwrite`, which skips over any bad blocks. To read back NAND memory, you should use `nanddump` which also skips bad blocks.

The MTD block device, mtdblock

The mtdblock driver is little used. Its purpose is to present flash memory as a block device which you can use to format and mount as a filesystem. However, it has severe limitations because it does not handle bad blocks in NAND flash, does not do wear leveling, and does not handle the mismatch in size between filesystem blocks and flash erase blocks. In other words, it does not have a flash translation layer, which is essential for reliable file storage. The only case where the mtdblock device is useful is to mount read-only filesystems such as Squashfs on top of reliable flash memory such as NOR.

 If you want a read-only filesystem on NAND flash, you should use the UBI driver, as described later in this chapter.

Logging kernel oops to MTD

Kernel errors, or oopsies, are normally logged via the `klogd` and `syslogd` daemons to a circular memory buffer or a file. Following a reboot, the log will be lost in the case of a ring buffer and, even in the case of a file, it may not have been properly written before the system crashed.

A more reliable method is to write oops and kernel panics to an MTD partition as a circular log buffer. You enable it with `CONFIG_MTD_OOPS` and you add `console=ttyMTDN` to the kernel command line, N being the MTD device number to write the messages to.

Simulating NAND memory

The NAND simulator emulates a NAND chip using system RAM. The main use is for testing code that has to be NAND-aware without access to physical NAND memory. In particular, the ability to simulate bad blocks, bit flips, and other errors allows you to test code paths that are difficult to exercise using real flash memory. For more information, the best place to look is in the code itself, which has a comprehensive description of the ways you can configure the driver. The code is in `drivers/mtd/nand/nandsim.c`. Enable it with the kernel configuration `CONFIG_MTD_NAND_NANDSIM`.

The MMC block driver

MMC/SD cards and eMMC chips are accessed using the mmcblk block driver. You need a host controller to match the MMC adapter you are using, which is part of the board support package. The drivers are located in the Linux source code in `drivers/mmc/host`.

MMC storage is partitioned using a partition table in exactly the same way you would for hard disks, using fdisk or a similar utility.

Filesystems for flash memory

There are several challenges when making efficient use of flash memory for mass storage: the mismatch between the size of an erase block and a disk sector, the limited number of erase cycles per erase block, and the need for bad block handling on NAND chips. These differences are resolved by a **Flash Translation Layer globally**, or **FTL**.

Flash translation layers

A flash translation layer has the following features:

- **Sub allocation**: Filesystems work best with a small allocation unit, traditionally a 512-byte sector. This is much smaller than a flash erase block of 128 KiB or more. Therefore erase blocks have to be sub-divided into smaller units to avoid wasting large amounts of space.

- **Garbage collection**: A consequence of sub-allocation is that an erase block will contain a mixture of good data and stale data after the filesystem has been in use for a while. Since we can only free up whole erase blocks, the only way to reclaim the free space is to coalesce the good data into one place and return the now empty erase block to the free list: this is garbage collection, and is usually implemented as a background thread.

- **Wear leveling**: There is a limit on the number of erase cycles for each block. To maximize the lifespan of a chip, it is important to move data around so that each block is erased roughly the same number of times.

- **Bad block handling**: On NAND flash chips, you have to avoid using any block marked bad and also mark good blocks as bad if they cannot be erased.

- **Robustness**: Embedded devices may be powered off or reset without warning, so any filesystem should be able to cope without corruption, usually by incorporating a journal or log of transactions.

There are several ways to deploy the flash translation layer:

- **In the filesystem**: as with JFFS2, YAFFS2, and UBIFS

- **In the block device driver**: the UBI driver, on which UBIFS depends, implements some aspects of a flash translation layer

- **In the device controller**: as with managed flash devices

When the flash translation layer is in the filesystem or the block driver, the code is part of the kernel and so it is open source, meaning that we can see how it works and we can expect that it will be improved over time. On the other hand, the FTL is inside a managed flash device; it is hidden from view and we cannot verify whether or not it works as we would want. Not only that, but putting the FTL into the disk controller means that it misses out on information that is held at the filesystem layer such as which sectors belong to files that have been deleted and so do not contain useful data anymore. The latter problem is solved by adding commands that pass this information between the filesystem and the device I will describe in the section on the TRIM command later, but the question of code visibility remains. If you are using managed flash, you just have to choose a manufacturer you can trust.

Filesystems for NOR and NAND flash memory

To use raw flash chips for mass storage, you have to use a filesystem that understands the peculiarities of the underlying technology. There are three such filesystems:

- **Journaling Flash File System 2, JFFS2**: This was the first flash filesystem for Linux, and is still in use today. It works for NOR and NAND memory, but is notoriously slow during mount.

- **Yet Another Flash File System 2, YAFFS2**: This is similar to JFFS2, but specifically for NAND flash memory. It was adopted by Google as the preferred raw flash filesystem on Android devices.

- **Unsorted Block Image File System, UBIFS**: This is the latest flash-aware filesystem for both NOR and NAND memory, which is used in conjunction with the UBI block driver. It generally offers better performance than JFFS2 or YAFFS2, and so should be the preferred solution for new designs.

All of these use MTD as the common interface to flash memory.

JFFS2

The Journaling Flash File System had its beginnings in the software for the Axis 2100 network camera in 1999. For many years, it was the only flash filesystem for Linux and has been deployed on many thousands of different types of devices. Today, it is not the best choice, but I will cover it first because it shows the beginning of the evolutionary path.

JFFS2 is a log-structured filesystem that uses MTD to access flash memory. In a log-structured filesystem, changes are written sequentially as nodes to the flash memory. A node may contain changes to a directory, such as the names of files created and deleted, or it may contain changes to file data. After a while, a node may be superseded by information contained in subsequent nodes and becomes an obsolete node.

Erase blocks are categorized into three types:

- **free**: It contains no nodes at all

- **clean**: It contains only valid nodes

- **dirty**: It contains at least one obsolete node

At any one time, there is one block receiving updates which is called the open block. If power is lost or the system is reset, the only data that can be lost is the last write to the open block. In addition, nodes are compressed as they are written, increasing the effective storage capacity of the flash chip, which is important if you are using expensive NOR flash memory.

When the number of free blocks falls below a threshold, a garbage collector kernel thread is started, which scans for dirty blocks and copies the valid nodes into the open block, and then frees up the dirty block.

At the same time, the garbage collector provides a crude form of wear leveling because it cycles valid data from one block to another. The way that the open block is chosen means that each block is erased roughly the same number of times so long as it contains data that changes from time to time. Sometimes a clean block is chosen for garbage collection to make sure that blocks containing static data that is seldom written are also wear leveled.

JFFS2 filesystems have a write through cache, meaning that writes are written to the flash memory synchronously as if they have been mounted with a `-o sync` option. While improving reliability, it does increase the time to write data. There is a further problem with small writes: if the length of a write is comparable to the size of the node header (40 bytes) the overhead becomes high. A well-known corner case is log files, produced, for example, by syslogd.

Summary nodes

There is one overriding disadvantage to JFFS2: since there is no on-chip index, the directory structure has to be deduced at mount-time by reading the log from start to finish. At the end of the scan, you have a complete picture of the directory structure of the valid nodes, but the time taken is proportional to the size of the partition. It is not uncommon to see mount times of the order of one second per megabyte, leading to total mount times of tens or hundreds of seconds.

To reduce the time to scan during mount, summary nodes became an option in Linux 2.6.15. A summary node is written at the end of the open erase block just before it is closed. The summary node contains all of the information needed for the mount-time scan, thereby reducing the amount of data to process during the scan. Summary nodes can reduce mount times by a factor of between two and five, at the expense of an overhead of about 5% of the storage space. They are enabled with the kernel configuration `CONFIG_JFFS2_SUMMARY`.

Clean markers

An erased block with all bits set to 1 is indistinguishable from a block that has been written with 1's, but the latter has not had its memory cells refreshed and cannot be programmed again until it is erased. JFFS2 uses a mechanism called clean markers to distinguish between these two situations. After a successful block erase, a clean marker is written, either to the beginning of the block, or to the OOB area of the first page of the block. If the clean marker exists then it must be a clean block.

Creating a JFFS2 filesystem

Creating an empty JFFS2 filesystem at runtime is as simple as erasing an MTD partition with clean markers and then mounting it. There is no formatting step because a blank JFFS2 filesystem consists entirely of free blocks. For example, to format MTD partition 6, you would enter these commands on the device:

```
# flash_erase -j /dev/mtd6 0 0
# mount -t jffs2 mtd6 /mnt
```

The -j option to flash_erase adds the clean markers, and mounting with type jffs2 presents the partition as an empty filesystem. Note that the device to be mounted is given as mtd6, not /dev/mtd6. Alternatively, you can give the block device node /dev/mtdblock6. This is just a peculiarity of JFFS2. Once mounted, you can treat it like any filesystem and, when you next boot and mount it, all the files will still be there.

You can create a filesystem image directly from the staging area of your development system using mkfs.jffs2 to write out the files in JFFS2 format and sumtool to add the summary nodes. Both of these are part of the mtd-utils package.

As an example, to create an image of the files in rootfs for a NAND flash device with an erase block size of 128 KB (0x20000) and with summary nodes, you would use these two commands:

```
$ mkfs.jffs2 -n -e 0x20000 -p -d ~/rootfs -o ~/rootfs.jffs2
$ sumtool -n -e 0x20000 -p -i ~/rootfs.jffs2 -o ~/rootfs-sum.jffs2
```

The -p option adds padding at the end of the image file to make it a whole number of erase blocks. The -n option suppresses the creation of clean markers in the image, which is normal for NAND devices as the clean marker is in the OOB area. For NOR devices, you would leave out the -n option. You can use a device table with mkfs.jffs2 to set the permissions and the ownership of files by adding -D [device table]. Of course, Buildroot and the Yocto Project will do all this for you.

You can program the image into flash memory from your bootloader. For example, if you have loaded a filesytem image into RAM at address 0x82000000 and you want to load it into a flash partition begins at 0x163000 bytes from the start of the flash chip and is 0x7a9d000 bytes long, the U-Boot commands would be:

```
nand erase clean 163000 7a9d000
nand write 82000000 163000 7a9d000
```

You can do the same thing from Linux using the mtd driver like this:

```
# flash_erase -j /dev/mtd6 0 0
# nandwrite /dev/mtd6 rootfs-sum.jffs2
```

To boot with a JFFS2 root filesystem, you need to pass the `mtdblock` device on the kernel command line for the partition and a root `fstype` because JFFS2 cannot be auto-detected:

```
root=/dev/mtdblock6 rootfstype=jffs2
```

YAFFS2

The YAFFS filesystem was written by Charles Manning beginning in 2001, specifically to handle NAND flash chips at a time when JFFS2 did not. Subsequent changes to handle larger (2 KiB) page sizes resulted in YAFFS2. The website for YAFFS is `http://www.yaffs.net`.

YAFFS is also a log-structured filesystem following the same design principles as JFFS2. The different design decisions mean that it has a faster mount-time scan, simpler and faster garbage collection, and has no compression, which speeds up reads and writes at the expense of less efficient use of storage.

YAFFS is not limited to Linux; it has been ported to a wide range of operating systems. It has a dual license: GPLv2 to be compatible with Linux, and a commercial license for other operating systems. Unfortunately, the YAFFS code has never been merged into mainline Linux so you will have to patch your kernel, as shown in the following code.

To get YAFFS2 and patch a kernel, you would:

```
$ git clone git://www.aleph1.co.uk/yaffs2

$ cd yaffs2

$ ./patch-ker.sh c m <path to your link source>
```

Then, configure the kernel with `CONFIG_YAFFS_YAFFS2`.

Creating a YAFFS2 filesystem

As with JFFS2, to create a YAFFS2 filesystem at runtime, you only need to erase the partition and mount it but note that, in this case, you do not enable clean markers:

```
# flash_erase /dev/mtd/mtd6 0 0
# mount -t yaffs2 /dev/mtdblock6 /mnt
```

To create a filesystem image, the simplest thing to do is use the `mkyaffs2` tool from `https://code.google.com/p/yaffs2utils` using the following command:

```
$ mkyaffs2 -c 2048 -s 64 rootfs rootfs.yaffs2
```

Here `-c` is the page size and `-s` the OOB size. There is a tool named `mkyaffs2image` that is part of the YAFFS code, but it has a couple of drawbacks. Firstly, the page and OOB size are hard-coded in the source: you will have to edit and recompile if you have memory that does not match the defaults of 2,048 and 64. Secondly, the OOB layout is incompatible with MTD, which uses the first two byes as a bad block marker, whereas `mkyaffs2image` uses those bytes to store part of the YAFFS metadata.

To copy the image to the MTD partition from a Linux shell prompt, follow these steps:

```
# flash_erase /dev/mtd6 0 0
# nandwrite -a /dev/mtd6 rootfs.yaffs2
```

To boot with a YAFFS2 root filesystem, add the following to the kernel command line:

```
root=/dev/mtdblock6 rootfstype=yaffs2
```

UBI and UBIFS

The **unsorted block image** (**UBI**) driver, is a volume manager for flash memory which takes care of bad block handling and wear leveling. It was implemented by Artem Bityutskiy and first appeared in Linux 2.6.22. In parallel with that, engineers at Nokia were working on a filesystem that would take advantage of the features of UBI which they called UBIFS; it appeared in Linux 2.6.27. Splitting the flash translation layer in this way makes the code more modular and also allows other filesystems to take advantage of the UBI driver, as we shall see later on.

UBI

UBI provides an idealized, reliable view of a flash chip by mapping **physical erase blocks** (**PEB**) to **logical erase blocks** (**LEB**). Bad blocks are not mapped to LEBs and so are never used. If a block cannot be erased, it is marked as bad and dropped from the mapping. UBI keeps a count of the number of times each PEB has been erased in the header of the LEB and changes the mapping to ensure that each PEB is erased the same number of times.

UBI accesses the flash memory through the MTD layer. As an extra feature, it can divide an MTD partition into a number of UBI volumes, which improves wear leveling in the following way. Imagine that you have two filesystems, one containing fairly static data, for example, a root filesystem, and the other containing data that is constantly changing. If they are stored in separate MTD partitions, the wear leveling only has an effect on the second one, whereas, if you choose to store them in two UBI volumes in a single MTD partition, the wear leveling takes place over both areas of the storage and the lifetime of the flash memory is increased. The following diagram illustrates this situation:

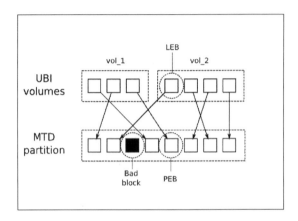

In this way, UBI fulfills two of the requirements of a flash translation layer: wear leveling and bad block handling.

To prepare an MTD partition for UBI, you don't use `flash_erase` as with JFFS2 and YAFFS2, instead you use the `ubiformat` utility, which preserves the erase counts that are stored in the PED headers. `ubiformat` needs to know the minimum unit of IO which, for most NAND flash chips, is the page size, but some chips allow reading and writing in sub pages that are a half or a quarter of the page size. Consult the chip data sheet for details and, if in doubt, use the page size. This example prepares `mtd6` using a page size of 2,048 bytes:

```
# ubiformat /dev/mtd6 -s 2048
```

You use the `ubiattach` command to load the UBI driver on an MTD partition that has been prepared in this way:

```
# ubiattach -p /dev/mtd6 -O 2048
```

This creates the device node `/dev/ubi0` through which you can access the UBI volumes. You can use `ubiattach` multiple times for other MTD partitions, in which case they can be accessed through `/dev/ubi1`, `/dev/ubi2`, and so on.

The PEB to LEB mapping is loaded into memory during the attach phase, a process that takes time proportional to the number of PEBs, typically a few seconds. A new feature was added in Linux 3.7 called the UBI fastmap which checkpoints the mapping to flash from time to time and so reduces the attach time. The kernel configuration option is CONFIG_MTD_UBI_FASTMAP.

The first time you attach to an MTD partition after a ubiformat there will be no volumes. You can create volumes using ubimkvol. For example, suppose you have a 128MB MTD partition and you want to split it into two volumes of 32 MB and 96 MB using a chip with 128 KB erase blocks and 2 KB pages:

```
# ubimkvol /dev/ubi0 -N vol_1 -s 32MiB
# ubimkvol /dev/ubi0 -N vol_2 -s 96MiB
```

Now, you have device the nodes /dev/ubi0_0 and /dev/ubi0_1. You can confirm the situation using ubinfo:

```
# ubinfo -a /dev/ubi0
ubi0
Volumes count:                             2
Logical eraseblock size:                   15360 bytes, 15.0 KiB
Total amount of logical eraseblocks:       8192 (125829120 bytes,
120.0 MiB)
Amount of available logical eraseblocks: 0 (0 bytes)
Maximum count of volumes                   89
Count of bad physical eraseblocks:         0
Count of reserved physical eraseblocks:    160
Current maximum erase counter value:       1
Minimum input/output unit size:            512 bytes
Character device major/minor:              250:0
Present volumes:                           0, 1
Volume ID:    0 (on ubi0)
Type:         dynamic
Alignment:    1
Size:         2185 LEBs (33561600 bytes, 32.0 MiB)
State:        OK
Name:         vol_1
Character device major/minor: 250:1
-------------------------------
Volume ID:    1 (on ubi0)
Type:         dynamic
Alignment:    1
Size:         5843 LEBs (89748480 bytes, 85.6 MiB)
State:        OK
Name:         vol_2
Character device major/minor: 250:2
```

Note that, since each LEB has a header to contain the meta information used by UBI, the LEB is smaller than the PEB by one page. For example, a chip with a PEB size of 128 KB and 2 KB pages would have an LEB of 126 KB. This is important information that you will need when creating a UBIFS image.

UBIFS

UBIFS uses a UBI volume to create a robust filesystem. It adds sub-allocation and garbage collection to create a complete flash translation layer. Unlike JFFS2 and YAFFS2, it stores index information on-chip and so mounting is fast, although don't forget that attaching the UBI volume beforehand may take a significant amount of time. It also allows for write-back caching like a normal disk filesystem, which means that writes are much faster, but with the usual problem of potential loss of data that has not been flushed from the cache to flash memory in the event of power down. You can resolve the problem by making careful use of the `fsync(2)` and `fdatasync(2)` functions to force a flush of file data at crucial points.

UBIFS has a journal for fast recovery in the event power down. The journal takes up some space, typically 4 MiB or more, so UBIFS is not suitable for very small flash devices.

Once you have created the UBI volumes, you can mount them using the device node for the volume, `/dev/ubi0_0`, or by using the device node for the whole partition plus the volume name, as shown here:

```
# mount -t ubifs ubi0:vol_1 /mnt
```

Creating a filesystem image for UBIFS is a two-stage process: first you create a UBIFS image using `mkfs.ubifs`, and then embed it into a UBI volume using `ubinize`.

For the first stage, `mkfs.ubifs` needs to be informed of the page size with `-m`, the size of the UBI LEB with `-e`, remembering that the LEB is usually one page shorter than the PEB, and the maximum number of erase blocks in the volume with `-c`. If the first volume is 32 MiB and an erase block is 128 KiB, then the number of erase blocks is 256. So, to take the contents of the directory rootfs and create a UBIFS image named `rootfs.ubi`, you would type the following:

```
$ mkfs.ubifs -r rootfs -m 2048 -e 126KiB -c 256 -o rootfs.ubi
```

The second stage requires you to create a configuration file for `ubinize` which describes the characteristics of each volume in the image. The help page (`ubinize -h`) gives details of the format. This example creates two volumes, `vol_1` and `vol_2`:

```
[ubifsi_vol_1]
mode=ubi
image=rootfs.ubi
```

```
vol_id=0
vol_name=vol_1
vol_size=32MiB
vol_type=dynamic

[ubifsi_vol_2]
mode=ubi
image=data.ubi
vol_id=1
vol_name=vol_2
vol_type=dynamic
vol_flags=autoresize
```

The second volume has an auto-resize flag and so will expand to fill the remaining space on the MTD partition. Only one volume can have this flag. From this information, `ubinize` will create an image file named by the -o parameter, with the PEB size -p, the page size -m, and the sub-page size -s:

```
$ ubinize -o ~/ubi.img -p 128KiB -m 2048 -s 512 ubinize.cfg
```

To install this image on the target, you would enter these commands on the target:

```
# ubiformat /dev/mtd6 -s 2048
# nandwrite /dev/mtd6 /ubi.img
# ubiattach -p /dev/mtd6 -O 2048
```

If you want to boot with a UBIFS root filesystem, you would give these kernel command line parameters:

```
ubi.mtd=6 root=ubi0:vol_1 rootfstype=ubifs
```

Filesystems for managed flash

As the trend towards managed flash technologies continues, particularly eMMC, we need to consider how to use it effectively. While they appear to have the same characteristics as hard disk drives, some NAND flash chips have the limitations of large erase blocks with limited erase cycles and bad block handling. And, of course, we need robustness in the event of losing power.

It is possible to use any of the normal disk filesystems but we should try to choose one that reduces disk writes and has a fast restart after an unscheduled shutdown, typically provided by a journal.

Flashbench

To make optimum use of the underlying flash memory, you need to know the erase block size and page size. Manufacturers do not publish these numbers, as a rule, but it is possible to deduce them by observing the behavior of the chip or card.

Flashbench is one such tool. It was initially written by Arnd Bergman, as described in the LWN article available at http://lwn.net/Articles/428584. You can get the code from https://github.com/bradfa/flashbench.

Here is a typical run on a SanDisk GiB SDHC card:

```
$ sudo ./flashbench -a  /dev/mmcblk0 --blocksize=1024
align 536870912 pre 4.38ms  on 4.48ms   post 3.92ms  diff 332µs
align 268435456 pre 4.86ms  on 4.9ms    post 4.48ms  diff 227µs
align 134217728 pre 4.57ms  on 5.99ms   post 5.12ms  diff 1.15ms
align 67108864  pre 4.95ms  on 5.03ms   post 4.54ms  diff 292µs
align 33554432  pre 5.46ms  on 5.48ms   post 4.58ms  diff 462µs
align 16777216  pre 3.16ms  on 3.28ms   post 2.52ms  diff 446µs
align 8388608   pre 3.89ms  on 4.1ms    post 3.07ms  diff 622µs
align 4194304   pre 4.01ms  on 4.89ms   post 3.9ms   diff 940µs
align 2097152   pre 3.55ms  on 4.42ms   post 3.46ms  diff 917µs
align 1048576   pre 4.19ms  on 5.02ms   post 4.09ms  diff 876µs
align 524288    pre 3.83ms  on 4.55ms   post 3.65ms  diff 805µs
align 262144    pre 3.95ms  on 4.25ms   post 3.57ms  diff 485µs
align 131072    pre 4.2ms   on 4.25ms   post 3.58ms  diff 362µs
align 65536     pre 3.89ms  on 4.24ms   post 3.57ms  diff 511µs
align 32768     pre 3.94ms  on 4.28ms   post 3.6ms   diff 502µs
align 16384     pre 4.82ms  on 4.86ms   post 4.17ms  diff 372µs
align 8192      pre 4.81ms  on 4.83ms   post 4.16ms  diff 349µs
align 4096      pre 4.16ms  on 4.21ms   post 4.16ms  diff 52.4µs
align 2048      pre 4.16ms  on 4.16ms   post 4.17ms  diff 9ns
```

Flashbench reads blocks of, in this case, 1,024 bytes just before and just after various power-of-two boundaries. As you cross a page or erase block boundary, the reads after the boundary take longer. The rightmost column shows the difference and is the one that is most interesting. Reading from the bottom, there is a big jump at 4 KiB, which is the most likely size of a page. There is a second jump from 52.4µs to 349µs at 8 KiB. This is fairly common and indicates that the card can use multi-plane accesses to read two 4 KiB pages at the same time. Beyond that, the differences are less well marked, but there is a clear jump from 485µs to 805µs at 512 KiB, which is probably the erase block size. Given that the card being tested is quite old, these are the sort of numbers you would expect.

Discard and TRIM

Usually, when you delete a file, only the modified directory node is written to storage while the sectors containing the file's contents remain unchanged. When the flash translation layer is in the disk controller, as with managed flash, it does not know that this group of disk sectors no longer contains useful data and so it ends up copying stale data.

In the last few years, the addition of transactions that pass information about deleted sectors down to the disk controller has improved the situation. The SCSI and SATA specifications have a TRIM command and MMC has a similar command named ERASE. In Linux, this feature is known as discard.

To make use of discard, you need a storage device that supports it – most current eMMC chips do – and a Linux device driver to match. You can check by looking at the block system queue parameters in /sys/block/<block device>/queue/. The ones of interest are as follows:

- discard_granularity: The size of the internal allocation unit of the device
- discard_max_bytes: The maximum number of bytes that can be discarded in one go
- discard_zeroes_data: If 1, discarded data will be set to zero

If the device or the device driver does not support discard, these values are all set to zero. These are the parameters you will see from the eMMC chip on the BeagleBone Black:

```
# grep -s "" /sys/block/mmcblk0/queue/discard_*
/sys/block/mmcblk0/queue/discard_granularity:2097152
/sys/block/mmcblk0/queue/discard_max_bytes:2199023255040
/sys/block/mmcblk0/queue/discard_zeroes_data:1
```

There is more information in the kernel documentation file, Documentation/block/queue-sysfs.txt.

You can enable discard when mounting a filesystem by adding the option -o discard to the mount command. Both ext4 and F2FS support it.

 Make sure that the storage device supports discard before using the -o discard mount option, otherwise data loss can occur.

It is also possible to force `discard` from the command line independently of how the partition is mounted, using the `fstrim` command which is part of the `util-linux` package. Typically, you would run this command periodically, once a week perhaps, to free up unused space. `fstrim` operates on a mounted filesystem so, to trim the root filesystem /, you would type the following:

```
# fstrim -v /
/: 2061000704 bytes were trimmed
```

The preceding example uses the verbose option, `-v`, so that it prints out the number of bytes potentially freed up. In this case 2,061,000,704 is the approximate amount of free space in the filesystem, so it is the maximum amount of storage that could have been freed.

Ext4

The extended filesystem, ext, has been the main filesystem for Linux desktops since 1992. The current version, ext4, is very stable, well tested and has a journal that makes recovery from an unscheduled shutdown fast and mostly painless. It is a good choice for managed flash devices and you will find that it is the preferred filesystem for Android devices that have eMMC storage. If the device supports `discard`, you should mount with the option `-o discard`.

To format and create an ext4 filesystem at runtime, you would type the following:

```
# mkfs.ext4 /dev/mmcblk0p2
# mount -t ext4 -o discard /dev/mmcblk0p1 /mnt
```

To create a filesystem image, you can use the `genext2fs` utility, available from `http://genext2fs.sourceforge.net`. In this example, I have specified the block size with `-B` and the number of blocks in the image with `-b`:

```
$ genext2fs -B 1024 -b 10000 -d rootfs rootfs.ext4
```

`genext2fs` can make use of a device table to set the file permissions and ownership, as described in *Chapter 5, Building a Root Filesystem*, with `-D [file table]`.

As the name implies, this will actually generate an image in `.ext2` format. You can upgrade using `tune2fs` as follows (details of the command options are in the main page for `tune2fs`):

```
$ tune2fs -j -J size=1 -O filetype,extents,uninit_bg,dir_index
rootfs.ext4
$ e2fsck -pDf rootfs.ext4
```

Both the Yocto Project and Buildroot use exactly these steps when creating images in `.ext4` format.

While a journal is an asset for devices that may power down without warning, it does add extra write cycles to each write transaction, wearing out the flash memory. If the device is battery-powered, especially if the battery is not removable, the chances of an unscheduled power down are small and so you may want to leave the journal out.

F2FS

The **Flash-Friendly File System**, **F2FS**, is a log-structured filesystem designed for managed flash devices, especially eMMC and SD. It was written by Samsung and was merged into mainline Linux in 3.8. It is marked experimental, indicating that it has not been extensively deployed as yet, but it seems that some Android devices are using it.

F2FS takes into account the page and erase block sizes and tries to align data on these boundaries. The log format gives resilience in the face of power down and also gives good write performance, in some tests showing a two-fold improvement over ext4. There is a good description of the design of F2FS in the kernel documentation in `Documentation/filesystems/f2fs.txt` and there are references at the end of the chapter.

The `mfs2.fs2` utility creates an empty F2FS filesystem with the label `-l`:

```
# mkfs.f2fs -l rootfs /dev/mmcblock0p1
# mount -t f2fs /dev/mmcblock0p1 /mnt
```

There isn't (yet) a tool to create F2FS filesystem images off-line.

FAT16/32

The old Microsoft filesystems, FAT16 and FAT32, continue to be important as a common format that is understood by most operating systems. When you buy an SD card or USB flash drive, it is almost certain to be formatted as FAT32 and, in some cases, the on-card microcontroller is optimized for FAT32 access patterns. Also, some boot ROMs require a FAT partition for the second stage bootloader, the TI OMAP-based chips for example. However, FAT formats are definitely not suitable for storing critical files because they are prone to corruption and make poor use of the storage space.

Linux supports FAT16 through the `msdos` filesystem and both FAT32 and FAT16 through the `vfat` filesystem. In most cases, you need to include the `vfat` driver. Then, to mount a device, say an SD card on the second `mmc` hardware adapter, you would type this:

```
# mount -t vfat /dev/mmcblk1p1 /mnt
```

In the past, there have been licensing issues with the `vfat` driver which may (or may not) infringe a patent held by Microsoft.

FAT32 has a limitation on the device size of 32 GiB. Devices of a larger capacity may be formatted using the Microsoft exFAT format and it is a requirement for SDXC cards. There is no kernel driver for exFAT, but it can be supported by means of a user-space FUSE driver. Since exFAT is proprietary to Microsoft there are certain to be licensing implications if you support this format on your device.

Read-only compressed filesystems

Compressing data is useful if you don't have quite enough storage to fit everything in. Both JFFS2 and UBIFS do on-the-fly data compression by default. However, if the files are never going to be written, as is usually the case with the root filesystem, you can achieve better compression ratios by using a read-only compressed filesystem. Linux supports several of these: `romfs`, `cramfs`, and `squashfs`. The first two are obsolete now, so I will describe only `squashfs`.

squashfs

`squashfs` was written by Phillip Lougher in 2002 as a replacement for `cramfs`. It existed as a kernel patch for a long time, eventually being merged into mainline Linux in version 2.6.29 in 2009. It is very easy to use: you create a filesystem image using `mksquashfs` and install it to the flash memory:

```
$ mksquashfs rootfs rootfs.squashfs
```

The resulting filesystem is read-only so there is no mechanism to modify any of the files at runtime. The only way to update a `squashfs` filesystem is to erase the whole partition and program in a new image.

`squashfs` is not bad block-aware and so must be used with reliable flash memory such as NOR flash. It can be used on NAND flash as long as you use UBI to create an emulated, reliable, MTD volume on top of UBI. You have to enable kernel configuration `CONFIG_MTD_UBI_BLOCK`, which will create a read-only MTD block device for each UBI volume. The following diagram shows two MTD partitions, each with accompanying `mtdblock` devices. The second partition is also used to create a UBI volume which is exposed as a third, reliable, `mtdblock` device, which you can use for any read-only filesystem that is not bad block-aware:

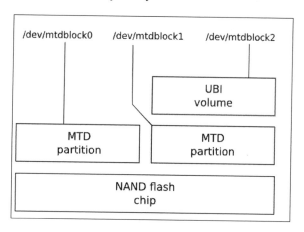

Temporary filesystems

There are always some files that have a short lifetime or which have no significance after a reboot. Many such files are put into `/tmp`, and so it makes sense to keep these files from reaching permanent storage.

The temporary filesystem, `tmpfs`, is ideal for this purpose. You can create a temporary RAM-based filesystem by simply mounting `tmpfs`:

```
# mount -t tmpfs tmp_files /tmp
```

As with `procfs` and `sysfs`, there is no device node associated with `tmpfs` so you have to supply a place-keeper string, `tmp_files` in the preceding example.

The amount of memory used will grow and shrink as files are created and deleted. The default maximum size is half the physical RAM. In most cases, it would be a disaster if `tmpfs` grew that large, so it is a very good idea to cap it with a `-o size` parameter. The parameter can be given in bytes, KiB (k), MiB (m), or GiB (g), for example:

```
mount -t tmpfs -o size=1m tmp_files /tmp
```

In addition to /tmp, some subdirectories of /var contain volatile data and it is good practice to use tmpfs for them as well, either by creating a separate filesystem for each or, more economically, by using symbolic links. Buildroot does it this way:

```
/var/cache -> /tmp
/var/lock ->  /tmp
/var/log ->   /tmp
/var/run ->   /tmp
/var/spool -> /tmp
/var/tmp ->   /tmp
```

In the Yocto Project, /run and /var/volatile are tmpfs mounts with symbolic links pointing to them as shown here:

```
/tmp ->       /var/tmp
/var/lock ->  /run/lock
/var/log ->   /var/volatile/log
/var/run ->   /run
/var/tmp ->   /var/volatile/tmp
```

Making the root filesystem read-only

You need to make your target device able to survive unexpected events including file corruption, and still be able to boot and achieve at least a minimum level of function. Making the root filesystem read-only is a key part of achieving this ambition because it eliminates accidental over-writes. Making it read-only is easy: replace rw with ro on the kernel command line or use an inherently read-only filesystem such as squashfs. However, you will find that there are a few files and directories that are traditionally writable:

- /etc/resolv.conf: This file is written by network configuration scripts to record the addresses of DNS name servers. The information is volatile, so you simply have to make it a symlink to a temporary directory, for example, /etc/resolv.conf -> /var/run/resolv.conf.

- /etc/passwd: This file, along with /etc/group, /etc/shadow, and /etc/gshadow, stores user and group names and passwords. They need to be symbolically linked to an area of persistent storage in the same way as resolv.conf.

- /var/lib: Many applications expect to be able to write to this directory and to keep permanent data here as well. One solution is to copy a base set of files to a tmpfs filesystem at boot time and then bind mount /var/lib to the new location by putting a sequence of commands such as these into one of the boot scripts:

```
mkdir -p /var/volatile/lib
cp -a /var/lib/* /var/volatile/lib
mount --bind /var/volatile/lib /var/lib
```

- `/var/log`: This is the place where syslog and other daemons keep their logs. Generally, logging to flash memory is not desirable because of the many small write cycles it generates. A simple solution is to mount `/var/log` using `tmpfs`, making all log messages volatile. In the case of `syslogd`, BusyBox has a version that can log to a circular ring buffer.

If you are using the Yocto Project, you can create a read-only root filesystem by adding `IMAGE_FEATURES = "read-only-rootfs"` to `conf/local.conf` or to your image recipe.

Filesystem choices

So far we have looked at the technology behind solid state memory and at the many types of filesystems. Now it is time to summarize the options.

In most cases, you will be able to divide your storage requirements into these three categories:

- **Permanent, readable, and writable data**: Runtime configuration, network parameters, passwords, data logs, and user data
- **Permanent, read-only data**: Programs, libraries, and configurations files that are constant, for example, the root filesystem
- **Volatile data**: Temporary storage for example `/tmp`

The choices for read-write storage are as follows:

- **NOR**: UBIFS or JFFS2
- **NAND**: UBIFS, JFFS2, or YAFFS2
- **eMMC**: ext4 or F2FS

For read-only storage, you can use all of the above mounted with the `ro` attribute. Additionally, if you want to save space, you could use `squashfs`, in the case of NAND flash using UBI `mtdblock` device emulation to handle the bad blocks for you.

Finally, for volatile storage, there is only one choice, `tmpfs`.

Updating in the field

There have been several well-publicized security flaws, including Heartbleed (a bug in the OpenSSL libraries) and Shellshock (a bug in the bash shell), both of which could have serious consequences for embedded Linux devices that are currently deployed. For this reason alone, it is highly desirable to have a mechanism to update devices in the field so that you can fix security problems as they arise. There are other good reasons as well: to deploy other bug fixes and feature updates.

The guiding principle of update mechanisms is that they should do no harm, remembering Murphy's Law: if it can go wrong, it will go wrong, eventually. Any update mechanism must be:

- **Robust**: It must not render the device inoperable. I will talk about updates being atomic; either the system is updated successfully or not updated at all and continues to run as before.
- **Failsafe**: It must handle interrupted updates gracefully.
- **Secure**: It must not allow unauthorized updates, otherwise it will become an attack mechanism.

Atomicity can be achieved by having duplicates of the things you want to update and switching to the new copy when safe to do so.

Failsafety requires there to be a mechanism to detect a failed update, such as a hardware watchdog, and a known good copy of software to fall back on.

Security can be achieved in the case of updates that are local and attended through authentication by a password or PIN code. But, if the update is remote and automatic, some level of authentication via the network is needed. Ultimately, you may want to add a secure bootloader and signed update binaries.

Some components are easier to update than others. The bootloader is very difficult to update since there are usually hardware constraints that mean there can only be one bootloader, and so there cannot be a backup if the update fails. On the other hand, bootloaders are not often a cause of runtime bugs. The best advice is to avoid bootloader updates in the field.

Granularity: file, package, or image?

This is the big question, and depends on your overall system design and your desired level of robustness.

File updates can be made atomic: the technique is to write the new content to a temporary file in the same filesystem and then use the POSIX `rename(2)` function to move it over the old file. It works because rename is guaranteed to be atomic. However, this is only one part of the problem because there will be dependencies between files which need to be considered.

Updating at the level of packages (`RPM`, `dpkg`, or `ipk`) is a better option, assuming that you have a runtime package manager. This, after all, is how desktop distributions have been doing it for years. The package manager has a database of updates and can keep track of those which have been updated and those that haven't. Each package has an update script that is designed to make sure that the package update is atomic. The great advantage is that you can update existing packages, install new ones, and delete obsolete ones with ease. If you are using a root filesystem that is mounted as read-only, you will have to temporarily remount read-write while updating, which opens up a small window for corruption.

Package managers do have downsides as well. They are not able to update kernel or other images in raw flash memory. After devices have been deployed and updated several times, you may end up with a large number of combinations of packages and package versions, which will complicate QA for each new update cycle. Package managers are not bulletproof in the event of power failure during an update.

The third option is to update whole system images: the kernel, the root filesystem, user applications, and so on.

Atomic image update

In order to make the update atomic, we need two things: a second copy of the operating system that can be used during the update, and a mechanism in the bootloader to select which copy of the operating system to load. The second copy may be exactly the same as the first, resulting in full redundancy of the operating system, or it may be a small operating system dedicated to updating the main one.

In the first scheme ,there are two copies of the operating system, each comprised of the Linux kernel, the root filesystem, and system applications, as shown in the following diagram:

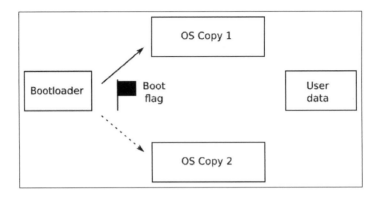

Initially, the boot flag is not set, so the bootloader loads copy 1. To install an update, the updater application, which is part of the operating system, overwrites copy 2. When complete, it sets the boot flag and reboots. Now, the bootloader will load the new operating system. When a further update is installed, the updater in copy 2 overwrites copy 1 and clears the boot flag and so you ping-pong between the two copies.

If an update fails, the boot flag is not changed and the last good operating system is used. Even if the update consists of several components, a kernel image, a DTB, a root filesystem, and a system application filesystem, the whole update is atomic because the boot flag is only updated when all updates are completed.

The main drawback with this scheme is that it requires storage for two copies of the operating system.

You can reduce storage requirements by keeping a minimal operating system purely for updating the main one, as shown in the following diagram:

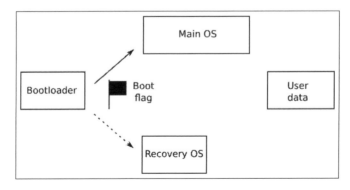

When you want to install an update, set the boot flag and reboot. Once the recovery operating system is running, it starts the updater which overwrites the main operating system images. When done, it clears the boot flag and reboots again, this time loading the new main operating system.

The recovery operating system is usually a lot smaller than the main operating system, maybe only a few megabytes, and so the storage overhead is not great. In fact, this is the scheme adopted by Android. The main operating system is several hundred megabytes, but the recovery mode operating system is a simple ramdisk of a few megabytes only.

Further reading

The following resources have further information about the topics introduced in this chapter:

- *XIP: The past, the present... the future?, Vitaly Wool,* presentation at FOSDEM 2007: `https://archive.fosdem.org/2007/slides/devrooms/embedded/Vitaly_Wool_XIP.pdf`

- *General MTD documentation,* `http://www.linux-mtd.infradead.org/doc/general.html`

- *Optimizing Linux with cheap flash drives, Arnd Bergmann:* `http://lwn.net/Articles/428584/`

- *Flash memory card design:* `https://wiki.linaro.org/WorkingGroups/KernelArchived/Projects/FlashCardSurvey`

- *eMMC/SSD File System Tuning Methodology:* `http://elinux.org/images/b/b6/EMMC-SSD_File_System_Tuning_Methodology_v1.0.pdf`

- *Flash-Friendly File System (F2FS):* `http://elinux.org/images/1/12/Elc2013_Hwang.pdf`

- *An f2fS teardown:* `http://lwn.net/Articles/518988/`

- *Building Murphy-compatible embedded Linux systems, Gilad Ben-Yossef:* `https://www.kernel.org/doc/ols/2005/ols2005v1-pages-21-36.pdf`

Summary

Flash memory has been the storage technology of choice for embedded Linux from the beginning and over the years Linux has gained very good support, from low-level drivers up to flash-aware filesystems, the latest being UBIFS.

However, as the rate at which new flash technologies are introduced increases, it is becoming harder to keep pace with the changes at the high end. System designers are increasingly turning to managed flash in the form of eMMC to provide a stable hardware and software interface which is independent of the memory chips inside. Embedded Linux developers are beginning to get to grips with these new chips. Support for TRIM in ext4 and F2FS is well established, and it is slowly finding its way into the chips themselves. Also, the appearance of new filesystems that are optimized to manage flash, such as F2FS, is a welcome step forward.

However, the fact remains that flash memory is not the same as a hard disk drive. You have to be careful to minimize the number of filesystem writes – especially as the higher density TLC chips may be able to support as few as 1,000 erase cycles.

Finally, it is essential to have a strategy for updating the files and images stored on the device in the field. A crucial part of this is the decision to use a package manager or not. A package manager gives you flexibility, but cannot give you a fully Murphy proof update solution. Your choice depends on the balance between convenience and robustness.

The next chapter describes how you control the hardware components of your system through the use of device drivers, both in the conventional sense of drivers that are part of the kernel, and also the extent to which you can control hardware from the user space.

8

Introducing Device Drivers

Kernel device drivers are the mechanism through which the underlying hardware is exposed to the rest of the system. As a developer of embedded systems, you need to know how device drivers fit into the overall architecture and how to access them from user space programs. Your system will probably have some novel pieces of hardware and you will have to work out a way of accessing them. In many cases, you will find that there are device drivers provided for you and you can achieve everything you want without writing any kernel code. For example, you can manipulate GPIO pins and LEDs using files in `sysfs`, and there are libraries to access serial buses, including SPI and I2C.

There are many places to find out how to write a device driver, but few to tell you why you would want to and the choices you have in doing so. That is what I want to cover here. However, remember that this is not a book dedicated to writing kernel device drivers and that the information given here is to help you navigate the territory but not necessarily to set up home there. There are many good books and articles that will help you to write device drivers, some of which are listed at the end of this chapter.

The role of device drivers

As mentioned in *Chapter 4*, *Porting and Configuring the Kernel*, one of the functions of the kernel is to encapsulate the many hardware interfaces of a computer system and present them in a consistent manner to user-space programs. There are frameworks designed to make it easy to write the interface logic for a device in the kernel and you can integrate it with the kernel: this is a device driver, the piece of code that mediates between the kernel above it and the hardware below. A device driver is a piece of software that controls physical devices such as a UART or an MMC controller, or virtual devices such as the null device (`/dev/null`) or a ramdisk. One driver may control multiple devices of the same kind.

Kernel device driver code runs at a high privilege level, as does the rest of the kernel. It has full access to the processor address space and hardware registers. It can handle interrupts and DMA transfers. It can make use of the sophisticated kernel infrastructure for synchronization and memory management. There is a downside to this, which is that if something goes wrong in a buggy driver, it can go really wrong and bring the system down. Consequently, there is a principle that device drivers should be as simple as possible, just providing information to applications where the real decisions are made. You often hear this being expressed as *no policy in the kernel*.

In Linux, there are three main types of device driver:

- **character**: This is for unbuffered I/O with a rich range of functions and a thin layer between the application code and the driver. It is the first choice when implementing custom device drivers.
- **block**: This has an interface tailored for block I/O to and from mass storage devices. There is a thick layer of buffering designed to make disk reads and writes as fast as possible, which makes it unsuitable for anything else.
- **network**: This is similar to a block device but is used for transmitting and receiving network packets rather than disk blocks.

There is also a fourth type that presents itself as a group of files in one of the pseudo filesystems. For example, you might access the GPIO driver through a group of files in /sys/class/gpio, as I will describe later on in this chapter. Let's begin by looking in more detail at the three basic device types.

Character devices

These devices are identified in user space by a filename: if you want to read from a UART, you open the device node, for example, the first serial port on the ARM Versatile Express would be /dev/ttyAMA0. The driver is identified differently in the kernel, using the major number which, in the example given, is 204. Since the UART driver can handle more than one UART, there is a second number, called the minor number, which identifies a specific interface, 64, in this case:

```
# ls -l /dev/ttyAMA*

crw-rw----    1 root      root       204,   64 Jan  1  1970 /dev/ttyAMA0
crw-rw----    1 root      root       204,   65 Jan  1  1970 /dev/ttyAMA1
crw-rw----    1 root      root       204,   66 Jan  1  1970 /dev/ttyAMA2
crw-rw----    1 root      root       204,   67 Jan  1  1970 /dev/ttyAMA3
```

The list of standard major and minor numbers can be found in the kernel documentation, in `Documentation/devices.txt`. The list does not get updated very often and does not include the `ttyAMA` device described in the preceding paragraph. Nevertheless, if you look at the source code in `drivers/tty/serial/amba-pl011.c`, you will see that the major and minor numbers are declared:

```
#define SERIAL_AMBA_MAJOR        204
#define SERIAL_AMBA_MINOR        64
```

Where there is more than one instance of a device, the naming convention for the device nodes is `<base name><interface number>`, for example, `ttyAMA0`, `ttyAMA1`, and so on.

As I mentioned in *Chapter 5, Building a Root Filesystem*, the device nodes can be created in several ways:

- `devtmpfs`: The node that is created when the device driver registers a new device interface using a base name supplied by the driver (`ttyAMA`) and an instance number.

- `udev` or `mdev` (without `devtmpfs`): Essentially the same as with `devtmpfs`, except that a user-space daemon program has to extract the device name from `sysfs` and create the node. I will talk about `sysfs` later.

- `mknod`: If you are using static device nodes, they are created manually using `mknod`.

You may have the impression from the numbers I have used above that both major and minor numbers are 8-bit numbers in the range 0 to 255. In fact, from Linux 2.6 onwards, the major number is 12 bits long, which gives valid numbers from 1 to 4,095, and the minor number is 20 bits, from 0 to 1,048,575.

When you open a device node, the kernel checks to see whether the major and minor numbers fall into a range registered by a device driver of that type (a character or block). If so, it passes the call to the driver, otherwise the open call fails. The device driver can extract the minor number to find out which hardware interface to use. If the minor number is out of range, it returns an error.

To write a program that accesses a device driver, you have to have some knowledge of how it works. In other words, a device driver is not the same as a file: the things you do with it change the state of the device. A simple example is the pseudo random number generator, `urandom`, which returns bytes of random data every time you read it. Here is a program that does just that:

```
#include <stdio.h>
#include <sys/types.h>
```

```
#include <sys/stat.h>
#include <fcntl.h>
#include <unistd.h>

int main(void)
{
  int f;
  unsigned int rnd;
  int n;
  f = open("/dev/urandom", O_RDONLY);
  if (f < 0) {
    perror("Failed to open urandom");
    return 1;
  }
  n = read(f, &rnd, sizeof(rnd));
  if (n != sizeof(rnd)) {
    perror("Problem reading urandom");
    return 1;
  }
  printf("Random number = 0x%x\n", rnd);
  close(f);
  return 0;
}
```

The nice thing about the Unix driver model is that, once we know that there is a device named urandom and that every time we read from it, it returns a fresh set of pseudo random data, we don't need to know anything else about it. We can just use normal functions such as open(2), read(2), and close(2).

We could use the stream I/O functions fopen(3), fread(3), and fclose(3) instead, but the buffering implicit in these functions often causes unexpected behavior. For example, fwrite(3) usually only writes to the user-space buffer, not to the device. We would need to call fflush(3) to force the buffer to be written out.

Don't use stream I/O functions such as fread(3) and fwrite(3) when calling device drivers.

Block devices

Block devices are also associated with a device node, which also has major and minor numbers.

Although character and block devices are identified using major and minor numbers, they are in different namespaces. A character driver with a major number 4 is in no way related to a block driver with a major number 4.

With block devices, the major number is used to identify the device driver and the minor number is used to identify the partition. Let's look at the MMC driver as an example:

```
# ls -l /dev/mmcblk*

brw-------    1 root root    179,    0 Jan  1  1970 /dev/mmcblk0
brw-------    1 root root    179,    1 Jan  1  1970 /dev/mmcblk0p1
brw-------    1 root root    179,    2 Jan  1  1970 /dev/mmcblk0p2
brw-------    1 root root    179,    8 Jan  1  1970 /dev/mmcblk1
brw-------    1 root root    179,    9 Jan  1  1970 /dev/mmcblk1p1
brw-------    1 root root    179,   10 Jan  1  1970 /dev/mmcblk1p2
```

The major number is 179 (look it up in `devices.txt`!). The minor numbers are used in ranges to identify different mmc devices and the partitions of the storage medium on that device. In the case of the mmcblk driver, the ranges are eight minor numbers per device: the minor numbers from 0 to 7 are for the first device, the numbers from 8 to 15 are for the second, and so on. Within each range, the first minor number represents the entire device as raw sectors, and the others represent up to seven partitions.

You are probably aware of the SCSI disk driver, known as sd, which is used to control a range of disks that use the SCSI command set, which includes SCSI, SATA, USB mass storage, and **UFS (universal flash storage)**. It has the major number eight and ranges of 16 minor numbers per interface (or disk). The minor numbers from 0 to 15 are for the first interface, with device nodes named sda up to sda15, the numbers from 16 to 31 are for the second disk with device nodes sdb up to sdb15, and so on. This continues up to the sixteenth disk from 240 to 255, with the node name sdp. There are other major numbers reserved for them because SCSI disks are so popular, but we needn't worry about that here.

The partitions are created using utilities such as fdisk, sfidsk, or parted. An exception is raw flash memory: the partition information for the MTD driver is part of the kernel command line or in the device tree, or one of the other methods described in *Chapter 7, Creating a Storage Strategy*.

A user-space program can open and interact directly with a block device through the device node. This is not a common thing to do, and is usually for performing administrative operations such as partitioning, formatting with a filesystem, and mounting. Once the filesystem is mounted, you interact with the block device indirectly through the files in that filesystem.

Network devices

Network devices are not accessed through device nodes and they do not have major and minor numbers. Instead, a network device is allocated a name by the kernel, based on a string and an instance number. Here is an example of the way a network driver registers an interface:

```
my_netdev = alloc_netdev(0, "net%d", NET_NAME_UNKNOWN,
netdev_setup);
ret = register_netdev(my_netdev);
```

This creates a network device named `net0` the first time it is called, `net1` the second, and so on. More common names are `lo`, `eth0`, and `wlan0`.

Note that this is the name it starts off with; device managers, such as `udev`, may change to something different later on.

Usually, the network interface name is only used when configuring the network using utilities such as `ip` and `ifconfig` to establish a network address and route. Thereafter, you interact with the network driver indirectly by opening sockets, and let the network layer decide how to route them to the right interface.

However, it is possible to access network devices directly from user space by creating a socket and using the `ioctl` commands listed in `include/linux/sockios.h`. For example, this program uses `SIOCGIFHWADDR` to query the driver for the hardware (MAC) address:

```
#include <stdio.h>
#include <stdlib.h>
#include <string.h>
#include <unistd.h>
#include <sys/ioctl.h>
#include <linux/sockios.h>
#include <net/if.h>
int main (int argc, char *argv[])
{
    int s;
    int ret;
    struct ifreq ifr;
    int i;
```

```
if (argc != 2) {
  printf("Usage %s [network interface]\n", argv[0]);
  return 1;
}
s = socket(PF_INET, SOCK_DGRAM, 0);
if (s < 0) {
  perror("socket");
  return 1;
}
strcpy(ifr.ifr_name, argv[1]);
ret = ioctl(s, SIOCGIFHWADDR, &ifr);
if (ret < 0) {
  perror("ioctl");
  return 1;
}
for (i = 0; i < 6; i++)
  printf("%02x:", (unsigned char)ifr.ifr_hwaddr.sa_data[i]);
printf("\n");
close(s);
return 0;
}
```

This is a standard device, `ioctl`, which is handled by the network layer on the driver's behalf, but it is possible to define your own `ioctl` numbers and handle them in a custom network driver.

Finding out about drivers at runtime

Once you have a running Linux system, it is useful to know which device drivers are loaded and what state they are in. You can find out a lot by reading the files in `/proc` and `/sys`.

First of all, you can list the character and block device drivers currently loaded and active by reading `/proc/devices`:

```
# cat /proc/devices

Character devices:

  1 mem
  2 pty
  3 ttyp
  4 /dev/vc/0
  4 tty
```

```
  4 ttyS
  5 /dev/tty
  5 /dev/console
  5 /dev/ptmx
  7 vcs
 10 misc
 13 input
 29 fb
 81 video4linux
 89 i2c
 90 mtd
116 alsa
128 ptm
136 pts
153 spi
180 usb
189 usb_device
204 ttySC
204 ttyAMA
207 ttymxc
226 drm
239 ttyLP
240 ttyTHS
241 ttySiRF
242 ttyPS
243 ttyWMT
244 ttyAS
245 ttyO
246 ttyMSM
247 ttyAML
248 bsg
249 iio
250 watchdog
251 ptp
252 pps
253 media
254 rtc

Block devices:

259 blkext
  7 loop
  8 sd
 11 sr
```

```
 31 mtdblock
 65 sd
 66 sd
 67 sd
 68 sd
 69 sd
 70 sd
 71 sd
128 sd
129 sd
130 sd
131 sd
132 sd
133 sd
134 sd
135 sd
179 mmc
```

For each driver, you can see the major number and the base name. However, this does not tell you how many devices each driver is attached to. It only shows ttyAMA but gives you no clue that it is attached to four real UARTS. I will come back to that later when I look at sysfs. If you are using a device manager such as mdev, udev, or devtmpfs, you can list the character and block device interfaces by looking in /dev.

You can also list network interfaces using ifconfig or ip:

```
# ip link show

1: lo: <LOOPBACK,UP,LOWER_UP> mtu 65536 qdisc noqueue state
UNKNOWN mode DEFAULT
    link/loopback 00:00:00:00:00:00 brd 00:00:00:00:00:00

2: eth0: <NO-CARRIER,BROADCAST,MULTICAST,UP> mtu 1500 qdisc
pfifo_fast state DOWN mode DEFAULT qlen 1000
    link/ether 54:4a:16:bb:b7:03 brd ff:ff:ff:ff:ff:ff

3: usb0: <BROADCAST,MULTICAST,UP,LOWER_UP> mtu 1500 qdisc
pfifo_fast state UP mode DEFAULT qlen 1000
    link/ether aa:fb:7f:5e:a8:d5 brd ff:ff:ff:ff:ff:ff
```

You can also find out about devices attached to USB or PCI buses using the well-known commands lsusb and lspci. There is information about them in the respective manuals and plenty of online guides, so I will not describe them any further here.

The really interesting information is in sysfs, which is the next topic.

Getting information from sysfs

You can define `sysfs` in a pedantic way as a representation of kernel objects, attributes and relationships. A kernel object is a directory, an attribute is a file, and a relationship is a symbolic link from one object to another.

From a more practical point of view, since the Linux device driver model, which was introduced in version 2.6, represents all devices and drivers as kernel objects. You can see the kernel's view of the system laid out before you by looking in `/sys`, as shown here:

```
# ls /sys

block   bus   class   dev   devices   firmware   fs   kernel   module
power
```

In the context of discovering information about devices and drivers, I will look at three of the directories: `devices`, `class`, and `block`.

The devices: /sys/devices

This is the kernel's view of the devices discovered since boot and how they are connected to each other. It is organized at the top level by the system bus, so what you see varies from one system to another. This is the QEMU emulation of the Versatile Express:

```
# ls
 /sys/devices
armv7_cortex_a9   platform    system
breakpoint        software    virtual
```

There are three directories that are present on all systems:

- `system`: This contains devices at the heart of the system, including CPUs and clocks.
- `virtual`: This contains devices that are memory-based. You will find the memory devices that appear as `/dev/null`, `/dev/random`, and `/dev/zero` in `virtual/mem`. You will find the loopback device, `lo`, in `virtual/net`.
- `platform`: This is a catch-all for devices that are not connected via a conventional hardware bus. This may be almost everything on an embedded device.

The other devices appear in directories that correspond to actual system buses. For example, the PCI root bus, if there is one, appears as `pci0000:00`.

Navigating this hierarchy is quite hard because it requires some knowledge of the topology of your system and the pathnames become quite long and hard to remember. To make life easier, /sys/class and /sys/block offer two different views of the devices.

The drivers: /sys/class

This is a view of the device drivers presented by their type, in other words, it is a software view rather than a hardware view. Each of the subdirectories represents a class of driver and is implemented by a component of the driver framework. For example, UART devices are managed by the tty layer and you will find them in /sys/class/tty. Likewise, you will find network devices in /sys/class/net, input devices such as the keyboard, the touchscreen, and the mouse in /sys/class/input, and so on.

There is a symbolic link in each subdirectory for each instance of that type of device pointing to its representation in /sys/device.

To take a concrete example, let's look at /sys/class/tty/ttyAMA0:

```
# cd   /sys/class/tty/ttyAMA0/
# ls
close_delay      flags            line             uartclk
closing_wait     io_type          port             uevent
custom_divisor   iomem_base       power            xmit_fifo_size
dev              iomem_reg_shift  subsystem
device           irq              type
```

The link device references the hardware node for the device and subsystem points back to /sys/class/tty. The others are attributes of the device. Some are specific to a UART, such as xmit_fifo_size and others apply to many types of device such as the interrupt number, irq, and the device number dev. Some attribute files are writable and allow you to tune parameters in the driver at runtime.

The dev attribute is particularly interesting. If you look at its value, you will find the following:

```
# cat /sys/class/tty/ttyAMA0/dev
204:64
```

These are the major and minor numbers of this device. This attribute is created when the driver registered this interface and it is from this file that udev and mdev read that information if they are being used without the help of devtmpfs.

The block drivers: /sys/block

There is one more view of the device model that is important: the block driver view that you will find in /sys/block. There is a subdirectory for each block device. This example is taken from a BeagleBone Black:

```
# ls /sys/block/

loop0   loop4   mmcblk0        ram0    ram12   ram2   ram6
loop1   loop5   mmcblk1        ram1    ram13   ram3   ram7
loop2   loop6   mmcblk1boot0   ram10   ram14   ram4   ram8
loop3   loop7   mmcblk1boot1   ram11   ram15   ram5   ram9
```

If you look into mmcblk1, which is the eMMC chip on this board, you can see the attributes of the interface and the partitions within it:

```
# cd /sys/block/mmcblk1
# ls

alignment_offset    ext_range       mmcblk1p1   ro
bdi                 force_ro        mmcblk1p2   size
capability          holders         power       slaves
dev                 inflight        queue       stat
device              mmcblk1boot0    range       subsystem
discard_alignment   mmcblk1boot1    removable   uevent
```

The conclusion, then, is that you can learn a lot about the devices (the hardware) and the drivers (the software) that are present on a system by reading sysfs.

Finding the right device driver

A typical embedded board is based on a reference design from the manufacturer with changes to make it suitable for a particular application. It may have a temperature sensor attached via I2C, lights and buttons connected via GPIO pins, an external Ethernet MAC, a display panel via a MIPI interface, or many other things. Your job is to create a custom kernel to control all of that, so where do you start?

Some things are so simple that you can write user space code to handle them. GPIOs and simple peripherals connected via I2C or SPI are easy to control from user space, as I will explain later.

Other things need a kernel driver so you need to know how to find one and incorporate it into your build. There is no simple answer, but here are some places to look.

The most obvious place to look is the driver support page on the manufacturer's website, or you could ask them directly. In my experience, this seldom gets the result you want; hardware manufacturers are not are not particularly Linux-savvy and they often give you misleading information. They may have proprietary drivers as binary blobs or they may have source code, but for a different version of the kernel than the one you have. So, by all means try this route. I will always try to find an open source driver for the task in hand.

There may be support in your kernel already: there are many thousands of drivers in mainline Linux and there are many vendor-specific drivers in the vendor kernels. Begin by running `make menuconfig` (or `xconfig`) and search for the product name or number. If you do not find an exact match, try more generic searches, allowing for the fact that most drivers handle a range of products from the same family. Next, try searching through the code in the drivers directory (`grep` is you friend here). Always make sure you are running the latest kernel for your board: later kernels generally have more device drivers.

If you still don't have a driver, you can try searching online and asking in the relevant forums to see if there is a driver for a different version of Linux. If you find one, you will have to backport it to your kernel. If the kernel versions are similar, it may be easy, but if they are more than 12 to 18 months apart, the chances are that the interfaces will have changed to the extent that you will have to rewrite a chunk of the driver to integrate it with your kernel. You may want to outsource this work. If all of the above fails, you will have to find a solution yourself.

Device drivers in user-space

Before you start writing a device driver, pause for a moment to consider whether it is really necessary. There are generic device drivers for many common types of device that allow you to interact with hardware directly from user space without having to write a line of kernel code. User space code is certainly easier to write and debug. It is also not covered by the GPL, although I don't feel that is a good reason in itself to do it this way.

They fall into two broad categories: those that you control through files in `sysfs`, including GPIO and LEDs, and serial buses that expose a generic interface through a device node, such as I2C.

GPIO

General Purpose Input/Output (GPIO) is the simplest form of digital interface since it gives you direct access to individual hardware pins, each of which can be configured as input or output. GPIO can even be used to create higher level interfaces such as I2C or SPI by manipulating each bit in the software, a technique that is called bit banging. The main limitation is the speed and accuracy of the software loops and the number of CPU cycles you want to dedicate to them. Generally speaking, it is hard to achieve timer accuracy better than a millisecond with kernels compiled with CONFIG_PREEMPT, and 100 microseconds with RT_PREEMPT, as we shall see in *Chapter 14, Real-time Programming*. More common use cases for GPIO are for reading push buttons and digital sensors and controlling LEDs, motors, and relays.

Most SoCs have a lot of GPIO bits which are grouped together in GPIO registers, usually 32 bits per register. On-chip GPIO bits are routed through to GPIO pins on the chip package via a multiplexer, known as a pin mux, which I will describe later. There may be additional GPIO bits available off-chip in the power management chip, and in dedicated GPIO extenders, connected through I2C or SPI buses. All this diversity is handled by a kernel subsystem known as gpiolib, which is not actually a library but the infrastructure GPIO drivers use to expose IO in a consistent way.

There are details about the implementation of gpiolib in the kernel source in Documentation/gpio and the drivers themselves are in drivers/gpio.

Applications can interact with gpiolib through files in the /sys/class/gpio directory. Here is an example of what you will see in there on a typical embedded board (a BeagleBone Black):

```
# ls /sys/class/gpio
export  gpiochip0  gpiochip32  gpiochip64  gpiochip96  unexport
```

The gpiochip0 to gpiochip96 directories represent four GPIO registers, each with 32 GPIO bits. If you look in one of the gpiochip directories, you will see the following:

```
# ls /sys/class/gpio/gpiochip96/
base  label  ngpio  power  subsystem  uevent
```

The file base contains the number of the first GPIO pin in the register and ngpio contains the number of bits in the register. In this case, gpiochip96/base is 96 and gpiochip96/ngpio is 32, which tells you that it contains GPIO bits 96 to 127. It is possible for there to be a gap between the last GPIO in one register and the first GPIO in the next.

To control a GPIO bit from user space, you first have to export it from kernel space, which you do by writing the GPIO number to `/sys/class/gpio/export`. This example shows the process for GPIO 48:

```
# echo 48 > /sys/class/gpio/export
# ls /sys/class/gpio
export       gpio48     gpiochip0    gpiochip32   gpiochip64
gpiochip96   unexport
```

Now there is a new directory, `gpio48`, which contains the files you need to control the pin. Note that if the GPIO bit is already claimed by the kernel, you will not be able to export it in this way.

The directory `gpio48` contains these files:

```
# ls /sys/class/gpio/gpio48
active_low   direction   edge   power   subsystem   uevent   value
```

The pin begins as an input. To change it to an output, write `out` to the `direction` file. The file `value` contains the current state of the pin, which is 0 for low and 1 for high. If it is an output, you can change the state by writing 0 or 1 to `value`. Sometimes, the meaning of low and high is reversed in hardware (hardware engineers enjoy doing that sort of thing), so writing 1 to `active_low` inverts the meaning so that a low voltage is reported as 1 in `value` and a high voltage as 0.

You can remove a GPIO from user space control by writing the GPIO number to `/sys/class/gpio/unexport`.

Handling interrupts from GPIO

In many cases, a GPIO input can be configured to generate an interrupt when it changes state, which allows you to wait for the interrupt rather than polling in an inefficient software loop. If the GPIO bit can generate interrupts, the file `edge` exists. Initially, it has the value `none`, meaning that it does not generate interrupts. To enable interrupts, you can set it to one of these values:

- **rising**: Interrupt on rising edge
- **falling**: Interrupt on falling edge
- **both**: Interrupt on both rising and falling edges
- **none**: No interrupts (default)

You can wait for an interrupt using the `poll()` function with POLLPRI as the event. If you want to wait for a rising edge on GPIO 48, you first enable interrupts:

```
# echo 48 > /sys/class/gpio/export
# echo rising > /sys/class/gpio/gpio48/edge
```

Then, you use `poll()` to wait for the change, as shown in this code example:

```c
#include <stdio.h>
#include <unistd.h>
#include <sys/types.h>
#include <sys/stat.h>
#include <fcntl.h>
#include <poll.h>

int main (int argc, char *argv[])
{
  int f;
  struct pollfd poll_fds [1];
  int ret;
  char value[4];
  int n;
  f = open("/sys/class/gpio/gpio48", O_RDONLY);
  if (f == -1) {
    perror("Can't open gpio48");
    return 1;
  }
  poll_fds[0].fd = f;
  poll_fds[0].events = POLLPRI | POLLERR;
  while (1) {
    printf("Waiting\n");
    ret = poll(poll_fds, 1, -1);
    if (ret > 0) {
        n = read(f, &value, sizeof(value));
        printf("Button pressed: read %d bytes, value=%c\n",
        n, value[0]);
    }
  }
  return 0;
}
```

LEDs

LEDs are often controlled though a GPIO pin, but there is another kernel subsystem that offers more specialized control specific to the purpose. The `leds` kernel subsystem adds the ability to set brightness, should the LED have that ability, and can handle LEDs connected in other ways than a simple GPIO pin. It can be configured to trigger the LED on an event such as block device access or just a heartbeat to show that the device is working. There is more information in `Documentation/leds/` and the drivers are in `drivers/leds/`.

As with GPIOs, LEDs are controlled through an interface in `sysfs`, in `/sys/class/leds`. The LEDs have names in the form `devicename:colour:function`, as shown here:

```
# ls /sys/class/leds
beaglebone:green:heartbeat    beaglebone:green:usr2
beaglebone:green:mmc0         beaglebone:green:usr3
```

This shows one individual LED:

```
# ls /sys/class/leds/beaglebone:green:usr2
brightness      max_brightness    subsystem      uevent
device          power             trigger
```

The `brightness` file controls the brightness of the LED and can be a number between 0 (off) and `max_brightness` (fully on). If the LED doesn't support intermediate brightness, any non-zero value turns it on and zero turns it off. The file `trigger` lists the events that trigger the LED to turn on. The list of triggers is implementation-dependent. Here is an example:

```
# cat /sys/class/leds/beaglebone:green:heartbeat/trigger
none mmc0 mmc1 timer oneshot [heartbeat] backlight gpio cpu0
default-on
```

The trigger currently selected is shown in square brackets. You can change it by writing one of the other triggers to the file. If you want to control the LED entirely through `brightness`, select `none`. If you set the trigger to `timer`, two extra files appear that allow you to set the on and off times in milliseconds:

```
# echo timer > /sys/class/leds/beaglebone:green:heartbeat/trigger
# ls /sys/class/leds/beaglebone:green:heartbeat
brightness  delay_on    max_brightness   subsystem    uevent
delay_off   device      power            trigger
# cat /sys/class/leds/beaglebone:green:heartbeat/delay_on
500
# cat /sys/class/leds/beaglebone:green:heartbeat/delay_off
500
#
```

If the LED has on-chip timer hardware, the blinking takes place without interrupting the CPU.

I2C

I2C is a simple low speed 2-wire bus that is common on embedded boards, typically used to access peripherals which are not on the SoC board such as display controllers, camera sensors, GPIO extenders, and the like. There is a related standard known as SMBus (system management bus) that is found on PCs, that is used to access temperature and voltage sensors. SMBus is a subset of I2C.

I2C is a master-slave protocol, with the master being one or more host controllers on the SoC. Slaves have a 7-bit address assigned by the manufacturer – read the data sheet – allowing up to 128 nodes per bus, but 16 are reserved, so only 112 nodes are allowed in practice. The bus speed is 100 KHz in standard mode, or up to 400 KHz in fast mode. The protocol allows read and write transactions between the master and slave of up to 32 bytes. Frequently, the first byte is used to specify a register on the peripheral and the remaining bytes are the data read from or written to that register.

There is one device node for each host controller, for example, this SoC has four:

```
# ls -l /dev/i2c*
crw-rw---- 1 root i2c 89, 0 Jan  1 00:18 /dev/i2c-0
crw-rw---- 1 root i2c 89, 1 Jan  1 00:18 /dev/i2c-1
crw-rw---- 1 root i2c 89, 2 Jan  1 00:18 /dev/i2c-2
crw-rw---- 1 root i2c 89, 3 Jan  1 00:18 /dev/i2c-3
```

The device interface provides a series of `ioctl` commands that query the host controller and send `read` and `write` commands to I2C slaves. There is a package named `i2c-tools` which uses this interface to provide basic command-line tools to interact with I2C devices. The tools are as follows:

- `i2cdetect`: This lists the I2C adapters and probes the bus
- `i2cdump`: This dumps data from all the registers of an I2C peripheral
- `i2cget`: This reads data from an I2C slave
- `i2cset`: This writes data to an I2C slave

The `i2c-tools` package is available in Buildroot and the Yocto Project, as well as most mainstream distributions. So long as you know the address and protocol of the slave, writing a user space program to talk to the device is straightforward:

```
#include <stdio.h>
#include <unistd.h>
#include <fcntl.h>
```

```
#include <i2c-dev.h>
#include <sys/ioctl.h>
#define I2C_ADDRESS 0x5d
#define CHIP_REVISION_REG 0x10

void main (void)
{
  int f_i2c;
  int val;

  /* Open the adapter and set the address of the I2C device */
  f_i2c = open ("/dev/i2c-1", O_RDWR);
  ioctl (f_i2c, I2C_SLAVE, I2C_ADDRESS);

  /* Read 16-bits of data from a register */
  val = i2c_smbus_read_word_data(f, CHIP_REVISION_REG);
  printf ("Sensor chip revision %d\n", val);
  close (f_i2c);
}
```

Note that the header `i2c-dev.h` is the one from the `i2c-tools` package, not the one from the Linux kernel headers. The `i2c_smbus_read_word_data()` function is written inline in `i2c-dev.h`.

There is more information about the Linux implementation of I2C in `Documentation/i2c/dev-interface`. The host controller drivers are in `drivers/i2c/busses`.

SPI

The serial peripheral interface bus is similar to I2C, but is a lot faster, up to the low MHz. The interface uses four wires with separate send and receive lines which allows it to operate in full duplex. Each chip on the bus is selected with a dedicated chip select line. It is commonly used to connect to touchscreen sensors, display controllers, and serial NOR flash devices.

As with I2C, it is a master-slave protocol, with most SoCs implementing one or more master host controllers. There is a generic SPI device driver which you can enable through the kernel configuration CONFIG_SPI_SPIDEV. It creates a device node for each SPI controller which allows you to access SPI chips from user space. The device nodes are named `spidev[bus].[chip select]`:

```
# ls -l /dev/spi*
crw-rw---- 1 root root 153, 0 Jan  1 00:29 /dev/spidev1.0
```

For examples of using the `spidev` interface, refer to the example code in `Documentation/spi`.

Writing a kernel device driver

Eventually, when you have exhausted all the user-space options above, you will find yourself having to write a device driver to access a piece of hardware attached to your device. While this is not the time or place to delve into details, it is worth considering the options. Character drivers are the most flexible and should cover 90% of all your needs; network devices apply if you are working with a network interface, and block devices are for mass storage. The task of writing a kernel driver is complex and beyond the scope of this book. There are some references at the end that will help you on your way. In this section, I want to outline the options available for interacting with a driver—a topic not normally covered—and show you the basic bones of a driver.

Designing a character device interface

The main character device interface is based on a stream of bytes, as you would have with a serial port. However, many devices don't fit this description: a controller for a robot arm needs functions to move and rotate each joint, for example. Luckily, there are other ways to communicate with device drivers that just read(2) and write(2):

- ioctl: The ioctl function allows you to pass two arguments to your driver which can have any meaning you like. By convention, the first argument is a command which selects one of several functions in your driver, and the second is a pointer to a structure which serves as a container for the input and output parameters. This is a blank canvas that allows you to design any program interface you like and it is pretty common when the driver and application are closely linked and written by the same team. However, ioctl is deprecated in the kernel and you will find it hard to get any drivers with new uses of ioctl accepted upstream. The kernel maintainers dislike ioctl because it makes kernel code and application code too interdependent, and it is hard to keep both of them in step across kernel versions and architectures.

- sysfs: This is the preferred way now, a good example being the GPIO interface described earlier. The advantages are that it is self-documenting, so long as you choose descriptive names for the files. It is also scriptable because the file contents are ASCII strings. On the other hand, the requirement for each file to contain a single value makes it hard to achieve atomicity if you need to change more than one value at a time. For example, if you want to set two values and then initiate an action, you would need to write to three files: two for the inputs and a third to trigger the action. Even then, there is no guarantee that the other two files have not been changed by someone else. Conversely, ioctl passes all its arguments in a structure in a single function call.

- `mmap`: You can get direct access to kernel buffers and hardware registers by mapping kernel memory into user-space, bypassing the kernel. You may still need some kernel code to handle interrupts and DMA. There is a subsystem that encapsulates this idea, known as `uio`, short for user I/O. There is more documentation in `Documentation/DocBook/uio-howto`, and there are example drivers in `drivers/uio`.

- `sigio`: You can send a signal from a driver using the kernel function `kill_fasync()` to notify applications of an event such as input becoming ready or an interrupt being received. By convention, signal SIGIO is used, but it could be anyone. You can see some examples in the UIO driver, `drivers/uio/uio.c`, and in the RTC driver, `drivers/char/rtc.c`. The main problem is that it is difficult to write reliable signal handlers and so it remains a little-used facility.

- `debugfs`: This is another pseudo filesystem that represents kernel data as files and directories, similar to `proc` and `sysfs`. The main distinction is that `debugfs` must not contain information that is needed for the normal operation of the system; it is for debug and trace information only. It is mounted as `mount -t debugfs debug /sys/kernel/debug`.

  There is a good description of `debugfs` in the kernel documentation, `Documentation/filesystems/debugfs.txt`.

- `proc`: The `proc` filesystem is deprecated for all new code unless it relates to processes, which was the original intended purpose for the filesystem. However, the you can use `proc` to publish any information you choose. And, unlike `sysfs` and `debugfs`, it is available to non-GPL modules.

- `netlink`: This is a socket protocol family. AF_NETLINK creates a socket that links kernel space to user-space. It was originally created so that network tools could communicate with the Linux network code to access the routing tables and other details. It is also used by udev to pass events from the kernel to the udev daemon. It is very rarely used in general device drivers.

There are many examples of all of the preceding filesystem in the kernel source code and you can design really interesting interfaces to your driver code. The only universal rule is the *principle of least astonishment*. In other words, application writers using your driver should find that everything works in a logical way with no quirks or oddities.

Anatomy of a device driver

It's time to draw some threads together by looking at the code for a simple device driver.

The source code is provided for a device driver named dummy which creates four devices that are accessed through /dev/dummy0 to /dev/dummy3. This is the complete code for the driver:

```c
#include <linux/kernel.h>
#include <linux/module.h>
#include <linux/init.h>
#include <linux/fs.h>
#include <linux/device.h>
#define DEVICE_NAME "dummy"
#define MAJOR_NUM 42
#define NUM_DEVICES 4

static struct class *dummy_class;
static int dummy_open(struct inode *inode, struct file *file)
{
  pr_info("%s\n", __func__);
  return 0;
}

static int dummy_release(struct inode *inode, struct file *file)
{
  pr_info("%s\n", __func__);
  return 0;
}

static ssize_t dummy_read(struct file *file,
  char *buffer, size_t length, loff_t * offset)
{
  pr_info("%s %u\n", __func__, length);
  return 0;
}

static ssize_t dummy_write(struct file *file,
  const char *buffer, size_t length, loff_t * offset)
{
  pr_info("%s %u\n", __func__, length);
  return length;
}
```

```
struct file_operations dummy_fops = {
  .owner = THIS_MODULE,
  .open = dummy_open,
  .release = dummy_release,
  .read = dummy_read,
  .write = dummy_write,
};

int __init dummy_init(void)
{
  int ret;
  int i;
  printk("Dummy loaded\n");
  ret = register_chrdev(MAJOR_NUM, DEVICE_NAME, &dummy_fops);
  if (ret != 0)
    return ret;
  dummy_class = class_create(THIS_MODULE, DEVICE_NAME);
  for (i = 0; i < NUM_DEVICES; i++) {
    device_create(dummy_class, NULL,
    MKDEV(MAJOR_NUM, i), NULL, "dummy%d", i);
  }
  return 0;
}

void __exit dummy_exit(void)
{
  int i;
  for (i = 0; i < NUM_DEVICES; i++) {
    device_destroy(dummy_class, MKDEV(MAJOR_NUM, i));
  }
  class_destroy(dummy_class);
  unregister_chrdev(MAJOR_NUM, DEVICE_NAME);
  printk("Dummy unloaded\n");
}

module_init(dummy_init);
module_exit(dummy_exit);
MODULE_LICENSE("GPL");
MODULE_AUTHOR("Chris Simmonds");
MODULE_DESCRIPTION("A dummy driver");
```

At the end of the code, the macros `module_init` and `module_exit` specify the functions to be called when the module is loaded and unloaded. The other three add some basic information about the module which can be retrieved from the compiled kernel module using the `modinfo` command.

When the module is loaded, the `dummy_init()` function is called.

You can see the point at which it becomes a character device by calling `register_chrdev`, passing a pointer to `struct file_operations` containing pointers to the four functions that the driver implements. While `register_chrdev` tells the kernel that there is a driver with a major number of 42, it doesn't say anything about the type of driver, and so it will not create an entry in `/sys/class`. Without an entry in `/sys/class`, the device manager cannot create device nodes. So, the next few lines of code create a device class, `dummy`, and four devices of that class called `dummy0` to `dummy3`. The result is the `/sys/class/dummy` directory, containing the `dummy0` to `dummy3` subdirectories, each containing a file, `dev`, with the major and minor numbers of the device. This is all that a device manager needs to create device nodes, `/dev/dummy0` to `/dev/dummy3`.

The `exit` function has to release the resources claimed by the `init` function which, here, means freeing up the device class and major number.

The file operation for this driver are implemented by `dummy_open()`, `dummy_read()`, `dummy_write()`, and `dummy_release()`, and are called when a user space program calls `open(2)`, `read(2)`, `write(2)`, and `close(2)`. They just print a kernel message so that you can see that they were called. You can demonstrate this from the command line using the `echo` command:

```
# echo hello > /dev/dummy0

[ 6479.741192] dummy_open
[ 6479.742505] dummy_write 6
[ 6479.743008] dummy_release
```

In this case, the messages appear because I was logged on to the console, and kernel messages are printed to the console by default.

The full source code for this driver is less than 100 lines, but it is enough to illustrate how the linkage between a device node and driver code works, how the device class is created, allowing a device manager to create device nodes automatically when the driver is loaded, and how data is moved between user and kernel spaces. Next, you need to build it.

Compile and load

At this point you have some driver code that you want to compile and test on your target system. You can copy it into the kernel source tree and modify makefiles to build it, or you can compile it as a module out of tree. Let's start by building out of tree.

You need a simple makefile which uses the kernel build system to do the hard work:

```
LINUXDIR := $(HOME)/MELP/build/linux

obj-m := dummy.o
all:
        make ARCH=arm CROSS_COMPILE=arm-cortex_a8-linux-gnueabihf- \
          -C $(LINUXDIR) M=$(shell pwd)
clean:
        make -C $(LINUXDIR) M=$(shell pwd) clean
```

Set LINUXDIR to the directory of the kernel for your target device that you will be running the module on. The code obj-m := dummy.o will invoke the kernel build rule to take the source file, dummy.c and create kernel module, dummy.ko. Note that kernel modules are not binary compatible between kernel releases and configurations, the module will only load on the kernel it was compiled with.

The end result of the build is the kernel dummy.ko which you can copy to the target and load as shown in the next section.

If you want to build a driver in the kernel source tree, the procedure is quite simple. Choose a directory appropriate to the type of driver you have. The driver is a basic character device, so I would put dummy.c in drivers/char. Then, edit the makefile in that directory and add a line to build the driver unconditionally as a module, as follows:

```
obj-m   += dummy.o
```

Or add the following line this to build it unconditionally as a built-in:

```
obj-y   += dummy.o
```

If you want to make the driver optional, you can add a menu option to the Kconfig file and make the compilation conditional on the configuration option, as I described in *Chapter 4, Porting and Configuring the Kernel*, when describing the kernel configuration.

Loading kernel modules

You can load, unload and list modules using the simple `insmod`, `lsmod`, and `rmmod` commands. Here they are shown loading the dummy driver:

```
# insmod /lib/modules/4.1.10/kernel/drivers/dummy.ko
# lsmod
dummy 1248 0 - Live 0xbf009000 (O)
# rmmod dummy
```

If the module is placed in a subdirectory in `/lib/modules/<kernel release>`, as in the example, you can create a modules dependency database using the command `depmod`:

```
# depmod -a
# ls /lib/modules/4.1.10/
kernel                   modules.builtin.bin    modules.order
modules.alias            modules.dep            modules.softdep
modules.alias.bin        modules.dep.bin        modules.symbols
modules.builtin          modules.devname        modules.symbols.bin
```

The information in the `module.*` files is used by the command `modprobe` to locate a module by name rather than the full path. `modprobe` has many other features which are described in the manual.

The module dependency information is also used by device managers, `udev` in particular. When new hardware is detected, for example a new USB device, the `udevd` daemon is alerted and passed the vendor, and product IDs are read from the hardware. `udevd` scans the module dependency files looking for a module that has registered those IDs. If one is found, it is loaded using `modprobe`.

Discovering hardware configuration

The dummy driver demonstrates the structure of a device driver, but it lacks interaction with real hardware since it only manipulates memory structures. Device drivers are usually written to interact with hardware and part of that is being able to discover the hardware in the first place, bearing in mind that it may be at different addresses in different configurations.

In some cases, the hardware provides the information itself. Devices on a discoverable bus such as PCI or USB have a query mode which returns resource requirements and a unique identifier. The kernel matches the identifier and possibly other characteristics with the device drivers, and marries them up.

However, most of the hardware blocks on an SoC do not have such identifiers. You have to provide the information yourself in the form of a device tree or as C structures known as platform data.

In the standard driver model for Linux, device drivers register themselves with the appropriate subsystem: PCI, USB, open firmware (device tree), platform device, and so on. The registration includes an identifier and a callback function called a probe function that is called if there is a match between the ID of the hardware and the ID of the driver. For PCI and USB, the ID is based on the vendor and the product IDs of the devices, for device tree and platform devices, it is a name (an ASCII string).

Device trees

I gave you an introduction to device trees in *Chapter 3, All About Bootloaders*. Here, I want to show you how the Linux device drivers hook up with that information.

As an example, I will use the ARM Versatile board, `arch/arm/boot/dts/versatile-ab.dts`, for which the Ethernet adapter is defined here:

```
net@10010000 {
  compatible = "smsc,lan91c111";
  reg = <0x10010000 0x10000>;
  interrupts = <25>;
};
```

Platform data

In the absence of device tree support, there is a fallback method of describing hardware using C structures, known as platform data.

Each piece of hardware is described by `struct platform_device`, which has a name and a pointer to an array of resources. The type of the resource is determined by flags, which include the following:

- `IORESOURCE_MEM`: The physical address of a region of memory
- `IORESOURCE_IO`: The physical address or port number of IO registers
- `IORESOURCE_IRQ`: The interrupt number

Here is an example of the platform data for an Ethernet controller taken from `arch/arm/mach-versatile/core.c`, which has been edited for clarity:

```
#define VERSATILE_ETH_BASE      0x10010000
#define IRQ_ETH                 25
static struct resource smc91x_resources[] = {
  [0] = {
    .start        = VERSATILE_ETH_BASE,
    .end          = VERSATILE_ETH_BASE + SZ_64K - 1,
    .flags        = IORESOURCE_MEM,
  },
  [1] = {
    .start        = IRQ_ETH,
    .end          = IRQ_ETH,
    .flags        = IORESOURCE_IRQ,
  },
};
static struct platform_device smc91x_device = {
  .name          = "smc91x",
  .id            = 0,
  .num_resources = ARRAY_SIZE(smc91x_resources),
  .resource      = smc91x_resources,
};
```

It has a memory area of 64 KiB and an interrupt. The platform data has to be registered with the kernel, usually when the board is initialized:

```
void __init versatile_init(void)
{
  platform_device_register(&versatile_flash_device);
  platform_device_register(&versatile_i2c_device);
  platform_device_register(&smc91x_device);
  [ ...]
```

Linking hardware with device drivers

You have seen in the preceding section how an Ethernet adapter is described using a device tree and using platform data. The corresponding driver code is in `drivers/net/ethernet/smsc/smc91x.c` and it works with both the device tree and platform data. Here is the initialization code, once again edited for clarity:

```
static const struct of_device_id smc91x_match[] = {
    { .compatible = "smsc,lan91c94", },
    { .compatible = "smsc,lan91c111", },
```

```
    {},
};
MODULE_DEVICE_TABLE(of, smc91x_match);
static struct platform_driver smc_driver = {
   .probe          = smc_drv_probe,
   .remove         = smc_drv_remove,
   .driver         = {
     .name   = "smc91x",
     .of_match_table = of_match_ptr(smc91x_match),
   },
};
static int __init smc_driver_init(void)
{
   return platform_driver_register(&smc_driver);
}
static void __exit smc_driver_exit(void) \
{
   platform_driver_unregister(&smc_driver);
}
module_init(smc_driver_init);
module_exit(smc_driver_exit);
```

When the driver is initialized, it calls `platform_driver_register()`, pointing to `struct platform_driver`, in which there is a callback to a probe function, a driver name, `smc91x`, and a pointer to `struct of_device_id`.

If this driver has been configured by the device tree, the kernel will look for a match between the `compatible` property in the device tree node and the string pointed to by the compatible structure element. For each match, it calls the `probe` function.

On the other hand, if it was configured through platform data, the `probe` function will be called for each match on the string pointed to by `driver.name`.

The `probe` function extracts information about the interface:

```
static int smc_drv_probe(struct platform_device *pdev)
{
   struct smc91x_platdata *pd = dev_get_platdata(&pdev->dev);
   const struct of_device_id *match = NULL;
   struct resource *res, *ires;
   int irq;

   res = platform_get_resource(pdev, IORESOURCE_MEM, 0);
   ires = platform_get_resource(pdev, IORESOURCE_IRQ, 0);
   [...]
```

```
        addr = ioremap(res->start, SMC_IO_EXTENT);
        irq = ires->start;
        [...]
   }
```

The calls to `platform_get_resource()` extract the memory and `irq` information from either the device tree or the platform data. It is up to the driver to map the memory and install the interrupt handler. The third parameter, which is zero in both of the previous cases, comes into play if there is more than one resource of that particular type.

Device trees allow you to configure more than just basic memory ranges and interrupts, however. There is a section of code in the `probe` function that extracts optional parameters from the device tree. In this snippet, it gets the `register-io-width` property:

```
   match = of_match_device(of_match_ptr(smc91x_match), &pdev->dev);
   if (match) {
     struct device_node *np = pdev->dev.of_node;
     u32 val;
     [...]
     of_property_read_u32(np, "reg-io-width", &val);
     [...]
   }
```

For most drivers, specific bindings are documented in `Documentation/devicetree/bindings`. For this particular driver, the information is in `Documentation/devicetree/bindings/net/smsc911x.txt`.

The main thing to remember here is that drivers should register a `probe` function and enough information for the kernel to call the `probe` as it finds matches with the hardware it knows about. The linkage between the hardware described by the device tree and the device driver is through the `compatible` property. The linkage between platform data and a driver is through the name.

Additional reading

The following resources have further information about the topics introduced in this chapter:

- *Linux Device Drivers, 4th edition*, by *Jessica McKellar, Alessandro Rubini, Jonathan Corbet*, and *Greg Kroah-Hartman*. This is not published at the time of writing, but if it is as good as the predecessor, it will be a good choice. However, the 3rd edition is too out of date to recommend.

- *Linux Kernel Development, 3rd edition* by *Robert Love*, Addison-Wesley Professional; (July 2, 2010) ISBN-10: 0672329468

- *Linux Weekly News*, lwn.net.

Summary

Device drivers have the job of handling devices, usually physical hardware but sometimes virtual interfaces, and presenting it to higher levels in a consistent and useful way. Linux device drivers fall into three broad categories: the character, the block, and the network. Of the three, the character driver interface is the most flexible and therefore, the most common. Linux drivers fit into a framework known as the driver model, which is exposed through sysfs. Pretty much the entire state of the devices and drivers is visible in /sys.

Each embedded system has its own unique set of hardware interfaces and requirements. Linux provides drivers for most standard interfaces, and by selecting the right kernel configuration, you can get the device operational very quickly. That leaves you with the non-standard components for which you will have to add your own device support.

In some cases, you can sidestep the issue by using generic drivers for GPIO, I2C, and so on, and write user space code to do the work. I recommend this as a starting point as it gives you the chance to get familiar with the hardware without writing kernel code. Writing kernel drivers is not particularly difficult but, if you do, you need to code carefully so as to not compromise the stability of the system.

I have talked about writing kernel driver code: if you go down that route, you will inevitably want to know how to check whether or not it is working correctly and detect any bugs. I will cover that topic in *Chapter 12, Debugging with GDB*.

The next chapter is all about user space initialization and the different options you have for the init program, from the simple BusyBox to the complex systemd.

Starting up - the init Program

I looked at how the kernel boots up to the point that it launches the first program, init, in *Chapter 4, Porting and Configuring the Kernel* and in *Chapter 5, Building a Root Filesystem* and *Chapter 6, Selecting a Build System*, I looked at creating root filesystems of varying complexity, all of which contained an init program. Now it is time to look at the init program in more detail and discover why it is so important to the rest of the system.

There are many possible implementations of init. I will describe the three main ones in this chapter: BusyBox init, System V init, and systemd. For each one, I will give an overview of how it works and the types of system it suits best. Part of that is balancing the trade-off between complexity and flexibility.

After the kernel has booted

We saw in *Chapter 4, Porting and Configuring the Kernel*, how the kernel bootstrap code seeks to find a root filesystem, either initramfs or a filesystem specified by root= on the kernel command line, and then to execute a program which, by default, is /init for initramfs, and /sbin/init for a regular filesystem. The init program has root privilege and since it is the first process to run, it has a process ID (PID) of 1. If, for some reason, init cannot be started, the kernel will panic.

The `init` program is the ancestor of all other processes, as shown here by the `pstree` command, which is part of the `psmisc` package in most distrubutions:

```
# pstree -gn

init(1)-+-syslogd(63)
        |-klogd(66)
        |-dropbear(99)
        `-sh(100)---pstree(109)
```

The job of the `init` program is to take control of the system and set it running. It may be as simple as a shell command running a shell script – there is an example at the start of *Chapter 5, Building a Root Filesystem* — but, in the majority of cases, you will be using a dedicated `init` daemon. The tasks it has to perform are as follows:

- At boot, it starts daemon programs, configures system parameters and the other things needed to get the system into a working state.
- Optionally, it launches daemons, such as `getty` on terminals which allow a login shell.
- It adopts processes that become orphaned as a result of their immediate parent terminating and there being no other processes in the thread group.
- It responds to any of `init`'s immediate children terminating by catching the signal `SIGCHLD` and collecting the return value to prevent them becoming zombie processes. I will talk more about zombies in *Chapter 10, Learning About Processes and Threads*.
- Optionally, it restarts those daemons that have terminated.
- It handles system shutdown.

In other words, `init` manages the lifecycle of the system, from boot up to shutdown. The current thinking is that `init` is well placed to handle other runtime events such as new hardware and the loading and unloading of modules. This is what `systemd` does.

Introducing the init programs

The three `init` programs that you are most likely to encounter in embedded devices are BusyBox `init`, System V `init`, and `systemd`. Buildroot has options to build all three with BusyBox `init` as the default. The Yocto Project allows you to choose between System V `init` and `systemd`, with System V `init` the default.

The following table gives some metrics to compare the three:

	BusyBox init	System V init	systemd
Complexity	Low	Medium	High
Boot-up speed	Fast	Slow	Medium
Required shell	ash	ash or bash	None
Number of executables	0	4	50(*)
libc	Any	Any	glibc
Size (MiB)	0	0.1	34(*)

(*) Based on the Buildroot configuration of `system`.

Broadly speaking, there is an increase in flexibility and complexity as you go from BusyBox `init` to `systemd`.

BusyBox init

BusyBox has a minimal `init` program that uses a configuration file, `/etc/inittab`, to define rules to start programs at boot up and to stop them at shutdown. Usually, the actual work is done by shell scripts which, by convention, are placed in the `/etc/init.d` directory.

`init` begins by reading the configuration file, `/etc/inittab`. This contains a list of programs to run, one per line, with this format:

```
<id>::<action>:<program>
```

The role of these parameters is as follows:

- `id`: The controlling terminal for the command
- `action`: The conditions to run this command, as shown in the following paragraph
- `program`: The program to run

The actions are as follows:

- `sysinit`: Run the program when `init` starts, before any of the other types of actions.
- `respawn`: Run the program and restart it if it terminates. It is used to run a program as a daemon.

- `askfirst`: This is the same as `respawn`, but prints the message **Please press Enter to activate this console** to the console and runs the program after *Enter* has been pressed. It is used to start an interactive shell on a terminal without prompting for a user name or password.
- `once`: Run the program once but do not attempt to restart it if it terminates.
- `wait`: Run the program and wait for it to complete.
- `restart`: Run the program when `init` receives the signal `SIGHUP`, indicating that it should reload the `inittab` file.
- `ctrlaltdel`: Run the program when `init` receives the signal `SIGINT`, usually as a result of pressing *Ctrl + Alt + Del* on the console.
- `shutdown`: Run the program when `init` shuts down.

Here is a small example that mounts `proc` and `sysfs` and runs a shell on a serial interface:

```
null::sysinit:/bin/mount -t proc proc /proc
null::sysinit:/bin/mount -t sysfs sysfs /sys
console::askfirst:-/bin/sh
```

For simple projects in which you want to launch a small number of daemons and perhaps start a login shell on a serial terminal, it is easy to write the scripts manually, and this is appropriate if you are creating a **RYO (roll your own)** embedded Linux. However, you will find that hand-written `init` scripts rapidly become unmaintainable as the number of things to be configured increases. They tend not to be very modular and so need updating each time a new component is added.

Buildroot init scripts

Buildroot has been making effective use of BusyBox `init` for many years. Buildroot has two scripts in `/etc/init.d` named `rcS` and `rcK`. The first one starts at boot-up and iterates over all the scripts beginning with a capital `S` followed by two digits, and runs them in numerical order. These are the start scripts. The `rcK` script is run at shutdown and iterates over all the scripts beginning with a capital `K` followed by two digits, and runs them in numerical order. These are the kill scripts.

With this in place, it becomes easy for Buildroot packages to supply their own start and kill scripts, using the two digit number to impose the order in which they should be run, and so the system becomes extensible. If you are using Buildroot, this is transparent. If not, you could use it as a model for writing your own BusyBox `init` scripts.

System V init

This init program was inspired by the one from UNIX System V, and so dates back to the mid 1980s. The version most often found in Linux distributions was written initially by Miquel van Smoorenburg. Until recently, it was considered the way to boot Linux, obviously including embedded systems, and BusyBox init is a trimmed down version of System V init.

Compared to BusyBox init, System V init has two advantages. Firstly, the boot scripts are written in a well-known, modular format, making it easy to add new packages at build time or runtime. Secondly, it has the concept of runlevels, which allow a collection of programs to be started or stopped in one go, by switching from one runlevel to another.

There are 8 runlevels numbered from 0 to 6, plus S:

- **S**: Single user mode
- **0**: Halt the system
- **1 to 5**: General use
- **6**: Reboot the system

Levels 1 to 5 can be used as you please. On desktop Linux distributions, they are conventionally assigned as follows:

- **1**: Single user
- **2**: Multi-user with no network configuration
- **3**: Multi-user with network configuration
- **4**: Not used
- **5**: Multi-user with graphical login

The init program starts the default runlevel given by the initdefault line in /etc/inittab. You can change the runlevel at runtime using the command telinit [runlevel] which sends a message to init. You can find the current runlevel, and the previous one, by using the runlevel command. Here is an example:

```
# runlevel
N 5
# telinit 3
INIT: Switching to runlevel: 3
# runlevel
5 3
```

On the first line, the output from `runlevel` is N 5, meaning that there is no previous runlevel because the `runlevel` has not changed since booting, and the current `runlevel` is 5. After changing the `runlevel`, the output is 5 3 showing that there has been a transition from 5 to 3. The `halt` and `reboot` commands switch to runlevels of 0 and 6 respectively. You can override the default `runlevel` by giving a different one on the kernel command line as a single digit from 0 to 6, or S for single user mode. For example, to force the `runlevel` to be for a single user, you would append S to the kernel command line and it would look something like this:

```
console=ttyAMA0 root=/dev/mmcblk1p2 S
```

Each runlevel has a number of scripts that stop things, called `kill` scripts, and another group that starts things, the `start` scripts. When entering a new `runlevel`, `init` first runs the `kill` scripts and then the `start` scripts. Running daemons which have neither a `start` script nor a `kill` script in the new `runlevel` are sent a SIGTERM signal. In other words, the default action on switching `runlevel` is to terminate the daemons unless told to do otherwise.

In truth, runlevels are not used that much in embedded Linux: most devices simply boot to the default `runlevel` and stay there. I have a feeling that it is partly because most people are not aware of them.

Runlevels are a simple and convenient way to switch between modes, for example, from production to maintenance mode.

System V `init` is an option in Buildroot and the Yocto Project. In both cases, the init scripts have been stripped of any bash specifics, so they work with the BusyBox ash shell. However, Buildroot cheats by replacing the BusyBox `init` program with SystemV `init` and adding `inittab` that mimics the behavior of BusyBox. Buildroot does not implement runlevels except that switching to levels 0 or 6 halts or reboots the system.

Next, let's look at some of the details. The following examples are taken from the fido version of the Yocto Project. Other distributions may implement the `init` scripts a little differently.

inittab

The `init` program begins by reading `/etc/inttab`, which contains entries that define what happens at each `runlevel`. The format is an extended version of the BusyBox `inittab` that I described in the preceding section, which is not surprising because BusyBox borrowed it from System V in the first place!

The format of each line in inittab is as follows:

```
id:runlevels:action:process
```

The fields are shown here:

- id: A unique identifier of up to four characters.
- runlevels: The runlevels for which this entry should be executed. (This was left blank in the BusyBox inittab)
- action: One of the keywords given as follows.
- process: The command to run.

The actions are the same as for BusyBox init: sysinit, respawn, once, wait, restart, ctrlaltdel, and shutdown. However, System V init does not have askfirst, which is specific to BusyBox.

As an example, this is the complete inttab supplied by the Yocto Project target core-image-minimal:

```
# /etc/inittab: init(8) configuration.
# $Id: inittab,v 1.91 2002/01/25 13:35:21 miquels Exp $

# The default runlevel.
id:5:initdefault:

# Boot-time system configuration/initialization script.
# This is run first except when booting in emergency (-b) mode.
si::sysinit:/etc/init.d/rcS

# What to do in single-user mode.
~~:S:wait:/sbin/sulogin
# /etc/init.d executes the S and K scripts upon change
# of runlevel.
#
# Runlevel 0 is halt.
# Runlevel 1 is single-user.
# Runlevels 2-5 are multi-user.
# Runlevel 6 is reboot.

l0:0:wait:/etc/init.d/rc 0
l1:1:wait:/etc/init.d/rc 1
l2:2:wait:/etc/init.d/rc 2
l3:3:wait:/etc/init.d/rc 3
l4:4:wait:/etc/init.d/rc 4
```

```
15:5:wait:/etc/init.d/rc 5
16:6:wait:/etc/init.d/rc 6
# Normally not reached, but fallthrough in case of emergency.
z6:6:respawn:/sbin/sulogin
AMA0:12345:respawn:/sbin/getty 115200 ttyAMA0
# /sbin/getty invocations for the runlevels.
#
# The "id" field MUST be the same as the last
# characters of the device (after "tty").
#
# Format:
#   <id>:<runlevels>:<action>:<process>
#

1:2345:respawn:/sbin/getty 38400 tty1
```

The fist entry, id:5:initdefault, sets the default runlevel to 5. The next entry, si::sysinit:/etc/init.d/rcS, runs the script rcS at boot up. There will be more about this later. A little further on, there is a group of six entries beginning with l0:0:wait:/etc/init.d/rc 0. They run the script /etc/init.d/rc each time there is a change in the runlevel: this script is responsible for processing the start and kill scripts. There is an entry for runlevel S which runs the single-user login program.

Towards the end of inittab, there are two entries that run a getty daemon to generate a login prompt on the devices /dev/ttyAMA0 and /dev/tty1 when entering runlevels 1 through to 5, thereby allowing you to log on and get an interactive shell:

```
AMA0:12345:respawn:/sbin/getty 115200 ttyAMA0
1:2345:respawn:/sbin/getty 38400 tty1
```

The device ttyAMA0 is the serial console on the ARM Versatile board we are emulating with QEMU, it will be different for other development boards. Tty1 is a virtual console which is often mapped to a graphical screen if you have built your kernel with CONFIG_FRAMEBUFFER_CONSOLE or VGA_CONSOLE. Desktop Linux usually spawns six getty processes on virtual terminals 1 to 6, which you can select with the key combination *Ctrl + Alt + F1* through *Ctrl + Alt + F6*, with virtual terminal 7 reserved for the graphical screen. Virtual terminals are seldom used on embedded devices.

The script /etc/init.d/rcS that is run by the sysinit entry does little more than enter runlevel S:

```
#!/bin/sh

[...]
exec /etc/init.d/rc S
```

Hence, the first run level entered is s, followed by the default runlevel of 5. Note that runlevel s is not recorded and is never displayed as a prior runlevel by the runlevel command.

The init.d scripts

Each component that needs to respond to a runlevel change has a script in /etc/ init.d to perform that change. The script should expect two parameters: start and stop. I will give an example of this later.

The runlevel handling script, /etc/init.d/rc, takes the runlevel it is switching to as a parameter. For each runlevel, there is a directory named rc<runlevel>.d:

```
# ls -d /etc/rc*
/etc/rc0.d  /etc/rc2.d  /etc/rc4.d  /etc/rc6.d
/etc/rc1.d  /etc/rc3.d  /etc/rc5.d  /etc/rcS.d
```

There you will find a set of scripts beginning with a capital s followed by two digits and you may also find scripts beginning with a capital k. These are start and kill scripts: Buildroot uses the same idea, borrowed from here:

```
# ls /etc/rc5.d
S01networking    S20hwclock.sh    S99rmnologin.sh S99stop-bootlogd
S15mountnfs.sh   S20syslog
```

These are in fact symbolic links back to the appropriate script in init.d. The rc script runs all the scripts beginning with a K first, adding the stop parameter , and then runs those beginning with an S adding the start parameter . Once again, the two digit code is there to impart the order in which the scripts should run.

Adding a new daemon

Imagine that you have a program named simpleserver which is written as a traditional Unix daemon, in other words, it forks and runs in the background. You will need an init.d script like this:

```
#! /bin/sh

case "$1" in
  start)
    echo "Starting simpelserver"
```

```
        start-stop-daemon -S -n simpleserver -a /usr/bin/simpleserver
        ;;
    stop)
        echo "Stopping simpleserver"
        start-stop-daemon -K -n simpleserver
        ;;
    *)
        echo "Usage: $0 {start|stop}"
    exit 1
esac

exit 0
```

Start-stop-daemon is a helper function that makes it easier to manipulate background processes such as this. It originally came from the Debian installer package, dpkg, but most embedded systems use the one from BusyBox. It starts the daemon with the -S parameter, making sure that there is never more than one instance running at any one time and it finds the daemon by name with -K and sends a signal, SIGTERM, by default. Place this script in /etc/init.d/simpleserver and make it executable.

Then, add symlinks from each of the run levels that you want to run this program from, in this case, only the default runlevel, 5:

```
# cd /etc/init.d/rc5.d
# ln -s ../init.d/simpleserver S99simpleserver
```

The number 99 means that this will be one of the last programs to be started. Bear in mind that there may be other links beginning S99, in which case the rc script will just run them in lexical order.

It is rare in embedded devices to have to worry too much about shutdown operations, but if there is something that needs to be done, add kill symlinks to levels 0 and 6:

```
# cd /etc/init.d/rc0.d
# ln -s ../init.d/simpleserver K01simpleserver
# cd /etc/init.d/rc6.d
# ln -s ../init.d/simpleserver K01simpleserver
```

Starting and stopping services

You can interact with the scripts in /etc/init.d by calling them directly with, for example, the syslog script which controls the syslogd and klogd daemons:

```
# /etc/init.d/syslog --help
Usage: syslog { start | stop | restart }

# /etc/init.d/syslog stop
Stopping syslogd/klogd: stopped syslogd (pid 198)
stopped klogd (pid 201)
done

# /etc/init.d/syslog start
Starting syslogd/klogd: done
```

All scripts implement start and stop and should implement help. Some implement status as well, which will tell you whether the service is running or not. Mainstream distributions that still use System V init have a command named service to start and stop services and hide the details of calling the scripts directly.

systemd

systemd defines itself as a system and service manager. The project was initiated in 2010 by Lennart Poettering and Kay Sievers to create an integrated set of tools for managing a Linux system including an init daemon. It also includes device management (udev) and logging, among other things. Some would say that it is not just an init program, it is a way of life. It is state of the art, and still evolving rapidly. systemd is common on desktop and server Linux distributions, and is becoming popular on embedded Linux systems too, especially on more complex devices. So, how is it better than System V init for embedded systems?

- Configuration is simpler and more logical (once you understand it), rather than the sometimes convoluted shell scripts of System V init, systemd has unit configuration files to set parameters

- There are explicit dependencies between services rather than a two digit code that merely sets the sequence in which the scripts are run

- It is easy to set the permissions and resource limits for each service, which is important for security

- systemd can monitor services and restart them if needed

- There are watchdogs for each service and for systemd itself

- Services are started in parallel, reducing boot time

A complete description of systemd is neither possible nor appropriate here. As with System V init, I will focus on embedded use-cases, with examples based on the configuration produced by Yocto Fido, which has systemd version 219. I will give a quick overview and then show you some specific examples.

Building systemd with the Yocto Project and Buildroot

The default init in Yocto Fido is System V. To select systemd, add these lines to your configuration, for example, in conf/local.conf:

```
DISTRO_FEATURES_append = " systemd"
VIRTUAL-RUNTIME_init_manager = "systemd"
```

Note that the leading space is important! Then rebuild.

Buildroot has systemd as the third init option. It requires glibc as the C library, and kernel version 3.7 or later with a particular set of configuration options enabled. There is a complete list of dependencies in the README file in the top level of the systemd source code.

Introducing targets, services, and units

Before I describe how systemd init works, I need to introduce these three key concepts.

Firstly, a target is a group of services, similar to, but more general than, a SystemV runlevel. There is a default target which is the group of services that are started at boot time.

Secondly, a service is a daemon that can be started and stopped, very much like a SystemV service.

Finally, a unit is a configuration file that describes a target, a service, and several other things. Units are text files that contain properties and values.

You can change states and find out what is going on by using the systemctl command.

Units

The basic item of configuration is the unit file. Unit files are found in three different places:

- `/etc/systemd/system`: Local configuration
- `/run/systemd/system`: Runtime configuration
- `/lib/systemd/system`: Distribution-wide configuration

When looking for a unit, `systemd` searches the directories in that order, stopping as soon as it finds a match, allowing you to override the behavior of a distribution-wide unit by placing a unit of the same name in `/etc/systemd/system`. You can disable a unit completely by creating a local file that is empty or linked to `/dev/null`.

All unit files begin with a section marked `[Unit]` which contains basic information and dependencies, for example:

```
[Unit]
Description=D-Bus System Message Bus
Documentation=man:dbus-daemon(1)
Requires=dbus.socket
```

Unit dependencies are expressed though `Requires`, `Wants`, and `Conflicts`:

- `Requires`: A list of units that this unit depends on, which is started when this unit is started
- `Wants`: A weaker form of `Requires`: the units listed are started but the current unit is not stopped if any of them fail
- `Conflicts`: A negative dependency: the units listed are stopped when this one is started and, conversely, if one of them is started, this one is stopped

Processing the dependencies produces a list of units that should be started (or stopped). The keywords `Before` and `After` determine the order in which they are started. The order of stopping is just the reverse of the start order:

- `Before`: This unit should be started before the units listed
- `After`: This unit should be started after the units listed

In the following example, the `After` directive makes sure that the web server is started after the network:

```
[Unit]
Description=Lighttpd Web Server
After=network.target
```

In the absence of `Before` or `After` directives, the units will be started or stopped in parallel with no particular ordering.

Services

A service is a daemon that can be started and stopped, equivalent to a System V `service`. A service is a type of unit file with a name ending in `.service`, for example, `lighttpd.service`.

A service unit has a `[Service]` section that describes how it should be run. Here is the relevant section from `lighttpd.service`:

```
[Service]
ExecStart=/usr/sbin/lighttpd -f /etc/lighttpd/lighttpd.conf -D
ExecReload=/bin/kill -HUP $MAINPID
```

These are the commands to run when starting the service and restarting it. There are many more configuration points you can add in here, so refer to the man page for `systemd.service`.

Targets

A target is another type of unit which groups services (or other types of unit). It is a type of unit that only has dependencies. Targets have names ending in `.target`, for example, `multi-user.target`. A target is a desired state, which performs the same role as System V runlevels.

How systemd boots the system

Now we can see how `systemd` implements the bootstrap. `systemd` is run by the kernel as a result of `/sbin/init` being symbolically linked to `/lib/systemd/systemd`. It runs the default target, `default.target`, which is always a link to a desired target such as `multi-user.target` for a text login or `graphical.target` for a graphical environment. For example, if the default target is `multi-user.target`, you will find this symbolic link:

```
/etc/systemd/system/default.target -> /lib/systemd/system/multi-
user.target
```

The default target may be overridden by passing `system.unit=<new target>` on the kernel command line. You can use `systemctl` to find out the default target, as shown here:

```
# systemctl get-default
multi-user.target
```

Starting a target such as `multi-user.target` creates a tree of dependencies that bring the system into a working state. In a typical system, `multi-user.target` depends on `basic.target`, which depends on `sysinit.target`, which depends on the services that need to be started early. You can print a graph using `systemctl list-dependencies`.

You can also list all the services and their current state using `systemctl list-units --type service`, and the same for targets using `systemctl list-units --type target`.

Adding your own service

Using the same `simpleserver` example as before, here is a service unit:

```
[Unit]
Description=Simple server

[Service]
Type=forking
ExecStart=/usr/bin/simpleserver

[Install]
WantedBy=multi-user.target
```

The `[Unit]` section only contains a description so that it shows up correctly when listed using `systemctl` and other commands. There are no dependencies; as I said, it is very simple.

The `[Service]` section points to the executable, and has a flag to indicate that it forks. If it were even simpler and ran in the foreground, `systemd` would do the daemonizing for us and `Type=forking` would not be needed.

The `[Install]` section makes it dependent on `multi-user.target` so that our server is started when the system goes into multi-user mode.

Once the unit is saved in `/etc/systemd/system/simpleserver.service`, you can start and stop it using the `systemctl start simpleserver` and `systemctl stop simpleserver` commands. You can use this command to find its current status:

```
# systemctl status simpleserver
  simpleserver.service - Simple server
  Loaded: loaded (/etc/systemd/system/simpleserver.service;
  disabled)
  Active: active (running) since Thu 1970-01-01 02:20:50 UTC; 8s
  ago
```

```
Main PID: 180 (simpleserver)
CGroup: /system.slice/simpleserver.service
        └─180 /usr/bin/simpleserver -n
```

```
Jan 01 02:20:50 qemuarm systemd[1]: Started Simple server.
```

At this point, it will only start and stop on command, as shown. To make it persistent, you need to add a permanent dependency to a target. That is the purpose of the [Install] section in the unit, it says that when this service is enabled it will become dependent on multi-user.target, and so will be started at boot time. You enable it using systemctl enable, like this:

```
# systemctl enable simpleserver
Created symlink from /etc/systemd/system/multi-
user.target.wants/simpleserver.service to
/etc/systemd/system/simpleserver.service.
```

Now you can see how dependencies are added at runtime without having to edit any unit files. A target can have a directory named <target_name>.target.wants which can contain links to services. This is exactly the same as adding the dependent unit to the [Wants] list in the target. In this case, you will find that this link has been created:

```
/etc/systemd/system/multi-user.target.wants/simpleserver.service
/etc/systemd/system/simpleserver.service
```

If this is were an important service you might want to restart if it failed. You can accomplish that by adding this flag to the [Service] section:

Restart=on-abort

Other options for Restart are on-success, on-failure, on-abnormal, on-watchdog, on-abort, or always.

Adding a watchdog

Watchdogs are a common requirement in embedded devices: you need to take action if a critical service stops working, usually by resetting the system. On most embedded SoCs, there is a hardware watchdog which can be accessed via the /dev/watchdog device node. The watchdog is initialized with a timeout at boot and then must be reset within that period, otherwise the watchdog will be triggered and the system will reboot. The interface with the watchdog driver is described in the kernel source in Documentation/watchdog, and the code for the drivers is in drivers/watchdog.

A problem arises if there are two or more critical services that need to be protected by a watchdog. systemd has a useful feature that distributes the watchdog between multiple services.

systemd can be configured to expect a regular keepalive call from a service and take action if it is not received, in other words, a per-service software watchdog. For this to work, you have to add code to the daemon to send the keepalive messages. It needs to check for a non-zero value in the WATCHDOG_USEC environment variable and then call sd_notify(false, "WATCHDOG=1") within that time (a period of half of the watchdog timeout is recommended). There are examples in the systemd source code.

To enable the watchdog in the service unit, add something like this to the [Service] section:

```
WatchdogSec=30s
Restart=on-watchdog
StartLimitInterval=5min
StartLimitBurst=4
StartLimitAction=reboot-force
```

In this example, the service expects a keepalive every 30 seconds. If it fails to be delivered, the service will be restarted, but if it is restarted more than four times in five minutes, systemd will force an immediate reboot. Once again, there is a full description of these settings in the systemd manual.

A watchdog like this takes care of individual services, but what if systemd itself fails, or the kernel crashes, or the hardware locks up. In those cases, we need to tell systemd to use the watchdog driver: just add RuntimeWatchdogSec=NN to /etc/systemd/system.conf. systemd will reset the watchdog within that period, and so the system will reset if systemd fails for some reason.

Implications for embedded Linux

systemd has a lot of features that are useful in embedded Linux, including many that I have not mentioned in this brief description such as resource control using slices (see the man page for systemd.slice(5) and systemd.resource-control(5)), device management (udev(7)) and system logging facilities (journald(5)).

You have to balance that with its size: even with a minimal build of just the core components, systemd, udevd, and journald, it is approaching 10 MiB of storage, including the shared libraries.

You also have to keep in mind that systemd development follows the kernel closely, so it will not work on a kernel more than a year or two older than the release of systemd.

Further reading

The following resource has further information about topics introduced in this chapter:

- *systemd system and Service Manager*: http://www.freedesktop.org/wiki/ Software/systemd/ (there are a lot of useful links at the bottom of that page)

Summary

Every Linux device needs an init program of some kind. If you are designing a system which only has to launch a small number of daemons at startup and remains fairly static after that, then BusyBox init is sufficient for your needs. It is usually a good choice if you are using Buildroot as the build system.

If, on the other hand, you have a system that has complex dependencies between services at boot time or runtime, and you have the storage space, then systemd would be the best choice. Even without the complexity, systemd has some useful features in the way it handles watchdogs, remote logging, and so on, so you should certainly give it a serious thought.

It is hard to make a case for System V init on its own merits, since it has few advantages over the simple BusyBox init. It will live on for a long time nevertheless, just because it is there. For example, if you are building using the Yocto Project and you decide against systemd then System V init is the alternative.

In terms of reducing boot time, systemd is faster than System V init for a similar workload. However, if you are looking for a very fast boot, nothing can beat a simple BusyBox init with minimal boot scripts.

This chapter is about one very important process, init. In the next chapter, I will describe what a process really is, how it relates to threads, how they cooperate, and how they are scheduled. Understanding these things is important if you want to create a robust and maintainable embedded system.

10
Learning About Processes and Threads

In the preceding chapters, we have considered the various aspects of creating an embedded Linux platform. Now it is time to start looking at how you can use the platform to create a working device. In this chapter, I will talk about the implications of the Linux process model and how it encompasses multi-threaded programs. I will look at the pros and cons of using single-threaded and multi-threaded processes. I will also look at scheduling and differentiate between timeshare and real-time scheduling policies.

While these topics are not specific to embedded computing, it is important for a designer of an embedded device to have an overview of these topics. There are many good reference works on the subject, some of which I reference at the end of the chapter, but in general, they do not consider the embedded use cases. In consequence, I will be concentrating on the concepts and design decisions rather than on the function calls and code.

Process or thread?

Many embedded developers who are familiar with **real-time operating systems (RTOS)** consider the Unix process model to be cumbersome. On the other hand, they see a similarity between an RTOS task and a Linux thread and they have a tendency to transfer an existing design using a one-to-one mapping of RTOS tasks to threads. I have, on several occasions, seen designs in which the entire application is implemented with one process containing 40 or more threads. I want to spend some time considering if this is a good idea or not. Let's begin with some definitions.

A process is a memory address space and a thread of execution, as shown in the following diagram. The address space is private to the process and so threads running in different processes. cannot access it. This memory separation is created by the memory management subsystem in the kernel, which keeps a memory page mapping for each process and re-programs the memory management unit on each context switch. I will describe how this works in detail in *Chapter 11, Managing Memory*. Part of the address space is mapped to a file which contains the code and static data that the program is running:

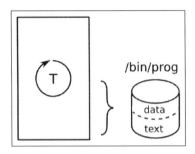

As the program runs, it will allocate resources such as stack space, heap memory, references to files, and so on. When the process terminates, these resources are reclaimed by the system: all the memory is freed up and all the file descriptors are closed.

Processes can communicate with each other using **inter process communication (IPC)** such as local sockets. I will talk about IPC later on.

A thread is a thread of execution within a process. All processes begin with one thread that runs the `main()` function and is called the main thread. You can create additional threads using the POSIX threads function `pthread_create(3)`, causing additional threads to execute in the same address space, as shown in the following diagram. Being in the same process, they share resources with each other. They can read and write the same memory and use the same file descriptors, and so communication between threads is easy, so long as you take care of the synchronization and locking issues:

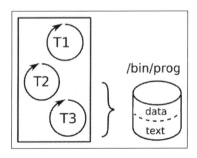

So, based on these brief details, you could imagine two extreme designs for a hypothetical system with 40 RTOS tasks being ported to Linux.

You could map tasks to processes, and have 40 individual programs communicating through IPC, for example with messages sent through sockets. You would greatly reduce memory corruption problems since the main thread running in each process is protected from the others, and you would reduce resource leakage since each process is cleaned up after it exits. However, the message interface between processes is quite complex and, where there is tight cooperation between a group of processes, the number of messages might be large and so become a limiting factor in the performance of the system. Furthermore, any one of the 40 processes may terminate, perhaps because of a bug causing it to crash, leaving the other 39 to carry on. Each process would have to handle the case that its neighbors are no longer running and recover gracefully.

At the other extreme, you could map tasks to threads and implement the system as a single process containing 40 threads. Cooperation becomes much easier because they share the same address space and file descriptors. The overhead of sending messages is reduced or eliminated and context switches between threads are faster than between processes. The downside is that you have introduced the possibility of one task corrupting the heap or the stack of another. If any one of the threads encounters a fatal bug, the whole process will terminate, taking all the threads with it. Finally, debugging a complex multi-threaded process can be a nightmare.

The conclusion you should draw is that neither design is ideal, and that there is a better way. But before we get to that point, I will delve a little more deeply into the APIs and the behavior of processes and threads.

Processes

A process holds the environment in which threads can run: it holds the memory mappings, the file descriptors, the user and group IDs, and more. The first process is the `init` process, which is created by the kernel during boot and has a PID of one. Thereafter, processes are created by duplication in an operation known as forking.

Creating a new process

The POSIX function to create a process is fork(2). It is an odd function because, for each successful call, there are two returns: one in the process that made the call, known as the parent, and one in the newly created process, known as the child as shown in the following diagram:

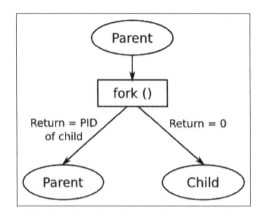

Immediately after the call, the child is an exact copy of the parent, it has the same stack, the same heap, the same file descriptors, and executes the same line of code, the one following fork(2). The only way the programmer can tell them apart is by looking at the return value of fork: it is zero for the child and greater than zero for the parent. Actually, the value returned in the parent is the PID of the newly created child process. There is a third possibility, which is that the return is negative, meaning that the fork call failed and there is still only one process.

Although the two processes are initially identical, they are in separate address spaces. Changes made to a variable by one will not be seen by the other. Under the hood, the kernel does not make a physical copy of the parent's memory, which would be quite a slow operation and consume memory unnecessarily. Instead, the memory is shared but marked with a **copy-on-write** (**CoW**) flag. If either parent or child modifies this memory, the kernel first makes a copy and then writes to the copy. This has the benefit of an efficient fork function while retaining the logical separation of process address spaces. I will discuss CoW in *Chapter 11, Managing Memory*.

Terminating a process

A process may be stopped voluntarily by calling the exit(3) function or, involuntarily, by receiving a signal that is not handled. One signal in particular, SIGKILL, cannot be handled and so will always kill a process. In all cases, terminating the process will stop all threads, close all file descriptors, and release all memory. The system sends a signal, SIGCHLD, to the parent so that it knows this has happened.

Processes have a return value which is composed of either the argument to exit(3), if it terminated normally, or the signal number if it was killed. The chief use for this is in shell scripts: it allows you to test the return from a program. By convention, 0 indicates success and other values indicate a failure of some sort.

The parent can collect the return value with the wait(2) or waitpid(2) functions. This causes a problem: there will be a delay between a child terminating and its parent collecting the return value. In that period, the return value must be stored somewhere, and the PID number of the now dead process cannot be reused. A process in this state is a zombie, state Z in ps or top. So long as the parent calls wait(2) or waitpid(2), whenever it is notified of a child's termination (by means of the SIGCHLD signal, see *Linux System Programming*, by *Robert Love, O'Reilly Media* or *The Linux Programming Interface*, by *Michael Kerrisk, No Starch Press* for details of handling signals), zombies exist for too short a time to show up in process listings. They will become a problem if the parent fails to collect the return value because you will not be able to create any more processes.

Here is a simple example, showing process creation and termination:

```c
#include <stdio.h>
#include <stdlib.h>
#include <unistd.h>
#include <sys/types.h>
#include <sys/wait.h>
int main(void)
{
  int pid;
  int status;
  pid = fork();
  if (pid == 0) {
    printf("I am the child, PID %d\n", getpid());
    sleep(10);
    exit(42);
  } else if (pid > 0) {
    printf("I am the parent, PID %d\n", getpid());
    wait(&status);
```

```
        printf("Child terminated, status %d\n",
        WEXITSTATUS(status));
    } else
        perror("fork:");
    return 0;
}
```

The `wait(2)` function blocks until a child process exits and stores the exit status. When you run it, you see something like this:

```
I am the parent, PID 13851
I am the child, PID 13852
Child terminated with status 42
```

The child process inherits most of the attributes of the parent, including the user and group IDs (UID and GID), all open file descriptors, signal handling, and scheduling characteristics.

Running a different program

The `fork` function creates a copy of a running program, but it does not run a different program. For that, you need one of the `exec` functions:

```
int execl(const char *path, const char *arg, ...);
int execlp(const char *file, const char *arg, ...);
int execle(const char *path, const char *arg,
           ..., char * const envp[]);
int execv(const char *path, char *const argv[]);
int execvp(const char *file, char *const argv[]);
int execvpe(const char *file, char *const argv[],
           char *const envp[]);
```

Each takes a path to the program file to load and run. If the function succeeds, the kernel discards all the resources of the current process, including memory and file descriptors, and allocates memory to the new program being loaded. When the thread that called `exec*` returns, it returns not to the line of code after the call, but to the `main()` function of the new program. Here is an example of a command launcher: it prompts for a command, for example, `/bin/ls`, and forks and executes the string you enter:

```
#include <stdio.h>
#include <stdlib.h>
#include <string.h>
#include <unistd.h>
#include <sys/types.h>
```

```
#include <sys/wait.h>
int main(int argc, char *argv[])
{
  char command_str[128];
  int pid;
  int child_status;
  int wait_for = 1;
  while (1) {
    printf("sh> ");
    scanf("%s", command_str);
    pid = fork();
    if (pid == 0) {
      /* child */
      printf("cmd '%s'\n", command_str);
      execl(command_str, command_str, (char *)NULL);
      /* We should not return from execl, so only get
      to this line if it failed */
      perror("exec");
      exit(1);
    }
    if (wait_for) {
      waitpid(pid, &child_status, 0);
      printf("Done, status %d\n", child_status);
    }
  }
  return 0;
}
```

It might seem odd to have one function that duplicates an existing process and another that discards its resources and loads a different program into memory, especially since it is common for a fork to be followed almost immediately by exec. Most operating systems combine the two actions into a single call.

There are distinct advantages, however. For example, it makes it very easy to implement redirection and pipes in the shell. Imagine that you want to get a directory listing, this is the sequence of events:

1. You type ls at the shell prompt.

2. The shell forks a copy of itself.

3. The child execs /bin/ls.

4. The ls program prints the directory listing to stdout (file descriptor 1) which is attached to the terminal. You see the directory listing.

5. The ls program terminates and the shell regains control.

Now, imagine that you want the directory listing to be written to a file by redirecting the output using the > character. The sequence is now as follows:

1. You type ls > listing.txt.

2. The shell forks a copy of itself.

3. The child opens and truncates the file listing.txt, and uses dup2(2) to copy the file descriptor of the file over file descriptor 1 (stdout).

4. The child execs /bin/ls.

5. The program prints the listing as before, but this time it is writing to listing.txt.

6. The ls program terminates and the shell regains control.

Note that there is an opportunity at step three to modify the environment of the child process before executing the program. The ls program does not need to know that it is writing to a file rather than a terminal. Instead of a file, stdout could be connected to a pipe and so the ls program, still unchanged, can send output to another program. This is part of the Unix philosophy of combining many small components that each do a job well, as described in *The Art of Unix Programming*, by *Eric Steven Raymond, Addison Wesley*; (23 Sept. 2003) ISBN 978-0131429017, especially in the section *Pipes, Redirection, and Filters*.

Daemons

We have encountered daemons in several places already. A daemon is a process that runs in the background, owned by the init process, PID1, and not connected to a controlling terminal. The steps to create a daemon are as follows:

1. Call fork() to create a new process, after which the parent should exit, thus creating an orphan which will be re-parented to init.

2. The child process calls setsid(2), creating a new session and process group of which it is the sole member. The exact details do not matter here, you can simply consider this as a way of isolating the process from any controlling terminal.

3. Change the working directory to the root.

4. Close all file descriptors and redirect stdin, stdout, and sterr (descriptors 0, 1, and 2) to /dev/null so that there is no input and all output is hidden.

Thankfully, all of the preceding steps can be achieved with a single function call, daemon(3).

Inter-process communication

Each process is an island of memory. You can pass information from one to another in two ways. Firstly, you can copy it from one address space to the other. Secondly, you can create an area of memory that both can access and so share the data.

The first is usually combined with a queue or buffer so that there is a sequence of messages passing between processes. This implies copying the message twice: first to a holding area and then to the destination. Some examples of this are sockets, pipes, and POSIX message queues.

The second way requires not only a method of creating memory that is mapped into two (or more) address spaces at once, but also a means of synchronizing access to that memory, for example, by using semaphores or mutexes. POSIX has functions for all of these.

There is an older set of APIs known as System V IPC, which provides message queues, shared memory, and semaphores, but it is not as flexible as the POSIX equivalents so I will not describe it here. The man page on svipc(7) gives an overview of the facilities and there is more detail in *The Linux Programming Interface*, by *Michael Kerrisk, No Starch Press* and *Unix Network Programming, Volume 2*, by *W. Richard Stevens*.

Message-based protocols are usually easier to program and debug than shared memory, but are slow if the messages are large.

Message-based IPC

There are several options which I will summarize as follows. The attributes that differentiate between them are:

- Whether the message flow is uni- or bi-directorial.
- Whether the data flow is a byte stream, with no message boundary, or discrete messages with boundaries preserved. In the latter case, the maximum size of a message is important.
- Whether messages are tagged with a priority.

The following table summarizes these properties for FIFOs, sockets, and message queues:

Property	FIFO	Unix socket: stream	Unix socket: datagram	POSIX message queue
Message boundary	Byte stream	Byte stream	Discrete	Discrete

Property	FIFO	Unix socket: stream	Unix socket: datagram	POSIX message queue
Uni/bi-directional	Uni	Bi	Uni	Uni
Max message size	Unlimited	Unlimited	In the range 100 KiB to 250 KiB	Default: 8 KiB, absolute maximum: 1 MiB
Priority levels	None	None	None	0 to 32767

Unix (or local) sockets

Unix sockets fulfill most requirements and, coupled with the familiarity of the sockets API, they are by far the most common mechanism.

Unix sockets are created with the address family AF_UNIX and bound to a path name. Access to the socket is determined by the access permission of the socket file. As with Internet sockets, the socket type can be SOCK_STREAM or SOCK_DGRAM, the former giving a bi-directional byte stream, and the latter providing discrete messages with preserved boundaries. Unix socket datagrams are reliable, meaning that they will not be dropped or reordered. The maximum size for a datagram is system-dependent and is available via /proc/sys/net/core/wmem_max. It is typically 100 KiB or more.

Unix sockets do not have a mechanism for indicating the priority of a message.

FIFOs and named pipes

FIFO and named pipe are just different terms for the same thing. They are an extension of the anonymous pipe that is used to communicate between parent and child and are used to implement piping in the shell.

A FIFO is a special sort of file, created by the command mkfifo(1). As with Unix sockets, the file access permissions determine who can read and write. They are uni-directional, meaning that there is one reader and usually one writer, though there may be several. The data is a pure byte stream but with a guarantee of atomicity of messages that are smaller than the buffer associated with the pipe. In other words, writes less than this size will not be split into several smaller writes and so the reader will read the whole message in one go, so long as the size of the buffer at the reader end is large enough. The default size of the FIFO buffer is 64 KiB on modern kernels and can be increased using fcntl(2) with F_SETPIPE_SZ up to the value in /proc/sys/fs/pipe-max-size, typically 1 MiB.

There is no concept of priority.

POSIX message queues

Message queues are identified by a name, which must begin with a forward slash / and contain only one / character: message queues are actually kept in a pseudo filesystem of the type `mqueue`. You create a queue and get a reference to an existing queue through `mq_open(3)`, which returns a file. Each message has a priority and messages are read from the queue in priority and then age order. Messages can be up to `/proc/sys/kernel/msgmax` bytes long. The default value is 8 KiB, but you can set it to be any size in the range 128 bytes to 1 MiB by writing the value to `/proc/sys/kernel/msgmax` bytes. Each message has a priority. They are read from the queue in priority then age order. Since the reference is a file descriptor, you can use `select(2)`, `poll(2)`, and other similar functions to wait for activity on the queue.

See the Linux man page *mq_overview(7)*.

Summary of message-based IPC

Unix sockets are the most often used because they offer all that is needed, except perhaps message priority. They are implemented on most operating systems, and so they confer maximum portability.

FIFOs are less used, mostly because they lack an equivalent to a datagram. On the other hand, the API is very simple, being the normal `open(2)`, `close(2)`, `read(2)`, and `write(2)` file calls.

Message queues are the least commonly used of this group. The code paths in the kernel are not optimized in the way that socket (network) and FIFO (filesystem) calls are.

There are also higher level abstractions, in particular dbus, which are moving from mainstream Linux into embedded devices. Dbus uses Unix sockets and shared memory under the surface.

Shared memory-based IPC

Sharing memory removes the need for copying data between address spaces but introduces the problem of synchronizing accesses to it. Synchronization between processes is commonly achieved using semaphores.

POSIX shared memory

To share memory between processes, you first have to create a new area of memory and then map it into the address space of each process that wants access to it, as in the following diagram:

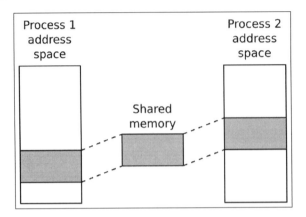

POSIX shared memory follows the pattern we encountered with message queues. The segments are identified by names that begin with a / character and have exactly one such character. The function shm_open(3) takes the name and returns a file descriptor for it. If it does not exist already and the O_CREAT flag is set, then a new segment is created. Initially it has a size of zero. Use the (misleadingly named) ftruncate(2) to expand it to the desired size.

Once you have a descriptor for the shared memory, you map it into the address space of the process using mmap(2), and so threads in different processes can access the memory.

Here is an example:

```
#include <stdio.h>
#include <stdlib.h>
#include <string.h>
#include <unistd.h>
#include <sys/mman.h>
#include <sys/stat.h>   /* For mode constants */
#include <fcntl.h>
#include <sys/types.h>
#include <errno.h>
#include <semaphore.h>
#define SHM_SEGMENT_SIZE 65536
#define SHM_SEGMENT_NAME "/demo-shm"
```

```
#define SEMA_NAME "/demo-sem"

static sem_t *demo_sem;
/*
 * If the shared memory segment does not exist already, create it
 * Returns a pointer to the segment or NULL if there is an error
 */

static void *get_shared_memory(void)
{
  int shm_fd;
  struct shared_data *shm_p;
  /* Attempt to create the shared memory segment */
  shm_fd = shm_open(SHM_SEGMENT_NAME, O_CREAT | O_EXCL | O_RDWR,
    0666);

  if (shm_fd > 0) {
    /* succeeded: expand it to the desired size (Note: dont't do
    "this every time because ftruncate fills it with zeros) */
    printf ("Creating shared memory and setting size=%d\n",
    SHM_SEGMENT_SIZE);

    if (ftruncate(shm_fd, SHM_SEGMENT_SIZE) < 0) {
      perror("ftruncate");
      exit(1);
    }
    /* Create a semaphore as well */
    demo_sem = sem_open(SEMA_NAME, O_RDWR | O_CREAT, 0666, 1);

    if (demo_sem == SEM_FAILED)
      perror("sem_open failed\n");
  }
  else if (shm_fd == -1 && errno == EEXIST) {
    /* Already exists: open again without O_CREAT */
    shm_fd = shm_open(SHM_SEGMENT_NAME, O_RDWR, 0);
    demo_sem = sem_open(SEMA_NAME, O_RDWR);

    if (demo_sem == SEM_FAILED)
      perror("sem_open failed\n");
  }

  if (shm_fd == -1) {
    perror("shm_open " SHM_SEGMENT_NAME);
    exit(1);
```

```
    }
    /* Map the shared memory */
    shm_p = mmap(NULL, SHM_SEGMENT_SIZE, PROT_READ | PROT_WRITE,
      MAP_SHARED, shm_fd, 0);

    if (shm_p == NULL) {
      perror("mmap");
      exit(1);
    }
    return shm_p;
  }
  int main(int argc, char *argv[])
  {
    char *shm_p;
    printf("%s PID=%d\n", argv[0], getpid());
    shm_p = get_shared_memory();

    while (1) {
      printf("Press enter to see the current contents of shm\n");
      getchar();
      sem_wait(demo_sem);
      printf("%s\n", shm_p);
      /* Write our signature to the shared memory */
      sprintf(shm_p, "Hello from process %d\n", getpid());
      sem_post(demo_sem);
    }
    return 0;
  }
```

The memory in Linux is taken from a `tmpfs` filesystem mounted in `/dev/shm` or `/run/shm`.

Threads

Now it is time to look at multi-threaded processes. The programming interface for threads is the POSIX threads API, which was first defined in IEEE POSIX 1003.1c standard (1995), commonly known as Pthreads. It was implemented as an additional part of the C library, `libpthread.so`. There have been two versions of Pthreads over the last 15 years or so, Linux Threads and the **Native POSIX Thread Library** (**NPTL**). The latter is much more compliant with the specification, particularly with regard to the handling of signals and process IDs. It is pretty dominant now, but you may come across some older versions of uClibc that use Linux Threads.

Creating a new thread

The function to create a thread is pthread_create(3):

```
int pthread_create(pthread_t *thread, const pthread_attr_t *attr,
  void *(*start_routine) (void *), void *arg);
```

It creates a new thread of execution which begins at the function start_routine
and places a descriptor in pthread_t pointed to by thread. It inherits the scheduling
parameters of the calling thread but these can be overridden by passing a pointer to
the thread attributes in attr. The thread will begin to execute immediately.

pthread_t is the main way to refer to the thread within the program but the thread
can also be seen from outside using a command like ps -eLf:

```
UID     PID   PPID   LWP   C  NLWP  STIME       TTY          TIME CMD
...
chris  6072   5648  6072   0   3    21:18  pts/0 00:00:00 ./thread-demo
chris  6072   5648  6073   0   3    21:18  pts/0 00:00:00 ./thread-demo
```

The program thread-demo has two threads. The PID and PPID columns show that
they all belong to the same process and have the same parent, as you would expect.
The column marked LWP is interesting, though. LWP stands for Light Weight Process
which, in this context, is another name for thread. The numbers in that column are
also known as **Thread IDs** or **TIDs**. In the main thread, the TID is the same as the PID,
but for the others it is a different (higher) value. Some functions will accept a TID in
places where the documentation states that you must give a PID, but be aware that
this behavior is specific to Linux and not portable. Here is the code for thread-demo:

```
#include <stdio.h>
#include <unistd.h>
#include <pthread.h>
#include <sys/syscall.h>

static void *thread_fn(void *arg)
{
  printf("New thread started, PID %d TID %d\n",
  getpid(), (pid_t)syscall(SYS_gettid));
  sleep(10);
  printf("New thread terminating\n");
  return NULL;
}
```

```
int main(int argc, char *argv[])
{
  pthread_t t;
  printf("Main thread, PID %d TID %d\n",
  getpid(), (pid_t)syscall(SYS_gettid));
  pthread_create(&t, NULL, thread_fn, NULL);
  pthread_join(t, NULL);
  return 0;
}
```

There is a man page for `getttid(2)` which explains that you have to make the Linux `syscall` directly because there isn't a C library wrapper for it, as shown.

There is a limit to the total number of threads that a given kernel can schedule. The limit scales according to the size of the system from around 1,000 on small devices up to tens of thousands on larger embedded devices. The actual number is available in `/proc/sys/kernel/threads-max`. Once you reach this limit, `fork()` and `pthread_create()` will fail.

Terminating a thread

A thread terminates when:

- It reaches the end of its `start_routine`
- It calls `pthread_exit(3)`
- It is canceled by another thread calling `pthread_cancel(3)`
- The process which contains the thread terminates, for example, because of a thread calling `exit(3)`, or the process receiving a signal that is not handled, masked or ignored

Note that, if a multi threaded program calls `fork(2)`, only the thread that made the call will exist in the new child process. Fork does not replicate all threads.

A thread has a return value, which is a void pointer. One thread can wait for another to terminate and collect its return value by calling `pthread_join(2)`. There is an example in the code for `thread-demo` mentioned in the preceding section. This produces a problem that is very similar to the zombie problem among processes: the resources of the thread, for example, the stack, cannot be freed up until another thread has joined with it. If threads remain unjoined there is a resource leak in the program.

Compiling a program with threads

The support for POSIX threads is part of the C library, in the library `libpthread.so`. However, there is more to building programs with threads than linking the library: there have to be changes to the way the compiler generates code to make sure that certain global variables, such as `errno`, have one instance per thread rather than one for the whole process.

 When building a threaded program, you must add the switch `-pthread` at the compile and link stages.

Inter-thread communication

The big advantage of threads is that they share the address space and so can share memory variables. This is also a big disadvantage because it requires synchronization to preserve data consistency, in a similar way to memory segments shared between processes but with the proviso that, with threads, all memory is shared. Threads can create private memory using **thread local storage (TLS)**.

The `pthreads` interface provides the basics necessary to achieve synchronization: mutexes and condition variables. If you want more complex structures, you will have to build them yourself.

It is worth noting that all of the IPC methods described earlier work equally well between threads in the same process.

Mutual exclusion

To write robust programs, you need to protect each shared resource with a mutex lock and make sure that every code path that reads or writes the resource has locked the mutex first. If you apply this rule consistently, most of the problems should be solved. The ones that remain are associated with the fundamental behavior of mutexes. I will list them briefly here, but will not go into detail:

- **Deadlock**: This occurs when mutexes become permanently locked. A classic situation is the deadly embrace in which two threads each require two mutexes and have managed to lock one of them but not the other. Each block waits for the lock the other has and so they remain as they are. One simple rule which avoids the deadly embrace problem is to make sure that mutexes are always locked in the same order. Other solutions involve timeouts and back off periods.

- **Priority inversion**: The delays caused by waiting for a mutex can cause a real-time thread to miss deadlines. The specific case of priority inversion happens when a high priority thread becomes blocked waiting for a mutex locked by a low priority thread. If the low priority thread is preempted by other threads of intermediate priority, the high priority thread is forced to wait for an unbounded length of time. There are mutex protocols called priority inheritance and priority ceiling which resolve the problem at the expense of greater processing overhead in the kernel for each lock and unlock call.

- **Poor performance**: Mutexes introduce minimal overhead to code as long as threads don't have to block on them most of the time. If your design has a resource that is needed by a lot of threads, however, the contention ratio becomes significant. This is usually a design issue which can be resolved by using finer grained locking or a different algorithm.

Changing conditions

Cooperating threads need a method of alerting one another that something has changed and needs attention. That thing is called a condition and the alert is sent through a condition variable, condvar.

A condition is just something that you can test to give a true or false result. A simple example is a buffer that contains either zero or some items. One thread takes items from the buffer and sleeps when it is empty. Another thread places items into the buffer and signals the other thread that it has done so, because the condition that the other thread is waiting on has changed. If it is sleeping, it needs to wake up and do something. The only complexity is that the condition is, by definition, a shared resource and so has to be protected by a mutex. Here is a simple example which follows the producer-consumer relationship described in the preceding section:

```
pthread_cond_t cv = PTHREAD_COND_INITIALIZER;
pthread_mutex_t mutx = PTHREAD_MUTEX_INITIALIZER;

void *consumer(void *arg)
{
  while (1) {
    pthread_mutex_lock(&mutx);
    while (buffer_empty(data))
      pthread_cond_wait(&cv, &mutx);
    /* Got data: take from buffer */
    pthread_mutex_unlock(&mutx);
    /* Process data item */
  }
```

```
    return NULL;
}

void *producer(void *arg)
{
  while (1) {
    /* Produce an item of data */
    pthread_mutex_lock(&mutx);
    add_data(data);
    pthread_mutex_unlock(&mutx);
    pthread_cond_signal(&cv);
  }
  return NULL;
}
```

Note that, when the consumer thread blocks on the condvar, it does so while holding a locked mutex, which would seem to be a recipe for deadlock the next time the producer thread tries to update the condition. To avoid this, pthread_condwait(3) unlocks the mutex after the thread is blocked and locks it again before waking it and returning from the wait.

Partitioning the problem

Now that we have covered the basics of processes and threads and the ways in which they communicate, it is time to see what we can do with them.

Here are some of the rules I use when building systems:

- **Rule 1**: Keep tasks that have a lot of interaction.

  Minimize overheads by keeping closely inter-operating threads together in one process.

- **Rule 2**: Don't put all your threads in one basket.

  On the other hand, try and keep components with limited interaction in separate processes, in the interests of resilience and modularity.

- **Rule 3**: Don't mix critical and non-critical threads in the same process.

  This is an amplification of Rule 2: the critical part of the system, which might be the machine control program, should be kept as simple as possible and written in a more rigorous way than other parts. It must be able to continue even if other processes fail. If you have real-time threads, they, by definition, must be critical and should go into a process by themselves.

- **Rule 4**: Threads shouldn't get too intimate.

  One of the temptations when writing a multi-threaded program is to intermingle the code and variables between threads because it is all in one program and easy to do. Don't keep threads modular with well-defined interactions.

- **Rule 5**: Don't think that threads are for free.

  It is very easy to create additional threads but there is a cost, not least in the additional synchronization necessary to coordinate their activities.

- **Rule 6**: Threads can work in parallel.

  Threads can run simultaneously on a multi-core processor, giving higher throughput. If you have a large computing job, you can create one thread per core and make maximum use of the hardware. There are libraries to help you do this, such as OpenMP. You probably shouldn't be coding parallel programming algorithms from scratch.

The Android design is a good illustration. Each application is a separate Linux process which helps to modularize memory management but especially ensures that one app crashing does not affect the whole system. The process model is also used for access control: a process can only access the files and resources which its UID and GIDs allow it to. There are a group of threads in each process. There is one to manage and update the user interface, one for handling signals from the operating system, several for managing dynamic memory allocation and the freeing up of Java objects and a worker pool of at least two threads for receiving messages from other parts of the system using the Binder protocol.

To summarize, processes provide resilience because each process has a protected memory space and, when the process terminates, all resources including memory and file descriptors are freed up, reducing resource leaks. On the other hand, threads share resources and so can communicate easily through shared variables, and can cooperate by sharing access to files and other resources. Threads give parallelism through worker pools and other abstractions which is useful on multi-core processors.

Scheduling

The second big topic I want to cover in this chapter is scheduling. The Linux scheduler has a queue of threads that are ready to run and its job is to schedule them on CPUs as they become available. Each thread has a scheduling policy which may be timeshared or real-time. The timeshared threads have a niceness value which increases or reduces their entitlement to CPU time. The real-time threads have a priority such that a higher priority thread will preempt a lower one. The scheduler works with threads, not processes. Each thread is scheduled regardless of which process it is running in.

The scheduler runs when:

- A thread blocks by calling `sleep()` or in a blocking I/O call
- A timeshare thread exhausts its time slice
- An interrupt causes a thread to be unblocked, for example, because of I/O completing

For background information on the Linux scheduler, I recommend reading the chapter on process scheduling in *Linux Kernel Development, 3rd edition by Robert Love, Addison-Wesley Professional*; (July 2, 2010) ISBN-10: 0672329468.

Fairness versus determinism

I have grouped the scheduling polices into categories of timeshare and real-time. Timeshare policies are based on the principal of fairness. They are designed to make sure that each thread gets a fair amount of processor time and that no thread can hog the system. If a thread runs for too long it is put to the back of the queue so that others can have a go. At the same time, a fairness policy needs to adjust to threads that are doing a lot of work and give them the resources to get the job done. Timeshare scheduling is good because of the way it automatically adjusts to a wide range of workloads.

On the other hand, if you have a real-time program, fairness is not helpful. Instead, you then want a policy that is deterministic, that will give you at least minimal guarantees that your real-time threads will be scheduled at the right time so that they don't miss their deadlines. This means that a real-time thread must preempt timeshare threads. Real-time threads also have a static priority that the scheduler can use to choose between them when there are several of them to run at once. The Linux real-time scheduler implements a fairly standard algorithm which runs the highest priority real-time thread. Most RTOS schedulers are also written in this way.

Both types of thread can coexist. Those requiring deterministic scheduling are scheduled first and the time remaining is divided between the timeshare threads.

Timeshare policies

Timeshare policies are designed for fairness. From Linux 2.6.23 onwards, the scheduler used has been the **Completely Fair Scheduler** (**CFS**). It does not use timeslices in the normal sense of the word. Instead, it calculates a running tally of the length of time a thread would be entitled to run if it had its fair share of CPU time, and balances that with the actual amount of time it has run. If it exceeds its entitlement, and there are other timeshare threads waiting to run, the scheduler will suspend the thread and run a waiting thread instead.

The timeshare policies are:

- `SCHED_NORMAL` (also known as `SCHED_OTHER`): This is the default policy. The vast majority of Linux threads use this policy.

- `SCHED_BATCH`: This is similar to `SCHED_NORMAL` except threads are scheduled with a larger granularity; that is they run for longer but have to wait longer until scheduled again. The intention is to reduce the number of context switches for background processing (batch jobs) and so reduce the amount of CPU cache churn.

- `SCHED_IDLE`: These threads are run only when there are no threads of any other policy ready to run. It is the lowest possible priority.

There are two pairs of functions to get and set the policy and priority of a thread. The first pair takes a PID as a parameter and affects the main thread in a process:

```
struct sched_param {
  ...
  int sched_priority;
  ...
};
int sched_setscheduler(pid_t pid, int policy,
const struct sched_param *param);
int sched_getscheduler(pid_t pid);
```

The second pair operates on `pthread_t` and so can change the parameters of the other threads in a process:

```
pthread_setschedparam(pthread_t thread, int policy,
  const struct sched_param *param);
pthread_getschedparam(pthread_t thread, int *policy,
  struct sched_param *param);
```

Niceness

Some timeshare threads are more important than others. You can indicate this with the `nice` value which multiplies a thread's CPU entitlement by a scaling factor. The name comes from the function call, `nice(2)`, which has been part of Unix since the early days. A thread becomes `nice` by reducing its load on the system, or moves in the opposite direction by increasing it. The range of values is from 19, which is really nice, to -20 which is really not nice. The default value is 0, which is averagely nice or so-so.

The `nice` value can be changed for `SCHED_NORMAL` and `SCHED_BATCH` threads. To reduce niceness, which increases the CPU load, you need the capability `CAP_SYS_NICE`, which is available to the root user.

Almost all the documentation for functions and commands that change the `nice` value (`nice(2)` and the `nice` and `renice` commands) talks in terms of processes. However, it really relates to threads. As mentioned in the preceding section, you can use a TID in place of a PID to change the `nice` value of an individual thread. One other discrepancy in the standard descriptions of `nice`: the `nice` value is referred to as the priority of a thread (or sometimes, mistakenly, a process). I believe this is misleading and confuses the concept with real-time priority which is a completely different thing.

Real-time policies

Real-time policies are intended for determinism. The real-time scheduler will always run the highest priority real-time thread that is ready to run. Real-time threads always preempt timeshare threads. In essence, by selecting a real-time policy over a timeshare policy, you are saying that you have inside knowledge of the expected scheduling of this thread and wish to override the scheduler's built-in assumptions.

There are two real-time policies:

- `SCHED_FIFO`: This is a run to completion algorithm, which means that, once the thread starts to run, it will continue until it is preempted by a higher priority real-time thread or blocks in a system call or terminates (completes).

- `SCHED_RR`: This is a round robin algorithm which will cycle between threads of the same priority if they exceed their time slice which, by default, is 100 ms. Since Linux 3.9, it has been possible to control the `timeslice` value through `/proc/sys/kernel/sched_rr_timeslice_ms`. Apart from this, it behaves in the same way as `SCHED_FIFO`.

Each real-time thread has a priority in the range 1 to 99, with 99 being the highest.

To give a thread a real-time policy, you need CAP_SYS_NICE which, by default, is given only to the root user.

One problem with real-time scheduling, both in Linux and elsewhere, is that of a thread that becomes compute bound, often because a bug has caused it to loop indefinitely, which prevents real-time threads of lower priority from running as well as all the timeshare threads. The system become erratic and may lock up completely. There are a couple of ways to guard against this possibility.

First, since Linux 2.6.25, the scheduler has, by default, reserved 5% of CPU time for non real-time threads, so that even a runaway real-time thread cannot completely halt the system. It is configured via two kernel controls:

- /proc/sys/kernel/sched_rt_period_us
- /proc/sys/kernel/sched_rt_runtime_us

They have default values of 1,000,000 (1 second) and 950,000 (950 ms) respectively, which means that out of every second, 50ms is reserved for non real-time processing. If you want real-time threads to be able to take 100% then set sched_rt_runtime_us to -1.

The second option is to use a watchdog, either hardware or software, to monitor the execution of key threads and to take action when they begin to miss deadlines.

Choosing a policy

In practice, timeshare policies satisfy the majority of computing workloads. Threads that are I/O bound spend a lot of time blocked and so always have some spare entitlement in hand. When they unblock they will be scheduled almost immediately. Meanwhile, CPU-bound threads will naturally take up any CPU cycles left over. Positive nice values can be applied to the less important threads and negative values to the important ones.

Of course, this is only average behavior, there are no guarantees that this will always be the case. If more deterministic behavior is needed, then real-time policies will be required. The things that mark out a thread as being real-time are:

- It has a deadline by which it must generate an output
- Missing the deadline would compromise the effectiveness of the system
- It is event-driven
- It is not compute bound

Examples of real-time tasks include the classic robot arm servo controller, multimedia processing, and communication processing.

Choosing a real-time priority

Choosing real-time priorities that work for all expected workloads is a tricky business and a good reason for avoiding real-time policies in the first place.

The most widely used procedure for choosing priorities is known as **Rate Monotonic Analysis (RMA)**, after the 1973 paper by Liu and Layland. It applies to real-time systems with periodic threads, which is a very important class. Each thread has a period, and a utilization, which is the proportion of the period it will be executing. The goal is to balance the load so that all threads can complete their execution phase before the next period. RMA states that this can be achieved if:

- The highest priorities are given to the threads with the shortest periods
- The total utilization is less than 69%

The total utilization is the sum of all of the individual utilizations. It also makes the assumption that the interaction between threads or the time spent blocked on mutexes and the like, is negligible.

Further reading

The following resources have further information about the topics introduced in this chapter:

- *The Art of Unix Programming*, by *Eric Steven Raymond, Addison Wesley*; (23 Sept. 2003) ISBN 978-0131429017
- *Linux System Programming, 2nd edition*, by *Robert Love, O'Reilly Media*; (8 Jun. 2013) ISBN-10: 1449339530
- *Linux Kernel Development, 3rd edition by Robert Love, Addison-Wesley Professional*; (July 2, 2010) ISBN-10: 0672329468
- *The Linux Programming Interface*, by *Michael Kerrisk, No Starch Press*; (October 2010) ISBN 978-1-59327-220-3
- *UNIX Network Programming: v. 2: Interprocess Communications, 2nd Edition*, by *W. Richard Stevens, Prentice Hall*; (25 Aug. 1998) ISBN-10: 0132974290
- *Programming with POSIX Threads*, by *Butenhof, David R, Addison-Wesley, Professional*
- *Scheduling Algorithm for multiprogramming in a Hard-Real-Time Environment*, by *C. L. Liu* and *James W. Layland, Journal of ACM*, 1973, vol 20, no 1, pp. 46-61

Summary

The long Unix heritage that is built into Linux and the accompanying C libraries provides almost everything you need to write stable and resilient embedded applications. The issue is that, for every job, there are at least two ways to achieve the end you desire.

In this chapter, I have focused on two aspects of system design: the partitioning into separate processes, each with one or more threads to get the job done, and the scheduling of those threads. I hope that I have shed some light on this, and given you the basis for further study into all of them.

In the next chapter, I will examine another important aspect of system design, memory management.

11
Managing Memory

This chapter covers issues relating to memory management, which is an important topic for any Linux system, but especially for embedded Linux where system memory is usually in limited supply. After a brief refresher on virtual memory, I will show you how to measure memory use, how to detect problems with memory allocation, including memory leaks, and what happens when you run out of memory. You will have to understand the tools that are available, from simple tools such as `free` and `top`, to complex tools such as mtrace and Valgrind.

Virtual memory basics

To recap, Linux configures the memory management unit of the CPU to present a virtual address space to a running program that begins at zero and ends at the highest address, `0xffffffff` on a 32-bit processor. That address space is divided into pages of 4 KiB (there are rare examples of systems using other page sizes).

Linux divides this virtual address space into an area for applications, called user space, and an area for the kernel, called kernel space. The split between the two is set by a kernel configuration parameter named `PAGE_OFFSET`. In a typical 32-bit embedded system, `PAGE_OFFSET` is `0xc0000000`, giving the lower three GiB to user space and the top one GiB to kernel space. The user address space is allocated per process, so that each process runs in a sandbox, separated from the others. The kernel address space is the same for all processes: there is only one kernel.

Pages in this virtual address space are mapped to physical addresses by the **memory management unit (MMU)**, which uses page tables to perform the mapping.

Each page of virtual memory may be:

- unmapped, in which access will result in a `SIGSEGV`
- mapped to a page of physical memory that is private to the process

- mapped to a page of physical memory that is shared with other processes
- mapped and shared with a `copy on write` flag set: a write is trapped in the kernel which makes a copy of the page and maps it to the process in place of the original page before allowing the write to take place
- mapped to a page of physical memory that is used by the kernel

The kernel may additionally map pages to reserved memory regions, for example, to access registers and buffer memory in device drivers.

An obvious question is, why do we do it this way instead of simply referencing physical memory directly, as typical RTOS would?

There are numerous advantages to virtual memory, some of which are described here:

- Invalid memory accesses are trapped and applications alerted by `SIGSEGV`
- Processes run in their own memory space, isolated from others
- Efficient use of memory through the sharing of common code and data, for example, in libraries
- The possibility of increasing the apparent amount of physical memory by adding swap files, although swapping on embedded targets is rare

These are powerful arguments, but we have to admit that there are some disadvantages as well. It is difficult to determine the actual memory budget of an application, which is one of the main concerns of this chapter. The default allocation strategy is to over-commit, which leads to tricky out-of-memory situations, which I will also discuss later on. Finally, the delays introduced by the memory management code in handling exceptions – page faults – make the system less deterministic, which is important for real-time programs. I will cover this in *Chapter 14, Real-time Programming*.

Memory management is different for kernel space and user space. The following sections describe the essential differences and the things you need to know.

Kernel space memory layout

Kernel memory is managed in a fairly straightforward way. It is not demand-paged, meaning that, for every allocation using `kmalloc()` or similar function, there is real physical memory. Kernel memory is never discarded or paged out.

Some architectures show a summary of the memory mapping at boot time in the kernel log messages. This trace is taken from a 32-bit ARM device (a BeagleBone Black):

```
Memory: 511MB = 511MB total
Memory: 505980k/505980k available, 18308k reserved, 0K highmem
Virtual kernel memory layout:
    vector  : 0xffff0000 - 0xffff1000   (    4 kB)
    fixmap  : 0xfff00000 - 0xfffe0000   (  896 kB)
    vmalloc : 0xe0800000 - 0xff000000   (  488 MB)
    lowmem  : 0xc0000000 - 0xe0000000   (  512 MB)
    pkmap   : 0xbfe00000 - 0xc0000000   (    2 MB)
    modules : 0xbf800000 - 0xbfe00000   (    6 MB)
      .text : 0xc0008000 - 0xc0763c90   ( 7536 kB)
      .init : 0xc0764000 - 0xc079f700   (  238 kB)
      .data : 0xc07a0000 - 0xc0827240   (  541 kB)
       .bss : 0xc0827240 - 0xc089e940   (  478 kB)
```

The figure of 505980 KiB available is the amount of free memory the kernel sees when it begins execution but before it begins making dynamic allocations.

Consumers of kernel-space memory include the following:

- The kernel itself, in other words, the code and data loaded from the kernel image file at boot time. This is shown in the preceding code in the segments .text, .init, .data, and .bss. The .init segment is freed once the kernel has completed initialization.

- Memory allocated through the slab allocator, which is used for kernel data structures of various kinds. This includes allocations made using kmalloc(). They come from the region marked lowmem.

- Memory allocated via vmalloc(), usually for larger chunks of memory than is available through kmalloc(). These are in the vmalloc area.

- Mapping for device drivers to access registers and memory belonging to various bits of hardware, which you can see by reading /proc/iomem. These come from the vmalloc area but since they are mapped to physical memory that is outside of main system memory, they do not take any real memory.

- Kernel modules, which are loaded into the area marked modules.

- Other low level allocations that are not tracked anywhere else.

How much memory does the kernel use?

Unfortunately, there isn't a complete answer to that question, but what follows is as close as we can get.

Firstly, you can see the memory taken up by the kernel code and data in the kernel log shown previously, or you can use the `size` command, as follows:

```
$ arm-poky-linux-gnueabi-size vmlinux
text        data      bss       dec        hex        filename
9013448     796868    8428144   18238460   1164bfc    vmlinux
```

Usually, the size is small when compared to the total amount of memory. If that is not the case, you need to look through the kernel configuration and remove those components that you don't need. There is an ongoing effort to allow small kernels to be built: search for Linux-tiny or Linux Kernel Tinification. There is a project page for the latter at https://tiny.wiki.kernel.org/.

You can get more information about memory usage by reading /proc/meminfo:

```
# cat /proc/meminfo
MemTotal:        509016 kB
MemFree:         410680 kB
Buffers:           1720 kB
Cached:           25132 kB
SwapCached:           0 kB
Active:           74880 kB
Inactive:          3224 kB
Active(anon):     51344 kB
Inactive(anon):    1372 kB
Active(file):     23536 kB
Inactive(file):    1852 kB
Unevictable:          0 kB
Mlocked:              0 kB
HighTotal:            0 kB
HighFree:             0 kB
LowTotal:        509016 kB
LowFree:         410680 kB
SwapTotal:            0 kB
SwapFree:             0 kB
Dirty:               16 kB
Writeback:            0 kB
AnonPages:        51248 kB
Mapped:           24376 kB
```

```
Shmem:              1452 kB
Slab:              11292 kB
SReclaimable:       5164 kB
SUnreclaim:         6128 kB
KernelStack:        1832 kB
PageTables:         1540 kB
NFS_Unstable:          0 kB
Bounce:                0 kB
WritebackTmp:          0 kB
CommitLimit:      254508 kB
Committed_AS:     734936 kB
VmallocTotal:     499712 kB
VmallocUsed:       29576 kB
VmallocChunk:     389116 kB
```

There is a description of each of these fields in the man page for `proc(5)`. The kernel memory usage is the sum of:

- **Slab**: The total memory allocated by the slab allocator
- **KernelStack**: The stack space used when executing kernel code
- **PageTables**: The memory used for storing page tables
- **VmallocUsed**: The memory allocated by `vmalloc()`

In the case of slab allocations, you can get more information by reading `/proc/slabinfo`. Similarly, there is a breakdown of allocations in `/proc/vmallocinfo` for the vmalloc area. In both cases, you need detailed knowledge of the kernel and its subsystems to see exactly which subsystem is making the allocations and why, which is beyond the scope of this discussion.

With modules, you can use `lsmod` to find out the memory space taken up by the code and data:

```
# lsmod
Module          Size   Used by
g_multi         47670  2
libcomposite    14299  1 g_multi
mt7601Usta      601404 0
```

That leaves the low level allocations of which there is no record, and which prevent us from generating an accurate account of kernel space memory usage. This will appear as missing memory when we add up all the kernel and user space allocations that we know about.

User space memory layout

Linux employs a lazy allocation strategy for user space, only mapping physical pages of memory when the program accesses it. For example, allocating a buffer of 1 MiB using `malloc(3)` returns a pointer to a block of memory addresses but no actual physical memory. A flag is set in the page table entries such that any read or write access is trapped by the kernel. This is known as a page fault. Only at this point does the kernel attempt to find a page of physical memory and add it to the page table mapping for the process. It is worthwhile demonstrating this with a simple program like this one:

```c
#include <stdio.h>
#include <stdlib.h>
#include <string.h>
#include <sys/resource.h>
#define BUFFER_SIZE (1024 * 1024)

void print_pgfaults(void)
{
  int ret;
  struct rusage usage;
  ret = getrusage(RUSAGE_SELF, &usage);
  if (ret == -1) {
    perror("getrusage");
  } else {
    printf ("Major page faults %ld\n", usage.ru_majflt);
    printf ("Minor page faults %ld\n", usage.ru_minflt);
  }
}

int main (int argc, char *argv[])
{
  unsigned char *p;
  printf("Initial state\n");
  print_pgfaults();
  p = malloc(BUFFER_SIZE);
  printf("After malloc\n");
  print_pgfaults();
  memset(p, 0x42, BUFFER_SIZE);
  printf("After memset\n");
  print_pgfaults();
  memset(p, 0x42, BUFFER_SIZE);
  printf("After 2nd memset\n");
  print_pgfaults();
  return 0;
}
```

When you run it, you will see something like this:

```
Initial state
Major page faults 0
Minor page faults 172
After malloc
Major page faults 0
Minor page faults 186
After memset
Major page faults 0
Minor page faults 442
After 2nd memset
Major page faults 0
Minor page faults 442
```

There were 172 minor page faults encountered initializing the program's environment, and a further 14 when calling getrusage(2) (these numbers will vary depending on the architecture and the version of the C library you are using). The important part is the increase when filling the memory with data: 442 – 186 = 256. The buffer is 1 MiB, which is 256 pages. The second call to memset(3) makes no difference because all the pages are now mapped.

As you can see, a page fault is generated when the kernel traps an access to a page that has not been mapped. In fact, there are two kinds of page fault: minor and major. With a minor fault, the kernel just has to find a page of physical memory and map it into the process address space, as shown in the preceding code. A major page fault occurs when the virtual memory is mapped to a file, for example using mmap(2), which I will describe shortly. Reading from this memory means that the kernel not only has to find a page of memory and map it in, but it also has to be filled with data from the file. Consequently, major faults are much more expensive in time and system resources.

Process memory map

You can see the memory map for a process through the proc filesystem. As an example, here is the map for the init process, PID 1:

```
# cat /proc/1/maps
00008000-0000e000 r-xp 00000000 00:0b 23281745   /sbin/init
00016000-00017000 rwxp 00006000 00:0b 23281745   /sbin/init
00017000-00038000 rwxp 00000000 00:00 0          [heap]
b6ded000-b6f1d000 r-xp 00000000 00:0b 23281695   /lib/libc-2.19.so
b6f1d000-b6f24000 ---p 00130000 00:0b 23281695   /lib/libc-2.19.so
```

```
b6f24000-b6f26000 r-xp 0012f000 00:0b 23281695    /lib/libc-2.19.so
b6f26000-b6f27000 rwxp 00131000 00:0b 23281695    /lib/libc-2.19.so
b6f27000-b6f2a000 rwxp 00000000 00:00 0
b6f2a000-b6f49000 r-xp 00000000 00:0b 23281359    /lib/ld-2.19.so
b6f4c000-b6f4e000 rwxp 00000000 00:00 0
b6f4f000-b6f50000 r-xp 00000000 00:00 0           [sigpage]
b6f50000-b6f51000 r-xp 0001e000 00:0b 23281359    /lib/ld-2.19.so
b6f51000-b6f52000 rwxp 0001f000 00:0b 23281359    /lib/ld-2.19.so
beea1000-beec2000 rw-p 00000000 00:00 0           [stack]
ffff0000-ffff1000 r-xp 00000000 00:00 0           [vectors]
```

The first three columns show the start and end virtual addresses and the permissions for each mapping. The permissions are shown here:

- r = read
- w = write
- x = execute
- s = shared
- p = private (copy on write)

If the mapping is associated with a file, the filename appears in the final column, and columns four, five, and six contain the offset from the start of the file, the block device number and the inode of the file. Most of the mappings are to the program itself and the libraries it is linked with. There are two areas where the program can allocate memory, marked [heap] and [stack]. Memory allocated using malloc(3) comes from the former (except for very large allocations, which we will come to later) ; allocations on the stack come from the latter. The maximum size of both areas is controlled by the process's ulimit:

- **heap**: ulimit -d, default unlimited
- **stack**: ulimit -s, default 8 MiB

Allocations that exceed the limit are rejected by SIGSEGV.

When running out of memory, the kernel may decide to discard pages that are mapped to a file and are read-only. If that page is accessed again, it will cause a major page fault and be read back in from the file.

Swap

The idea of swapping is to reserve some storage where the kernel can place pages of memory that are not mapped to a file, so that it can free up the memory for other uses. It increases the effective size of physical memory by the size of the swap file. It is not a panacea: there is a cost to copying pages to and from a swap file which becomes apparent on a system that has too little real memory for the workload it is carrying and begins *disk thrashing*.

Swap is seldom used on embedded devices because it does not work well with flash storage where constant writing would wear it out quickly. However, you may want to consider swapping to compressed RAM (zram).

Swap to compressed memory (zram)

The zram driver creates RAM-based block devices named /dev/zram0, /dev/zram1, and so on. Pages written to these devices are compressed before being stored. With compression ratios in the range of 30% to 50%, you can expect an overall increase in free memory of about 10%, at the expense of more processing and a corresponding increase in power usage. It is used in some low memory Android devices.

To enable zram, configure the kernel with these options:

```
CONFIG_SWAP
CONFIG_CGROUP_MEM_RES_CTLR
CONFIG_CGROUP_MEM_RES_CTLR_SWAP
CONFIG_ZRAM
```

Then, mount zram at boot time by adding this to /etc/fstab:

```
/dev/zram0 none swap defaults zramsize=<size in
    bytes>,swapprio=<swap partition priority>
```

You can turn swap on and off by using these commands:

```
# swapon /dev/zram0
# swapoff /dev/zram0
```

Mapping memory with mmap

A process begins life with a certain amount of memory mapped to the text (the code) and data segments of the program file, together with the shared libraries that it is linked with. It can allocate memory on its heap at runtime using `malloc(3)` and on the stack through locally scoped variables and memory allocated through `alloca(3)`. It may also load libraries dynamically at runtime using `dlopen(3)`. All of these mappings are taken care of by the kernel. However, a process can also manipulate its memory map in an explicit way using `mmap(2)`:

```
void *mmap(void *addr, size_t length, int prot, int flags,
    int fd, off_t offset);
```

It maps `length` bytes of memory from the file with the descriptor `fd`, starting at `offset` in the file, and returns a pointer to the mapping, assuming it is successful. Since the underlying hardware works in pages, the `length` is rounded up to the nearest whole number of pages. The protection parameter, `prot`, is a combination of read, write, and execute permissions and the `flags` parameter contains at least `MAP_SHARED` or `MAP_PRIVATE`. There are many other flags, which are described in the man page.

There are many things you can do with mmap. Here are a few of them.

Using mmap to allocate private memory

You can use mmap to allocate an area of private memory by setting the `MAP_ANONYMOUS` flag and the `fd` file descriptor to `-1`. This is similar to allocating memory from the heap using `malloc(3)` except that the memory is page-aligned and in multiples of pages. The memory is allocated in the same area as that used for libraries. In fact, that area is referred to by some as the mmap area for this reason.

Anonymous mappings are better for large allocations because they do not pin down the heap with chunks of memory, which would make fragmentation more likely. Interestingly, you will find that `malloc(3)` (in glibc at least) stops allocating memory from the heap for requests over 128 KiB and uses mmap in this way, so in most cases, just using malloc is the right thing to do. The system will choose the best way of satisfying the request.

Using mmap to share memory

As we saw in *Chapter 10, Learning About Processes and Threads*, POSIX shared memory requires mmap to access the memory segment. In this case, you set the MAP_SHARED flag and use the file descriptor from shm_open():

```
int shm_fd;
char *shm_p;

shm_fd = shm_open("/myshm", O_CREAT | O_RDWR, 0666);
ftruncate(shm_fd, 65536);
shm_p = mmap(NULL, 65536, PROT_READ | PROT_WRITE,
  MAP_SHARED, shm_fd, 0);
```

Using mmap to access device memory

As I mentioned in Chapter 8, *Introducing Device Drivers*, it is possible for a driver to allow its device node to be mmaped and so share some of the device memory with an application. The exact implementation is dependent on the driver.

One example is the Linux frame buffer, /dev/fb0. The interface is defined in /usr/include/linux/fb.h, including an ioctl function to get the size of the display and the bits per pixel. You can then use mmap to ask the video driver to share the frame buffer with the application and read and write pixels:

```
int f;
int fb_size;
unsigned char *fb_mem;

f = open("/dev/fb0", O_RDWR);
/* Use ioctl FBIOGET_VSCREENINFO to find the display dimensions
  and calculate fb_size */
fb_mem = mmap(0, fb_size, PROT_READ | PROT_WRITE, MAP_SHARED, f,
  0);
/* read and write pixels through pointer fb_mem */
```

A second example is the streaming video interface, Video 4 Linux, version 2, or V4L2, which is defined in /usr/include/linux/videodev2.h. Each video device has a node named /dev/videoN, starting with /dev/video0. There is an ioctl function to ask the driver to allocate a number of video buffers which you can mmap into user space. Then, it is just a question of cycling the buffers and filling or emptying them with video data, depending on whether you are playing back or capturing a video stream.

How much memory does my application use?

As with kernel space, the different ways of allocating, mapping and sharing user space memory make it quite difficult to answer this seemingly simple question.

To begin with, you can ask the kernel how much memory it thinks is available, which you can do by using the `free` command. Here is a typical example of the output:

```
                 total      used       free   shared  buffers   cached
Mem:            509016    504312       4704        0    26456   363860
-/+ buffers/cache:        113996     395020
Swap:                0         0          0
```

At first sight, this looks like a system that is almost out of memory with only 4704 KiB free out of 509,016 KiB: less than 1%. However, note that 26,456 KiB is in buffers and a whopping 363,860 KiB is in cache. Linux believes that free memory is wasted memory and so the kernel uses free memory for buffers and caches, in the knowledge that they can be shrunk when the need arises. Removing buffers and cache from the measurement gives the true free memory, which is 395,020 KiB; 77% of the total. When using free, the numbers on the second line marked `-/+ buffers/cache` are the important ones.

You can force the kernel to free up caches by writing a number between 1 and 3 to `/proc/sys/vm/drop_caches`:

```
# echo 3 > /proc/sys/vm/drop_caches
```

The number is actually a bit mask which determines which of the two broad types of cache you want to free: 1 for the page cache and 2 for the dentry and inode caches combined. The exact roles of those caches is not particularly important here, only that there is memory that the kernel is using but which can be reclaimed at short notice.

Per-process memory usage

There are several metrics to measure the amount of memory a process is using. I will begin with the two that are easiest to obtain— the **virtual set size (vss)** and the **resident memory size (rss)**, both of which are available in most implementations of the ps and top commands:

- **Vss**: called VSZ in the ps command and VIRT in top, is the total amount of memory mapped by a process. It is the sum of all the regions shown in /proc/<PID>/map. This number is of limited interest, since only part of the virtual memory is committed to physical memory at any one time.

- **Rss**: called RSS in ps and RES in top, is the sum of memory that is mapped to physical pages of memory. This gets closer to the actual memory budget of the process, but there is a problem, if you add up the Rss of all the processes, you will get an overestimate the memory in use because some pages will be shared.

Using top and ps

The versions of top and ps from BusyBox give very limited information. The examples that follow use the full version from the procps pacakge.

The ps command shows Vss (VSZ) and Rss (RSS) with the options, -Aly, and a custom format which includes vsz and rss, as shown here:

```
# ps -eo pid,tid,class,rtprio,stat,vsz,rss,comm

  PID   TID CLS RTPRIO STAT   VSZ   RSS COMMAND
    1     1 TS       -  Ss    4496  2652 systemd
  ...
  205   205 TS       -  Ss    4076  1296 systemd-journal
  228   228 TS       -  Ss    2524  1396 udevd
  581   581 TS       -  Ss    2880  1508 avahi-daemon
  584   584 TS       -  Ss    2848  1512 dbus-daemon
  590   590 TS       -  Ss    1332   680 acpid
  594   594 TS       -  Ss    4600  1564 wpa_supplicant
```

Likewise, `top` shows a summary of the free memory and memory usage per process:

```
top - 21:17:52 up 10:04,  1 user,  load average: 0.00, 0.01, 0.05
Tasks:  96 total,   1 running,  95 sleeping,   0 stopped,   0
zombie
%Cpu(s):  1.7 us,  2.2 sy,  0.0 ni, 95.9 id,  0.0 wa,  0.0 hi,
0.2 si,  0.0 st
KiB Mem:    509016 total,   278524 used,   230492 free,    25572
buffers
KiB Swap:        0 total,        0 used,        0 free,   170920
cached

PID USER      PR  NI  VIRT  RES  SHR S  %CPU %MEM    TIME+
   COMMAND
1098 debian   20   0 29076  16m 8312 S   0.0  3.2   0:01.29
   wicd-client
  595 root    20   0 64920 9.8m 4048 S   0.0  2.0   0:01.09 node
  866 root    20   0 28892 9152 3660 S   0.2  1.8   0:36.38 Xorg
```

These simple commands give you a feel of the memory usage and give the first indication that you have a memory leak when you see that the Rss of a process keeps on increasing. However, they are not very accurate in the absolute measurements of memory usage.

Using smem

In 2009, Matt Mackall began looking at the problem of accounting for shared pages in process memory measurement and added two new metrics called the **unique set size** or **Uss**, and the **proportional set size** or **Pss**:

- **Uss**: This is the amount of memory that is committed to physical memory and is unique to a process; it is not shared with any other. It is the amount of memory that would be freed if the process were to terminate.

- **Pss**: This splits the accounting of shared pages that are committed to physical memory between all the processes that have them mapped. For example, if an area of library code is 12 pages long and is shared by six processes, each will accumulate two pages in Pss. Thus, if you add the Pss numbers for all processes, you will get the actual amount of memory being used by those processes. In other words, Pss is the number we have been looking for.

The information is available in `/proc/<PID>/smaps`, which contains additional information for each of the mappings shown in `/proc/<PID>/maps`. Here is one section from such a file which provides information about the mapping for the `libc` code segment:

```
b6e6d000-b6f45000 r-xp 00000000 b3:02 2444 /lib/libc-2.13.so
Size:                 864 kB
Rss:                  264 kB
Pss:                    6 kB
Shared_Clean:         264 kB
Shared_Dirty:           0 kB
Private_Clean:          0 kB
Private_Dirty:          0 kB
Referenced:           264 kB
Anonymous:              0 kB
AnonHugePages:          0 kB
Swap:                   0 kB
KernelPageSize:         4 kB
MMUPageSize:            4 kB
Locked:                 0 kB
VmFlags: rd ex mr mw me
```

 Note that the Rss is 264 KiB but because it is shared between many other processes, the Pss is only 6 KiB.

There is a tool named smem that collates the information from the `smaps` files and presents it in various ways, including as pie or bar charts. The project page for smem is `https://www.selenic.com/smem`. It is available as a package in most desktop distributions. However, since it is written in Python, installing it on an embedded target requires a Python environment, which may be too much trouble for just one tool. To help with this, there is a small program named `smemcap` that captures the state from `/proc` on the target and saves it to a TAR file which can be analyzed later on the host computer. It is part of BusyBox, but it can also be compiled from the `smem` source.

Running `smem` natively, as `root`, you will see these results:

```
# smem -t
  PID User  Command                      Swap    USS   PSS   RSS
  610 0     /sbin/agetty -s ttyO0 11        0    128   149   720
 1236 0     /sbin/agetty -s ttyGS0 1        0    128   149   720
  609 0     /sbin/agetty tty1 38400         0    144   163   724
  578 0     /usr/sbin/acpid                 0    140   173   680
  819 0     /usr/sbin/cron                  0    188   201   704
  634 103   avahi-daemon: chroot hel        0    112   205   500
```

980	0	/usr/sbin/udhcpd -S /etc	0	196	205	568
	...					
836	0	/usr/bin/X :0 -auth /var	0	7172	7746	9212
583	0	/usr/bin/node autorun.js	0	8772	9043	10076
1089	1000	/usr/bin/python -O /usr/	0	9600	11264	16388
53	6		0	65820	78251	146544

You can see from the last line of the output that, in this case, the total Pss is about a half of the Rss.

If you don't have or don't want to install Python on your target, you can capture the state using smemcap, again as root:

```
# smemcap > smem-bbb-cap.tar
```

Then, copy the TAR file to the host and read it using smem -S, though this time there is no need to run as root:

```
$ smem -t -S smem-bbb-cap.tar
```

The output is identical to that when running it natively.

Other tools to consider

Another way to display Pss is via ps_mem (https://github.com/pixelb/ps_mem), which prints much the same information but in a simpler format. It is also written in Python.

Android also has a tool named procrank, which can be cross compiled for embedded Linux with a few small changes. You can get the code from https://github.com/csimmonds/procrank_linux.

Identifying memory leaks

A memory leak occurs when memory is allocated but not freed when it is no longer needed. Memory leakage is by no means unique to embedded systems, but it becomes an issue partly because targets don't have much memory in the first place, and partly because they often run for long periods of time without rebooting, allowing the leaks to become a large puddle.

You will realize that there is a leak when you run free or top and see that free memory is continually going down, even if you drop caches, as shown in the preceding section. You will be able to identify the culprit (or culprits) by looking at the Uss and Rss per process.

There are several tools for identifying memory leaks in a program. I will look at two: `mtrace` and `Valgrind`.

mtrace

`mtrace` is a component of glibc that traces calls to `malloc(3)`, `free(3)`, and related functions, and identifies areas of memory not freed when the program exits. You need to call the `mtrace()` function from within the program to begin tracing and then at runtime, write a path name to the `MALLOC_TRACE` environment variable in which the trace information is written. If `MALLOC_TRACE` does not exist or of the file cannot be opened, `mtrace` hooks are not not installed. While the trace information is written in ASCII, it is usual to use the `mtrace` command to view it.

Here is an example:

```
#include <mcheck.h>
#include <stdlib.h>
#include <stdio.h>

int main(int argc, char *argv[])
{
  int j;
  mtrace();
  for (j = 0; j < 2; j++)
    malloc(100);  /* Never freed:a memory leak */
  calloc(16, 16);  /* Never freed:a memory leak */
  exit(EXIT_SUCCESS);
}
```

Here is what you might see when running the program and looking at the trace:

```
$ export MALLOC_TRACE=mtrace.log
$ ./mtrace-example
$ mtrace mtrace-example mtrace.log

Memory not freed:
-----------------
          Address     Size     Caller
0x0000000001479460    0x64   at /home/chris/mtrace-example.c:11
0x00000000014794d0    0x64   at /home/chris/mtrace-example.c:11
0x0000000001479540    0x100  at /home/chris/mtrace-example.c:15
```

Unfortunately, `mtrace` does not tell you about leaked memory while the program runs. It has to terminate first.

Valgrind

Valgrind is a very powerful tool for discovering memory problems including leaks, and other things besides. One advantage is that you don't have to recompile the programs and libraries that you want to check, although it does work better if they have been compiled with the -g option so that they include debug symbol tables. It works by running the program in an emulated environment and trapping execution at various points. This leads to the big downside of Valgrind, which is that the program runs at a fraction of normal speed which makes it less useful for testing anything with real-time constraints.

 Incidentally, the name is often mispronounced: it says in the Valgrind FAQ that the *grind* is pronounced with a short *i* -- as in *grinned* (rhymes with *tinned*) rather than *grined* (rhymes with *find*). The FAQ, documentation and downloads are available at http://valgrind.org.

Valgrind contains several diagnostic tools:

- **memcheck**: This is the default tool, and detects memory leaks and general misuse of memory
- **cachegrind**: This calculates the processor cache hit rate
- **callgrind**: This calculates the cost of each function call
- **helgrind**: This highlights misuse of the Pthread API, potential deadlocks, and race conditions
- **DRD**: This is another Pthread analysis tool
- **massif**: This profiles usage of the heap and stack

You can select the tool you want with the -tool option. Valgrind runs on the major embedded platforms: ARM (Cortex A), PPC, MIPS, and x86 in 32- and 64-bit variants. It is available as a package in both the Yocto Project and Buildroot.

To find our memory leak, we need to use the default memcheck tool, with the option --leakcheck=full to print out the lines where the leak was found:

```
$ valgrind --leak-check=full ./mtrace-example
==17235== Memcheck, a memory error detector
==17235== Copyright (C) 2002-2013, and GNU GPL'd, by Julian Seward
  et al.
==17235== Using Valgrind-3.10.0.SVN and LibVEX; rerun with -h for
  copyright info
==17235== Command: ./mtrace-example
==17235==
```

```
==17235==
==17235== HEAP SUMMARY:
==17235==   in use at exit: 456 bytes in 3 blocks
==17235==   total heap usage: 3 allocs, 0 frees, 456 bytes
  allocated
==17235==
==17235== 200 bytes in 2 blocks are definitely lost in loss record
  1 of 2
==17235==     at 0x4C2AB80: malloc (in
  /usr/lib/valgrind/vgpreload_memcheck-linux.so)
==17235==     by 0x4005FA: main (mtrace-example.c:12)
==17235==
==17235== 256 bytes in 1 blocks are definitely lost in loss record
  2 of 2
==17235==     at 0x4C2CC70: calloc (in
  /usr/lib/valgrind/vgpreload_memcheck-linux.so)
==17235==     by 0x400613: main (mtrace-example.c:14)
==17235==
==17235== LEAK SUMMARY:
==17235==    definitely lost: 456 bytes in 3 blocks
==17235==    indirectly lost: 0 bytes in 0 blocks
==17235==      possibly lost: 0 bytes in 0 blocks
==17235==    still reachable: 0 bytes in 0 blocks
==17235==         suppressed: 0 bytes in 0 blocks
==17235==
==17235== For counts of detected and suppressed errors, rerun
  with: -v
==17235== ERROR SUMMARY: 2 errors from 2 contexts (suppressed: 0
  from 0)
```

Running out of memory

The standard memory allocation policy is to **over-commit**, meaning that the kernel will allow more memory to be allocated by applications than there is physical memory. Most of the time, this works fine because it is common for applications to request more memory than they really need. It also helps in the implementation of fork(2): it is safe to make a copy of a large program because the pages of memory are shared with the copy-on-write flag set. In the majority of cases, fork is followed by an exec function call, which unshares the memory and then loads a new program.

However, there is always the possibility that a particular workload will cause a group of processes to try to cash in on the allocations they have been promised simultaneously and so demand more than there really is. This is an **out of memory** situation, or **OOM**. At this point, there is no other alternative but to kill off processes until the problem goes away. This is the job of the out of memory killer.

Before we get to that, there is a tuning parameter for kernel allocations in
`/proc/sys/vm/overcommit_memory`, which you can set to:

- `0`: heuristic over-commit (this is the default)
- `1`: always over-commit, never check
- `2`: always check, never over-commit

Option 1 is only really useful if you run programs that work with large sparse arrays
and so allocate large areas of memory but write to a small proportion of them. Such
programs are rare in the context of embedded systems.

Option 2, never over-commit, seems to be a good choice if you are worried about
running out of memory, perhaps in a mission or safety-critical application. It will
fail allocations that are greater than the commit limit, which is the size of swap space
plus total memory multiplied by the over-commit ratio. The over-commit ratio is
controlled by `/proc/sys/vm/overcommit_ratio` and has a default value of 50%.

As an example, suppose you have a device with 512 MB of system RAM and you set
a really conservative ratio of 25%:

```
# echo 25 > /proc/sys/vm/overcommit_ratio
# grep -e MemTotal -e CommitLimit /proc/meminfo
MemTotal:          509016 kB
CommitLimit:       127252 kB
```

There is no swap so the commit limit is 25% of `MemTotal`, as expected.

There is another important variable in `/proc/meminfo`: `Committed_AS`. This is
the total amount of memory that is needed to fulfill all the allocations made so far.
I found the following on one system:

```
# grep -e MemTotal -e Committed_AS /proc/meminfo
MemTotal:          509016 kB
Committed_AS:      741364 kB
```

In other words, the kernel has already promised more memory than the available
memory. Consequently, setting `overcommit_memory` to 2 means that all allocations
fail, regardless of `overcommit_ratio`. To get to a working system, I would have to
either install double the amount of RAM or severely reduce the number of running
processes, of which there are about 40.

In all cases, the final defense is the OOM killer. It uses a heuristic method to calculate a badness score between 0 and 1,000 for each process and then terminates those with the highest score until there is enough free memory. You should see something like this in the kernel log:

```
[44510.490320] eatmem invoked oom-killer: gfp_mask=0x200da,
order=0, oom_score_adj=0
...
```

You can force an OOM event using `echo f > /proc/sysrq-trigger`.

You can influence the badness score for a process by writing an adjustment value to `/proc/<PID>/oom_score_adj`. A value of `-1000` means that the badness score can never be greater than zero and so it will never be killed; a value of `+1000` means that it will always be greater than 1000 and so will always be killed.

Further reading

The following resources have further information about the topics introduced in this chapter:

- *Linux Kernel Development, 3rd Edition,* by *Robert Love, Addison Wesley, O'Reilly Media;* (Jun. 2010) ISBN-10: 0672329468

- *Linux System Programming, 2nd Edition,* by *Robert Love, O'Reilly Media;* (8 Jun. 2013) ISBN-10: 1449339530

- *Understanding the Linux VM Manager* by *Mel Gorman:* `https://www.kernel.org/doc/gorman/pdf/understand.pdf`

- *Valgrind 3.3 - Advanced Debugging and Profiling for Gnu/Linux Applications* by *J Seward, N. Nethercote,* and *J. Weidendorfer, Network Theory Ltd;* (1 Mar. 2008) ISBN 978-0954612054

Summary

Accounting for every byte of memory used in a virtual memory system is just not possible. However, you can find a fairly accurate figure for the total amount of free memory, excluding that taken by buffers and cache, by using the `free` command. By monitoring it over a period of time and with different workloads, you should become confident that it will remain within a given limit.

When you want to tune memory usage or identify sources of unexpected allocations, there are resources that give more detailed information. For kernel space, the most useful information is in `/proc:` `meminfo`, `slabinfo`, and `vmallocinfo`.

When it comes to getting accurate measurements for user space, the best metric is Pss, as shown by smem and other tools. For memory debugging, you can get help from simple tracers such as mtrace, or you have the heavyweight option of the Valgrind memcheck tool.

If you have concerns about the consequence of an out of memory situation, you can fine-tune the allocation mechanism via /proc/sys/vm/overcommit_memory and you can control the likelihood of particular processes being killed though the oom_score_adj parameter.

The next chapter is all about debugging user space and kernel code using the GNU debugger, and the insights you can gain from watching code as it runs, including the memory management functions I have described here.

12
Debugging with GDB

Bugs happen. Identifying and fixing them is part of the development process. There are many different techniques for finding and characterizing program defects, including static and dynamic analysis, code review, tracing, profiling, and interactive debugging. I will look at tracers and profilers in the next chapter, but here I want to concentrate on the traditional approach of watching code execution through a debugger, in our case, the **GNU debugger**, **GDB**. GDB is a powerful and flexible tool. You can use it to debug applications, examine the postmortem files (core files) that are created after a program crash, and even step through kernel code.

In this chapter, I will show you how to use GDB to debug applications, how to look at core files and how to debug kernel code, in all cases, emphasizing the aspects that are relevant for embedded Linux.

The GNU debugger

GDB is a source-level debugger for the compiled languages, primarily C and C++, although there is also support for a variety of other languages such as Go and Objective. You should read the notes for the version of GDB you are using to find out the current status of support for the various languages. The project website is http://www.gnu.org/software/gdb and contains a lot of useful information, including the GDB manual.

Out of the box, GDB has a command-line user interface which some people find off-putting although, in reality, it is easy to use with a little practice. If command-line interfaces are not to your liking, there are a lot of front-end user interfaces to GDB and I will describe three of them later.

Preparing to debug

You need to compile the code you want to debug with debug symbols. GCC offers two options for this: -g and -ggdb. The latter adds debug information that is specific to GDB, whereas the former generates information in an appropriate format for whichever target operating system you are using, making it the more portable option. In our particular case, the target operating system is always Linux and it makes little difference whether you use -g or -ggdb. Of more interest is the fact that both options allow you to specify the level of debug information, from 0 to 3:

- 0: This produces no debug information at all and is equivalent to omitting the -g or -ggdb switch

- 1: This produces little information but which includes function names and external variables which is enough to generate a back trace

- 2: This is the default and includes information about local variables and line numbers so that you can do source level debugging and a single step through the code

- 3: This includes extra information which, among other things, means that GDB handles macro expansions correctly

In most cases, -g suffices but reserve -g3 or -ggdb3 if you are having problems stepping through code, especially if it contains macros.

The next issue to consider is the level of code optimization. Compiler optimization tends to destroy the relationship between lines of source code and machine code, which makes stepping through the source unpredictable. If you experience problems like this you will most likely need to compile without optimization, leaving out the -O compile switch, or at least reduce it to level 1, using the compile switch -O1.

A related issue is that of stack frame pointers, which are needed by GDB to generate a back trace of function calls up to the current one. On some architectures, GCC will not generate stack frame pointers with higher levels of optimization (-O2). If you find yourself in the situation that you really have to compile with -O2 but still want back traces, you can override the default behavior with -fno-omit-frame-pointer. Also look out for code that has been hand optimized to leave out frame pointers through the addition of -fomit-frame-pointer: you may want to temporarily remove them.

Debugging applications using GDB

You can use GDB to debug applications in one of two ways. If you are developing code to run on desktops and servers, or indeed any environment where you compile and run the code on the same machine, it is natural to run GDB natively. However, most embedded development is done using a cross toolchain and hence you want to debug code running on the device, but control it from the cross-development environment where you have the source code and the tools. I will focus on the latter case since it is not so well documented and yet it is the most likely scenario for embedded developers. I am not going to describe the basics of using GDB here since there are many good references on that topic already, including the GDB manual and the suggested further reading at the end of the chapter.

I will begin with some details on working with gdbserver and then show you how to configure the Yocto Project and Buildroot for remote debug.

Remote debugging using gdbserver

The key component for remote debugging is the debug agent, gdbserver, which runs on the target and controls execution of the program being debugged. Gdbserver connects to a copy of GDB running on the host machine via a network connection or an RS-232 serial interface.

Debugging through gdbserver is almost, but not quite, the same as debugging natively. The differences are mostly centered around the fact that there are two computers involved and they have to be in the right state for debugging to take place. Here are some things to look out for:

- At the start of a debug session you need to load the program you want to debug on the target using gdbserver and then separately load GDB from your cross toolchain on the host.

- GDB and gdbserver need to connect to each other before a debug session can begin.

- GDB, running onto the host, needs to be told where to look for debug symbols and source code, especially for shared libraries.

- The GDB run command does not work as expected.

- gdbserver will terminate when the debug session ends and you will need to restart it if you want another debug session.

- You need debug symbols and source code for the binaries you want to debug on the host, but not necessarily on the target. Often there is not enough storage space for them on the target and they will need to be stripped before deploying to the target.

- The GDB/gdbserver combination does not have all the features of GDB running natively: for example, gdbserver cannot follow the child after `fork()` whereas native GDB can.

- Odd things can happen if GDB and gdbserver are different versions or are the same version but configured differently. Ideally they should be built from the same source using your favorite build tool.

Debug symbols increase the size of executables dramatically, sometimes by a factor of 10. As mentioned in *Chapter 5, Building a Root Filesystem*, it can be useful to remove debug symbols without recompiling everything. The tool for the job is strip from your cross toolchain. You can control the aggressiveness of the strip with these switches:

- `--strip-all`: (default) removes all symbols
- `--strip-unneeded`: removes symbols not needed for relocation processing
- `--strip-debug`: removes only debug symbols

> For applications and shared libraries, `--strip-all` (the default) is fine, but when it comes to kernel modules you will find that it will stop the module loading. Use `--strip-unneeded` instead. I am still working on a use case for `-strip-debug`.

With that in mind, let's look at the specifics involved in debugging with the Yocto Project and Buildroot.

Setting up the Yocto Project

The Yocto Project builds a cross GDB for the host as part of the SDK, but you will have to make changes to your target configuration to include gdbserver in the target image. You can add the package explicitly, for example by adding this to `conf/local.conf`, noting once again that there must be a leading space at the start of this string:

```
IMAGE_INSTALL_append = " gdbserver"
```

Or, you can add `tools-debug` to `EXTRA_IMAGE_FEATURES`, which will add both gdbserver and strace to the target image (I will talk about `strace` in the next chapter):

```
EXTRA_IMAGE_FEATURES = "debug-tweaks tools-debug"
```

Setting up Buildroot

With Buildroot, you need to enable options both to build the cross GDB for the host (assuming that you are using the Buildroot internal toolchain) and to build gdbserver for the target. Specifically you need to enable:

- BR2_PACKAGE_HOST_GDB, in the menu **Toolchain | Build cross gdb for the host**

- BR2_PACKAGE_GDB, in the menu **Target packages | Debugging, profiling and benchmark | gdb**

- BR2_PACKAGE_GDB_SERVER in the menu **Target packages | Debugging, profiling and benchmark | gdbserver**

Starting to debug

Now that you have gdbserver installed on the target and a cross GDB on the host you can start a debug session.

Connecting GDB and gdbserver

The connection between GDB and gdbserver can be through a network or a serial interface. In the case of a network connection, you launch gdbserver with the TCP port number to listen on and, optionally, an IP address to accept connections from. In most cases you don't care which IP address is going to connect, so you can just give the port number. In this example gdbserver waits for a connection on port 10000 from any host:

```
# gdbserver :10000 ./hello-world
Process hello-world created; pid = 103
Listening on port 10000
```

Next, start the copy of GDB from your toolchain, giving the same program as an argument so that GDB can load the symbol table:

```
$ arm-poky-linux-gnueabi-gdb hello-world
```

In GDB, you use the command target remote to make the connection, giving the IP address or host name of the target and the port it is waiting on:

```
(gdb) target remote 192.168.1.101:10000
```

When gdbserver sees the connection from the host it prints the following:

```
Remote debugging from host 192.168.1.1
```

The procedure is similar for a serial connection. On the target, you tell gdbserver which serial port to use:

```
# gdbserver /dev/tty00 ./hello-world
```

You may need to configure the port baud rate beforehand using `stty` or a similar program. A simple example would be as follows:

```
# stty -F /dev/tty01 115200
```

There are many other options to `stty`, please read the man page for more details. It is worthwhile noting that the port must not be used for anything else, for example, you can't use a port that is being used as the system console. On the host, you make the connection to gdbserver using `target remote` plus the serial device at the host end of the cable. In most cases you will want to set the baud rate of the host serial port using the GDB command `set remotebaud`:

```
(gdb) set remotebaud 115200
(gdb) target remote /dev/ttyUSB0
```

Setting the sysroot

GDB needs to know where to find debug symbols and source code for shared libraries. When debugging natively the paths are well known and built in to GDB, but when using a cross toolchain, GDB has no way to guess where the root of the target filesystem is. You do so by setting the sysroot. The Yocto Project and Buildroot have different ways of handling library symbols so the location of the sysroot is quite different.

The Yocto Project includes debug information in the target filesystem image, so you need to unpack the target image tar file that is generated in `build/tmp/deploy/images`, for which you would need to do something like this:

```
$ mkdir ~/rootfs
$ cd ~/rootfs
$ sudo tar xf ~/poky/build/tmp/deploy/images/beaglebone/core-image-minimal-
beaglebone.tar.bz2Then you can point sysroot to the root of the unpacked
files:
```

```
(gdb) set sysroot /home/chris/MELP/rootfs
```

Buildroot compiles libraries with minimal or full debug symbols, depending on `BR2_ENABLE_DEBUG`, puts them into the staging directory, then strips them as they are copied into target image. So, for Buildroot, the sysroot is always the staging area regardless of where the root filesystem is extracted.

GDB command files

There are some things that you need to do each time you run GDB, for example, setting the sysroot. It is convenient to put such commands into a command file and run them each time GDB is started. GDB reads commands from `$HOME/.gdbinit`, then from `.gdbinit` in the current directory and then from files specified on the command line with the `-x` parameter. However, recent versions of GDB will refuse to load `.gdbinit` from the current directory for security reasons. You can override that behavior for a single directory by adding a line like this to your `$HOME/.gdbinit`:

```
add-auto-load-safe-path /home/chris/myprog/.gdbinit
```

You can also disable the check globally by adding:

```
set auto-load safe-path /
```

My personal preference is use the `-x` parameter to point to the command file, which exposes the location of the file so I don't forget about it.

To help you set up GDB, Buildroot creates a GDB command file containing the correct sysroot command in `output/staging/usr/share/buildroot/gdbinit`. It will contain a command similar to this one:

```
set sysroot /home/chris/buildroot/output/host/usr/arm-buildroot-linux-
gnueabi/sysroot
```

Overview of GDB commands

GDB has a great many commands, which are described in the online manual and in the resources mentioned in the *Further Reading* section. To help you get going as quickly as possible, here is a list of the most commonly used commands. In most cases there is a short-hand for the command, which is listed underneath the full command.

Breakpoints

The following table shows the commands for breakpoints:

Commands	Use
`break <location>` `b <location>`	Set a breakpoint on a function name, line number or line. Examples are: `"main"`, `"5"`, and `"sortbug.c:42"`
`info break` `i b`	List breakpoints
`delete break <N>` `d b <N>`	Delete breakpoint N

Running and stepping

The following table shows the commands for running and stepping:

Commands	Use
run r	Load a fresh copy of the program into memory and start it running. This does not work for remote debug using gdbserver
continue c	Continue execution from a breakpoint
Ctrl-C	Stop the program being debugged
step s	Step one line of code, stepping into any function that is called
next n	Step one line of code, stepping over a function call
finish	Run until the current function returns

Information commands

The following table shows the commands for getting information:

Commands	Use
backtrace bt	List the call stack
info threads	Continue execution from a breakpoint
Info libs	Stop the program
print <variable> p <variable>	Print the value of a variable, e.g. print foo
list	List lines of code around the current program counter

Running to a breakpoint

Gdbserver loads the program into memory and sets a breakpoint at the first instruction, then waits for a connection from GDB. When the connection is made you enter into a debug session. However, you will find that if you try to single step immediately you will get this message:

```
Cannot find bounds of current function
```

This is because the program is halted in code written in assembly that creates the run time environment for C and C++ programs. The first line of C or C++ code is the main() function. Supposing that you want to stop at main(), you would set a breakpoint there and then use the continue command (abbreviation c) to tell gdbserver to continue from the breakpoint at the start of the program and stop at main:

```
(gdb) break main
Breakpoint 1, main (argc=1, argv=0xbefffe24) at helloworld.c:8
8 printf("Hello, world!\n");
```

If at this point you see the following:

```
warning: Could not load shared library symbols for 2 libraries,
e.g. /lib/libc.so.6.
```

That means that you have forgotten the set sysroot!

This is all very different to starting a program natively, where you just type run. In fact, if you try typing run in a remote debug session, you will either see a message saying that the remote target does not support run, or in older versions of GDB it will just hang without any explanation.

Debugging shared libraries

To debug the libraries that are built by the build tool you will have to make a few changes to the build configuration. For libraries built outside the build environment you will have to do some extra work.

The Yocto Project

The Yocto Project builds debug variants of binary packages and puts them into build/tmp/deploy/<package manager>/<target architecture>. Here is an example of the debug package, for the C library in this case:

build/tmp/deploy/rpm/armv5e/libc6-dbg-2.21-r0.armv5e.rpm

You can add these debug packages selectively to your target image by adding <package name-dbg> to your target recipe. For glibc, the package is named glibc-dbg. Alternatively, you can simply tell the Yocto Project to install all debug packages by adding dbg-pkgs to EXTRA_IMAGE_FEATURES. Be warned that this will increase the size of the target image dramatically, perhaps by several hundred megabytes.

The Yocto Project places the debug symbols in a hidden directory named `.debug` in both the `lib` and `usr/lib`, directories. GDB knows to look for symbol information in these locations within the sysroot.

The debug packages also contain a copy of the source code which is installed into directory `usr/src/debug/<package name>` in the target image, which is one of the reasons for the increase in size. You can prevent it from happening by adding to your recipes:

```
PACKAGE_DEBUG_SPLIT_STYLE = "debug-without-src"
```

Remember, though, that when you are debugging remotely with gdbserver, you only need the debug symbols and source code on the host, not on the target. There is nothing to stop you from deleting the `lib/.debug`, `usr/lib/.debug` and `usr/src` directories from the copy of the image that is installed on the target.

Buildroot

Buildroot is characteristically straightforward. You just need to rebuild with line-level debug symbols, for which you need to enable the following:

* `BR2_ENABLE_DEBUG` in the menu **Build options | build packages with debugging symbols**

This will create the libraries with debug symbols in `output/host/usr/<arch>/sysroot`, but the copies in the target image are still stripped. If you need debug symbols on the target, perhaps to run GDB natively, you can disable stripping by setting **Build options | strip command for binaries on target** to none.

Other libraries

In addition to building with debug symbols you will have to tell GDB where to find the source code. GDB has a search path for source files, which you can see using the command `show directories`:

```
(gdb) show directories
Source directories searched: $cdir:$cwd
```

These are the default search paths: `$cdir` is the compile directory, which is the directory where the source was compiled; `$cwd` is the current working directory of GDB.

Normally these are sufficient, but if the source code has been moved you will have to use the directory command as shown here:

```
(gdb) dir /home/chris/MELP/src/lib_mylib
Source directories searched:
/home/chris/MELP/src/lib_mylib:$cdir:$cwd
```

Just-in-time debugging

Sometimes a program will start to misbehave after it has been running for a while and you would like to know what it is doing. The GDB attach feature does exactly that. I call it just-in-time debugging. It is available with both native and remote debug sessions.

In the case of remote debugging, you need to find the PID of the process to be debugged and pass it to gdbserver with the --attach option. For example, if the PID is 109 you would type:

```
# gdbserver --attach :10000 109

Attached; pid = 109

Listening on port 10000
```

That forces the process to stop as if it were at a breakpoint, allowing you to start your cross GDB in the normal way and connect to gdbserver.

When you are done you can detach, allowing the program to continue running without the debugger:

```
(gdb) detach
Detaching from program: /home/chris/MELP/helloworld/helloworld,
process 109
Ending remote debugging.
```

Debugging forks and threads

What happens when the program you are debugging forks? Does the debug session follow the parent or the child? The behavior is controlled by follow-fork-mode which may be parent or child, with parent being the default. Unfortunately, current versions of gdbserver do not support this option, so it only works for native debugging. If you really need to debug the child process while using gdbserver, a workaround is to modify the code so that the child loops on a variable immediately after the fork, giving you the opportunity to attach a new gdbserver session to it and then to set the variable so that it drops out of the loop.

When a thread in a multithreaded process hits a breakpoint, the default behavior is for all threads to halt. In most cases this is the best thing to do as it allows you to look at static variables without them being changed by the other threads. When you recommence execution of the thread, all the stopped threads start up, even if you are single stepping, and it is especially this last case that can cause problems. There is a way to modify the way GDB handles stopped threads, through a parameter called `scheduler-locking`. Normally it is `off`, but if you set it to `on`, only the thread that was stopped at the breakpoint is resumed and the others remain stopped, giving you a chance to see what the thread alone does without interference. This continues to be the case until you turn scheduler-locking off. Gdbserver supports this feature.

Core files

Core files capture the state of a failing program at the point that it terminates. You don't even have to be in the room with a debugger when the bug manifests itself. So when you see `Segmentation fault (core dumped)`, don't shrug; investigate the core file and extract the goldmine of information in there.

The first observation is that core files are not created by default, but only when the core file resource limit for the process is non-zero. You can change it for the current shell using `ulimit -c`. To remove all limits on the size of core files, type the following:

```
$ ulimit -c unlimited
```

By default, the core file is named `core` and is placed in the current working directory of the process, which is the one pointed to by `/proc/<PID>/cwd`. There are a number of problems with this scheme. Firstly, when looking at a device with several files named `core` it is not obvious which program generated each one. Secondly, the current working directory of the process may well be in a read-only filesystem, or there may not be enough space to store the `core` file, or the process may not have permissions to write to the current working directory.

There are two files that control the naming and placement of `core` files. The first is `/proc/sys/kernel/core_uses_pid`. Writing a `1` to it causes the PID number of the dying process to be appended to the filename, which is somewhat useful as long as you can associate the PID number with a program name from log files.

Much more useful is `/proc/sys/kernel/core_pattern`, which gives you a lot more control over `core` files. The default pattern is `core` but you can change it to a pattern composed of these meta characters:

- `%p`: the PID
- `%u`: the real UID of the dumped process

- %g: the real GID of the dumped process
- %s: number of the signal causing the dump
- %t: the time of dump, expressed as seconds since the Epoch, 1970-01-01 00:00:00 +0000 (UTC)
- %h: the hostname
- %e: the executable filename
- %E: the pathname of the executable, with slashes (/) replaced by exclamation marks (!)
- %c: the core file size soft resource limit of the dumped process

You can also use a pattern that begins with an absolute directory name so that all core files are gathered together in one place. As an example, the following pattern puts all core files into the /corefiles directory and names them with the program name and the time of the crash:

```
# echo /corefiles/core.%e.%t > /proc/sys/kernel/core_pattern
```

Following a core dump, you would find something like this:

```
$ ls /corefiles/
core.sort-debug.1431425613
```

For more information, refer to the man page *core(5)*.

For more sophisticated processing of core files you can pipe them to a program that does some post processing. The core pattern begins with a pipe symbol | followed by the program name and parameters. My Ubuntu 14.04, for example, has this core pattern:

```
|/usr/share/apport/apport %p %s %c %P
```

Apport is the crash reporting tool used by Canonical. A crash reporting tool run in this way is run while the process is still in memory, and the kernel passes the core image data to it on standard input. Thus, this program can process the image, possibly stripping parts of it to reduce the size in the filesystem, or just scanning it at the time of the core dump for specific information. The program can look at various pieces of system data, for example, reading the /proc filesystem entries for the program, and can use ptrace system calls to operate on the program and read data from it. However, once the core image data is read from standard in, the kernel does various cleanups that make information about the process no longer available.

Using GDB to look at core files

Here is a sample GDB session looking at a core file:

```
$ arm-poky-linux-gnueabi-gdb sort-debug
/home/chris/MELP/rootdirs/rootfs/corefiles/core.sort-debug.1431425613
[...]
Core was generated by `./sort-debug'.
Program terminated with signal SIGSEGV, Segmentation fault.
#0  0x000085c8 in addtree (p=0x0, w=0xbeac4c60 "the") at sort-
debug.c:41
41       p->word = strdup (w);
```

That shows that the program stopped at line 43. The `list` command shows the code in the immediate vicinity:

```
(gdb) list
37       static struct tnode *addtree (struct tnode *p, char *w)
38       {
39           int cond;
40
41           p->word = strdup (w);
42           p->count = 1;
43           p->left = NULL;
44           p->right = NULL;
45
```

The `backtrace` command (shortened to `bt`) shows how we got to this point:

```
(gdb) bt
#0  0x000085c8 in addtree (p=0x0, w=0xbeac4c60 "the") at sort-
debug.c:41
#1  0x00008798 in main (argc=1, argv=0xbeac4e24) at sort-debug.c:89
```

An obvious mistake: `addtree()` was called with a null pointer.

GDB user interfaces

GDB is controlled at a low level through the GDB machine interface, GDB/MI, which is used to wrap GDB in a user interface or as part of a larger program and considerably extends the range of options available to you.

I have only mentioned those which have features that are useful in embedded development.

Terminal user interface

Terminal user interface (**TUI**), is an optional part of the standard GDB package. The main feature is a code window which shows the line of code about to be executed, together with any breakpoints. It is a definite improvement on the `list` command in command-line mode GDB.

The attraction of TUI is that it just works and doesn't need any extra set-up and, since it is in text mode, it is possible to use over an ssh terminal session when running `gdb` natively on a target. Most cross toolchains configure GDB with TUI. Simply add `-tui` to the command line and you will see the following:

```
        Terminal
 File  Edit  View  Search  Terminal  Help
    ┌─sort-debug.c─────────────────────────────────────────────┐
    │36        * the count, otherwise add a new node */          │
    │37        static struct tnode *addtree (struct tnode *p, char *w)│
    │38        {                                                  │
    │39              int cond;                                    │
    │40                                                           │
B+> │41              p->word = strdup (w);                        │
    │42              p->count = 1;                                │
    │43              p->left = NULL;                              │
    │44              p->right = NULL;                             │
    │45                                                           │
    │46              cond = strcmp (w, p->word);                  │
    │47                                                           │
    │48              if (cond == 0)                               │
    └──────────────────────────────────────────────────────────┘
remote Thread 95 In: addtree                    Line: 41    PC: 0x85b4
Breakpoint 1, main (argc=1, argv=0xbefffe24) at sort-debug.c:72
(gdb) break addtree
Breakpoint 2 at 0x85b4: file sort-debug.c, line 41.
(gdb) c
Continuing.

Breakpoint 2, addtree (p=0x0, w=0xbefffc60 "the") at sort-debug.c:41
(gdb)
```

Data display debugger

Data display debugger (DDD), is a simple standalone program that gives you a graphical user interface to GDB with minimal fuss and bother and, although the UI controls look dated, it does everything that is necessary.

The `--debugger` option tells DDD to use GDB from your toolchain and you can use the `-x` argument for GDB command files:

```
$ ddd --debugger arm-poky-linux-gnueabi-gdb -x gdbinit sort-debug
```

The following screenshot shows off one of the nicest features: the data window which contains items in a grid that you can rearrange as you wish. If you double-click on a pointer, it is expanded into a new data item and the link is shown with an arrow:

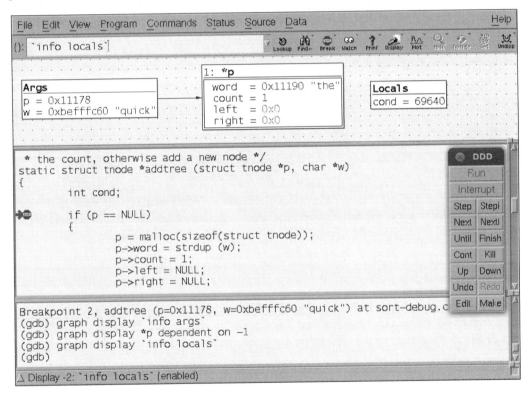

Eclipse

Eclipse, with the **C development toolkit (CDT)** plug-in, supports debugging with GDB, including remote debugging. If you use Eclipse for all your code development, this is the obvious tool to use but, if you are not a regular Eclipse user it is probably not worth the effort of setting it up just for this task. It would take me a whole chapter to explain adequately how to configure CDT to work with a cross toolchain and connect to a remote device, so I will refer you to the references at the end of the chapter for more information. The screenshot that follows shows the debug perspective of CDT. In the the top right window you see the stack frames for each of the threads in the process, and at the top right is the watch window showing variables. In the middle is the code window, showing the line of code where the debugger has stopped the program.

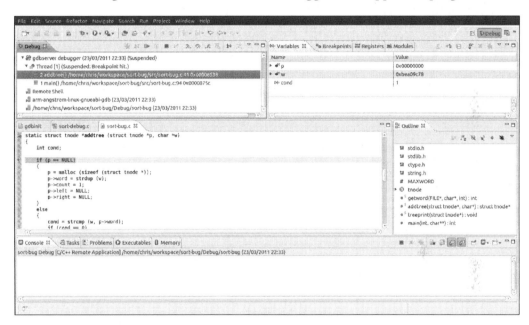

Debugging kernel code

Debugging application code helps you gain insight into the way code works and what is happening when it misbehaves and you can do the same with the kernel, with some limitations.

You can use `kgdb` for source level debugging, in a manner similar to remote debugging with `gdbserver`. There is also a self-hosted kernel debugger, `kdb`, that is handy for lighter weight tasks such as seeing if an instruction is executed and getting the backtrace to find out how it got there. Finally, there are kernel oops messages and panics, which tell you a lot about the cause of a kernel exception.

Debugging kernel code with kgdb

When looking at kernel code using a source debugger, you must remember that the kernel is a complex system, with real-time behaviors. Don't expect debugging to be as easy as it is for applications. Stepping through code that changes the memory mapping or switches context is likely to produce odd results.

kgdb is the name given to the kernel GDB stubs that have been part of mainline Linux for many years now. There is a user manual in the kernel DocBook and you can find an online version at https://www.kernel.org/doc/htmldocs/kgdb/index.html.

The widely supported way to connect to kgdb is over the serial interface, which is usually shared with the serial console, and so this implementation is called kgdboc, meaning kgdb over console. To work, it requires a platform tty driver that supports I/O polling instead of interrupts, since kgdb has to disable interrupts when communicating with GDB. A few platforms support kgdb over USB and there have been versions that work over Ethernet but, unfortunately, none of those have found their way into mainline Linux.

The same caveats about optimization and stack frames apply to the kernel, with the limitation that the kernel is written to assume an optimization level of at least -O1. You can override the kernel compile flags by setting KCGLAGS before running make.

These, then, are the kernel configuration options you will need for kernel debugging:

- CONFIG_DEBUG_INFO is in the **Kernel hacking | Compile-time checks and compiler options | Compile the kernel with debug info menu**

- CONFIG_FRAME_POINTER may be an option for your architecture, and is in the **Kernel hacking | Compile-time checks and compiler options | Compile the kernel with frame pointers menu**

- CONFIG_KGDB is in the **Kernel hacking | KGDB: kernel debugger menu**

- CONFIG_KGDB_SERIAL_CONSOLE is in the **Kernel hacking | KGDB: kernel debugger | KGDB: use kgdb over the serial console menu**

In addition to the uImage or zImage compressed kernel image, you will need the kernel image in ELF object format so that GDB can load the symbols into memory. That is the file called vmlinux that is generated in the directory where Linux is built. In the Yocto Project, you can request that a copy be included in the target image, which is convenient for this and other debug tasks. It is built into a package named kernel-vmlinux, which you can install like any other, for example by adding it to the IMAGE_INSTALL_append list. The file is put into the boot directory, with a name like this:

```
boot/vmlinux-3.14.26ltsi-yocto-standard
```

In Buildroot, you will find `vmlinux` in the directory where the kernel was built, which is in `output/build/linux-<version string>/vmlinux`.

A sample debug session

The best way to show you how it works is with a simple example.

You need to tell `kgdb` which serial port to use, either through the kernel command line or at runtime via `sysfs`. For the first option, add `kgdboc=<tty>,<baud rate>` to the command line, as shown:

```
kgdboc=ttyO0,115200
```

For the second option, boot the device up and write the terminal name to the `/sys/module/kgdboc/parameters/kgdboc` file, as shown:

```
# echo ttyO0 > /sys/module/kgdboc/parameters/kgdboc
```

Note that you cannot set the baud rate in this way. If it is the same `tty` as the console then it is set already, if not use `stty` or a similar program.

Now you can start GDB on the host, selecting the `vmlinux` file that matches the running kernel:

```
$ arm-poky-linux-gnueabi-gdb ~/linux/vmlinux
```

GDB loads the symbol table from `vmlinux` and waits for further input.

Next, close any terminal emulator that is attached to the console: you are about to use it for GDB and, if both are active at the same time, some of the debug strings might get corrupted.

Now, you can return to GDB and attempt to connect to `kgdb`. However, you will find that the response you get from `target remote` at this time is unhelpful:

```
(gdb) set remotebaud 115200
(gdb) target remote /dev/ttyUSB0
Remote debugging using /dev/ttyUSB0
Bogus trace status reply from target: qTStatus
```

The problem is that `kgdb` is not listening for a connection at this point. You need to interrupt the kernel before you can enter into an interactive GDB session with it. Unfortunately, just typing *Ctrl + C* in GDB, as you would with an application, does not work. You have to force a trap into the kernel by launching another shell on the target, via ssh, for example, and writing a `g` to `/proc/sysrq-trigger` on the target board:

```
# echo g > /proc/sysrq-trigger
```

The target stops dead at this point. Now you can connect to kgdb via the serial device at the host end of the cable:

```
(gdb) set remotebaud 115200
(gdb) target remote /dev/ttyUSB0
Remote debugging using /dev/ttyUSB0
0xc009a59c in arch_kgdb_breakpoint ()
```

At last, GDB is in charge. You can set breakpoints, examine variables, look at backtraces, and so on. As an example, set a break on sys_sync, as follows:

```
(gdb) break sys_sync
Breakpoint 1 at 0xc0128a88: file fs/sync.c, line 103.
(gdb) c
Continuing.
```

Now the target comes back to life. Typing sync on the target calls sys_sync and hits the breakpoint.

```
[New Thread 87]
[Switching to Thread 87]


Breakpoint 1, sys_sync () at fs/sync.c:103
```

If you have finished the debug session and want to disable kgdboc, just set the kgdboc terminal to null:

```
# echo "" > /sys/module/kgdboc/parameters/kgdboc
```

Debugging early code

The preceding example works in cases where the code you are interested in is executed when the system is fully booted. If you need to get in early, you can tell the kernel to wait during boot by adding kgdbwait to the command line, after the kgdboc option:

```
kgdboc=ttyO0,115200 kgdbwait
```

Now, when you boot, you will see this on the console:

```
    1.103415] console [ttyO0] enabled
[    1.108216] kgdb: Registered I/O driver kgdboc.
[    1.113071] kgdb: Waiting for connection from remote gdb...
```

At this point, you can close the console and connect from GDB in the usual way.

Debugging modules

Debugging kernel modules presents an additional challenge because the code is relocated at runtime and so you need to find out at what address it resides. The information is presented via sysfs. The relocation addresses for each section of the module are stored in /sys/module/<module name>/sections. Note that, since ELF sections begin with a dot, '.', they appear as hidden files and you will have to use ls -a if you want to list them. The important ones are .text, .data, and .bss.

Take as an example a module named mbx:

```
# cat /sys/module/mbx/sections/.text
0xbf000000
# cat /sys/module/mbx/sections/.data
0xbf0003e8
# cat /sys/module/mbx/sections/.bss
0xbf0005c0
```

Now you can use these numbers in GDB to load the symbol table for the module at those addresses:

```
(gdb) add-symbol-file /home/chris/mbx-driver/mbx.ko 0xbf000000 \
-s .data 0xbf0003e8 -s .bss 0xbf0005c0
add symbol table from file "/home/chris/mbx-driver/mbx.ko" at
  .text_addr = 0xbf000000
  .data_addr = 0xbf0003e8
  .bss_addr = 0xbf0005c0
```

Everything should now work as normal: you can set breakpoints and inspect global and local variables in the module just as you can in vmlinux:

```
(gdb) break mbx_write


Breakpoint 1 at 0xbf00009c: file /home/chris/mbx-driver/mbx.c,
line 93.


(gdb) c
Continuing.
```

Then, force the device driver to call mbx_write and it will hit the breakpoint:

```
Breakpoint 1, mbx_write (file=0xde7a71c0, buffer=0xadf40 "hello\n\n",
    length=6, offset=0xde73df80)
    at /home/chris/mbx-driver/mbx.c:93
```

Debugging kernel code with kdb

Although kdb does not have the features of kgdb and GDB, it does have its uses and, being self-hosted, there are no external dependencies to worry about. kdb has a simple command-line interface which you can use on a serial console. You can use it to inspect memory, registers, process lists, dmesg, and even set breakpoints to stop in a certain location.

To configure kgd for access via a serial console, enable kgdb as shown previously and then enable this additional option:

*   CONFIG_KGDB_KDB, which is in the **KGDB: Kernel hacking | kernel debugger | KGDB_KDB: include kdb frontend for kgdb** menu

Now, when you force the kernel to a trap, instead of entering into a GDB session, you will see the kdb shell on the console:

```
# echo g > /proc/sysrq-trigger
[   42.971126] SysRq : DEBUG

Entering kdb (current=0xdf36c080, pid 83) due to Keyboard Entry
kdb>
```

There are quite a few things you can do in the kdb shell. The help command will print all of the options. Here is an overview.

Getting information:

*   ps: displays active processes
*   ps A: displays all processes
*   lsmod: lists modules
*   dmesg: displays the kernel log buffer

Breakpoints:

*   bp: sets a breakpoint
*   bl: lists breakpoints
*   bc: clears a breakpoint
*   bt: prints a backtrace
*   go: continues execution

Inspect memory and registers:

*   md: displays memory
*   rd: displays registers

Here is a quick example of setting a break point:

```
kdb> bp sys_sync
Instruction(i) BP #0 at 0xc01304ec (sys_sync)
    is enabled  addr at 00000000c01304ec, hardtype=0 installed=0


kdb> go
```

The kernel returns to life and the console shows the normal bash prompt. If you type sync, it hits the breakpoint and enters kdb again:

```
Entering kdb (current=0xdf388a80, pid 88) due to Breakpoint @
0xc01304ec
```

kdb is not a source debugger so you can't see the source code, or single step. However, you can display a backtrace using the bt command, which is useful to get an idea of program flow and call hierarchy.

When the kernel performs an invalid memory access or executes an illegal instruction, a kernel oops message is written to the kernel log. The most useful part of this is the backtrace, and I want to show you how to use the information there to locate the line of code that caused the fault. I will also address the problem of preserving oops messages if they cause the system to crash.

Looking at an oops

An oops message looks like this:

```
[   56.225868] Unable to handle kernel NULL pointer dereference at
virtual address 00000400[   56.229038] pgd = cb624000[   56.229454]
[00000400] *pgd=6b715831, *pte=00000000, *ppte=00000000[   56.231768]
Internal error: Oops: 817 [#1] SMP ARM[   56.232443] Modules linked
in: mbx(O)[   56.233556] CPU: 0 PID: 98 Comm: sh Tainted: G   O   4.1.10
#1[   56.234234] Hardware name: ARM-Versatile Express[   56.234810]
task: cb709c80 ti: cb71a000 task.ti: cb71a000[   56.236801] PC is at
mbx_write+0x14/0x98 [mbx][   56.237303] LR is at __vfs_write+0x20/0xd8[
56.237559] pc : [<bf0000a0>]    lr : [<c0307154>]    psr: 800f0013[
56.237559] sp : cb71bef8  ip : bf00008c  fp : 00000000[   56.238183] r10:
00000000  r9 : cb71a000  r8 : c02107c4[   56.238485] r7 : cb71bf88  r6 :
000afb98  r5 : 00000006  r4 : 00000000[   56.238857] r3 : cb71bf88  r2 :
00000006  r1 : 000afb98  r0 : cb61d600

[   56.239276] Flags: Nzcv  IRQs on  FIQs on  Mode SVC_32  ISA ARM
Segment user[   56.239685] Control: 10c5387d  Table: 6b624059  DAC:
00000015[   56.240019] Process sh (pid: 98, stack limit = 0xcb71a220)
```

`PC is at mbx_write+0x14/0x98 [mbx]` tells you most of what you want to know: the last instruction was in the `mbx_write` function in a kernel module named `mbx`. Furthermore, it was at offset `0x14` bytes from the start of the function, which is `0x98` bytes long.

Next, take a look at the backtrace:

```
[   56.240363] Stack: (0xcb71bef8 to 0xcb71c000)[   56.240745] bee0:
cb71bf88 cb61d600[   56.241331] bf00: 00000006 c0307154 00000000 c020a308
cb619d88
00000301 00000000 00000042[   56.241775] bf20: 00000000 cb61d608 cb709c80
cb709c78 cb71bf60
c0250a54 00000000 cb709ee0[   56.242190] bf40: 00000003 bef4f658 00000000
cb61d600 cb61d600
00000006 000afb98 cb71bf88[   56.242605] bf60: c02107c4 c030794c 00000000
00000000 cb61d600
cb61d600 00000006 000afb98[   56.243025] bf80: c02107c4 c0308174 00000000
00000000 00000000
000ada10 00000001 000afb98[   56.243493] bfa0: 00000004 c0210640 000ada10
00000001 00000001
000afb98 00000006 00000000[   56.243952] bfc0: 000ada10 00000001 000afb98
00000004 00000001
00000020 000ae274 00000000[   56.244420] bfe0: 00000000 bef4f49c 0000fcdc
b6f1aedc 600f0010
00000001 00000000 00000000[   56.245653] [<bf0000a0>] (mbx_write [mbx])
from [<c0307154>]
(__vfs_write+0x20/0xd8)[   56.246368] [<c0307154>]
(__vfs_write) from [<c030794c>]
(vfs_write+0x90/0x164)[   56.246843] [<c030794c>] (vfs_write) from
[<c0308174>]
(SyS_write+0x44/0x9c)[   56.247265] [<c0308174>] (SyS_write) from
[<c0210640>]
(ret_fast_syscall+0x0/0x3c)[   56.247737] Code: e5904090 e3520b01
23a02b01 e1a05002 (e5842400)[   56.248372] ---[ end trace
999c378e4df13d74 ]---
```

In this case, we don't learn much more, merely that `mbx_write` is called from the virtual filesystem code.

It would be very nice to find the line of code that relates to `mbx_write+0x14`, for which we can use `objdump`. We can see from `objdump -S` that `mbx_write` is at offset `0x8c` in `mbx.ko`, so that last instruction executed is at `0x8c + 0x14 = 0xa0`. Now, we just need to look at that offset and see what is there:

```
$ arm-poky-linux-gnueabi-objdump -S mbx.kostatic ssize_t mbx_write(struct
file *file,const char *buffer, size_t length, loff_t * offset){   8c:
e92d4038        push    {r3, r4, r5, lr}  struct mbx_data *m = (struct
mbx_data *)file->private_data;   90:    e5904090         ldr     r4, [r0,
#144]   ; 0x90  94:    e3520b01        cmp     r2, #1024       ; 0x400  98:
23a02b01       movcs    r2, #1024      ; 0x400  if (length > MBX_LEN)
length = MBX_LEN;     m->mbx_len = length;  9c:    e1a05002        mov
r5, r2  a0:    e5842400        str     r2, [r4, #1024] ; 0x400
```

This shows the instruction where it stopped. The last line of code is shown here:

```
m->mbx_len = length;
```

You can see that m has the type `struct mbx_data *`. Here is the place where that structure is defined:

```
#define MBX_LEN 1024 struct mbx_data {   char mbx[MBX_LEN];   int mbx_
len;};
```

So, it looks like the m variable is a null pointer, and that is causing the oops.

Preserving the oops

Decoding an oops is only possible if you can capture it in the first place. If the system crashes during boot before the console is enabled, or after a suspend, you won't see it. There are mechanisms to log kernel oops and messages to an MTD partition or to persistent memory, but here is a simple technique that works in many cases and needs little prior thought.

So long as the contents of memory are not corrupted during a reset (and usually they are not), you can reboot into the bootloader and use it to display memory. You need to know the location of the kernel log buffer, remembering that it is a simple ring buffer of text messages. The symbol is __log_buf. Look this up in `System.map` for the kernel:

```
$ grep __log_buf System.mapc0f72428 b __log_buf
```

Then, map that kernel logical address into a physical address that U-Boot can understand by subtracting PAGE_OFFSET, 0xc0000000, and adding the physical start of RAM, 0x80000000 on a BeagleBone, so c0f72428 - 0xc0000000 + 0x80000000 = 80f72428.

Then use the U-Boot md command to show the log:

```
U-Boot# md 80f7242880f72428: 00000000 00000000 00210034
c6000000     ........4.!.....80f72438: 746f6f42 20676e69 756e694c
6e6f2078    Booting Linux on80f72448: 79687020 61636973 5043206c
78302055     physical CPU 0x80f72458: 00000030 00000000 00000000 00730084
0.............s.80f72468: a6000000 756e694c 65762078 6f697372     ....
Linux versio80f72478: 2e34206e 30312e31 68632820 40736972     n 4.1.10
(chris@80f72488: 6c697562 29726564 63672820 65762063    builder)
(gcc ve80f72498: 6f697372 2e34206e 20312e39 6f726328    rsion 4.9.1
(cro80f724a8: 6f747373 4e2d6c6f 2e312047 302e3032    sstool-NG
1.20.080f724b8: 20292029 53203123 5720504d 4f206465    ) ) #1 SMP Wed
O80f724c8: 32207463 37312038 3a31353a 47203335    ct 28 17:51:53 G
```

> From Linux 3.5 onwards, there is a 16-byte binary header for each line in the kernel log buffer which encodes a timestamp, a log level and other things. There is a discussion about it in the Linux Weekly News titled *Toward more reliable logging* at `https://lwn.net/Articles/492125/`.

Additional reading

The following resources have further information about the topics introduced in this chapter:

- *The Art of Debugging with GDB, DDD, and Eclipse*, by *Norman Matloff* and *Peter Jay Salzman, No Starch Press*; 1 edition (28 Sept. 2008), ISBN 978-1593271749

- *GDB Pocket Reference* by *Arnold Robbins, O'Reilly Media*; 1st edition (12 May 2005), ISBN 978-0596100278

- *Getting to grips with Eclipse: cross compiling*, `http://2net.co.uk/tutorial/eclipse-cross-compile`

- *Getting to grips with Eclipse: remote access and debugging*, `http://2net.co.uk/tutorial/eclipse-rse`

Summary

GDB for interactive debugging is a useful tool in the embedded developer's tool chest. It is a stable, well-documented and well-known entity. It has the ability to debug remotely by placing an agent on the target, be it `gdbserver` for applications or `kgdb` for kernel code and, although the default command-line user interface takes a while to get used to, there are many alternative front-ends. The three I mentioned were TUI, DDD, and Eclipse, which should cover most situations, but there are other front-ends around that you can try.

A second and equally important way to approach debugging is to collect crash reports and analyze them offline. In this category, I have looked at application core dumps and kernel oops messages.

However, this is only one way of identifying flaws in programs. In the next chapter, I will talk about profiling and tracing as ways of analyzing and optimizing programs.

13
Profiling and Tracing

Interactive debugging using a source level debugger, as described in the previous chapter, can give you an insight into the way a program works, but it constrains your view to a small body of code. In this chapter, I will look at the larger picture to see if the system is performing as intended.

Programmers and system designers are notoriously bad at guessing where bottlenecks are. So, if your system has performance issues, it is wise to start by looking at the full system and then work down, using more sophisticated tools. In this chapter I begin with the well-known command, `top`, as a means of getting an overview. Often the problem can be localized to a single program, which you can analyze using the Linux profiler, `perf`. If the problem is not so localized and you want to get a broader picture, `perf` can do that as well. To diagnose problems associated with the kernel, I will describe the trace tools, `Ftrace` and `LTTng`, as a means of gathering detailed information.

I will also cover Valgrind which, because of its sandboxed execution environment, can monitor a program and report on code as it runs. I will complete the chapter with a description of a simple trace tool, `strace`, which reveals the execution of a program by tracing the system calls it makes.

The observer effect

Before diving into the tools, let's talk about what the tools will show you. As is the case in many fields, measuring a certain property affects the observation itself. Measuring the electric current in a line requires measuring the voltage drop over a small resistor. However, the resistor itself affects the current. The same is true for profiling: every system observation has a cost in CPU cycles and that resource is no longer spent on the application. Measurement tools also mess up caching behavior, eat memory space, and write to disk, which all make it worse. There is no measurement without overhead.

I've often heard engineers say that the results of a profiling job were totally misleading. That is usually because they were performing the measurements on something approaching a real situation. Always try to measure on the target, using release builds of the software, with a valid data set, using as few extra services as possible.

Symbol tables and compile flags

We will hit a problem immediately. While it is important to observe the system in its natural state, the tools often need additional information to make sense of the events.

Some tools require special kernel options, specifically from those listed in the introduction, `perf`, Ftrace, and LTTng. Therefore, you will probably have to build and deploy a new kernel for these tests.

Debug symbols are very helpful in translating raw program addresses into function names and lines of code. Deploying executables with debug symbols does not change the execution of the code but it does require that you have copies of the binaries and the kernel compiled with `debug`, at least for the components you want to profile. Some tools work best if you have these installed on the target system, `perf`, for example. The techniques are the same as for general debugging, as I discussed in *Chapter 12, Debugging with GDB*.

If you want a tool to generate call graphs, you may have to compile with stack frames enabled. If you want the tool to attribute addresses with lines of code accurately, you may need to compile with lower levels of optimization.

Finally, some tools require instrumentation to be inserted into the program to capture samples, so you will have to recompile those components. This applies to `gprof` for applications, and Ftrace and LTTng for the kernel.

Be aware that, the more you change the system you are observing, the harder it is to relate the measurements you make to the production system.

It is best to adopt a wait-and-see approach, making changes only when the need is clear, and being mindful that each time you do so, you will change what you are measuring.

Beginning to profile

When looking at the entire system, a good place to start is with a simple tool like top, which gives you an overview very quickly. It shows you how much memory is being used, which processes are eating CPU cycles, and how this is spread across different cores and time.

If top shows that a single application is using up all the CPU cycles in user space then you can profile that application using perf.

If two or more processes have a high CPU usage, there is probably something that is coupling them together, perhaps data communication. If a lot of cycles are spent in system calls or handling interrupts, then there may be an issue with the kernel configuration or with a device driver. In either case you need to start by taking a profile of the whole system, again using perf.

If you want to find out more about the kernel and the sequencing of events there, you would use Ftrace or LTTng.

There could be other problems that top will not help you with. If you have multi-threaded code and there are problems with lockups, or if you have random data corruption then Valgrind plus the Helgrind plug-in might be helpful. Memory leaks also fit into this category: I covered memory-related diagnosis in *Chapter 11, Managing Memory*.

Profiling with top

top is a simple tool that doesn't require any special kernel options or symbol tables. There is a basic version in BusyBox, and a more functional version in the procps package which is available in the Yocto Project and Buildroot. You may also want to consider using htop which is functionally similar to top but has a nicer user interface (some people think).

To begin with, focus on the summary line of top, which is the second line if you are using BusyBox and the third line if using procps top. Here is an example, using BusyBox top:

```
Mem: 57044K used, 446172K free, 40K shrd, 3352K buff, 34452K cached
CPU:  58% usr   4% sys   0% nic   0% idle  37% io   0% irq   0% sirq
Load average: 0.24 0.06 0.02 2/51 105
  PID  PPID USER     STAT    VSZ %VSZ %CPU COMMAND
  105   104 root     R     27912   6%  61% ffmpeg -i track2.wav
  [...]
```

The summary line shows the percentage of time spent running in various states, as shown in this table:

procps	Busybox	
us	usr	User space programs with default nice value
sy	sys	Kernel code
ni	nic	User space programs with non-default nice value
id	idle	Idle
wa	io	I/O wait
hi	irq	Hardware interrupts
si	sirq	Software interrupts
st	--	Steal time: only relevant in virtualized environments

In the preceding example, almost all of the time (58%) is spent in user mode, with a small amount (4%) in system mode, so this is a system that is CPU-bound in user space. The first line after the summary shows that just one application is responsible: ffmpeg. Any efforts towards reducing CPU usage should be directed there.

Here is another example:

```
Mem: 13128K used, 490088K free, 40K shrd, 0K buff, 2788K cached
CPU:   0% usr  99% sys   0% nic   0% idle   0% io   0% irq   0% sirq
Load average: 0.41 0.11 0.04 2/46 97
  PID  PPID USER     STAT    VSZ %VSZ %CPU COMMAND
   92    82 root     R      2152   0% 100% cat /dev/urandom
  [...]
```

This system is spending almost all of the time in kernel space, as a result of cat reading from /dev/urandom. In this artificial, case, profiling cat by itself would not help, but profiling the kernel functions that cat calls might be.

The default view of top shows only processes, so the CPU usage is the total of all the threads in the process. Press *H* to see information for each thread. Likewise, it aggregates the time across all CPUs. If you are using procps top, you can see a summary per CPU by pressing the *1* key.

Imagine that there is a single user space process taking up most of the time and look at how to profile that.

Poor man's profiler

You can profile an application just by using GDB to stop it at arbitrary intervals and see what it is doing. This is the *poor man's profiler*. It is easy to set up and it is one way of gathering profile data.

The procedure is simple and explained here:

1. Attach to the process using `gdbserver` (for a remote debug) or gbd (for a native debug). The process stops.
2. Observe the function it stopped in. You can use the `backtrace` GDB command to see the call stack.
3. Type `continue` so that the program resumes.
4. After a while, type *Ctrl + C* to stop it again and go back to step 2.

If you repeat steps 2 to 4 several times, you will quickly get an idea of whether it is looping or making progress and, if you repeat them often enough, you will get an idea of where the hotspots in the code are.

There is a whole web page dedicated to the idea at `http://poormansprofiler.org`, together with scripts which make it a little easier. I have used this technique many times over the years with various operating systems and debuggers.

This is an example of statistical profiling, in which you sample the program state at intervals. After a number of samples, you begin to learn the statistical likelihood of the functions being executed. It is surprising how few you really need. Other statistical profilers are `perf record`, `OProfile`, and `gprof`.

Sampling using a debugger is intrusive because the program is stopped for a significant period while you collect the sample. Other tools can do that with much lower overhead.

I will now consider how to use `perf` to do statistical profiling.

Introducing perf

`perf` is an abbreviation of the **Linux performance event counter subsystem**, `perf_events`, and also the name of the command-line tool for interacting with `perf_events`. Both have been part of the kernel since Linux 2.6.31. There is plenty of useful information in the Linux source tree in `tools/perf/Documentation`, and also at `https://perf.wiki.kernel.org`.

The initial impetus for developing `perf` was to provide a unified way to access the registers of the **performance measurement unit (PMU)**, which is part of most modern processor cores. Once the API was defined and integrated into Linux, it became logical to extend it to cover other types of performance counters.

At its heart, `perf` is a collection of event counters with rules about when they actively collect data. By setting the rules, you can capture data from the whole system, or just the kernel, or just one process and its children, and do it across all CPUs or just one CPU. It is very flexible. With this one tool you can start by looking at the whole system, then zero in on a device driver that seems to be causing problems, or an application that is running slowly, or a library function that seems to being taking longer to execute than you thought.

The code for the `perf` command-line tool is part of the kernel, in the `tools/perf` directory. The tool and the kernel subsystem are developed hand-in-hand, meaning that they must be from the same version of the kernel. `perf` can do a lot. In this chapter, I will examine it only as a profiler. For a description of its other capabilities, read the `perf` man pages and refer to the documentation mentioned in the previous paragraph.

Configuring the kernel for perf

You need a kernel that is configured for `perf_events` and you need the `perf` command cross compiled to run on the target. The relevant kernel configuration is `CONFIG_PERF_EVENTS` present in the menu **General setup | Kernel Performance Events And Counters**.

If you want to profile using tracepoints — more on this subject later — also enable the options described in the section about `Ftrace`. While you are there, it is worthwhile enabling `CONFIG_DEBUG_INFO` as well.

The `perf` command has many dependencies which makes cross compiling it quite messy. However, both the Yocto Project and Buildroot have target packages for it.

You will also need debug symbols on the target for the binaries that you are interested in profiling, otherwise `perf` will not be able to resolve addresses to meaningful symbols. Ideally, you want debug symbols for the whole system including the kernel. For the latter, remember that the debug symbols for the kernel are in the `vmlinux` file.

Building perf with the Yocto Project

If you are using the standard linux-yocto kernel, `perf_events` is enabled already, so there is nothing more to do.

To build the `perf` tool, you can add it explicitly to the target image dependencies, or you can add the tools-profile feature which also brings in `gprof`. As I mentioned previously, you will probably want debug symbols on the target image, and also the kernel `vmlinux` image. In total, this is what you will need in `conf/local.conf`:

```
EXTRA_IMAGE_FEATURES = "debug-tweaks dbg-pkgs tools-profile"
IMAGE_INSTALL_append = " kernel-vmlinux"
```

Building perf with Buildroot

Many Buildroot kernel configurations do not include `perf_events`, so you should begin by checking that your kernel includes the options mentioned in the preceding section.

To cross compile perf, run the Buildroot `menuconfig` and select the following:

- `BR2_LINUX_KERNEL_TOOL_PERF` in **Kernel | Linux Kernel Tools**. To build packages with debug symbols and install them unstripped on the target, select these two settings.

- `BR2_ENABLE_DEBUG` in the menu **Build options | build packages with debugging symbols** menu.

- `BR2_STRIP = none` in the menu **Build options | strip command for binaries on target**.

Then, run `make clean`, followed by `make`.

When you have built everything, you will have to copy `vmlinux` into the target image manually.

Profiling with perf

You can use `perf` to sample the state of a program using one of the event counters and accumulate samples over a period of time to create a profile. This is another example of statistical profiling. The default event counter is called cycles, which is a generic hardware counter that is mapped to a PMU register representing a count of cycles at the core clock frequency.

Creating a profile using `perf` is a two stage process: the `perf record` command captures samples and writes them to a file named `perf.data` (by default) and then `perf report` analyzes the results. Both commands are run on the target. The samples being collected are filtered for the process and its children, for a command you specify. Here is an example profiling a shell script that searches for the string `linux`:

```
# perf record sh -c "find /usr/share | xargs grep linux >
/dev/null"
[ perf record: Woken up 2 times to write data ]
[ perf record: Captured and wrote 0.368 MB perf.data (~16057
samples) ]
# ls -l perf.data
-rw-------    1 root      root        387360 Aug 25  2015 perf.data
```

Now you can show the results from `perf.data` using the command `perf report`. There are three user interfaces which you can select on the command line:

- `--stdio`: This is a pure text interface with no user interaction. You will have to launch `perf report` and annotate for each view of the trace.

- `--tui`: This is a simple text-based menu interface with traversal between screens.

- `--gtk`: This is a graphical interface that otherwise acts in the same way as `--tui`.

The default is TUI, as shown in this example:

```
Samples: 9K of event 'cycles', Event count (approx.): 2006177260
 11.29%   grep  libc-2.20.so        [.] re_search_internal
  8.80%   grep  busybox.nosuid      [.] bb_get_chunk_from_file
  5.55%   grep  libc-2.20.so        [.] _int_malloc
  5.40%   grep  libc-2.20.so        [.] _int_free
  3.74%   grep  libc-2.20.so        [.] realloc
  2.59%   grep  libc-2.20.so        [.] malloc
  2.51%   grep  libc-2.20.so        [.] regexec@@GLIBC_2.4
  1.64%   grep  busybox.nosuid      [.] grep_file
  1.57%   grep  libc-2.20.so        [.] malloc_consolidate
  1.33%   grep  libc-2.20.so        [.] strlen
  1.33%   grep  libc-2.20.so        [.] memset
  1.26%   grep  [kernel.kallsyms]   [k] __copy_to_user_std
  1.20%   grep  libc-2.20.so        [.] free
  1.10%   grep  libc-2.20.so        [.] _int_realloc
  0.95%   grep  libc-2.20.so        [.] re_string_reconstruct
  0.79%   grep  busybox.nosuid      [.] xrealloc
  0.75%   grep  [kernel.kallsyms]   [k] __do_softirq
  0.72%   grep  [kernel.kallsyms]   [k] preempt_count_sub
  0.68%   find  [kernel.kallsyms]   [k] __do_softirq
  0.53%   grep  [kernel.kallsyms]   [k] __dev_queue_xmit
  0.52%   grep  [kernel.kallsyms]   [k] preempt_count_add
  0.47%   grep  [kernel.kallsyms]   [k] finish_task_switch.isra.85
Press '?' for help on key bindings
```

`perf` is able to record the kernel functions executed on behalf of the processes because it collects samples in kernel space.

The list is ordered with the most active functions first. In this example, all but one are captured while `grep` is running. Some are in a library, `libc-2.20`, some in a program, `busybox.nosuid`, and some are in the kernel. We have symbol names for program and library functions because all the binaries have been installed on the target with debug information, and kernel symbols are being read from `/boot/vmlinux`. If you have `vmlinux` in a different location, add `-k <path>` to the `perf report` command. Rather than storing samples in `perf.data`, you can save them to a different file using `perf record -o <file name>` and analyze them using `perf report -i <file name>`.

By default, `perf record` samples at a frequency of 1000Hz using the cycles counter.

> A sampling frequency of 1000Hz may be higher than you really need, and may be the cause of an observer effect. Try with lower rates: 100Hz is enough for most cases, in my experience. You can set the sample frequency using the `-F` option.

Call graphs

This is still not really making life easy; the functions at the top of the list are mostly low level memory operations and you can be fairly sure that they have already been optimized. It would be nice to step back and see where these functions are being called from. You can do that by capturing the backtrace from each sample, which you can do with the `-g` option to `perf record`.

Now `perf report` shows a plus sign (**+**) where the function is part of a call chain. You can expand the trace to see the functions lower down in the chain:

```
Samples: 10K of event 'cycles', Event count (approx.): 2256721655
-   9.95%   grep  libc-2.20.so      [.] re_search_internal          ◄
   - re_search_internal
         95.96% 0
          3.50% 0x208
+   8.19%   grep  busybox.nosuid    [.] bb_get_chunk_from_file
+   5.07%   grep  libc-2.20.so      [.] _int_free
+   4.76%   grep  libc-2.20.so      [.] _int_malloc
+   3.75%   grep  libc-2.20.so      [.] realloc
+   2.63%   grep  libc-2.20.so      [.] malloc
+   2.04%   grep  libc-2.20.so      [.] regexec@@GLIBC_2.4
+   1.43%   grep  busybox.nosuid    [.] grep_file
+   1.37%   grep  libc-2.20.so      [.] memset
+   1.29%   grep  libc-2.20.so      [.] malloc_consolidate
+   1.22%   grep  libc-2.20.so      [.] _int_realloc
+   1.15%   grep  libc-2.20.so      [.] free
+   1.01%   grep  [kernel.kallsyms] [k] __copy_to_user_std
+   0.98%   grep  libc-2.20.so      [.] strlen
+   0.89%   grep  libc-2.20.so      [.] re_string_reconstruct
+   0.73%   grep  [kernel.kallsyms] [k] preempt_count_sub
+   0.68%   grep  [kernel.kallsyms] [k] finish_task_switch.isra.85
+   0.62%   grep  busybox.nosuid    [.] xrealloc
+   0.57%   grep  [kernel.kallsyms] [k] __do_softirq
Press '?' for help on key bindings
```

 Generating call graphs relies on the ability to extract call frames from the stack, just as is necessary for backtraces in GDB. The information needed to unwind stacks is encoded in the debug information of the executables but not all combinations of architecture and toolchains are capable of doing so.

perf annotate

Now that you know which functions to look at, it would be nice to step inside and see the code and to have hit counts for each instruction. That is what `perf annotate` does, by calling down to a copy of `objdump` installed on the target. You just need to use `perf annotate` in place of `perf report`.

`perf annotate` requires symbol tables for the executables and vmlinux. Here is an example of an annotated function:

```
re_search_internal   /lib/libc-2.20.so
                  cmp     r1,
                  beq     c362c <gai_strerror+0xcaf8>
                  str     r3, [fp, #-40]          ; 0x28
                  b       c3684 <gai_strerror+0xcb58>
         0.65     ldr     ip, [fp, #-256]         ; 0x100
         0.16     ldr     r0, [fp, #-268]         ; 0x10c
         2.44     add     r3,
         4.15     cmp     r0,
         3.91     strle   r3, [fp, #-40]          ; 0x28
                  ble     c3684 <gai_strerror+0xcb58>
         4.72     ldrb    r1, [r2, #1]!
        10.26     ldrb    r1, [ip, r1]
         6.68     cmp     r1,
                  beq     c3660 <gai_strerror+0xcb2c>
         0.90     str     r3, [fp, #-40]          ; 0x28
         2.12     ldr     r3, [fp, #-40]          ; 0x28
         0.08     ldr     r2, [fp, #-268]         ; 0x10c
         0.33     cmp     r2,
                  bne     c3804 <gai_strerror+0xccd0>
         0.08     mov     r3,
                  ldr     r2, [fp, #-280]         ; 0x118
         0.08     cmp     r3,
 press 'h' for help on key bindings
```

If you want to see the source code interleaved with the assembler, you can copy the relevant parts to the target device. If you are using the Yocto Project and build with the extra image feature dbg-pkgs, or have installed the individual -dbg package, then the source will have been installed for you in /usr/src/debug. Otherwise, you can examine the debug information to see the location of the source code:

```
$ arm-buildroot-linux-gnueabi-objdump --dwarf lib/libc-2.19.so   |
grep DW_AT_comp_dir

  <3f>    DW_AT_comp_dir : /home/chris/buildroot/output/build/host-
gcc-initial-4.8.3/build/arm-buildroot-linux-gnueabi/libgcc
```

The path on the target should be exactly the same as the path you can see in DW_AT_comp_dir.

Here is an example of annotation with source and assembler code:

```
re_search_internal   /lib/libc-2.20.so
                        ++match_first;
                        goto forward_match_found_start_or_reached_end;

                      case 6:
                        /* Fastmap without translation, match forward.  */
                        while (BE (match_first < right_lim, 1)
         4.15     cmp     r0,
         3.91     strle   r3, [fp, #-40]          ; 0x28
                  ble     c3684 <gai_strerror+0xcb50>
                              && !fastmap[(unsigned char) string[match_first]])
         4.72     ldrb    r1, [r2, #1]!
        10.26     ldrb    r1, [ip, r1]
         6.68     cmp     r1,
                  beq     c3660 <gai_strerror+0xcb2c>
         0.90     str     r3, [fp, #-40]          ; 0x28
                          ++match_first;

                        forward_match_found_start_or_reached_end:
                          if (BE (match_first == right_lim, 0))
         2.12     ldr     r3, [fp, #-40]          ; 0x28
         0.08     ldr     r2, [fp, #-268]         ; 0x10c
         0.33     cmp     r2,
 press 'h' for help on key bindings
```

Other profilers: OProfile and gprof

These two statistical profilers predate `perf`. They are both subsets of the functionality of `perf`, but they are still quite popular. I will mention them only briefly.

OProfile is a kernel profiler that started out in 2002. Originally, it had its own kernel sampling code, but recent versions use the `perf_events` infrastructure for that purpose. There is more information about it at `http://oprofile.sourceforge.net`. OProfile consists of a kernel-space component and a user space daemon and analysis commands.

OProfile needs these two kernel options to be enabled:

- `CONFIG_PROFILING` in **General setup** | **Profiling support**
- `CONFIG_OPROFILE` in **General setup** | **OProfile system profiling**

If you are using the Yocto Project, the user-space components are installed as part of the `tools-profile` image feature. If you are using Buildroot, the package is enabled by `BR2_PACKAGE_OPROFILE`.

You can collect samples by using this command:

```
# operf <program>
```

Wait for your application to finish, or press *Ctrl* + *C*, to stop profiling. The profile data is stored in `<cur-dir>/oprofile_data/samples/current`.

Use `opreport` to generate a profile summary. There are various options which are documented in the OProfile manual.

`gprof` is part of the GNU toolchain and was one of the earliest open source code profiling tools. It combines compile-time instrumentation and sampling techniques, using a 100 Hz sample rate. It has the advantage that it does not require kernel support.

To prepare a program for profiling with `gprof`, you add `-pg` to the compile and link flags, which injects code that collects information about the call tree into the function preamble. When you run the program, samples are collected and stored in a buffer, which is written to a file named `gmon.out`, when the program terminates.

You use the `gprof` command to read the samples from `gmon.out` and the debug information from a copy of the program.

As an example, if you wanted to profile the BusyBox `grep` applet. you would rebuild BusyBox with the `-pg` option, run the command, and view the results:

```
# busybox grep "linux" *
# ls -l gmon.out
-rw-r--r-- 1 root root    473 Nov 24 14:07 gmon.out
```

Then, you would analyze the captured samples on either the target or the host, using the following:

```
# gprof busybox
Flat profile:


Each sample counts as 0.01 seconds.
 no time accumulated


  %   cumulative   self              self     total
 time   seconds   seconds    calls  Ts/call  Ts/call  name
 0.00     0.00     0.00      688     0.00     0.00   xrealloc
 0.00     0.00     0.00      345     0.00     0.00   bb_get_chunk_from_file
 0.00     0.00     0.00      345     0.00     0.00   xmalloc_fgetline
 0.00     0.00     0.00       6      0.00     0.00   fclose_if_not_stdin
 0.00     0.00     0.00       6      0.00     0.00   fopen_for_read
 0.00     0.00     0.00       6      0.00     0.00   grep_file
[...]
     Call graph


granularity: each sample hit covers 2 byte(s) no time propagated


index  % time    self  children    called     name
                 0.00    0.00     688/688    bb_get_chunk_from_file [2]
[1]      0.0     0.00    0.00     688             xrealloc [1]
-----------------------------------------------------
                 0.00    0.00     345/345    xmalloc_fgetline [3]
```

```
[2]        0.0     0.00    0.00      345      bb_get_chunk_from_file [2]
                   0.00    0.00    688/688    xrealloc [1]
-----------------------------------------------------------------
                   0.00    0.00    345/345    grep_file [6]
[3]        0.0     0.00    0.00      345      xmalloc_fgetline [3]
                   0.00    0.00    345/345    bb_get_chunk_from_file
[2]
-----------------------------------------------------------------
                   0.00    0.00      6/6      grep_main [12]
[4]        0.0     0.00    0.00       6       fclose_if_not_stdin
[4]
[...]
```

Note that the execution times are all shown as zero, because most of the time was spent in system calls, which are not traced by gprof.

> gprof does not capture samples from threads other than the main thread of a multi-threaded process, and it does not sample kernel space, all of which limits its usefulness.

Tracing events

The tools we have seen so far all use statistical sampling. You often want to know more about the ordering of events so that you can see them and relate them to each other. Function tracing involves instrumenting the code with trace points which capture information about the event, and may include some or all of the following:

- Timestamp
- Context, such as the current PID
- Function parameters and return value
- Callstack

It is more intrusive than statistical profiling and it can generate a large amount of data. The latter can be mitigated by applying filters when the sample is captured, and later on when viewing the trace.

I will cover two trace tools here: the kernel function tracers, Ftrace and LTTng.

Introducing Ftrace

The kernel function tracer, Ftrace, evolved from work done by Steven Rostedt, and many others, as they were tracking down the causes of high latency. Ftrace appeared in Linux 2.6.27 and has been actively developed since then. There are a number of documents describing kernel tracing in the kernel source in Documentation/trace.

Ftrace consists of a number of tracers that can log various types of activity in the kernel. Here, I am going to talk about the function and function_graph tracers, and about the event tracepoints. In *Chapter 14, Real-time Programming,* I will revisit Ftrace and use it to show real-time latencies.

The function tracer instruments each kernel function so that calls can be recorded and timestamped. As a matter of interest, it compiles the kernel with the -pg switch to inject the instrumentation, but there the resemblance to gprof ends. The function_graph tracer goes further and records both the entry and exit of functions so that it can create a call graph. The event tracepoints feature also records parameters associated with the call.

Ftrace has a very embedded-friendly user interface that is entirely implemented through virtual files in the debugfs filesystem, meaning that you do not have to install any tools on the target to make it work. Nevertheless, there are other user interfaces if you prefer: trace-cmd is a command-line tool which records and views traces and is available in Buildroot (BR2_PACKAGE_TRACE_CMD) and the Yocto Project (trace-cmd). There is a graphical trace viewer named KernelShark which is available as a package for the Yocto Project.

Preparing to use Ftrace

Ftrace and its various options are configured in the kernel configuration menu. You will need the following as a minimum:

- CONFIG_FUNCTION_TRACER in the menu **Kernel hacking | Tracers | Kernel Function Tracer**

For reasons that will become clear later, you would be well advised to turn on these options as well:

- CONFIG_FUNCTION_GRAPH_TRACER in the menu **Kernel hacking | Tracers | Kernel Function Graph Tracer**
- CONFIG_DYNAMIC_FTRACE in the menu **Kernel hacking | Tracers | enable/disable function tracing dynamically**

Since the whole thing is hosted in the kernel, there is no user space configuration to be done.

Using Ftrace Before you can use `Ftrace`, you have to mount the `debugfs` filesystem which, by convention, goes in the `/sys/kernel/debug` directory:

```
# mount -t debugfs none /sys/kernel/debug
```

All the controls for `Ftrace` are in the `/sys/kernel/debug/tracing` directory; there is even a mini HOWTO in the README file.

This is the list of tracers available in the kernel:

```
# cat /sys/kernel/debug/tracing/available_tracers
blk function_graph function nop
```

The active tracer is shown by `current_tracer`, which, initially, will be the null tracer, `nop`.

To capture a trace, select the tracer by writing the name of one of the `available_tracers` to `current_tracer`, then enable tracing for a short while, as shown here:

```
# echo function > /sys/kernel/debug/tracing/current_tracer
# echo 1 > /sys/kernel/debug/tracing/tracing_on
# sleep 1
# echo 0 > /sys/kernel/debug/tracing/tracing_on
```

In that one second, the trace buffer will have been filled with the details of every function called by the kernel. The format of the trace buffer is plain text, as described in `Documentation/trace/ftrace.txt`. You can read the trace buffer from the `trace` file:

```
# cat /sys/kernel/debug/tracing/trace
# tracer: function
#
# entries-in-buffer/entries-written: 40051/40051    #P:1
#
#                              _-----=> irqs-off
#                             / _----=> need-resched
#                            | / _---=> hardirq/softirq
#                            || / _--=> preempt-depth
```

```
#                              ||| /   delay
#          TASK-PID   CPU#   ||||    TIMESTAMP  FUNCTION
#           | |         |     ||||       |          |
          sh-361    [000]  ...1   992.990646: mutex_unlock <-
rb_simple_write

          sh-361    [000]  ...1   992.990658: __fsnotify_parent
<-vfs_write

          sh-361    [000]  ...1   992.990661: fsnotify <-
vfs_write

          sh-361    [000]  ...1   992.990663: __srcu_read_lock
<-fsnotify

          sh-361    [000]  ...1   992.990666: preempt_count_add
<-__srcu_read_lock

          sh-361    [000]  ...2   992.990668: preempt_count_sub
<-__srcu_read_lock

          sh-361    [000]  ...1   992.990670: __srcu_read_unlock
<-fsnotify

          sh-361    [000]  ...1   992.990672: __sb_end_write <-
vfs_write

          sh-361    [000]  ...1   992.990674: preempt_count_add
<-__sb_end_write
[...]
```

You can capture a large number of data points in just one second.

As with profilers, it is difficult to make sense of a flat function list like this. If you select the function_graph tracer, Ftrace captures call graphs like this:

```
# tracer: function_graph
#
# CPU  DURATION                  FUNCTION CALLS
#|      |   |                    |   |   |   |
 0) + 63.167 us   |               } /* cpdma_ctlr_int_ctrl */
 0) + 73.417 us   |               } /* cpsw_intr_disable */
 0)               |               disable_irq_nosync() {
 0)               |                 __disable_irq_nosync() {
 0)               |                   __irq_get_desc_lock() {
 0)    0.541 us   |                     irq_to_desc();
 0)    0.500 us   |                     preempt_count_add();
 0) + 16.000 us   |                   }
```

```
0)                    |              __disable_irq() {
0)    0.500 us        |                irq_disable();
0)    8.208 us        |              }
0)                    |              __irq_put_desc_unlock() {
0)    0.459 us        |                preempt_count_sub();
0)    8.000 us        |              }
0) + 55.625 us        |            }
0) + 63.375 us        |          }
```

Now you can see the nesting of the function calls, delimited by parentheses, { and }. At the terminating brace, there is a measurement of the time taken in the function, annotated with a plus sign, +, if it takes more than 10 µs, and an exclamation mark, !, if it takes more than 100 µs.

You are often only interested in the kernel activity caused by a single process or thread, in which case you can restrict the trace to the one thread by writing the thread ID to set_ftrace_pid.

Dynamic Ftrace and trace filters

Enabling CONFIG_DYNAMIC_FTRACE allows Ftrace to modify the function trace sites at runtime, which has a couple of benefits. Firstly, it triggers additional build-time processing of the trace function probes which allows the Ftrace subsystem to locate them at boot time and overwrite them with NOP instructions, thus reducing the overhead of the function trace code to almost nothing. You can then enable Ftrace in production or near production kernels with no impact on performance.

The second advantage is that you can selectively enable function trace sites rather than trace everything. The list of functions is put into available_filter_functions; there are several tens of thousands of them. You can selectively enable function traces as you need them by copying the name from available_filter_functions to set_ftrace_filter, and then stop tracing that function by writing the name to set_ftrace_notrace. You can also use wildcards and append names to the list. For example, suppose you are interested in tcp handling:

```
# cd /sys/kernel/debug/tracing
# echo "tcp*" > set_ftrace_filter
# echo function > current_tracer
# echo 1 > tracing_on
```

Run some tests and then look at the trace:

```
# cat trace
# tracer: function
#
# entries-in-buffer/entries-written: 590/590    #P:1
#
#                                _-----=> irqs-off
#                               / _----=> need-resched
#                              | / _---=> hardirq/softirq
#                              || / _--=> preempt-depth
#                              ||| /     delay
#           TASK-PID   CPU#    ||||    TIMESTAMP  FUNCTION
#              | |       |     ||||       |          |
        dropbear-375   [000]  ...1 48545.022235: tcp_poll <-sock_poll
        dropbear-375   [000]  ...1 48545.022372: tcp_poll <-sock_poll
        dropbear-375   [000]  ...1 48545.022393: tcp_sendmsg <-
          inet_sendmsg
        dropbear-375   [000]  ...1 48545.022398: tcp_send_mss <-
          tcp_sendmsg
        dropbear-375   [000]  ...1 48545.022400: tcp_current_mss <-
          tcp_send_mss
[...]
```

set_ ftrace_filter can also contain commands, for example, to start and stop tracing when certain functions are executed. There isn't space to go into these details here but, if you want to find out more, please read the **Filter commands** section in Documentation/trace/ftrace.txt.

Trace events

The function and function_graph tracers described in the preceding section record only the time at which the function was executed. The trace events feature also records parameters associated with the call, making the trace more readable and informative. For example, instead of just recording that the function kmalloc had been called, a trace event will record the number of bytes requested and the returned pointer. Trace events are used in perf and LTTng as well as Ftrace, but the development of the trace events subsystem was prompted by the LTTng project.

It takes effort from kernel developers to create trace events since each one is different. They are defined in the source code using the TRACE_EVENT macro: there are over a thousand of them now. You can see the list of events available at runtime in /sys/ kernel/debug/tracing/available_events. They are named subsystem:function, for example, kmem:kmalloc. Each event is also represented by a subdirectory in tracing/events/[subsystem]/[function], as demonstrated here:

```
# ls events/kmem/kmalloc
enable    filter    format    id    trigger
```

The files are as follows:

- enable: You write a 1 to this file to enable the event.
- filter: This is an expression which must evaluate to true for the event to be traced.
- format: This is the format of the event and parameters.
- id: This is a numeric identifier.
- trigger: This is a command that is executed when the event occurs using the syntax defined in the **Filter commands** section of Documentation/trace/ ftrace.txt. I will show you a simple example involving kmalloc and kfree.

Event tracing does not depend on the function tracers, so begin by selecting the nop tracer:

```
# echo nop > current_tracer
```

Next, select the events to trace by enabling each one individually:

```
# echo 1 > events/kmem/kmalloc/enable
# echo 1 > events/kmem/kfree/enable
```

You can also write the event names to set_event, as shown here:

```
# echo "kmem:kmalloc kmem:kfree" > set_event
```

Now, when you read the trace, you can see the functions and their parameters:

```
# tracer: nop
#
# entries-in-buffer/entries-written: 359/359     #P:1
#
#                              _-----=> irqs-off
#                             / _----=> need-resched
#                            | / _---=> hardirq/softirq
#                            || / _--=> preempt-depth
```

```
#                           ||| /     delay
#            TASK-PID    CPU#  ||||      TIMESTAMP  FUNCTION
#               | |        |    ||||        |          |
             cat-382     [000] ...1  2935.586706: kmalloc:
call_site=c0554644 ptr=de515a00 bytes_req=384 bytes_alloc=512
gfp_flags=GFP_ATOMIC|GFP_NOWARN|GFP_NOMEMALLOC
             cat-382     [000] ...1  2935.586718: kfree:
call_site=c059c2d8 ptr=  (null)
```

Exactly the same trace events are visible in perf as *tracepoint events*.

Using LTTng

The Linux Trace Toolkit project was started by Karim Yaghmour as a means of tracing kernel activity and was one of the first trace tools generally available for the Linux kernel. Later, Mathieu Desnoyers took up the idea and re-implemented it as the next generation trace tool, LTTng. It was then expanded to cover user space traces as well as the kernel. The project website is at `http://lttng.org/` and contains a comprehensive user manual.

LTTng consists of three components:

- A core session manager
- A kernel tracer implemented as a group of kernel modules
- A user space tracer implemented as a library

In addition to those, you will need a trace viewer such as Babeltrace (`http://www.efficios.com/babeltrace`) or the Eclipse Trace Compaas plug-in to display and filter the raw trace data on the host or target.

LTTng requires a kernel configured with `CONFIG_TRACEPOINTS`, which is enabled when you select **Kernel hacking | Tracers | Kernel Function Tracer**.

The description that follows refers to LTTng version 2.5; other versions may be different.

LTTng and the Yocto Project

You need to add these packages to the target dependencies, for example, in `conf/local.conf`:

```
IMAGE_INSTALL_append = " lttng-tools lttng-modules lttng-ust"
```

If you want to run Babeltrace on the target, also append the package `babeltrace`.

LTTng and Buildroot

You need to enable the following:

- `BR2_PACKAGE_LTTNG_MODULES` in the menu **Target packages | Debugging, profiling and benchmark | lttng-modules**.
- `BR2_PACKAGE_LTTNG_TOOLS` in the menu **Target packages | Debugging, profiling and benchmark | lttng-tools**.

For user space trace tracing, enable this:

- `BR2_PACKAGE_LTTNG_LIBUST` in the menu **Target packages | Libraries | Other**, enable **lttng-libust**.

There is a package called `lttng-babeltrace` for the target. Buildroot builds the host `babeltrace` automatically and places in `output/host/usr/bin/babeltrace`.

Using LTTng for kernel tracing

LTTng can use the set of `ftrace` events described above as potential trace points. Initially, they are disabled.

The control interface for LTTng is the `lttng` command. You can list the kernel probes using the following:

```
# lttng list --kernel
Kernel events:
------------

      writeback_nothread (loglevel: TRACE_EMERG (0)) (type:
tracepoint)
      writeback_queue (loglevel: TRACE_EMERG (0)) (type:
tracepoint)
      writeback_exec (loglevel: TRACE_EMERG (0)) (type:
tracepoint)
[...]
```

Traces are captured in the context of a session which, in this example, is called `test`:

```
# lttng create test
Session test created.
Traces will be written in /home/root/lttng-traces/test-20150824-
140942
# lttng list
Available tracing sessions:
```

```
    1) test (/home/root/lttng-traces/test-20150824-140942)
[inactive]
```

Now enable a few events in the current session. You can enable all kernel tracepoints using the `--all` option but remember the warning about generating too much trace data. Let's start with a couple of scheduler-related trace events:

```
# lttng enable-event --kernel sched_switch,sched_process_fork
```

Check that everything is set up:

```
# lttng list test
Tracing session test: [inactive]
    Trace path: /home/root/lttng-traces/test-20150824-140942
    Live timer interval (usec): 0


=== Domain: Kernel ===


Channels:
-------------
- channel0: [enabled]


    Attributes:
      overwrite mode: 0
      subbufers size: 26214
      number of subbufers: 4
      switch timer interval: 0
      read timer interval: 200000
      trace file count: 0
      trace file size (bytes): 0
      output: splice()


    Events:
      sched_process_fork (loglevel: TRACE_EMERG (0)) (type:
tracepoint) [enabled]
      sched_switch (loglevel: TRACE_EMERG (0)) (type: tracepoint)
[enabled]
```

Now start tracing:

```
# lttng start
```

Run the test load and then stop tracing:

```
# lttng stop
```

Traces for the session are written to the session directory, lttng-traces/<session>/ kernel.

You can use the Babeltrace viewer to dump the raw trace data in text format, in this case, I ran it on the host computer:

```
$ babeltrace  lttng-traces/test-20150824-140942/kernel
```

The output is too verbose to fit on this page, so I will leave it as an exercise for you, the reader, to capture and display a trace in this way. The text output from eBabeltrace does have the advantage that it is easy to search for strings using grep and similar commands.

A good choice for a graphical trace viewer is the Trace Compass plug-in for Eclipse, which is now part of the Eclipse IDE for C/C++ Developers bundle. Importing the trace data into Eclipse is characteristically fiddly. Briefly, you need to follow these steps:

1. Open the tracing perspective.
2. Create a new project by selecting **File | New | Tracing project**.
3. Enter a project name and click **Finish**.
4. Right-click on the **New Project** option in the **Project Explorer** menu and select **Import**.
5. Expand **Tracing** and then select **Trace Import**.
6. Browse to the directory containing the traces (for example, test-20150824-140942), tick the box to indicate which sub-directories you want (it might be the kernel) and click **Finish**.
7. Now, expand the project and, within that, expand **Traces[1]** and, within that, double-click on **kernel**.

8. You should see the trace data shown in the following screenshot:

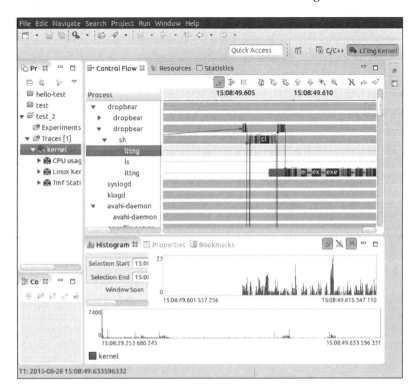

In the preceding screenshot, I have zoomed in on the control flow view to show state transitions between `dropbear` and a shell, and also some activity of the `lttng` daemon.

Using Valgrind for application profiling

I introduced Valgrind in *Chapter 11, Managing Memory*, as a tool for identifying memory problems using the memcheck tool. Valgrind has other useful tools for application profiling. The two I am going to look at here are **Callgrind** and **Helgrind**. Since Valgrind works by running the code in a sandbox, it is able to check the code as it runs and report certain behaviors, which native tracers and profilers cannot do.

Callgrind

Callgrind is a call-graph generating profiler that also collects information about processor cache hit rate and branch prediction. Callgrind is only useful if your bottleneck is CPU-bound. It's not useful if heavy I/O or multiple processes are involved.

Valgrind does not require kernel configuration but it does need debug symbols. It is available as a target package in both the Yocto Project and Buildroot (`BR2_PACKAGE_ VALGRIND`).

You run Callgrind in Valgrind on the target, like so:

```
# valgrind --tool=callgrind <program>
```

This produces a file called `callgrind.out.<PID>` which you can copy to the host and analyze with `callgrind_annotate`.

The default is to capture data for all the threads together in a single file. If you add option `--separate-threads=yes` when capturing, there will be profiles for each of the threads in files named `callgrind.out.<PID>-<thread id>`, for example, `callgrind.out.122-01`, `callgrind.out.122-02`, and so on.

Callgrind can simulate the processor L1/L2 cache and report on cache misses. Capture the trace with the `--simulate-cache=yes` option. L2 misses are much more expensive than L1 misses, so pay attention to code with high D2mr or D2mw counts.

Helgrind

This is a thread error detector for detecting synchronization errors in C, C++, and Fortran programs that include POSIX threads.

Helgrind can detect three classes of error. Firstly, it can detect the incorrect use of the API. For example, it can unlock a mutex that is already unlocked, unlock a mutex that was locked by a different thread, not checking the return value of certain Pthread functions. Secondly, it monitors the order in which threads acquire locks and thus detects potential deadlocks which could arise from the formation of cycles of locks. Finally, it detects data races which can happen when two threads access a shared memory location without using suitable locks or other synchronization to ensure single-threaded access.

Using Helgrind is simple, you just need this command:

```
# valgrind --tool=helgrind <program>
```

It prints problems and potential problems as it finds them. You can direct these messages to a file by adding `--log-file=<filename>`.

Using strace to show system calls

I started the chapter with the simple and ubiquitous tool, `top`, and I will finish with another: `strace`. It is a very simple tracer that captures system calls made by a program and, optionally, its children. You can use it to do the following:

- Learn which system calls a program makes.

- Find those system calls that fail together with the error code. I find this useful if a program fails to start but doesn't print an error message or if the message is too general. `strace` shows the failing syscall.

- Find which files a program opens.

- Find out what syscalls a running program is making, for example to see if it is stuck in a loop.

There are many more examples online, just search for `strace` tips and tricks. Everybody has their own favorite story, for example, `http://chadfowler.com/blog/2014/01/26/the-magic-of-strace`

`strace` uses the `ptrace(2)` function to hook calls from user space to the kernel. If you want to know more about how `ptrace` works, the man page is detailed and surprisingly legible.

The simplest way to get a trace is to run the command with `strace` as shown here (the listing has been edited to make it clearer):

```
# strace ./helloworld
execve("./helloworld", ["./helloworld"], [/* 14 vars */]) = 0
brk(0)                                  = 0x11000
uname({sys="Linux", node="beaglebone", ...}) = 0
mmap2(NULL, 4096, PROT_READ|PROT_WRITE, MAP_PRIVATE|MAP_ANONYMOUS, -
1, 0) = 0xb6f40000
access("/etc/ld.so.preload", R_OK)      = -1 ENOENT (No such file or
directory)
open("/etc/ld.so.cache", O_RDONLY|O_CLOEXEC) = 3
fstat64(3, {st_mode=S_IFREG|0644, st_size=8100, ...}) = 0
mmap2(NULL, 8100, PROT_READ, MAP_PRIVATE, 3, 0) = 0xb6f3e000
close(3)                                = 0
open("/lib/tls/v7l/neon/vfp/libc.so.6", O_RDONLY|O_CLOEXEC) = -1
ENOENT (No such file or directory)
[...]
open("/lib/libc.so.6", O_RDONLY|O_CLOEXEC) = 3
read(3,
"\177ELF\1\1\1\0\0\0\0\0\0\0\0\0\3\0(\0\1\0\0\0$`\1\0004\0\0\0"...,
512) = 512
fstat64(3, {st_mode=S_IFREG|0755, st_size=1291884, ...}) = 0
```

```
mmap2(NULL, 1328520, PROT_READ|PROT_EXEC, MAP_PRIVATE|MAP_DENYWRITE,
3, 0) = 0xb6df9000

mprotect(0xb6f30000, 32768, PROT_NONE)   = 0

mmap2(0xb6f38000, 12288, PROT_READ|PROT_WRITE,
MAP_PRIVATE|MAP_FIXED|MAP_DENYWRITE, 3, 0x137000) = 0xb6f38000

mmap2(0xb6f3b000, 9608, PROT_READ|PROT_WRITE,
MAP_PRIVATE|MAP_FIXED|MAP_ANONYMOUS, -1, 0) = 0xb6f3b000

close(3)
[...]
write(1, "Hello, world!\n", 14Hello, world!
)            = 14
exit_group(0)                               = ?
+++ exited with 0 +++
```

Most of the trace shows how the runtime environment is created. In particular
you can see how the library loader hunts for libc.so.6, eventually finding it in
/lib. Finally, it gets to running the main() function of the program, which prints
its message and exits.

If you want strace to follow any child processes or threads created by the original
process, add the -f option.

> If you are using strace to trace a program that creates threads,
> you almost certainly want the -f option. Better still, use -ff and
> -o <file name> so that the output for each child process or thread
> is written to a separate file named <filename>.<PID | TID>.

A common use of strace is to discover which files a program tries to open at start
up. You can restrict the system calls that are traced through the -e option, and you
can write the trace to a file instead of stdout by using the -o option:

```
# strace -e open -o ssh-strace.txt ssh localhost
```

This shows the libraries and configuration files ssh opens when it is setting up
a connection.

You can even use strace as a basic profile tool: if you use the -c option, it
accumulates the time spent in system calls and prints out a summary like this:

```
# strace -c grep linux /usr/lib/* > /dev/null
% time     seconds  usecs/call     calls    errors syscall
------ ----------- ----------- --------- --------- ----------
 78.68    0.012825           1     11098        18    read
```

11.03	0.001798	1	3551		write
10.02	0.001634	8	216	15	open
0.26	0.000043	0	202		fstat64
0.00	0.000000	0	201		close
0.00	0.000000	0	1		execve
0.00	0.000000	0	1	1	access
0.00	0.000000	0	3		brk
0.00	0.000000	0	199		munmap
0.00	0.000000	0	1		uname
0.00	0.000000	0	5		mprotect
0.00	0.000000	0	207		mmap2
0.00	0.000000	0	15	15	stat64
0.00	0.000000	0	1		getuid32
0.00	0.000000	0	1		set_tls
------	-----------	-----------	---------	---------	-----------
100.00	0.016300		15702	49	total

Summary

Nobody can complain that Linux lacks options to profile and trace. This chapter has given you an overview of some of the most common ones.

When faced with a system that is not performing as well as you would like, start with top and try to identify the problem. If it proves to be a single application, then you can use perf record/report to profile it, bearing in mind that you will have to configure the kernel to enable perf and you will need debug symbols for the binaries and kernel. OProfile is an alternative to perf record and can tell you similar things. gprof is, frankly, outdated but it does have the advantage of not requiring kernel support. If the problem is not so well localized, use perf (or OProfile) to get a system-wide view.

Ftrace comes into its own when you have specific questions about the behavior of the kernel. The function and function_graph tracers give a detailed view of the relationship and sequence of function calls. The event tracers allow you to extract more information about functions including the parameters and return values. LTTng performs a similar role, making use the event trace mechanism, and adds high speed ring buffers to extract large quantities of data from the kernel. Valgrind has the particular advantage that it runs code in a sandbox and can report on errors that are hard to track down in other ways.

Using the Callgrind tool, it can generate call graphs and report on processor cache usage and, with Helgrind, it can report on thread-related problems. Finally, don't forget strace. It is a good standby for finding out what system calls a program is making, from tracking file open calls to find file path names to checking for system wake ups and incoming signals.

All the while, be aware of, and try to avoid, the observer effect: make sure that the measurements you are making are valid for a production system. In the next chapter, I will continue the theme as I delve into the latency tracers that help us quantify the real-time performance of a target system.

14
Real-time Programming

Much of the interaction between a computer system and the real world happens in real-time and so this is an important topic for developers of embedded systems. I have touched on real-time programming in several places so far: in *Chapter 10*, *Learning About Processes and Threads*, I looked at scheduling policies and priority inversion, and in *Chapter 11*, *Managing Memory*, I described the problems with page faults and the need for memory locking. Now, it is time to bring these topics together and look at real-time programming in some depth.

In this chapter, I will begin with a discussion about the characteristics of real-time systems and then consider the implications for system design, both at the application and kernel levels. I will describe the real-time kernel patch, PREEMPT_RT, and show how to get it and apply it to a mainline kernel. The last sections will describe how to characterize system latencies using two tools: cyclictest and Ftrace.

There are other ways to achieve real-time behavior on an embedded Linux device, for instance, using a dedicated micro-controller or a separate real-time kernel alongside the Linux kernel in the way that Xenomai and RTAI do. I am not going to discuss these here because the focus of this book is on using Linux as the core for embedded systems.

What is real-time?

The nature of real-time programming is one of the subjects that software engineers love to discuss at length, often giving a range of contradictory definitions. I will begin by setting out what I think is important about real-time.

A task is a real-time task if it has to complete before a certain point in time, known as the deadline. The distinction between real-time and non real-time tasks is shown by considering what happens when you play an audio stream on your computer while compiling the Linux kernel.

The first is a real-time task because there is a constant stream of data arriving at the audio driver and blocks of audio samples have to be written to the audio interface at the playback rate. Meanwhile, the compilation is not real-time because there is no deadline. You simply want it to complete as soon as possible; whether it takes 10 seconds or 10 minutes does not affect the quality of the kernel.

The other important thing to consider is the consequence of missing the deadline, which can range from mild annoyance through to system failure and death. Here are some examples:

- **Playing an audio stream**: There is a deadline in the order of tens of milliseconds. If the audio buffer under-runs you will hear a click, which is annoying, but you will get over it.

- **Moving and clicking a mouse**: The deadline is also in the order of tens of milliseconds. If it is missed, the mouse moves erratically and button clicks will be lost. If the problem persists, the system will become unusable.

- **Printing a piece of paper**: The deadlines for the paper feed are in the millisecond range, which, if missed, may cause the printer to jam and somebody will have to go and fix it. Occasional jams are acceptable but nobody is going to buy a printer that keeps on jamming.

- **Printing sell-by dates on bottles on a production line**: If one bottle is not printed the whole production line has to be halted, the bottle removed and the line restarted, which is expensive.

- **Baking a cake**: There is a deadline of 30 minutes or so. If you miss it by a few minutes, the cake might be ruined. If you miss it by a large amount, the house will burn down.

- **A power surge detection system**: If the system detects a surge, a circuit breaker has to be triggered within 2 milliseconds. Failing to do so causes damage to the equipment and may injure or kill personnel.

In other words, there are many consequences to missed deadlines. We often talk about these different categories:

- **soft real-time**: The deadline is desirable but is sometimes missed without the system being considered a failure. First two examples are like this.

- **hard real-time**: Here, missing a deadline has a serious effect. We can further subdivide hard real-time into mission-critical systems in which there is a cost to missing the deadline, such as the fourth example, and safety critical-systems in which there is a danger to life and limb, such as the last two examples. I put in the banking example to show that not all hard real-time systems have deadlines measured in microseconds.

Software written for safety-critical systems has to conform to various standards that seek to ensure that it is capable of performing reliably. It is very difficult for a complex operating system such as Linux to meet those requirements.

When it comes to mission-critical systems, it is possible, and common, for Linux to be used for a wide range of control systems. The requirements of the software depend on the combination of the deadline and the confidence level, which can usually be determined through extensive testing.

Therefore, to say that a system is real-time, you have to measure its response times under the maximum anticipated load, and show that it meets the deadline for an agreed proportion of the time. As a rule of thumb, a well configured Linux system using a mainline kernel is good for soft real-time tasks with deadlines down to tens of milliseconds and a kernel with the PREEMPT_RT patch is good for soft and hard real-time mission-critical systems with deadlines down to several hundreds of microseconds.

The key to creating a real-time system is to reduce the variability in response times so that you have greater confidence that they will not be missed; in other words, you need to make the system more deterministic. Often, this is done at the expense of performance. For example, caches make systems run faster by making the average time to access an item of data shorter, but the maximum time is longer in the case of a cache miss. Caches make a system faster but less deterministic, which is the opposite of what we want.

 It is a myth of real-time computing that it is fast. This is not so, the more deterministic a system is, the lower the maximum throughput.

The remainder of this chapter is concerned with identifying the causes of latency and the things you can do to reduce it.

Identifying the sources of non-determinism

Fundamentally, real-time programming is about making sure that the threads controlling the output in real-time are scheduled when needed and so can complete the job before the deadline. Anything that prevents this is a problem. Here are some problem areas:

- **Scheduling**: Real-time threads must be scheduled before others so they must have a real-time policy, SCHED_FIFO, or SCHED_RR. Additionally they should have priorities assigned in descending order starting with the one with the shortest deadline, according to the theory of Rate Monotonic Analysis that I described in *Chapter 10, Learning About Processes and Threads*.

- **Scheduling latency**: The kernel must be able to reschedule as soon as an event such as an interrupt or timer occurs, and not be subject to unbounded delays. Reducing scheduling latency is a key topic later on in this chapter.

- **Priority inversion**: This is a consequence of priority-based scheduling, which leads to unbounded delays when a high priority thread is blocked on a mutex held by a low priority thread, as I described in *Chapter 10, Learning About Processes and Threads*. User space has priority inheritance and priority ceiling mutexes; in kernel space we have rt-mutexes which implement priority inheritance and which I will talk about in the section on the real-time kernel.

- **Accurate timers**: If you want to manage deadlines in the region of low milliseconds or microseconds, you need timers that match. High resolution timers are crucial and are a configuration option on almost all kernels.

- **Page faults**: A page fault while executing a critical section of code will upset all timing estimates. You can avoid them by locking memory, as I describe later on.

- **Interrupts**: They occur at unpredictable times and can result in unexpected processing overhead if there is a sudden flood of them. There are two ways to avoid this. One is to run interrupts as kernel threads, and the other, on multi-core devices, is to shield one or more CPUs from interrupt handling. I will discuss both possibilities later.

- **Processor caches**: Provide a buffer between the CPU and the main memory and, like all caches, are a source of non-determinism, especially on multi-core devices. Unfortunately, this is beyond the scope of this book but, refer to the references at the end of the chapter.

- **Memory bus contention**: When peripherals access memory directly through a DMA channel they use up a slice of memory bus bandwidth, which slows down access from the CPU core (or cores) and so contributes to non-deterministic execution of the program. However, this is a hardware issue and is also beyond the scope of this book.

I will expand on the important problems and see what can be done about them in the next sections.

One item missing from the list is power management. The needs of real-time and power management pull in opposite directions. Power management often leads to high latencies when switching between sleep states, since setting up power regulators and waking up processors all takes time, as does changing the core clock frequency because the clocks take time to settle. But, surely you wouldn't expect a device to respond immediately to an interrupt from suspend state? I know I can't get going in the morning until after at least one cup of coffee.

Understanding scheduling latency

Real-time threads need to be scheduled as soon as they have something to do. However, even if there are no other threads of the same or higher priority, there is always a delay from the point at which the wake up event occurs – an interrupt or system timer – to the time that the thread starts to run. This is called scheduling latency. It can be broken down into several components, as shown in the following diagram:

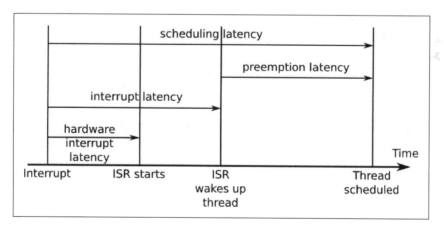

Firstly, there is the hardware interrupt latency from the point at which an interrupt is asserted until the **ISR (interrupt service routine)** begins to run. A small part of this is the delay in the interrupt hardware itself but the biggest problem is interrupts disabled in the software. Minimizing this *IRQ off time* is important.

The next is interrupt latency, which is the length of time until the ISR has serviced the interrupt and woken up any threads waiting on this event. It is mostly dependent on the way the ISR was written. Normally it should take only a short time, measured in micro-seconds.

The final delay is the preemption latency, which is the time from the point that the kernel is notified that a thread is ready to run to that at which the scheduler actually runs the thread. It is determined by whether the kernel can be preempted or not. If it is running code in a critical section then the reschedule will have to wait. The length of the delay is dependent on the configuration of kernel preemption.

Kernel preemption

The preemption latency occurs because it is not always safe or desirable to preempt the current thread of execution and call the scheduler. Mainline Linux has three settings for preemption, selected via the **Kernel Features | Preemption Model** menu:

- CONFIG_PREEMPT_NONE: no preemption
- CONFIG_PREEMPT_VOLUNTARY: enables additional checks for requests for preemption
- CONFIG_PREEMPT: allows the kernel to be preempted

With preemption set to none, kernel code will continue without rescheduling until it either returns via a syscall back to user space, where preemption is always allowed, or it encounters a sleeping wait which stops the current thread. Since it reduces the number of transitions between the kernel and user space and may reduce the total number of context switches, this option results in the highest throughput at the expense of large preemption latencies. It is the default for servers and some desktop kernels where throughput is more important than responsiveness.

The second option enables more explicit preemption points where the scheduler is called if the need_resched flag is set, which reduces the worst case preemption latencies at the expense of slightly lower throughput. Some distributions set this option on desktops.

The third option makes the kernel preemptible, meaning that an interrupt can result in an immediate reschedule so long as the kernel is not executing in an atomic context, which I will describe in the following section. This reduces worst case preemption latencies and, therefore, overall scheduling latencies, to something in the order of a few milliseconds on typical embedded hardware. This is often described as a soft real-time option and most embedded kernels are configured in this way. Of course, there is a small reduction in overall throughput but that is usually less important than having more deterministic scheduling for embedded devices.

The real-time Linux kernel (PREEMPT_RT)

There is a long-standing effort to reduce latencies still further which goes by the name of the kernel configuration option for these features, `PREEMPT_RT`. The project was started by Ingo Molnar, Thomas Gleixner, and Steven Rostedt and has had contributions from many more developers over the years. The kernel patches are at `https://www.kernel.org/pub/linux/kernel/projects/rt` and there is a wiki, including an FAQ (slightly out of date), at `https://rt.wiki.kernel.org`.

Many parts of the project have been incorporated into mainline Linux over the years, including high resolution timers, kernel mutexes, and threaded interrupt handlers. However, the core patches remain outside of the mainline because they are rather intrusive and (some claim) only benefit a small percentage of the total Linux user base. Maybe, one day, the whole patch set will be merged upstream.

The central plan is to reduce the amount of time the kernel spends running in an atomic context, which is where it is not safe to call the scheduler and switch to a different thread. Typical atomic contexts are when the kernel:

- is running an interrupt or trap handler
- is holding a spin lock or in an RCU critical section. Spin lock and RCU are kernel locking primitives, the details of which are not relevant here
- is between calls to `preempt_disable()` and `preempt_enable()`
- hardware interrupts are disabled

The changes that are part of `PREEMPT_RT` fall into two main areas: one is to reduce the impact of interrupt handlers by turning them into kernel threads and the other is to make locks preemptible so that a thread can sleep while holding one. It is obvious that there is a large overhead in these changes, which makes average case interrupt handling slower but much more deterministic, which is what we are striving for.

Threaded interrupt handlers

Not all interrupts are triggers for the real-time tasks but all interrupts steal cycles from the real-time task. Threaded interrupt handlers allow a priority to be associated with the interrupt and for it to be scheduled at an appropriate time as shown in the following diagram:

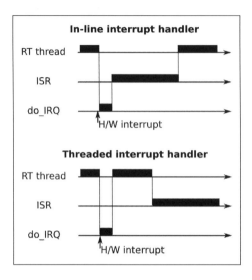

If the interrupt handler code is run as a kernel thread there is no reason why it cannot be preempted by a user space thread of higher priority, and so the interrupt handler does not contribute towards scheduling latency of the user space thread. Threaded interrupt handlers have been a feature of mainline Linux since 2.6.30. You can request that an individual interrupt handler is threaded by registering it with `request_threaded_irq()` in place of the normal `request_irq()`. You can make threaded IRQs the default by configuring the kernel with `CONFIG_IRQ_FORCED_THREADING=y` which makes all handlers into threads unless they have explicitly prevented this by setting the `IRQF_NO_THREAD` flag. When you apply the `PREEMPT_RT` patches, interrupts are, by default, configured as threads in this way. Here is an example of what you might see:

```
# ps -Leo pid,tid,class,rtprio,stat,comm,wchan | grep FF
PID     TID     CLS     RTPRIO  STAT    COMMAND         WCHAN
3       3       FF      1       S       ksoftirqd/0     smpboot_th
7       7       FF      99      S       posixcputmr/0   posix_cpu_
19      19      FF      50      S       irq/28-edma     irq_thread
20      20      FF      50      S       irq/30-edma_err irq_thread
42      42      FF      50      S       irq/91-rtc0     irq_thread
```

43	43	FF	50	S	irq/92-rtc0	irq_thread
44	44	FF	50	S	irq/80-mmc0	irq_thread
45	45	FF	50	S	irq/150-mmc0	irq_thread
47	47	FF	50	S	irq/44-mmc1	irq_thread
52	52	FF	50	S	irq/86-44e0b000	irq_thread
59	59	FF	50	S	irq/52-tilcdc	irq_thread
65	65	FF	50	S	irq/56-4a100000	irq_thread
66	66	FF	50	S	irq/57-4a100000	irq_thread
67	67	FF	50	S	irq/58-4a100000	irq_thread
68	68	FF	50	S	irq/59-4a100000	irq_thread
76	76	FF	50	S	irq/88-OMAP UAR	irq_thread

In this case, a BeagleBone running `linux-yocto-rt`, only the `gp_timer` interrupt was not threaded. It is normal that the timer interrupt handler be run in-line.

> Note that the interrupt threads have all been given the default policy `SCHED_FIFO` and a priority of `50`. It doesn't make sense to leave them with the defaults, however; now is your chance to assign priorities according to the importance of the interrupts compared to real-time user space threads.

Here is a suggested order of descending thread priorities:

- The POSIX timers thread, `posixcputmr`, should always have the highest priority.
- Hardware interrupts associated with the highest priority real-time thread.
- The highest priority real-time thread.
- Hardware interrupts for the progressively lower priority real-time threads followed by the thread itself.
- Hardware interrupts for non-real-time interfaces.
- The soft IRQ daemon, `ksoftirqd`, which on RT kernels is responsible for running delayed interrupt routines and, prior to Linux 3.6, was responsible for running the network stack, the block I/O layer, and other things. You may need to experiment with different priority levels to get a balance.

You can change the priorities using the `chrt` command as part of the boot script, using a command like this:

```
# chrt -f -p 90 `pgrep irq/28-edma`
```

The `pgrep` command is part of the `procps` package.

Preemptible kernel locks

Making the majority of kernel locks preemptible is the most intrusive change that PREEMPT_RT makes and this code remains outside of the mainline kernel.

The problem occurs with spinlocks, which are used for much of the kernel locking. A spinlock is a busy-wait mutex which does not require a context switch in the contended case and so is very efficient as long as the lock is held for a short time. Ideally, they should be locked for less than the time it would take to reschedule twice. The following diagram shows threads running on two different CPUs contending the same spinlock. **CPU0** gets it first, forcing **CPU1** to spin, waiting until it is unlocked:

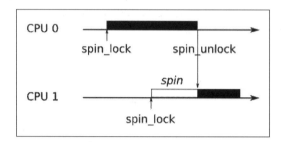

The thread that holds the spinlock cannot be preempted since doing so may make the new thread enter the same code and deadlock when it tries to lock the same spinlock. Consequently, in mainline Linux, locking a spinlock disables kernel preemption, creating an atomic context. This means that a low priority thread that holds a spinlock can prevent a high priority thread from being scheduled.

> The solution adopted by PREEMPT_RT is to replace almost all spinlocks with rt-mutexes. A mutex is slower than a spinlock but it is fully preemptible. Not only that, but rt-mutexes implement priority inheritance and so are not susceptible to priority inversion.

Getting the PREEMPT_RT patches

The RT developers do not create patch sets for every kernel version because of the amount of effort involved. On average, they create patches for every other kernel. The most recent kernels that are supported at the time of writing are as follows:

- 4.1-rt
- 4.0-rt
- 3.18-rt

- 3.14-rt
- 3.12-rt
- 3.10-rt

The patches are available at `https://www.kernel.org/pub/linux/kernel/projects/rt`.

If you are using the Yocto Project, there is an `rt` version of the kernel already. Otherwise, it is possible that the place you got your kernel from already has the `PREEMPT_RT` patch applied. Otherwise, you will have to apply the patch yourself. Firstly, make sure that the `PREEMPT_RT` patch version and your kernel version match exactly, otherwise you will not be able to apply the patches cleanly. Then you apply it in the normal way, as shown here:

```
$ cd linux-4.1.10
$ zcat patch-4.1.10-rt11.patch.gz | patch -p1
```

You will then be able to configure the kernel with `CONFIG_PREEMPT_RT_FULL`.

There is a problem in the last paragraph. The RT patch will only apply if you are using a compatible mainline kernel. You are probably not because that is the nature of embedded Linux kernels and so you will have to spend some time looking at failed patches and fixing them, and then analyzing the board support for your target and adding any real-time support that is missing. These details are, once again, outside the scope of this book. If you are not sure what to do, you should inquire of the developers of the kernel you are using and on kernel developer's forums.

The Yocto Project and PREEMPT_RT

The Yocto Project supplies two standard kernel recipes: `linux-yocto` and `linux-yoco-rt`, the latter having the real-time patches already applied. Assuming that your target is supported by these kernels, then you just need to select `linux-yocto-rt` as your preferred kernel and declare that your machine is compatible, for example, by adding lines similar to these to your `conf/local.conf`:

```
PREFERRED_PROVIDER_virtual/kernel = "linux-yocto-rt"
COMPATIBLE_MACHINE_beaglebone = "beaglebone"
```

High resolution timers

Timer resolution is important if you have precise timing requirements which is typical for real-time applications. The default timer in Linux is a clock that runs at a configurable rate, typically 100 Hz for embedded systems and 250 Hz for servers and desktops. The interval between two timer ticks is known as a **jiffy** and, in the examples given above, is 10 milliseconds on an embedded SoC and four milliseconds on a server.

Linux gained more accurate timers from the real-time kernel project in version 2.6.18 and now they are available on all platforms, providing that there is a high resolution timer source and device driver for it – which is almost always the case. You need to configure the kernel with `CONFIG_HIGH_RES_TIMERS=y`.

With this enabled, all the kernel and user space clocks will be accurate down to the granularity of the underlying hardware. Finding the actual clock granularity is difficult. The obvious answer is the value provided by `clock_getres(2)` but that always claims a resolution of one nanosecond. The `cyclictest` tool that I will describe later has an option to analyze the times reported by the clock to guess the resolution:

```
# cyclictest -R
# /dev/cpu_dma_latency set to 0us
WARN: reported clock resolution: 1 nsec
WARN: measured clock resolution approximately: 708 nsec
You can also look at the kernel log messages for strings like this:
# dmesg | grep clock
OMAP clockevent source: timer2 at 24000000 Hz
sched_clock: 32 bits at 24MHz, resolution 41ns, wraps every
178956969942ns
OMAP clocksource: timer1 at 24000000 Hz
Switched to clocksource timer1
```

The two methods give rather different numbers, for which I have no good explanation but, since both are below one microsecond, I am happy.

Avoiding page faults in a real-time application

A page fault occurs when an application reads or writes memory that is not committed to physical memory. It is impossible (or very hard) to predict when a page fault will happen so they are another source of non-determinism in computers.

Fortunately, there is a function that allows you to commit all memory for a process and lock it down so that it cannot cause a page fault. It is mlockall(2). These are its two flags:

- MCL_CURRENT: locks all pages currently mapped
- MCL_FUTURE: locks pages that are mapped in later

You usually call mlockall(2) during the start up of the application with both flags set to lock all current and future memory mappings.

 Note that MCL_FUTURE is not magic in that there will still be non-deterministic delay when allocating or freeing heap memory using malloc()/free() or mmap(). Such operations are best done at start up and not in the main control loops.

Memory allocated on the stack is trickier because it is done automatically and if you call a function that makes the stack deeper than before, you will encounter more memory management delays. A simple fix is to grow the stack to a size larger than you think you will ever need at start up. The code would look like this:

```
#define MAX_STACK (512*1024)
static void stack_grow (void)
{
  char dummy[MAX_STACK];
  memset(dummy, 0, MAX_STACK);
  return;
}

int main(int argc, char* argv[])
{
  [...]
  stack_grow ();
  mlockall(MCL_CURRENT | MCL_FUTURE);
  [...]
```

The stack_grow() function allocates a large variable on the stack and then zeroes it to force those pages of memory to be committed to this process.

Interrupt shielding

Using threaded interrupt handlers helps mitigate interrupt overhead by running some threads at a higher priority than interrupt handlers that do not impact the real-time tasks. If you are using a multi-core processor, you can take a different approach and shield one or more cores from processing interrupts completely, allowing them to be dedicated to real-time tasks instead. This works either with a normal Linux kernel or a PREEMPT_RT kernel.

Achieving this is a question of pinning the real-time threads to one CPU and the interrupt handlers to a different one. You can set the CPU affinity off a thread or process using the command line tool taskset, or you can use the sched_setaffinity(2) and pthread_setaffinity_np(3) functions.

To set the affinity of an interrupt, first note that there is a subdirectory for each interrupt number in /proc/irq/<IRQ number>. The control files for the interrupt are in there, including a CPU mask in smp_affinity. Write a bitmask to that file with a bit set for each CPU that is allowed to handle that IRQ.

Measuring scheduling latencies

All the configuration and tuning you may do will be pointless if you cannot show that your device meets the deadlines. You will need your own benchmarks for the final testing but I will describe here two important measurement tools: cyclictest and Ftrace.

cyclictest

cyclictest was originally written by Thomas Gleixner and is now available on most platforms in a package named rt-tests. If you are using the Yocto Project, you can create a target image that includes rt-tests by building the real-time image recipe like this:

```
$ bitbake core-image-rt
```

If you are using Buildroot, you need to add the package, BR2_PACKAGE_RT_TESTS in the menu **Target packages | Debugging, profiling and benchmark | rt-tests**.

cyclictest measures scheduling latencies by comparing the actual time taken for a sleep to the requested time. If there was no latency they would be the same and the reported latency would be zero. cyclictest assumes a timer resolution of less than one microsecond.

It has a large number of command-line options. To start with, you might try running this command as root on the target:

```
# cyclictest -l 100000 -m -n -p 99
# /dev/cpu_dma_latency set to 0us
policy: fifo: loadavg: 1.14 1.06 1.00 1/49 320


T: 0 (  320) P:99 I:1000 C: 100000 Min:  9 Act:  13 Avg:  15
Max:  134
```

The options selected are as follows:

- `-l N`: loop N times: the default is unlimited
- `-m`: lock memory with mlockall
- `-n`: use `clock_nanosleep(2)` instead of `nanosleep(2)`
- `-p N`: use the real-time priority N

The result line shows the following, reading from left to right:

- `T: 0`: this was thread 0, the only thread in this run. You can set the number of threads with parameter `-t`.
- `(320)`: this was PID 320.
- `P:99`: the priority was 99.
- `I:1000`: the interval between loops was 1,000 microseconds. You can set the interval with parameter `-i N`.
- `C:100000`: the final loop count for this thread was 100,000.
- `Min:  9`: the minimum latency was 9 microseconds.
- `Act:13`: the actual latency was 13 microseconds. The actual latency is the most recent latency measurement, which only makes sense if you are watching `cyclictest` run.
- `Avg:15`: the average latency was 15 microseconds.
- `Max:134`: the maximum latency was 134 microseconds.

This was obtained on an idle system running an unmodified `linux-yocto` kernel as a quick demonstration of the tool. To be of real use, you would run tests over a 24 hour period or more while running a load representative of the maximum you expect.

Of the numbers produced by `cyclictest`, the maximum latency is the most interesting, but it would be nice to get an idea of the spread of the values. You can get that by adding `-h <N>` to obtain a histogram of samples that are up to N microseconds late. Using this technique, I obtained three traces for the same target board running kernels with no preemption, with standard preemption, and with RT preemption while being loaded with Ethernet traffic from a flood ping. The command line was as shown here:

```
# cyclictest -p 99 -m -n -l 100000 -q -h 500 > cyclictest.data
```

The following is the output generated with no preemption:

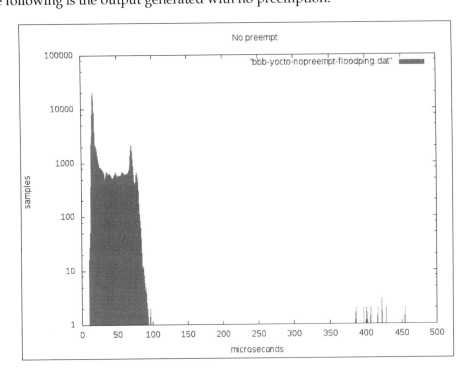

Without preemption, most samples are within 100 microseconds of the deadline, but there are some outliers of up to 500 microseconds, which is pretty much what you would expect.

This is the output generated with standard preemption:

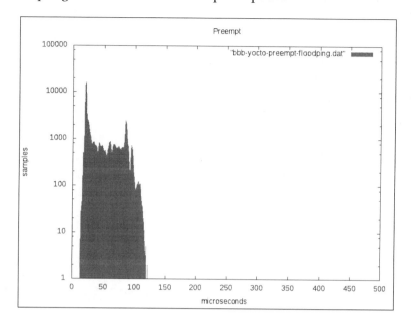

With preemption, the samples are spread out at the lower end but there is nothing beyond 120 microseconds.

Here is the output generated with RT preemption:

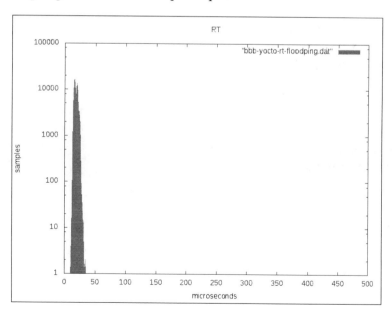

The RT kernel is a clear winner because everything is tightly bunched around the 20 microsecond mark and there is nothing later than 35 microseconds.

`cyclictest`, then, is a standard metric for scheduling latencies. However, it cannot help you identify and resolve specific problems with kernel latency. To do that, you need `Ftrace`.

Using Ftrace

The kernel function tracer has tracers to help track down kernel latencies — that is what it was originally written for, after all. These tracers capture the trace for the worst case latency detected during a run, showing the functions that caused the delay. The tracers of interest, together with the kernel configuration parameters, are as follows:

- `irqsoff`: `CONFIG_IRQSOFF_TRACER` traces code that disables interrupts, recording the worst case
- `preemptoff`: `CONFIG_PREEMPT_TRACER` is similar to `irqsoff`, but traces the longest time that kernel preemeption is disabled (only available on preemptible kernels)
- `preemptirqsoff`: it combines the previous two traces to record the largest time either `irqs` and/or preemption is disabled
- `wakeup`: traces and records the maximum latency that it takes for the highest priority task to get scheduled after it has been woken up
- `wakeup_rt`: the same as wake up but only for real-time threads with the `SCHED_FIFO`, `SCHED_RR`, or `SCHED_DEADLINE` policies
- `wakeup_dl`: the same but only for deadline-scheduled threads with the `SCHED_DEADLINE` policy

Be aware that running `Ftrace` adds a lot of latency, in the order of tens of milliseconds, every time it captures a new maximum which `Ftrace` itself can ignore. However, it skews the results of user-space tracers such as `cyclictest`. In other words, ignore the results of `cyclictest` if you run it while capturing traces.

Selecting the tracer is the same as for the function tracer we looked at in *Chapter 13, Profiling and Tracing*. Here is an example of capturing a trace for the maximum period with preemption disabled for a period of 60 seconds:

```
# echo preemptoff > /sys/kernel/debug/tracing/current_tracer
# echo 0 > /sys/kernel/debug/tracing/tracing_max_latency
# echo 1 > /sys/kernel/debug/tracing/tracing_on
# sleep 60
# echo 0 > /sys/kernel/debug/tracing/tracing_on
```

The resulting trace, heavily edited, looks like this:

```
# cat /sys/kernel/debug/tracing/trace
# tracer: preemptoff
#
# preemptoff latency trace v1.1.5 on 3.14.19-yocto-standard
# --------------------------------------------------------------------
# latency: 1160 us, #384/384, CPU#0 | (M:preempt VP:0, KP:0, SP:0 HP:0)
#    -----------------
#    | task: init-1 (uid:0 nice:0 policy:0 rt_prio:0)
#    -----------------
# => started at: ip_finish_output
# => ended at:    __local_bh_enable_ip
#
#
#
#                    _------=> CPU#
#                   / _-----=> irqs-off
#                  | / _----=> need-resched
#                  || / _---=> hardirq/softirq
#                  ||| / _--=> preempt-depth
#                  |||| /     delay
# cmd      pid     ||||| time  |  caller
#    \     /       |||||  \    |  /
    init-1       0..s.    1us+: ip_finish_output
    init-1       0d.s2   27us+: preempt_count_add <-cpdma_chan_submit
    init-1       0d.s3   30us+: preempt_count_add <-cpdma_chan_submit
    init-1       0d.s4   37us+: preempt_count_sub <-cpdma_chan_submit

[...]

    init-1       0d.s2 1152us+: preempt_count_sub <-__local_bh_enable
    init-1       0d..2 1155us+: preempt_count_sub <-__local_bh_enable_ip
    init-1       0d..1 1158us+: __local_bh_enable_ip
    init-1       0d..1 1162us!: trace_preempt_on <-__local_bh_enable_ip
    init-1       0d..1 1340us : <stack trace>
```

Here, you can see that the longest period with kernel preemption disabled while running the trace was 1,160 microseconds. This simple fact is available by reading `/sys/kernel/debug/tracing/tracing_max_latency`, but the trace above goes further and gives you the sequence of kernel function calls that lead up to that measurement. The column marked `delay` shows the point on the trail where each function was called, ending with the call to `trace_preempt_on()` at 1162us, at which point kernel preemption is once again enabled. With this information, you can look back through the call chain and (hopefully) work out if this is a problem or not.

The other tracers mentioned work in the same way.

Combining cyclictest and Ftrace

If `cyclictest` reports unexpectedly long latencies you can use the `breaktrace` option to abort the program and trigger `Ftrace` to obtain more information.

You invoke breaktrace using `-b<N>` or `--breaktrace=<N>` where `N` is the number of microseconds of latency that will trigger the trace. You select the `Ftrace` tracer using `-T[tracer name]` or one of the following:

- `-C`: context switch
- `-E`: event
- `-f`: function
- `-w`: wakeup
- `-W`: wakeup-rt

For example, this will trigger the `Ftrace` function tracer when a latency greater than 100 microseconds is measured:

```
# cyclictest -a -t -n -p99 -f -b100
```

Further reading

The following resources have further information about the topics introduced in this chapter:

- *Hard Real-Time Computing Systems: Predictable Scheduling Algorithms and Applications* by *Buttazzo, Giorgio, Springer*, 2011
- *Multicore Application Programming* by *Darryl Gove, Addison Wesley*, 2011

Summary

The term real-time is meaningless unless you qualify it with a deadline and an acceptable miss rate. When you know that you can determine whether or not Linux is a suitable candidate for the operating system and, if so, begin to tune your system to meet the requirements. Tuning Linux and your application to handle real-time events means making it more deterministic so that it can process data reliably inside deadlines. Determinism usually comes at the price of total throughput so a real-time system is not going to be able to process as much data as a non-real-time system.

It is not possible to provide mathematical proof that a complex operating system like Linux will always meet a given deadline, so the only approach is through extensive testing using tools such as `cyclictest` and `Ftrace`, and, more importantly, using your own benchmarks for your own application.

To improve determinism, you need to consider both the application and the kernel. When writing real-time applications, you should follow the guidelines given in this chapter about scheduling, locking, and memory.

The kernel has a large impact on the determinism of your system. Thankfully, there has been a lot of work on this over the years. Enabling kernel preemption is a good first step. If you still find that it is missing deadlines more often than you would like, then you might want to consider the `PREEMPT_RT` kernel patches. They can certainly produce low latencies but the fact that they are not in mainline yet means that you may have problems integrating them with the vendor kernel for your particular board. You may instead, or in addition, need to embark on the exercise of finding the cause of the latencies using `Ftrace` and similar tools.

That brings me to the end of this dissection of embedded Linux. Being an engineer of embedded systems requires a very wide range of skills, which range from a low level knowledge of hardware, how the system bootstrap works and how the kernel interacts with it, to being an excellent system engineer who is able to configure user applications and tune them to work in an efficient manner. All of this has to be done with hardware that is, almost always, only just capable of the task. There is a quotation that sums this up, *An engineer can do for a dollar what anyone else can do for two*. I hope that you will be able to achieve that with the information I have presented during the course of this book.

Index

Thank you for buying
Mastering Embedded Linux Programming

About Packt Publishing

Packt, pronounced 'packed', published its first book, *Mastering phpMyAdmin for Effective MySQL Management*, in April 2004, and subsequently continued to specialize in publishing highly focused books on specific technologies and solutions.

Our books and publications share the experiences of your fellow IT professionals in adapting and customizing today's systems, applications, and frameworks. Our solution-based books give you the knowledge and power to customize the software and technologies you're using to get the job done. Packt books are more specific and less general than the IT books you have seen in the past. Our unique business model allows us to bring you more focused information, giving you more of what you need to know, and less of what you don't.

Packt is a modern yet unique publishing company that focuses on producing quality, cutting-edge books for communities of developers, administrators, and newbies alike. For more information, please visit our website at www.packtpub.com.

About Packt Open Source

In 2010, Packt launched two new brands, Packt Open Source and Packt Enterprise, in order to continue its focus on specialization. This book is part of the Packt Open Source brand, home to books published on software built around open source licenses, and offering information to anybody from advanced developers to budding web designers. The Open Source brand also runs Packt's Open Source Royalty Scheme, by which Packt gives a royalty to each open source project about whose software a book is sold.

Writing for Packt

We welcome all inquiries from people who are interested in authoring. Book proposals should be sent to author@packtpub.com. If your book idea is still at an early stage and you would like to discuss it first before writing a formal book proposal, then please contact us; one of our commissioning editors will get in touch with you.

We're not just looking for published authors; if you have strong technical skills but no writing experience, our experienced editors can help you develop a writing career, or simply get some additional reward for your expertise.

[PACKT] open source ✿
PUBLISHING
community experience distilled

BeagleBone Essentials

ISBN: 978-1-78439-352-6   Paperback: 240 pages

Harness the power of the BeagleBone Black to manage external environments using C, Bash, and Python/PHP programming

1. Learn the fundamentals of Beaglebone Black via a detailed tutorial that provides practical examples, from initial board setup to device driver management.

2. Access external peripherals to monitor and control an electronic device.

3. Monitor and control several electronic devices with one of the best embedded computers.

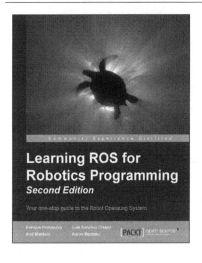

Learning ROS for Robotics Programming
Second Edition

ISBN: 978-1-78398-758-0   Paperback: 458 pages

Your one-stop guide to the Robot Operating System

1. Model your robot on a virtual world and learn how to simulate it.

2. Create, visualize, and process Point Cloud information.

3. Easy-to-follow, practical tutorials to program your own robots.

Please check **www.PacktPub.com** for information on our titles

Learning Embedded Linux Using the Yocto Project

ISBN: 978-1-78439-739-5   Paperback: 334 pages

Develop powerful embedded Linux systems with the Yocto Project components

1. A hands-on guide to enhance your ability to develop captivating embedded Linux projects.

2. Learn about the compelling features offered by the Yocto Project, such as customization, virtualization, and many more.

3. Illustrates concepts such device-emulation and cross-compiling in a pragmatic and lucid way.

Using Yocto Project with BeagleBone Black

ISBN: 978-1-78528-973-6   Paperback: 144 pages

Unleash the power of the BeagleBone Black embedded platform with Yocto Project

1. Build real world embedded system projects using the impressive combination of Yocto Project and Beaglebone Black.

2. Learn how to effectively add multimedia to your board and save time by exploiting layers from the existing ones.

3. A step-by-step, comprehensive guide for embedded system development with hands-on examples.

Please check **www.PacktPub.com** for information on our titles

49248376R00233

Made in the USA
Middletown, DE
10 October 2017